C. T. R. Hayward is Reader i. ... ... Testament
Theology at Durham University.

Jacket illustration: St Jerome in his study by Ghirlandaio, from the
church of the Ognissanti, Florence. Photo: Mansell Collection.

OXFORD EARLY CHRISTIAN STUDIES

General Editors

Henry Chadwick   Andrew Louth

THE OXFORD EARLY CHRISTIAN STUDIES series
will include scholarly volumes on the thought and history of
the early Christian centuries. Covering a wide range of
Greek, Latin, and Oriental sources, the books will be of
interest to theologians, ancient historians, and specialists in
the classical and Jewish worlds.

Titles in the series include:

Saint Jerome's *Hebrew Questions on Genesis*

Translated with Introduction and Commentary
by
C. T. R. HAYWARD

CLARENDON PRESS · OXFORD
1995

Oxford University Press, Walton Street, Oxford OX2 6DP
Oxford New York
Athens Auckland Bangkok Bombay
Calcutta Cape Town Dar es Salaam Delhi
Florence Hong Kong Istanbul Karachi
Kuala Lumpur Madras Madrid Melbourne
Mexico City Nairobi Paris Singapore
Taipei Tokyo Toronto
and associated companies in
Berlin Ibadan

Oxford is a trade mark of Oxford University Press

Published in the United States
by Oxford University Press Inc., New York

British Library Cataloguing in Publication Data
Data available

Library of Congress Cataloging in Publication Data
Jerome, Saint, d. 419 or 20.
[Quaestiones hebraicae in Genesim. English]
Saint Jerome's Hebrew questions on Genesis / translated with
introduction and commentary by C. T. R. Hayward.
(Oxford early Christian studies)
Includes bibliographical references and index.
1. Bible. O.T. Genesis—Criticism, interpretation, etc.
I. Hayward, Robert, 1948– . II. Title. III. Series.
BS1235.J4713 1995 222'.1106—dc20 94-45753
ISBN 0-19-826350-3

1 3 5 7 9 10 8 6 4 2

Typeset by Best-set Typesetter Ltd., Hong Kong
Printed in Great Britain on acid-free paper by
Bookcraft (Bath) Ltd., Midsomer Norton

Magistris Meis
Antonio Gelston, DD
et
Geza Vermes, DD
Hoc Opus Dicatum

Notus in Judaea Deus: in Israel magnum Nomen ejus
Ps. 75: 1

PREFACE

This translation of Jerome's *Hebrew Questions on Genesis*, with commentary and introduction, is offered to students of Patristics and Judaica in the hope that what is an unusual, even in some respects unique, writing might become better known. In undertaking this enterprise, the richness and depth of Jerome's knowledge, especially his appreciation of the Jewish tradition, has impressed itself upon me with every passing day. Indeed, the commentary offered in the following pages represents only a fraction of what could have been written, space permitting, on almost any of the verses which Jerome chose to expound. The treatise is of particular interest for our own times, when Jewish–Christian relations seem to be entering a new era. For this little book of Jerome's, when viewed as a whole, confronts the reader with the question: what exactly was Jerome's relationship with the Jews of his day, and why were they willing to acquaint him with their teachings? Perhaps the present work will encourage others to grant this problem the attention it deserves.

By custom, this is the point at which thanks are offered to those who have helped the author in the course of his work. It is a particular pleasure for me to express my gratitude to my colleagues Carol Harrison and George Dragas, whose advice and assistance with regard to the patristic material in this book has been generous and invaluable. Special thanks are also due to Gerald Bonner, whose advice and criticisms were particularly encouraging when I began work on the book. To both Tony Gelston and Walter Moberly, fellow Hebraists, I owe important insights in this work, and I have been particularly helped by their willingness to discuss individual points of detail at length. To all these I owe much; but for the mistakes, omissions, and other imperfections which must surely attend a work of this kind they are not responsible.

My thanks are also due to David Hunt, Tessa Rajak, David Brown, Jeremy Black, and Jan Rhodes for their help in the elucidation of individual details, and to my pupil Keith Holland for his assistance in preparing the typescript. I am indebted also to Eric

Halladay, Principal of St Chad's College, for ensuring with good-humoured advice that I kept this work within its proper limits. Finally, and most especially, I wish to thank the staff of the Library of the University of Durham for their efficiency, dedication, and never failing courtesy: without their help, this book would never have been written.

C.T.R.H.

St Chad's College
Feast of the Epiphany 1994

CONTENTS

ABBREVIATIONS

Bible and Versions

For the text of Genesis in Hebrew and in the Versions, the following abbreviations have been used in discussion of Jerome's *Hebrew Questions on Genesis*, itself hereafter referred to as *QHG*.

Field	F. Field (ed.), *Origenis Hexaplorum Quae Supersunt*, 2 vols. (Oxford, 1875)
FTP, FTV	The Fragment Targums preserved respectively in MS Paris, Bibliothèque nationale Hébreu 110, and MS Vatican Ebr. 440, ed. M. L. Klein, in *The Fragment-Targums of the Pentateuch*, 2 vols. (Rome, 1980)
GM (Klein)	M. L. Klein (ed.), *Genizah Manuscripts of Palestinian Targum to the Pentateuch*, 2 vols. (Cincinnati, 1986)
LXX (Wevers)	*Septuaginta Vetus Testamentum Graecum*, i: *Genesis*, ed. J. W. Wevers (Göttingen, 1974)
MT	Masoretic Text. *Biblia Hebraica Stuttgartensia* (Stuttgart, 1966–77)
Ngl	Marginal and interlinear glosses of TN
Pesh	*The Peshitta Version* (United Bible Societies; London, 1979)
PJ	Targum Pseudo-Jonathan. *Targum Pseudo-Jonathan of the Pentateuch*, ed. E. G. Clarke, W. E. Aufrecht, J. C. Hurd, and F. Spitzer (Hoboken, NJ, 1984)
TN	Targum Neofiti 1. *Ms. Neophyti I*, ed. A. Díez Macho, 5 vols. (Madrid and Barcelona, 1968–78)
TO	Targum Onkelos. *The Bible in Aramaic*, i: *The Pentateuch according to Targum Onkelos*, ed. A. Sperber (Leiden, 1959)
Vg	*Biblia Sacra iuxta Vulgatam Versionem*, 2 vols. (Stuttgart, 1969)
VL (Fischer)	*Vetus Latina: Die Reste der altlateinischen Bibel*, ii: *Genesis*, ed. B. Fischer (Freiburg i.B., 1951)

Greek and Latin Sources

Abbreviations as follows have been used for authors and sources most frequently cited.

Augustine, QG	*Quaestionum in Heptateuchum Liber i*, in *Sancti Aurelii Augustini . . . Opera Omnia*, iii, ed. Monks of

	St Benedict, Maurist Congregation (Paris, 1836); questions on Genesis followed by question number
Devreesse	Fragments of Eusebius of Emesa, ed. R. Devreesse, in *Les Anciens Commentateurs grecs de l'Octateuque et des Rois (Fragments tirés des chaînes)* (Studi e Testi, 201; Vatican, 1959)
LAB	Pseudo-Philo, *Liber Antiquitatum Biblicarum*, ed. D. J. Harrington, *Pseudo-Philon: Les Antiquités bibliques*, i (Sources chrétiennes, 229; Paris, 1976)
Lib. Heb. Nom.	Jerome's *Liber Interpretationis Hebraicorum Nominum*, ed. P. de Lagarde (CCSL 72; Tournai, 1959); cited by page number
Lib. Loc.	Jerome's *Liber de Situ et Nominibus Locorum Hebraicorum*; cited from PL 23 by column number
Petit, i	*Catenae Graecae in Genesim et Exodum*, i: *Catena Sinaitica*, ed. F. Petit (CCSG 2; Louvain, 1977)
Petit, ii	*Catenae Graecae in Genesim et Exodum*, ii: *Collectio Coisliniana in Genesim*, ed. F. Petit (CCSG 15; Louvain, 1986)
Petit, *La Chaîne*	*La Chaîne sur La Genèse, édition intégrale*, i, ed. F. Petit (Louvain, 1991)
Philo, *QG*	Philo, *Questions and Answers on Genesis*, trans. R. Marcus, in *Philo Supplement*, i (Loeb Classical Library; Cambridge, Mass. and London, 1961)
Theodoret, *QG*	*Theodoreti Cyrensis Quaestiones in Octateuchum*, ed. N. Fernández Marcos and A. Sáenz-Badillos (Madrid, 1979); questions relating to Genesis, followed by appropriate question number

Hebrew Sources

References to the Mishnah (= *m.*), Tosefta (= *t.*), Baylonian Talmud (= *b.*), and Jerusalem Talmud (= *jer.*) are followed by names of tractates (here listed in traditional order) abbreviated as follows:

Ber.	Berakhot	MQ	Mo'ed Qaṭan
Kil.	Kilaim	Ḥag.	Ḥagigah
Sheb.	Shebi'it	Yeb.	Yebamot
Ḥall.	Ḥallah	Ket.	Ketubot
Bikk.	Bikkurim	Ned.	Nedarim
Shabb.	Shabbat	Soṭ.	Soṭah
'Erub.	'Erubin	Giṭṭ.	Giṭṭin
Pes.	Pesaḥim	Qidd.	Qiddushin
Shek.	Shekalim	BM	Baba Metzia

Sukk.	*Sukkah*	*BB*	*Baba Batra*
RS	*Rosh Ha-Shanah*	*Sanh.*	*Sanhedrin*
Ta͑an.	*Ta͑anit*	*AZ*	*Abodah Zarah*
Meg.	*Megillah*	*Zeb.*	*Zebahim*

References to Midrash Rabbah are indicated by the name of the biblical book, followed by *Rab*. References to and quotations from *Genesis Rab.* follow J. Theodor and H. Albeck, *Bereschit Rabba mit kritischem Apparat und Kommentar*, 4 vols. (Berlin 1903–36).

Mekhilta de R. Ishmael is cited according to the edition of J. Z. Lauterbach, *Mekilta de-Rabbi Ishmael*, 3 vols. (Philadelphia, 1933–5). *Mekhilta de Rabbi Simeon bar Yohai* is cited by page number according to the edition of J. N. Epstein and E. Z. Melamed (Jerusalem, 1955).

Later Midrashim are abbreviated as follows:

ARNa	*Abot de Rabbi Nathan, recension a*
ARNb	*Abot de Rabbi Nathan, recension b*
MHG	*Midrash Ha-Gadol*
PR	*Pᵉsiqta Rabbati*
PRE	*Pirqe de Rabbi Eliezer*
PRK	*Pᵉsiqta de Rab Kahana*
Tanḥ.	*Tanḥuma Yashen*
Tanḥ. B.	*Tanḥuma, ed. S. Buber* (Wilna, 1885)

Modern Works

CCSG	Corpus Christianorum Series Graeca
CCSL	Corpus Christianorum Series Latina
CSEL	Corpus Scriptorum Ecclesiasticorum Latinorum
JBL	*Journal of Biblical Literature*
JJS	*Journal of Jewish Studies*
JQR	*Jewish Quarterly Review*
JSJ	*Journal for the Study of Judaism*
JSS	*Journal of Semitic Studies*
JTS	*Journal of Theological Studies*
MGWJ	*Monatsschrift für Geschichte und Wissenschaft des Judenthums*
PG	Patrologia Graeca
PIBA	*Proceedings of the Irish Biblical Academy*
PL	Patrologia Latina
RB	*Revue biblique*
REA	*Revue des études augustiniennes*
RHE	*Revue d'histoire ecclésiastique*
RHR	*Revue de l'histoire des religions*
RSR	*Recherches de science religieuse*

RTP	*Revue de théologie et de philosophie*
SVT	Supplement series to *Vetus Testamentum*
TDOT	*Theological Dictionary of the Old Testament*, ed. G. J. Botterweck and H. Ringgren, 6 vols. (Grand Rapids, 1974–90)
TU	Texte und Untersuchungen
VT	*Vetus Testamentum*

INTRODUCTION

The closing decades of the fourth century were a time of growing disappointment and sadness for Jews who were now subjects of the Christian Empire of Rome. As early as the reign of Constantine I, an imperial law of 315 had decreed that Jews should not proselytize. The Emperor Constantius had enacted (in 338) that Jews who had married Christian women working in the imperial weaving factories should divorce their wives; he also threatened with death Jewish men who sought Christian wives. The same emperor had forbidden Jews to own a Christian slave. Laws like these marked the beginnings of anti-Jewish legislation which gathered momentum with the passing years: by the year 439, the Emperor Theodosius II was preventing Jews from undertaking public office, unless it required the expenditure of large sums of money which the Roman authorities would not reimburse. Jews could have had few doubts about the bleakness of their prospects; and no clearer sign of things to come could have been given than the emperor's reversal, at Ambrose's prompting, of his decision that Christians should pay for damage they had inflicted on a Jewish synagogue at Callinicum.[1] This last incident took place in the year 388.

By that year, Jerome was settled in the Land of Israel, immersing himself in Hebrew studies, consorting with Jewish teachers, acquiring Jewish texts, and learning all he could about the Hebrew language and Jewish exegesis of Scripture. That itself was extraordinary, given the climate of the times; even more remarkable was his composition of an entire work devoted to things Jewish. For *Hebrew Questions on Genesis* (hereafter *QHG*) represents the most ordered and sustained attempt by any Christian writer, up to Jerome's time, to transmit to the Church Jewish scholarship in its own terms. *QHG* is thus an unusual work. At first blush, it would seem appropriate to relate it in some way to Jerome's greatest enterprise, his translation of the Old Testament into Latin direct from the Hebrew. It was with that end in view that he had first

---

[1] See Ambrose, *Epistles* 40 and 41.

laboured to learn about Hebrew language and Jewish Bible interpretation. Might he not have meant *QHG*, then, to offer some
rationale, even justification, for his evidently consuming interest in
the ways of a people increasingly humiliated and despised by his co-
religionists? The answer to this question will depend in some
measure on proper appraisal of the literary character of *QHG*, of
its subject-matter, and of the circumstances in which it was
composed.

The Literary Character of QHG

Jerome described his work as a book of Hebrew *quaestiones*: see,
for example, *De Vir. Illust.* 135; *Lib. Heb. Nom.*, preface; ibid., p.
75. In so doing, he seems to invite comparison of this book with
works of other Christian writers which were entitled *Quaestiones
et Solutiones* or *Quaestiones et Responsiones*. By the mid-second
century BC, collections of 'problems and solutions' or 'questions
and answers' were familiar enough to contemporary pagans; and
they had a distinguished pedigree. The poems of Homer and the
writings of Aristotle, in particular, had come to occupy such pre-
eminence in Hellenistic culture that scholars began to scrutinize
their texts, and the texts of certain other writers, with great attention to detail. Apparent inconsistencies, obscurities, anachronisms,
repetitions, and other difficulties needed explanation. Rare words
and expressions required elucidation. Complex philosophical and
ethical ideas, especially in the matter of Aristotle's works, were ripe
for interpretation. To accommodate these needs, grammarians and
commentators developed treatises in question and answer form;
and the form proved so popular that Roman scholars and rhetori-
cians deemed it a suitable means of explicating Virgil's poetry. Its
distinctive characteristics, and the modifications which these under-
went through the passing centuries, have been rehearsed elsewhere;
and it is unnecessary to repeat them here.[2]

The Church Fathers eventually adopted this type of treatise to
deal with all kinds of problems raised by the texts of both the Old
and the New Testaments. Possibly they were goaded into doing so

---

[2] See A. Kamesar, *Jerome, Greek Scholarship, and the Hebrew Bible: A Study of
the* Quaestiones Hebraicae in Genesim (Oxford, 1993), 82–92, and the literature
there cited.

by heretics like Marcion, Apelles, and Tatian, who seem to have written books of 'questions and answers' as polemic against the Catholics. Be that as it may, in the questions and answers which the Fathers produced, the same scriptural verses are often cited as problematic; so much so that the lists of questions can, on occasions, appear stereotyped. Sometimes the questions appear artificial, manufactured by the exegete himself as a peg on which to hang his own commentary. On other occasions, they are real difficulties which individuals bring to an acknowledged authority for solution. But in either case, the question and answer framework is evident.[3]

Jerome does not present his *QHG* to us, however, in the form of questions and answers. Although Bardy speaks of 220 *questions* which Jerome poses in the treatise, he immediately qualifies his words by speaking of the questions as a true commentary on Genesis in the form of scholia. Indeed, he hesitates to call them questions at all. The monograph consists of sets of difficulties followed by their solutions. The author does not respond to specific questions or to objections which have been raised as regards the text: he offers explanations of controversial passages which illuminate the literal meaning of particular verses.[4] Yet might not the 'questions and answers' genre still best account for the form of *QHG*? Bardy suggests that *QHG* is indeed dealing with real *questions*, ones which arise from the comparison of the Hebrew text with the LXX version. And to indicate that Jerome was no stranger to the 'questions and answers' form, he quotes passages from his *Epistles* which show his familiarity with some 'classics' of the genre, inspired by earlier Greek commentators.[5]

That the 'questions and answers' form was a major influence on Jerome in writing *QHG* has recently received strong support from Adam Kamesar. He has noted that in 'questions' literature the standard 'question and answer' form need not always be used, and that questions may be 'hidden', without being explicitly formulated. Furthermore, questions may be implied in expressions not obviously belonging to the genre, some of which Jerome occasionally uses; and sometimes solutions may be offered alone, without a

---

[3] For all this, see G. Bardy, 'La Littérature patristique des "Quaestiones et Responsiones" sur l'Écriture Sainte', *RB* 41 (1932), 210–36, 341–69, 515–37; *RB* 42 (1933), 14–30, 211–29, 328–52.

[4] See Bardy, 'La Littérature patristique', (*RB* 41), 358.

[5] Ibid. 358–69. He cites especially *Eps.* 19–21, 25–6, 28–30, 35–6, 120–1.

statement of the problem.[6] Even so, Kamesar accepts that *QHG* cannot be explained entirely by the standard 'question' genre, however broadly that genre might have been interpreted by the ancients; and that a large portion of the work must be accounted for in another way.[7] Accordingly, Kamesar suggests that *QHG* is a work of mixed genre, which combines the form 'questions and answers' in its broadest and most generous definition with *excerpta* or scholia, succinct observations on difficulties and obscurities in the scriptural text. This, he argues, is confirmed by a letter of Jerome written in 392/3 to Aurelius, bishop of Carthage, where he refers to *QHG* as *commentarioli*. This word probably refers to scholia, since Jerome used it on other occasions apparently to describe *excerpta* by Origen.[8] The exegetical content of *QHG*, therefore, is unmistakable.

Although Kamesar's argument is impressive, there is more to be said, as analysis of Jerome's use of the words *quaero*, *quaestio*, *solvo*, *solutio*, and related forms in *QHG* soon reveals. These words occur very rarely: there are only two occurrences of *solvo* and its noun *solutio* (12: 4; 13: 1–4), and eight of *quaestio* and related terms (5: 25–7; 12: 4; 14: 18–19; 15: 16; 19: 30; 32: 28; 37: 36; 41: 50–2). Kamesar notes some of these passages, but fails to notice a crucial aspect of what they are saying.[9] For in each of them a textual or exegetical difficulty is explained, with reference either to the Hebrew text (5: 25–7; 13: 1–4; 15: 16, referring the reader to his *Ep.* 36 to Pope Damasus; and 41: 50–2) or to Jewish interpretation of Scripture either implied (see 32: 28 and commentary) or frankly acknowledged. Thus at 12: 4 he speaks of a Jewish tradition (*traditio*) which is 'true'; at 19: 30 of a Jewish inference (*conjectura*) which is true; and at 37: 36 of Jews handing on a tradition (*tradunt*) which he accepts. Most important is 14: 18–19, where he describes his little book as 'a collection of Hebrew ques-

[6] See Kamesar, *Jerome*, 82–8. He correctly rejects Bardy's view that the differences between the Hebrew text and LXX constitute 'problems'. The latter, for Jerome, consist in differences between various translations of the Hebrew: see ibid. 88.

[7] Ibid. 91.

[8] Ibid. 91–5. The letter of Jerome to Aurelius was published by J. Divjak, *Sancti Aureli Augustini Opera* (sect. 2, pt. 6) in CSEL 88 (Vienna, 1981), 130–3, as *Ep.* 27. See esp. p. 132, lines 7–8: 'misi opuscula, id est in psalmum decimum et quaestionum Hebraicarum in Genesin commentariolos'.

[9] Ibid. 86–7.

tions or traditions' ('quaestionum hebraicarum vel traditionum congregatio').[10]

This evidence is important, because Jerome uses the words 'tradition' (*traditio*) and 'hand on as tradition' (*trado*) frequently in *QHG* of the Jewish material which he transmits. The noun *traditio* is found at 12: 4; 14: 8–9, and forms of the verb *trado* at 11: 28; 14: 2–3; 22: 20; 24: 9; 27: 15; 33: 18; 37: 36; 41: 43. The association of 'traditions' with 'questions' in 14: 18–19, therefore, requires further investigation. Here it should be noted that the word *quaestio* need not necessarily imply reference to a literary genre of 'questions and solutions'. In any event, the rarity of the words *solvo* and *solutio* in *QHG* has already been recorded. *Quaestio* may simply mean an act of searching, scientific investigation, examination of witnesses, research of disputed opinions, or an object of enquiry. And Jerome is keen to present his book as the fruits of investigations: so much is clear from 22: 13, where he refers to his careful searching. Again at 32: 28–9 he speaks of his careful research which, as a glance at the commentary on those verses will show, included investigation of Jewish scriptural exegesis and Jewish teaching. Now *traditio* may mean precisely an item of teaching, an instruction handed down from the past. The verb *trado* describes the bequeathing of this teaching to others, and may even suggest that the teaching is authoritative. Jerome uses the verb with this particular force at 31: 7–8, where he quotes a line of Virgil as an authoritative statement of fact.[11]

That Jerome's 'questions' may, at least in some cases, be properly understood as investigations of authoritative Hebrew teachings is supported by evidence from the Preface to *QHG*. Towards the end of this lengthy introduction, he speaks of his work in metaphorical terms as foreign merchandise made up of balsam, pepper, and the fruits of palm trees brought by boat to those who desire it. In this way, he suggests that *QHG* is an assemblage of items not easily available in the West. These are exotic, little known except by hearsay, and possibly unsettling: at 22: 13 and 32: 28 these 'foreign

---

[10] See also F. Cavallera, 'Les "Quaestiones Hebraicae in Genesim" de saint Jérôme et les "Quaestiones in Genesim" de Saint Augustin', *Miscellanea Augustiniana*, pt. 2 (Rome, 1931), 361–2.

[11] That sheep may bear offspring twice in the year is proved from *Georgics* 2. 150, where Jerome says it is handed on as tradition (*traditur*) that they do so.

imports' reveal certain authorities accepted in Christian scholarship as being in the wrong. And earlier in the preface he had spoken of *QHG* as 'opus novum' ('a new work'), indicating its unusual character. *QHG*'s individuality is unambiguously heralded in the Preface to *Lib. Heb. Nom.*, a treatise which Jerome completed shortly before publishing the former. There, *QHG* is described as 'opus novum inauditum tam Graecis tam Latinis' ('a new work, unheard of both among the Greeks and the Latins').[12]

The description of *QHG* as 'opus novum' sets the treatise on a par with Jerome's direct translation of the Scriptures into Latin from the original Hebrew: in the Preface to his translation of the Books of Chronicles (*Paraleipomenon*), he refers to this Vulgate as *novum opus*, and proceeds to attack his detractors. Now it should be noted that Jerome begins his Preface to *QHG* with a sustained polemic against unnamed critics who had accused him of plagiarism.[13] His stress on the newness of *QHG*, on its unparalleled character as an 'exotic' work bringing hitherto unheard of delicacies to the West, seems clearly designed to answer his critics' charge that he was a thief of other people's ideas, a plagiarist, a jaded scholarly magpie. And it was entirely natural that he should labour the utter originality of *QHG*, when the other works on which he was engaged at the time of its composition were indeed translations or editions of other people's writings. Thus he had recently finished translating Didymus the Blind's treatise *On the Holy Ghost* and Origen's thirty-nine *Homilies on Saint Luke*, and had published *Lib. Heb. Nom.* and *Liber Locorum*, both of which were translations and revisions of already existing works.[14] *QHG* differs in conception *toto caelo* from all of these.

In the light of the foregoing observations, it is easy to appreciate why Bardy, Kamesar, and others have encountered such difficulties in defining the literary genre of *QHG*. Indeed, the single title *Quaestiones* without an accompanying *Solutiones* (a word very

[12] For the dates of *QHG* and *Lib. Heb. Nom.*, see below, pp. 23–27. G. Grützmacher, *Hieronymus: Eine biographische Studie zur alten Kirchengeschichte*, ii (Berlin, 1906), 63–6, points to the novel character of *QHG* as conveying Jewish tradition to a Christian public.

[13] For the meaning of plagiarism, and the problem of *contaminatio*, see the Commentary on Jerome's preface below, pp. 88–99.

[14] For these works, which occupied Jerome before and during the composition of *QHG*, see F. Cavallera, *Saint Jérôme: Sa vie et son œuvre*, i (Paris, 1992), 138–50; and J. Gribomont, 'The Translations: Jerome and Rufinus', in A. di Bernardino (ed.), *Patrology*, iv, trans. P. Solari (Westminster, Md., 1991), 227–33.

rarely used in the work), and Jerome's own description of the book as *inauditum*, 'unheard of', suggest that *QHG* is not a simple reworking of the 'questions and answers' genre. The latter was very familiar to fourth-century Christians and pagans alike: the evidence which Kamesar adduces renders this indisputable. So the question arises: would Jerome have regarded as 'unheard of' a work composed in a very familiar form, even if that form had been modified to include 'hidden questions', and expanded to such an extent that it had come to resemble commentary? The same question applies to scholia or *excerpta*. These also are too well known to count as 'unheard of' or as making up a 'new work'; and we should recall that Jerome is defending himself against charges of plagiarism which he evidently took fully to heart.

Speaking of *QHG* as a 'mixed' genre, as does Kamesar, goes some way towards resolving the difficulty, in that there seem to be no other works known which fall precisely into the mixture. But this solution may not give sufficient weight to Jerome's own description of the book in 14: 18–19 as 'semel . . . vel quaestionum hebraicarum vel traditionum congregatio est'. The meanings of *quaestio* and *traditio* are qualified by the adjective 'Hebrew'. It is thus specifically Hebrew researches and Hebrew teachings which he is transmitting, and he uses *semel* to underline the point. This word may mean 'once' or 'once for all', 'in a word' or 'briefly', and 'first' in order of succession.[15] In the present setting, it serves to describe the little book's form and function succinctly, 'in a word', as a collection of Hebrew lore; and it may suggest that *QHG* is the first in a unique series of such treatises. But why should Jerome have embarked on such a project? Was he attempting to refute charges of plagiarism by writing something absolutely new and hitherto unparalleled; or had he other motives as well?

The Purpose of QHG

The likelihood of a connection between Jerome's work of translating the Hebrew Scriptures directly into Latin and *QHG* is suggested

[15] A. Souter, *A Glossary of Late Latin to 600 AD* (Oxford, 1949), 371, notes an occurrence of *semel* in Jerome's *Vita Hilarionis* 10 where the meaning of the word is equivalent to *aliquando*, 'sometimes, at some time or other'. This sense is unsuitable in *QHG* since, as a glance at the Commentary will show, almost every comment which Jerome makes owes something to Jewish teachings.

by the description of both enterprises as 'opus novum'.[16] In 1685, R. Simon suggested that Jerome wrote *QHG* as an apology for his Vulgate translation, and as a critique of translations adopted by the LXX. Kamesar has revived this explanation in a much revised, highly sophisticated, and rigorously argued form, urging that *QHG* was written to defend the entirely new philological system which Jerome had perforce to adopt in translating directly from Hebrew into Latin. This philology underlies the whole of his Latin version of the Old Testament. It is a philology forged out of the translations of Aquila, Symmachus, and Theodotion, also owing much to Rabbinic explanations of grammar, syntax, and the meanings of words and phrases. It is therefore entirely different from, and alternative to, the standard approach of the Greeks, who based their philology on the LXX. *QHG*, therefore, is probably a conscious description of this new philological system; for the Vulgate required 'novi scribendi genus', 'a new species of writing, philology' (Preface to Isaiah), and *QHG* is precisely such a 'new work', hitherto 'unheard of among both Greeks and Latins'.[17]

The strength of Kamesar's thesis is evident when set against other explanations of *QHG*'s purpose. Believing that Jerome began work on *QHG* by composing its preface, and noting therein remarks which apparently absolve the LXX translators of error, L. Schade argued that the first part of the book displays a balanced attitude to the differences between LXX and the Hebrew text. It was these which had spurred him to write the work in the first place; and he is capable of adopting a 'neutral' attitude to LXX's renderings on many occasions in *QHG*. But he interrupted work on *QHG* to translate Origen's homilies on Luke and to write *Lib. Heb. Nom.*[18] By the time he resumed work on *QHG*, Jerome had begun to question the value of further revision of the Old Latin version in the light of a restored LXX, and had veered completely towards the Hebrew text. The second part of *QHG*, therefore, abandons any appeal to LXX, and is entirely partial to the Hebrew. In this way, Jerome's work on *QHG* provided the catalyst for his decision to translate the Old Testament direct from the Hebrew.[19]

[16] See above, p. 6.
[17] See Kamesar, *Jerome* 76–81. On p. 77, he notes the earlier articulation of the basic theory by R. Simon, *Histoire critique du Vieux Testament*[2] (Rotterdam, 1685).
[18] See L. Schade, *Die Inspirationslehre des heiligen Hieronymus* (Freiburg i.B., 1910), 149–53.
[19] For the questions of chronology raised here, see below, pp. 23–27.

But as Kamesar rightly objects, there is no evidence that the Preface of *QHG* was written before the rest of the work; and the seemingly pro-LXX remarks which it contains need be understood no differently from the closely similar remarks he makes in the prefaces to books in his Vulgate. Furthermore, the facts do not bear out Schade's contention that *QHG* begins with pro-LXX sympathies which are altered in favour of the Hebrew. There are numerous 'anti-LXX' remarks in the early pages. Never in this book does Jerome prefer LXX to Hebrew text; and the texts which Schade describes as 'neutral' are in reality in favour of the Hebrew.[20] Analysis of the evidence confirms Kamesar's contention. A careful reading of the Preface of *QHG* reveals that Jerome asserts that LXX altered the text of Scripture in certain places; and work on the translation offered in this volume has revealed not one instance of Jerome's preferring a LXX reading to what he knew as the Hebrew text.[21]

There is also no doubt that a philology based on a combination of the Three (Aquila, Symmachus, and Theodotion) and Hebrew tradition forms a central element in *QHG*. Jerome is patently concerned with Hebrew idiom and etymology, words which feature prominently in the text of the work. Expressions like allegory, metaphor, tropology, figure, and type, which in Jerome's commentaries form the stock-in-trade of exegetical vocabulary, appear seldom, if at all. Many of the problems, absurdities, and obscurities found in LXX or VL, when set by the side of the original Hebrew text, are convincingly resolved. The author is keen to elucidate the meaning of names of people and places, and sometimes 'corrects' in *QHG* what he has come to regard as errors in earlier writings.[22] And his overall plan of allowing the Hebrew to show up the 'superfluities', gaps, and errors of LXX is evident on every page. There is nothing transitional or experimental in this: Jerome is out to prove a point.

Yet Cavallera, somewhat in the manner of Schade, views *QHG* precisely as a transitional work. Communicating Hebrew lore to the West, it provided a starting-point for Jerome's later commentar-

---

[20] See Kamesar, *Jerome*, 77–80.

[21] See below, Commentary on the preface, pp. 92–94.

[22] A good example may be found in *QHG* 30: 19–20, where he corrects an interpretation of the name Zebulon given in *Lib. Heb. Nom.* See further Grützmacher, *Hieronymus*, ii. 62.

ies, and represented a first attempt at translation according to the 'Hebrew truth'. It is thus a hybrid work, a staging-post along the way to Jerome's translation of the Bible independent of commentary on the one hand, and his writing of full scale commentaries on the other. When Jerome finally began to undertake these latter enterprises, he abandoned plans for further 'Hebrew questions' altogether.[23] Grützmacher argued that *QHG* was designed primarily to remove suspicion of the Hebrew text among Jerome's contemporaries: he regarded it as a commentary, a rich depository of Haggadah, explaining names, places, and objects by means of the Hebrew language.[24] With this Kelly agrees, also seeing in *QHG* the point at which Jerome relinquished confidence in LXX, and began to argue in favour of the Hebrew text.[25]

All this, however, overlooks the significance of Jerome's early Roman letters, which already in the years around 382–5 demonstrate Jerome's 'conversion' to the idea that Hebrew is the indispensable key to proper understanding of the Scriptures. Kamesar sifts and discusses this crucial and often neglected evidence, and points out that although the expression 'Hebrew truth' does not occur in these writings, the principle is certainly enunciated in *Ep.* 20. 2, 34. 2. His assessment of these letters leaves little room for doubt that Jerome was convinced, years before he composed *QHG* around 392, that knowledge of Hebrew was essential, and that it should be rigorously promoted and defended against those who believed otherwise.[26] The purpose of *QHG* must be evaluated in the light of this early evidence of Jerome's 'conversion' to Hebrew; for then the treatise must be regarded as much more than a 'transitional' work, or a further defence of the Hebrew text against LXX.

Kamesar's explanation of the work's purpose is firmly grounded in a mass of detailed evidence drawn from *QHG*, in the historical facts of Jerome's development as a student of Hebrew, and in a realistic appraisal of the latter's regard for LXX at the time of *QHG*'s composition. It has a powerful appeal. Yet despite its evident strengths, it may be doubted whether it tells the whole story. For once *QHG*'s translations of particular words and

---

[23] See Cavallera, *Saint Jérôme*, i. 144–6.

[24] See Grützmacher, *Hieronymus*, ii. 62–3.

[25] See J. N. D. Kelly, *Jerome: His Life, Writings, and Controversies* (London, 1975), 155–6.

[26] See Kamesar, *Jerome*, 41–3.

phrases are systematically compared with the translations of those same words and phrases in Vg, problems appear. Details of what follows can be found in the Commentary; but the following summary may help to make the point. On approximately 99 occasions, *QHG* and Vg agree entirely in their renderings of the same Hebrew word or phrase. But I estimate at least 80 cases in *QHG* where a 'solution' of the text is given which does not correspond to the Vg translation; and on approximately 24 occasions Jerome prefers to follow LXX in his Vg, even though in *QHG* he has expressed reservations about the former. One or two examples will suffice to show the difficulties.

Jerome discusses in *QHG* the meaning of the obscure Hebrew word *merahepet* (1: 2), which he translates as 'was brooding over' or 'was keeping warm'; in Vg, however, he has put 'moved', which is the LXX translation of the word. At 2: 17 in *QHG* he praises Symmachus for translating the Hebrew *mōt tāmūt* as 'you shall be mortal', although his Vg has 'you shall die by death', which is virtually a translation of LXX. The latter add at 4: 8 the words 'let us go out into the plain', which Jerome in *QHG* notes as superfluous to the Hebrew; notwithstanding this, he adds in Vg the words 'let us go outside'. The Hebrew of 6: 3, he tells us in *QHG*, means 'My Spirit shall not judge...'; but in Vg he translates as 'My Spirit shall not remain...', which is LXX's rendering, criticized in *QHG*. Although *QHG* praises Aquila's translation 'he halved' at 33: 1 as correctly expressing Jacob's apportionment of his family before his meeting with Esau, Vg has 'he divided', which Jerome in *QHG* regarded as inadequate and possibly misleading. Again, Aquila's rendering of *šelēmīm* as 'perfect, complete' receives Jerome's unqualified approval in *QHG* 34: 20–1; yet the Vg of 34: 21 follows LXX and takes the word as 'peaceful'.

In the matter of names of people and places, to which Jerome attaches some importance, there is often discrepancy between *QHG* and Vg. Thus in *QHG* of 14: 5 Jerome insists that the Hebrew text refers to a place named Hom, and goes to some lengths to explain why LXX have translated the word as 'with them'; this last, however, forms his own translation of the word in Vg. Despite noting at some length a meaning of the Patriarchal name Gad deriving from 'troop' or 'arms', and quoting Aquila to that effect in *QHG* 30: 10–11, in Vg Jerome still essentially follows LXX in relating the name to luck or chance. The name Zabulon is explained in *QHG* 30: 20 as 'the dwelling place'; yet this sense is not clearly transferred to the Vg of that verse. The description of Issachar as a 'bony ass', which is ably set out with its accompanying Jewish Haggadah in *QHG* 49: 14–15, is not reflected in Vg 49: 14, where the Patriarch is somewhat weakly called a 'strong ass'. Finally, Vg of 26: 26 still refers to Ochozath his (sc. Abraham's) friend, even though *QHG* on this verse notes that the Hebrew means 'the association of his friends'. In this case, Ochozath is not a proper noun, but a word meaning 'company'.

Such mismatches between *QHG* and Vg must prompt the question whether the former can be regarded purely and simply as a philological exercise in defence of the latter. And this question is made more urgent by the observation that verses of Genesis which are well known precisely for their philological difficulties receive not so much as a passing mention in *QHG*. An obvious case is 1: 2, where the Hebrew describes the earth before creation as *tōhū wābōhū*. The versions had difficulty with the meaning of these words: LXX had taken them to mean 'invisible and unfashioned', while Aquila put 'empty space and nothing', and Symmachus 'idle (untilled?) and confused'. Given the importance of this verse in Christian thinking on *creatio ex nihilo* (see Hermas, *Visions* 1.6, Mandates 1.1), Jerome's silence about the meaning of the Hebrew is astonishing. Equally puzzling is omission of 3: 22, 'Behold, the man has become like one of us to know good and evil', where the wording of the Hebrew text may be ambiguous, LXX and Symmachus differ greatly in their renderings, and a rich tradition of Jewish exegesis exists to which Jerome could have appealed. Again, 21: 33 has the Hebrew word *ʾēšel*, 'tamarisk', which also occasioned discussion in antiquity: LXX had taken it as 'field', but Aquila put 'tree', Symmachus 'plantation', and the Palestinian Targums 'pleasure garden' (*pardēs*). Jerome rendered it in Vg as 'grove', 'plantation'; but of his reasons for doing so *QHG* gives no hint. The point need not be laboured: Jerome's choice of verses for discussion in *QHG* appears somewhat haphazard. If philology was the pre-eminent unifying principle in his construction of the book, it may reasonably be asked why the treatment of difficult verses is not carried through more systematically?[27]

---

[27] Kamesar, ibid. 200, takes me to task for suggesting that *QHG* 'reveals no obvious discernible over-arching plan or theme'. But it was Jerome's choice of some verses, yet not of others equally worthy of 'question', which led to my remark. The

Further, many of the Jewish traditions which Jerome records cast no light on philological matters. Thus the discussion of Ishmael and his weaning (21: 14) is used primarily to explain a chronological difficulty; the traditions that Melchizedek is identified with Shem (14: 18–19) and that Esau's garments were priestly vestments (27: 15) carry no philological implications; and the identification of Migdal-Eder with the site of the Temple (35: 21) is brought forward simply as an example of Jewish exegesis without reference to philology. And on the few occasions when Jerome uses some form of the verb *quaero*, or the noun *quaestio*, he seems more often engaged in exegesis than in philological research. So the question about Methuselah's age (5: 25–7) is one of chronology, answered by reference to the Hebrew text. The question at 12: 4 concerns Abraham's age, and is answered from the Haggadah. As we have already seen, 14: 18–19 on Shem and Melchizedek is a question unrelated to philology; and the question in 15: 16 is again one of chronology. The question why Lot left Segor for the mountain (19: 30) is an exegetical one, the Haggadah supplying the answer; and the question why Potiphar the eunuch had a wife (37: 36), not at all a matter of philology, is explained from the Haggadah. The question raised at 41: 50–2 concerns the number of Jacob's descendants who went to Egypt. In all these cases, where the title-word *quaestio* of Jerome's treatise occurs, the text deals not with philology, but with exegesis.

These observations lead one to conclude, albeit with some reluctance, that *QHG* was not composed simply as a philological justification of Jerome's translating the Old Testament into Latin direct from the Hebrew. The literary character of the work and its purpose seem to be intimately connected to one another; and of the former Jerome himself gives us an accurate description. He says that *QHG* is, 'in a word, a collection of Hebrew researches or traditions' (14: 18–19). The opening sentences of his Preface to *QHG* strongly suggest that one of his reasons for writing the treatise was to refute charges of plagiarism. In this work, he introduces to the whole Christian world, not simply to the West, a world of scholarship hitherto unknown. This scholarship without doubt includes the fruits of philological research; but there is more besides. For Jerome's purpose in *QHG* is not so much the compara-

Father's selection of excerpts for comment is not nearly so deliberate as Kamesar's exposition of *QHG* would surely require.

tively narrow one of defending his Latin translation of the Old Testament: this he carries out quite successfully in his prefaces to the translated biblical books themselves, and in his later commentaries. His purpose seems to be nothing less than an attempt to justify his dealings with Judaism and the Jews, when the ecclesiastical and civil authorities were intent on pushing that nation to the margins of Christian society. It is well known that Jerome's dealings with the Jews and their scholars led some of his contemporaries to regard him with the very deepest suspicion; and it is to disarm this suspicion of his work that he composed *QHG*. As if this were not enough, *QHG* aims to show his detractors that Jewish understanding of the Scriptures is often correct. The staggering originality of this thesis demanded that Jerome defend, from first principles, his dealings with Jews and their teachings, and his acceptance of the latter.

Thus *QHG* argues not only for the primacy of the Hebrew text over LXX, but significantly emphasizes the importance of Jewish tradition, the authoritative exposition of Scripture by Jewish teachers.[28] Philology plays an important part in all this, but it is not alone. The strong exegetical element in *QHG* is a reminder that theological concerns are never far from Jerome's agenda. Hebrew text and Jewish tradition for him combine to bring to light the *mysterium* (14: 18; 18: 6; 35: 21; 49: 9, 19), the *sacramentum* (15: 10; 26: 17), or the 'spiritual meaning' (25: 8) of particular words and phrases. They reveal the true character of the Scriptures as prophetic of Christian life (9: 27; 35: 21; 49: 9), and above all they convey the 'Hebraica veritas', the 'Hebrew truth', a famous phrase which Jerome uses for the first time in his Preface to *QHG*. It includes not only the philological aspects of Jerome's work, but also the exegetical, as its appearance in his comments on 13: 1–4; 19: 14; 49: 5–6 demonstrates. And it should never be forgotten that Jerome's interest in the biblical text was never merely philological: theological concerns are never far from the surface.[29] With this in mind, we turn to consider the sources which Jerome used in compiling this book.

[28] For the way in which this affects Jerome's estimate of LXX, see Commentary on his preface below, pp. 95–96.

[29] See S. Kamin, 'The Theological Significance of the *Hebraica Veritas* in Jerome's Thought', in M. Fishbane and E. Tov (eds.), with assistance of W. W. Fields, '*Sha-'arei Talmon*': *Studies in the Bible, Qumran, and the Ancient Near East presented to Shemaryahu Talmon* (Winona Lake, Ind., 1992), 243–53.

The Sources of QHG

Jerome sometimes names explicitly those who provided him with information set out in *QHG*. Most obviously, he proclaims his debts to Aquila, Symmachus, and Theodotion when he reports their several translations of Hebrew words and phrases; but this practice is not invariable. At 40: 16, for example, he gives the meaning of Hebrew *ḥōrī* as 'flour' without recording Aquila's very similar rendering of the word. Likewise Symmachus was probably the direct source of his translation of the rare *lāśūaḥ* as 'to speak' in 24: 63; but that translator receives no mention. He also refers directly to Josephus, in the preface and at 32: 28–9; but in his comments on the Table of Nations in Gen. 10 and on many other verses noted in the Commentary, where he owes a good deal to this author, Jerome fails to name him. His use of Josephus, often unacknowledged, is none the less original: he is not content simply to reproduce his source, but omits portions, adds to it, and in other ways significantly modifies it. So much is clear from his exposition of the Table of Nations, which is by no means a mere copy of the latter's work. Further, Jerome often disagrees with Josephus, although he does not refer directly to him: so much is evident from his discussion of the sources of the Jordan (14: 14), the meaning of the name Israel (32: 28–9), and the interpretation of the name Zaphnath-Paneah (41: 45).

Jerome names Eusebius of Emesa, singling him out for ridicule at 22: 13; and he thoroughly criticizes Origen under the nickname Adamantius at the end of the preface. But more commonly he speaks of individuals whom he does not name. Thus he refers to a 'certain person' who had identified Gog and Magog in 10: 21 as the Goths: he was thinking of Ambrose of Milan, who made the identification in his *De Fide* 2. 16. He says that 'certain people' interpreted 49: 7 as prophetic of the deaths of the Apostles and Christ: here he had in mind Tertullian, Hippolytus, and Origen. In a similarly unspecific way he refers to unnamed persons, who turn out to have included Josephus, as holding that Jacob divided his family into three parts, not two, before he met with Esau (33: 1–3). Yet in all this he indicates that others have provided him with interpretations which need correction.

For the most part, however, Jerome does not refer to his Christian or Jewish sources for *QHG* either directly or indirectly. Since he is silent about some of his possible sources for this work, the question must be asked whether material for which he claims Jewish origin might not derive from writers like Origen and Eusebius of Emesa? It has long been known that Jerome sometimes claimed to have derived material direct from Hebrew masters, when in fact he had probably received it from the hands of other Christian writers.[30] As a possible example of his following this course in *QHG* his exegesis of 38: 29 may be cited. There he connects the name Pharez with the Pharisees through the Hebrew root *prẓ*, 'to break through'. Origen, too, had related the two words in similar fashion (*Comm. Series in Matt.* 9, 20, 27; *Comm. in Joh.* 1. 13). Origen's allegorical interpretation of the word Pharisee, however, does not appear in *QHG*. While this passage possibly betrays Jerome's knowledge of Origen, his very next comment on the name Zerah (38: 30) is entirely concerned with the philological problem of the name and its meaning: by contrast, Origen's Christological interpretation of Zerah (*Comm. Series in Matt.* 125) is nowhere in Jerome's sight.

Close inspection of *QHG* reveals that Origen does not feature as a major source; and when in this treatise Jerome discusses the same texts as Origen, the former's textual, philological, and historical interests almost always differ significantly from Origen's allegorical or homiletic purposes.[31] Much more in Jerome's mind were Antiochene exegetes like Eusebius of Emesa, Diodore of Tarsus, and the authors of fragments of exegesis now preserved in the Greek Catenae. Significantly, both Eusebius and Diodore often quote as authorities 'the Hebrew' or 'the Syrian'. Many of Jerome's comments in *QHG* seem designed either to correct or dismiss altogether their exegesis, which he appears to regard as based not on direct knowledge of the Hebrew text and authentic Jewish tradition, but on second-hand interpretations.[32] For example, at 2: 8 he may be countering the view of Eusebius that God created Eden after he had created Adam; at 3: 24 he may be refuting the opinion, again held by Eusebius, that God left Adam close to paradise to punish him; at 24: 9 he may be disagreeing with an implied view of

[30] See especially G. Bardy, 'Saint Jérôme et ses maîtres hébreux', *RB* 46 (1934), 145–64; and most recently D. Brown, *Vir Trilinguis: A Study in the Biblical Exegesis of Saint Jerome* (Kampen, 1992), 71–82.
[31] See Commentary on 2: 23; 6: 16; 18: 6; 19: 30; 22: 3–4; 23: 2; 24: 62–3; 26: 12; 31: 7–8, 46–7; 37: 3; 40: 9–10; 47: 31; and Kamesar, *Jerome*, 98–103.
[32] The case for this is convincingly argued by Kamesar, *Jerome*, 126–75.

Eusebius that the Hebrew text of that verse refers to the mark of Abraham's circumcision; and at 47: 31 he seems to attack Eusebius's understanding of Joseph's staff. More often than not, he invokes Jewish tradition and the Hebrew text to support his own interpretations of these verses.

Jerome's discussion of the place named Bale and Segor admirably illustrates what has been said. In 14: 2–3, he tells us that Bale is Hebrew and means 'swallowing down'; and that Hebrew tradition identifies it with a place called Salissa. This was because it was swallowed up in a third earthquake, and was eventually named Segor, which in the Syrian tongue means 'small'. At 19: 30 he repeats the Jewish tradition. The town was often undermined by earthquake, was first called Bale, and then Salissa. Eusebius of Emesa (Devreesse, pp. 71–2) knows a tradition superficially similar to the one which Jerome recounts; but close inspection reveals profound differences between the two writers. First, Eusebius links his comments to 19: 21–3, not to 14: 2–3, and states that God had promised through an angel not to overthrow Segor for the sake of Lot. Jerome relates nothing of the kind, and contradicts Eusebius by noting the Jewish tradition that the place was often overturned by earthquake (19: 30). Second, Eusebius fails to identify the place with Salissa. Rather, he says that Scripture called it Zogor, Syrian Zaar, and that it is Balak (which stands for LXX's Bale), 'the one which swallows up', because its inhabitants were swallowed. Here Eusebius suggests that Zogor or the Syrian Zaar may be equivalent in meaning to Bale: Jerome, by contrast, is careful to keep the meanings of the words, and their respective languages, quite separate and distinct. Third, Eusebius introduces further confusion by saying that the city was called 'swallowing' because Lot derived his food from it. Later, in his comment on 19: 30, he returns to the alleged promise that it would not be overturned, and tells us that some people consequently alleged that it was not faced with a catastrophe, but was swallowed up, which is the meaning of the name Balak. This combination of philological vagueness and exegetical farrago is far removed from Jerome's clarity. The presumption is reasonable that the latter intended to dispel the confusion which Eusebius had created, for he insists (19: 30) that the Hebrew tradition which he represents is true.

Whence, then, did Jerome derive the Jewish traditions which feature in *QHG*? As the commentary shows, almost every comment

which he offers shows some contact with Jewish learning; and it
would appear that Origen, Eusebius, and other Christian writers
only partly account for a small proportion of the teachings trans-
mitted under the name of Hebrew tradition. While it is often
impossible to point with certainty to Jewish texts or collections of
tradition as the sources for Jerome's knowledge, an appraisal of
QHG as a whole does permit certain tentative conclusions. First,
Philo's influence, although unacknowledged, can be detected in
comments such as that on 25: 8, which discusses the seemingly
tautologous language of LXX as referring to Abraham's virtue (cf.
Philo, *QG* 4. 152). At 26: 12 Jerome's interpretation of Isaac's
barley stocks as an increase in his virtues probably owes something
to Philo's comments in *De Mut. Nom.* 268–9 and *QG* 4. 189–90.
Jerome also disagrees with Philo: the latter's understanding of the
name Israel as 'a man seeing God' (cf. *Leg. All.* 2. 34, 3. 15), and
of Benjamin as 'son of days' (cf. *De Somn.* 2. 36) earn his rebuke in
comments on 32: 28–9 and 35: 18 respectively.

   Second, Philo and the matter of names leads naturally to
consideration of the *Liber Nominum*, the *Book of Names*. Jerome
had translated this work, no longer extant in its original form,
believing that Philo had composed it. In his preface to the translation (PL 23: 815–16), which was published shortly before the
appearance of *QHG* under the title *Liber de Nominibus Hebraicis*,
he cites Origen as having revised this work: he therefore presumably regarded it as an authentic Jewish text with Christian additions.[33] He himself introduced new material relating to the Old
Testament, and added interpretations of New Testament names.
The meanings of these names, Jerome and his contemporaries believed, could shed light on profound scriptural mysteries. But the
information which Jerome found in the *Book of Names* was sometimes inaccurate and misleading; and he made some efforts to
correct it.[34] His use of this source in *QHG* is most evident when he

[33] See N. R. M. de Lange, *Origen and the Jews: Studies in Jewish–Christian
Relations in third-century Palestine* (Cambridge, 1976), 118–21 for the *Book of
Names* and a discussion of Rabbinic interest in the meaning of biblical names. He
suggests that the *Book of Names* is of Alexandrian Greek-Jewish origin; indeed,
modern scholars do not accept Philo as author of the work. See F. X. Wutz,
*Onomastica Sacra: Untersuchungen zum Liber Interpretationis Nominum
Hebraicorum des heiligen Hieronymus* (TU 41; Leipzig, 1914–15), 14–24; Kamesar,
Jerome, 104; and P. Jay, *L'Exégèse de saint Jérôme d'après son 'Commentaire sur
Isaïe'* (Paris, 1985), 292–3.
[34] See Kelly, *Jerome*, 153–5.

discusses the meanings of the Patriarchal names in comments from 29: 32 to 30: 21, where he takes further steps to correct it. Thus in his comment on the name Zabulon (30: 19–20) he explicitly states that the explanation given in the *Book of Names* is incorrect. Among the many other examples of corrections of the *Book of Names* which may be found in *QHG*, Jerome defines Eve's name (3: 20) as meaning 'life', and thus sets aside the additional senses of 'calamity or woe' offered by the *Book of Names*. Likewise the name Seth was defined by the latter as 'a placing, or placed, or goblet, or grass, or seed, or resurrection': *QHG* 4: 25 rejects most of these senses in favour of 'a placing'.

It would seem, then, that when he came to incorporate materials into *QHG* from the sources so far examined, Jerome felt able to modify them to greater or lesser degrees, to add to them, to disagree with them, and to interpret them with a certain freedom. Herein lies one important aspect of his scholarly originality: he does not simply reproduce his sources, but brings to them both critical judgement and additional information. Much of the latter he seems to have acquired directly from his Jewish teachers, and it is largely responsible for the distinctive character of *QHG*. It is impossible to know whether Jerome derived this information from written or oral sources, or from a combination of both of these; but analysis of the traditions themselves is highly informative.

It is evident to a reader of *QHG* that the treatise includes virtually no legal material. It is true that the comment on Jacob's blessing of Benjamin (49: 27) includes an halakhic point relating to sacrifice; but it is most likely that Jerome has recorded the matter only because it featured in a larger Haggadic explanation of the verse. The same could be said of his explanations (11: 29; 20: 12) of Abraham's marriage to his 'sister'. He offers not a full legal interpretation of the Patriarch's action, but adopts an Haggadah which identifies Sarah with Iesca daughter of Aran, such that Sarah becomes Abraham's niece. And he appears to be unaware of the legal implications of the Haggadah; for Lev. 18: 13 tacitly permits the marriage of uncle and niece.

Much of what Jerome tells us in the name of the Hebrews, and a good deal else, can still be recognized in Haggadic comments of the Tannaitic Midrashim, the Midrash Rabbah, the two Talmuds, and later Midrashim. Sometimes what he writes is almost identical with extant Jewish sources; on other occasions, he hands on teaching which differs from known Jewish sources only in small individual details. On yet other occasions, he relays to us the general outline of known Haggadah combined with material, said to be of Jewish origin, not now attested in extant sources. Collections of some of this material were made in the last century by Rahmer, Ginzberg, and Krauss, and many further examples of it will be found in the Commentary to Jerome's text.[35] It may, none the less, be useful at this point to give a few representative examples of Jerome's use of the Haggadah.

As examples of Jerome's almost complete accord with the Haggadah we may note his interpretation of 4: 26, that in the days of Enosh idolatry began, a sentiment shared with *Gen. Rab.* 23: 7. His identification of Lasha as Callirhoe (10: 19) agrees with *Gen. Rab.* 37: 6, *Sifre Deut.* 6, and *jer. Meg.* 1: 9; his statement that Sarah is Iesca (11: 29) is of a piece with *b. Sanh.* 69b and many other sources; Shem is identified with Melchizedek (14: 18–19) in *b. Ned.* 32b, *Gen. Rab.* 43: 6, and many other texts; the tradition that Esau's garments were priestly vestments (27: 15) is found in *jer. Meg.* 1: 11; and the Haggadah of Potiphar's punishment on account of his unnatural desire for Joseph (37: 36) is found, among other sources, in *Gen. Rab.* 86: 3 and *b. Soṭ.* 13b.

Examples of Jerome's quotation of known Haggadah with details which differ from extant accounts of it include the story of Abraham's escape from the fiery furnace of the Chaldeans (11: 28; 12: 4), which may be compared with *Gen. Rab.* 38: 13. The interpretation of Abraham's removal of birds from the scene of sacrifice (15: 10–11) as symbolic of his merits protecting Israel from the Gentiles is similar to material in *Gen. Rab.* 44: 6. The names of the four Patriarchs buried at Kiriath-Arba (23: 2) corresponds with one interpretation of several listed in *Gen. Rab.* 58: 4; and the interpretation of Jacob's gaining of Shechem by his bow and sword as symbolizing his righteousness is similar to *Mekh. de R. Ishmael Beshallah* 3: 40–4. It is also possible that he was aware of differences of opinion between teachers. His comment on

[35] See M. Rahmer, *Die hebräischen Traditionen in den Werken des Hieronymus durch einen Vergleichung mit den jüdischen Quellen*, i: *Die 'Quaestiones in Genesin'* (Breslau, 1861). More critical in his estimate of Jerome's use of Jewish sources is L. Ginzberg, 'Die Haggada bei den Kirchenvätern und in der apokryphischen Literatur', *MGWJ* NS 6 (1898), 537–50; NS 7 (1899), 17–22, 61–75, 117–25, 149–59, 217–31, 292–303, 409–16, 461–70, 485–504, 529–47. See also S. Krauss, 'The Jews in the Works of the Church Fathers', *JQR* 6 (1894), 225–61.

Mamre (14: 13) may imply that he knew of its interpretation now as the name of a person, now as a place, a difference emerging in the debate between R. Nehemiah and R. Judah in *Gen. Rab.* 42: 8. Finally, we may note his ascription to the Jews of a view that Zoar is Shalishah, so called because it was swallowed up in the third earthquake (14: 2–3): this precise tradition is not found in extant Jewish sources, but is reflected in the Haggadah that Zoar was spared while earthquakes happened elsewhere (*Gen. Rab.* 49: 6) and remained untouched after the other Cities of the Plain were destroyed (*b. Shabb.* 10b).

All of these, and the scores of other examples listed in the Commentary, suggest that Jerome was well informed about the Haggadah current in his day. One source for some of these which he almost certainly had at his disposal, directly or indirectly, was the tradition of the Aramaic Targums. The purpose, form, and content of these translations-cum-interpretations of the biblical books into Aramaic have often been described.[36] Instruction of the people was certainly one of their functions. The Targums often represent the commonly accepted meaning of a biblical verse as it was expounded to the public. It is therefore improbable, to say the least, that Jerome's Hebrew teachers did not pass on to him, consciously or unconsciously, some accepted renderings of the contemporary Targum. We should expect them to have done this especially in the case of difficult or obscure expressions. Indeed, there are many passages in QHG which appear to presuppose Targumic tradition, and some which may even preserve Targumic language and terminology. A striking example of this last may be found at 25: 3. Jerome reports that 'they', presumably his Jewish informants, think that the Asshurim and Letushim of that verse 'should be *translated* as traders . . . and forgers of metals of bronze and iron', while Leummim means 'chiefs of many tribes and peoples'. These renderings reflect almost exactly the Aramaic translation of the words in FTV, and have close affinity with PJ's translation.

The influence of Targumic tradition may perhaps be discerned in Jerome's understanding of single difficult words. Thus his translation of *qīṭōr* at 19: 28 by a Greek word meaning 'a rising of vapour, an exhalation', and as 'steam, smoke, or ashes' reflects the

---

[36] For a comprehensive, convenient, and recent description of Targums and their methods, see P. S. Alexander, s.v. 'Targum, Targumim', in *The Anchor Bible Dictionary*, vi (New York, 1992), 320–31.

word chosen by TO in its particular range of meanings. The rare word *šārīg* at 40: 10, 12 he interprets as 'vine-shoots, branches, or shoots', a variety of meanings found in PJ, TO, and TN respectively. And his otherwise puzzling comment on the drunkenness of Joseph and his brothers (43: 34) is most easily understood on the assumption that Jerome knew that Hebrew *škr*, 'become drunk', is almost always translated in Aramaic Targums by the root *rwy*, whose primary meaning is 'be saturated'.

Furthermore, particular expressions in *QHG* closely echo the Targums. Thus Noah's blessing of Japheth (9: 27) Jerome takes as a prophecy of the conversion of the Gentiles in very much the same way as PJ and the margin of TN. The setting of his comment is now Christian; but in isolation his remark could almost be a quotation of the Targum. His comment on Esau's eventual casting off of Jewish dominion (27: 40) includes expressions like 'to be subject to the Jews' and 'yoke of servitude' which are non-scriptural, but feature in the Targums of this verse. As yet another example we may compare PJ's interpretation of the place Petah 'Enayim (38: 14) as 'the crossroads, where all eyes gaze forth' with Jerome's explanation of the place as 'a crossroads, where a traveller has to look more carefully which road he should take to walk along'.

The forms in which he hands on Haggadic material are sometimes more akin to the Targumic tradition than to other extant types. Thus his understanding of Phaleg as 'division' (10: 24–5) in the sense that human languages were divided in his day is not at all common in the Midrash or Talmud, but is attested by PJ of Deut. 32: 8. The precise form and wording of the blessing of Benjamin (49: 27) is very close to TO's exegesis, including a particular halakhic point about sacrifice which Jerome has apparently understood correctly. His seemingly fluid interpretation of the verb *yādōn* in 6: 3, now as 'will judge', now as 'will remain', quite possibly reflects Targumic tradition of the kind found in FTP, where other words and phrases closely similar to those in Jerome's commentary also occur. These examples, and the many others noted in the Commentary, strongly suggest that Targums in particular may have been the ultimate source of some of Jerome's knowledge of the Haggadah.

The Jewish material incorporated in *QHG* is wide-ranging in scope and content. Its prominence strengthens the suggestion already made, that Jerome intended his work primarily as a collection of Jewish traditions and teachings, compiled as the direct result of his own researches, whose ultimate aim was to convince his readers of two things. First, he set out to demonstrate his own scholarly originality: he alone among his contemporaries was capable of comprehending, gathering together, and applying to the urgent needs of the Church's theology such complex material, which was utterly unfamiliar to his fellow Christians. Second, he sought to prove beyond any reasonable doubt that knowledge and proper use of those Jewish materials was absolutely necessary for a correct understanding of the Scriptures. In a word, *QHG* is his means of answering his detractors, and insisting against the doubters that *veritas* is most certainly *Hebraica*.

The Date of QHG

Jerome lists *QHG* as an already published work in a catalogue of his writings given in *De Vir. Illust.* 135. This last was almost certainly completed in the earlier part of 393; *QHG*, therefore, must have been written at the very latest in the first months of that year.[37] This date is to some degree confirmed by Jerome's letter to Aurelius of Carthage on the latter's consecration to the episcopate: it refers explicitly to *QHG*, a copy of which Jerome had sent to Aurelius.[38] At the latest, this letter dates from the end of 393; and it is possible, though not certain, that it speaks of *QHG* and other writings of Jerome as though they were of recent composition.[39]

It is, however, far from easy to determine how long before the first part of 393 *QHG* may have been written. Jerome was certainly engaged in work on this enterprise around 390, since it was linked with his revisions of two well-known and much used etymological works on the names of Hebrew persons and places, which were to become the extant *Lib. Loc.* and *Lib. Heb. Nom.*[40] The preface of the latter speaks of his being occupied in producing *books* of

---

[37] This dating of *De Vir. Illust.* was argued by P. Nautin, 'La Date du "De Viris Inlustribus" de Jérôme, de la mort de Cyrille de Jérusalem et de celle de Grégoire de Nazianze', *RHE* 56 (1961), 33–5; and is accepted by P. Jay, 'La Datation des premières traductions de l'Ancien Testament sur l'hébreu par saint Jérôme', *REA* 28 (1982), 208; Gribomont, 'The Translations', 228–9; and Kamesar, *Jerome*, 73. T. D. Barnes, *Tertullian* (Oxford, 1971), 235–6, offers a different dating which is refuted by Nautin, 'Études de chronologie hiéronymienne', *REA* 20 (1974), 280–4.

[38] See above, n. 8.   [39] For this, see Kamesar, *Jerome*, 76.

[40] See Gribomont, 'The Translations', 228.

Hebrew Questions.[41] The plural is certain, and is confirmed later in the same treatise when he comments on the names Galaad and Israel. For both these entries he uses almost identical words to say that he has spoken more fully about these names in the books of Hebrew Questions.[42] His use of the perfect tense 'we have spoken' (*diximus*) may indicate that he had already written his comments on Galaad and Israel in *QHG* by the time *Lib. Heb. Nom.* was published. The comments in *QHG* (31: 46–7; 32: 28–9) come close together, about two-thirds of the way through the book. Such a conclusion, however, would not necessarily be well founded, as evidence from *Lib. Loc.* may indicate. Jerome remarks in *Lib. Loc.* 924 of the places Bethel and Bala that he *has spoken* of them more fully in the books of Hebrew Questions; but in the next breath (*Lib. Loc.* 925) he notes of Beelphegor, a place named in the book Exodus: 'and there *has been fuller discussion* of this in the books of Hebrew Questions'. But Jerome has left us no record of a comment on Beelphegor in any extant 'Hebrew Questions' on Exodus, nor do we know if such was ever written. The same observation holds good for his comments on Carchedon, Elmoni, and Mello (*Lib. Loc.* 934, 942, and 958 respectively), names which do not occur in Genesis.

Thus while it is possible that Jerome may have completed much of *QHG* by the time he had published *Lib. Heb. Nom.* and *Lib. Loc.*, his language will not permit certainty in the matter. What both these texts imply, however, is that Jerome envisaged 'Hebrew Questions' extending far beyond Genesis; and in the Preface to *QHG* he plainly states that such was his aim. There he refers to 'the book of Hebrew Questions which I have set out to write on the whole of Holy Scripture'; and he was still speaking of *books* of Hebrew Questions much later, when writing his commentary on Isaiah.[43]

It is not known whether these books were ever written. If they were, there is no way of discovering how much of the biblical text they may have covered, nor of inferring why they did not survive. But they may never have been composed in the first place; in which

[41] See *Lib. Heb. Nom.* (p. 59): 'Libros enim hebraicarum quaestionum nunc in manus habeo . . .'

[42] See *Lib. Heb. Nom.* (p. 75): 'Galaad . . . Super hoc in libris hebraicarum quaestionum plenius diximus . . . Israhel . . . Et de hoc in libris hebraicarum quaestionum plenius diximus.' See also an earlier entry (p. 67) under Galaad.

[43] See *In Esa.* 5. 15: 5, and below, p. 92.

case *QHG* is the sole representative of Jerome's intended, much larger project. This uncertainty is sufficiently frustrating, the more so because it complicates interpretation of what should be vital information about *QHG*'s date. This is a note in the Preface to his translation of ·Origen's *Homilies on Saint Luke*, indicating that Jerome has set aside for a little 'the books of Hebrew Questions' while he puts these homilies into Latin.[44]

The translation of Origen's homilies was urged upon Jerome by Paula and Eustochium, who had been deeply disappointed on reading Ambrose's new work, *Expositio Evangelii secundum Lucam*. It is difficult to be sure when the final form of this work was published, not least because it refers to another work of Ambrose whose date is hotly debated, *De Apologia Prophetae David*. M. G. Mara lists suggestions of dates for the latter between 383 and 394, and herself proposes a date for the *Expositio* before 389.[45] But there are grounds for supposing that *De Apologia* was written after the battle of Thessalonica, which took place in 390; the *Expositio*, therefore, must have been published either later that year or sometime in the following one.[46] Paula and Eustochium were in Palestine when they read it. We do not know how long it took for the text to reach them there; possibly they had seen it by late 391, but it may have been 392 before it came into their possession.[47]

When Jerome says that he set aside work on 'books of Hebrew Questions' in 392 to turn his attention to Origen's homilies, what exactly does he mean? If *QHG* was the only book of 'Hebrew Questions' which he ever wrote, then we must conclude that he interrupted work on it, probably sometime in 392, to put Origen's homilies into Latin. In that case, *QHG* would have been completed probably late in 392 or early in 393, after he had finished his translation and before he published *De Viris Illustribus*.

But it is evident that Jerome insisted on speaking of *books* of 'Hebrew Questions'; and this permits another solution to the problem. Whether or not Jerome in truth composed further books of

---

[44] See PL 26: 219, 'Praetermisi paululum Hebraicarum Quaestionum libros...'

[45] See G. M. Mara, 'Ambrose of Milan, Ambrosiaster, and Nicetas', in *Patrology*, iv. 162, 164.

[46] See F. Claus, 'La Datation de l'Apologia Prophetae David et l'Apologia David altera: Deux œuvres authentiques de saint Ambroise', *Studia Patristica Mediolanensia*, 7 (Milan, 1976), 168–93.

[47] So P. Nautin, 'L'Activité littéraire de Jérôme de 387–392', *RTP* 115 (1983), 252, followed by Kamesar, *Jerome*, 74.

'Hebrew Questions' does not affect this solution: it is enough that he should have intended to do so. When Paula and Eustochium made their request, it is possible that Jerome had already finished *QHG*, and interrupted work on further 'Hebrew Questions', meaning to resume his labours when he had translated Origen's homilies. With this solution, we still do not know whether he resumed work on 'Hebrew Questions'; but we should be able to suggest a date for the completed *QHG* late in 391 (assuming that Paula and Eustochium had read Ambrose's work by then), or during the earlier part of 392.

It would seem most likely, then, that Jerome finished *QHG* sometime between the later part of 391 and the early months of 393: the complexities of the evidence allow nothing more definite to be said.[48] Here, however, we have spoken only of the date of *QHG*'s completion. It should not be forgotten that his researches for this work are likely to belong to the period before 391–3. The manner in which he refers to 'Hebrew Questions' in *Lib. Loc.* and *Lib. Heb. Nom.* strongly implies that his work on these questions had been in hand for some time. Jerome is familiar with it. He can speak of it in the perfect tense, which invites the reader to understand that he already has a store of Hebrew knowledge which is as good as ready for the Christian public to read. It would not be exceeding the evidence, in our view, to suggest that Jerome was determining the principles and groundwork of *QHG* long before 390. Given the amount of knowledge which *QHG* presupposes, and the great range of interests on Jerome's part which the monograph expresses, it is possible that he spent a number of years preparing for this unique work. Indeed, his own words to Aurelius

---

[48] Compare Kamesar, *Jerome*, 73–6. Formerly scholars worked with a chronology which tended to date *QHG* slightly earlier. Thus Grützmacher, *Hieronymus*, i. 63, dated the three treatises *Lib. Heb. Nom.*, *QHG*, and *Lib. Loc.* generally between 386 and 392, Ambrose's *Expositio* in 388, and Jerome's rendering of Origen's homilies on Luke between 388 and 392. He noted that Vallarsi had dated the three treatises to 389–90, without giving evidence. His opinion was clear, however, that Jerome had published *QHG* before translating Origen's homilies (vol. ii, p. 80 and n. 3). Cavallera, *Saint Jérôme*, ii. 26–8 dates it to 389–92, arguing against Grützmacher that Jerome had interrupted *QHG* to translate Origen's work which he thinks arrived in Bethlehem around 389. More recently, Kelly, *Jerome*, p. 153, has followed Cavallera's view, suggesting that Jerome was working on *QHG*, *Lib. Heb. Nom.*, and *Lib. Loc.* c.389–91, and that he suspended work on *QHG* to translate Origen's homilies.

of Carthage, in offering to him a copy of *QHG*, may indicate as much.[49]

Notes on the Translation

The text translated here is that edited by D. Vallarsi in J.-P. Migne's PL 23, *Sancti Eusebii Hieronymi Stridonensis Presbyteri Liber Hebraicarum Quaestionum in Genesim* (Paris, 1865). The text published under the auspices of P. Antin in Corpus Christianorum Series Latina (Tournai, 1959), a reprint of the edition of P. de Lagarde (Leipzig, 1868), displays a number of errors, misprints, and inaccuracies, especially in the transmission of Greek and Hebrew forms. The critical apparatus of the latter, however, is of particular value; and where reference is made to it, or to Lagarde's text, this is clearly indicated in the Commentary or the accompanying footnotes.

Jerome's language in *QHG* often reflects the wording and phraseology of his sources. The Jewish background and ethos of many of his remarks is revealed by his mode of expression, which to Latin ears must have sounded strange. A translation of the Latin, however literal, may not be sufficient wholly to convey the underlying drift of Jerome's meaning; and the Commentary, at least in part, is therefore designed to explore the ramifications of his choice of vocabulary and the range of his sources.

---

[49] He says: 'Itaque si qua nunc scripsimus maturiora et aetati nostrae convenientia aestimare debes . . .', contrasting his literary gifts to Aurelius with the writings of his youth: see *Ep.* 27 in Divjak's edition (cited above, n. 8), 131, lines 20–1. The language could imply that *QHG* is the product of mature reflection on his work.

Hebrew Questions on the Book of Genesis by Saint Jerome the Presbyter

At the beginning of my books, I ought to set forth the subject-matter of the work which follows; but I am compelled first of all to reply to things which have been said by way of abuse, and thereby I uphold something of the attitude of Terence, who used to put on stage the prologues of his comedies as a defence of his own work. For Luscius Lanvinus, who is like our Luscius, used to press him and charge him with being a poet-thief from the public treasury. The Mantuan bard also suffered this same thing from his rivals, so that he was dubbed a 'plunderer of the ancients' when he translated certain verses of Homer in a literal fashion. In reply, he told these men that it takes great strength to wrench the club of Hercules from his hand. And even Cicero, who stood at the very height of Roman eloquence as king of public speakers and as one who made glorious the Latin language, is accused by the Greeks of expropriation.

So it is not astonishing if filthy swine grunt against me as being a tiny little man, and trample pearls with their feet; since spite flames out against the most learned men and those who should have to overcome jealousy with renown. But justly did this happen to those men whose eloquence used to thunder forth in the theatres, the Senate House, the public assembly, and at the speakers' platform: for bravery in the public arena always has those who are jealous of it, *and lightning-flashes strike the highest mountains.* But I am far away from the cities, the market-place, the lawcourts, and the crowds; even so, as Quintilian says: *Jealousy discovers the one who lies hidden from view.* Wherefore I beseech the reader (*if, however, anyone shall read these things, held captive by love*) that, in the Book of Hebrew Questions which I have set out to write on the whole of Holy Scripture, he should not seek eloquence, nor the charm of public speakers; but rather that he should himself make reply to our enemies on our behalf, that pardon be granted to a new work. For just as we ourselves are lowly and poor little ones, and neither have riches, nor are worthy to receive them when they are presented; so they also should recognize that they cannot put knowledge of the Scriptures (that is, the riches of Christ) on a par with the riches of the world.

Therefore it shall be my concern both to rebut the errors of those who make different kinds of conjectures about the Hebrew books, and to restore to their proper authority those things which in the Latin and Greek codices seem to burst forth in abundance; and to make plain through consideration of the native language the etymologies of objects, of names, and of territories which have no meaning in our own language. And so that the improvement be more easily recognized, we shall set out first of all the witnesses as they exist among us. And we shall show, by comparison with what follows, what in them is either less, or more, or different. But we neither charge the Septuagint with errors, as jealous people slander us; nor do we regard our own work as a censure of them, since they were unwilling to make known to Ptolemy, king of Alexandria, mystical teachings in the Holy Scriptures, and especially those things which promised the coming of Christ, lest the Jews might appear to worship a second God also. For the king, being a follower of Plato, used to make much of the Jews, on the grounds that they were said to worship one God.

Yet even the Evangelists, and also Our Lord and Saviour, as well as the Apostle Paul, quote many things as if from the Old Testament, which are not contained in our codices; about which we shall offer fuller discussion in their proper places. Consequently, it is clear that those copies are the more reliable which agree with the authority of the New Testament; add to this the fact that Josephus, who sets forth the history of the Septuagint, reports that only the five Books of Moses were translated by them, books which we too acknowledge as agreeing more than the others with the Hebrew. But also those interpreters who lived afterwards, I mean Aquila and Symmachus and Theodotion, have something very different from what we read.

Finally, (something that may appease even those who disparage us), let foreign merchandise come by boat only to those who desire it: peasants may not buy balsam, pepper, and the fruits of palm trees. I remain silent about Adamantius, whose name (*if it be permitted to compare little things with great*) is more hateful than my name: this is because in his sermons which he delivers to the common folk he follows the common edition [of the Scriptures]; but in his books, that is, in more important debate, he is overcome

by the Hebrew truth and surrounded by their armies, and sometimes seeks the help of a foreign language. This one thing I say: that
I should wish, along with hatred of his name, also to have knowledge of the Scriptures, and to value as a trifle the images and
shadows of ghosts, whose nature is said to be to terrify little
children and to chatter in dark corners.

1: 1 *In the beginning, God made the heaven and the earth.* As it
is written in the dispute between Jason and Papiscus, and as
Tertullian reckons in the book against Praxeas, and as Hilary also
asserts in the exposition of a certain Psalm, most people think that
in the Hebrew is contained *In the Son, God made heaven and earth,*
which the facts of the matter itself prove to be mistaken. For both
the Septuagint, and Symmachus and Theodotion, translated it as *In
the beginning*; and in the Hebrew is written *bresith* (which Aquila
understands as *In the chapter*) and not *baben,* which would mean
In the Son. So the verse can be applied to Christ more in respect of
its intention than following its literal translation: to Christ who is
proved to be founder of heaven and earth both at the very front of
Genesis, which is the head of all the books, and also at the beginning of John the Evangelist's work. Consequently He says of Himself, both in the Psalter *In the chapter of the book it is written
concerning Me,* that means, at the beginning of Genesis; and in the
Gospel, *All things were made by Him, and without Him nothing
was made.* But this should also be known, that among the Hebrews
this book is called *bresith,* because they have this custom of giving
names to scrolls from their opening words.
2 *And the Spirit of God moved over the waters.* In place of what is
written in our codices as *moved,* the Hebrew has *merefeth,* which
we can render as 'was brooding over' or 'was keeping warm', in the
likeness of a bird giving life to its eggs with warmth. Consequently
we understand that this is said not about the spirit of the world, as
some suppose, but about the Holy Spirit, Who is also said from the
beginning Himself to be *The Life-giver to all things.* If, then, He is
the Life-giver, He is therefore also the Author [of life]; and if the
Author, then He is also God: *For send forth Thy Spirit,* says
Scripture, *and they shall be created.*
10 *And the gatherings together of the waters He called seas.* It is to
be observed that every gathering together of waters, be they salt
or sweet, is named 'seas' according to the idiom of the Hebrew

language. It is therefore to no purpose that Porphyry misrepresents the Evangelists as having called Genesareth 'a sea' instead of 'a lake', so as to concoct a miracle for the ignorant to the effect that the Lord walked on the sea; for every lake and every gathering of waters is called 'seas'.

2: 2 *And on the sixth day God brought to completion His works which He had made.* In the Hebrew, it has 'the seventh day' instead of *on the sixth day.* Therefore we shall press the Jews who boast of the repose of the Sabbath, because already then, in the beginning, the Sabbath was broken while God laboured on the Sabbath by bringing his works to completion on it and by blessing the day itself; since on that day He completed the universe.

8 *And the Lord God planted a paradise in Eden over against the east.* Instead of *a paradise,* in Hebrew it has 'a garden', that is, *gan.* Then they understand Eden as 'delights': for this word, Symmachus offered the translation 'a flowering paradise'. And what follows, *over against the east,* is written in Hebrew as *mekedem.* Aquila took it as *apo archēs* (and we can translate it as 'from the outset'), but Symmachus as *ek prōtēs,* and Theodotion as *en prōtois,* which also in fact means not 'the east', but 'the beginning'. From this it is most clearly established that God had previously founded paradise before He set about making heaven and earth, as indeed one reads in the Hebrew: *Moreover the Lord God had planted, from the beginning, a paradise in Eden.*

11 *The name of the one is Phison.* They believe that this is the River Ganges of India.

12 *Where there is carbuncle and prasine stone.* Instead of *carbuncle* and *prasine stone,* the others have translated as *bdellion* and *onyx.*

15 *And the Lord took up the man, and placed him in the paradise of pleasure.* In the Hebrew it has 'Eden' instead of *pleasure.* Now the Septuagint themselves explained *eden* as meaning 'pleasure'; but Symmachus, who a little earlier had translated it as 'flowering paradise', put here *en tōi paradeisōi tēs aktēs,* which itself has overtones of both 'charm' and 'delights'.

17 *For on whatever day you shall eat of it, you shall die by death.* Symmachus translated more appropriately when he rendered it as *you shall be mortal.*

21 *And the Lord God sent extasim upon Adam.* Instead of *extasis,* that is, 'departure of the mind', in the Hebrew it has *thardema,*

which Aquila has translated as *kataphoran* and Symmachus as *karon*, that is, 'heavy and deep sleep'. Then there follows *and he slept*. This very same word is used in Jonah of a man snoring in his sleep.

23 *This now is bone from my bones and flesh from my flesh: this one shall be called woman, because she was taken from man.* In Greek and Latin it does not seem to make sense why she should be called woman because she was taken from man; but in the Hebrew language the *etymology* [derivation of the word] is observed, since man is called *is* and woman *issa*. Therefore woman is rightly called *issa*, as from *is*. Consequently Symmachus also was determined to preserve the *etymology* in an elegant manner, even in Greek, when he translated: *This one shall be called andris, hoti apo andros elēphthē*. In Latin, we can express it as: 'This one shall be called *virago*, because she was taken from *vir*.' On the other hand, Theodotion supposed another derivation, and translated: *This one shall be called taking up, because she was taken up out of man*; since in fact *issa* can also be understood as 'taking up' according to a different manner of accentuation.

3: 1 *Now the serpent was wiser than all the beasts upon the earth*. Instead of *wise* in the Hebrew it has *arom*, which Aquila and Theodotion have understood as *panourgon*, that is, 'worthless' and 'sly'. So by means of this word are described cunning and slyness rather than wisdom.

8 *And they heard the voice of the Lord God walking in paradise towards the evening*. In the majority of the codices belonging to the Latins it has *after noon* instead of *towards the evening*, which we have set down here. This is because we cannot translate exactly the Greek expression *to deilinon*, instead of which is written in Hebrew *larue aiom*. Aquila understood this as *en tōi anemōi tēs hēmeras*, that is, 'in the wind of the day'; but Symmachus translated it as *dia pneumatos hēmeras*, that is, 'through the spirit of the day'. Finally, Theodotion rendered it more clearly as *en tōi pneumati pros katapsuxin tēs hēmeras* to indicate the coolness of the breeze which blows when the noonday heat is past.

14 *On your breast and on your belly you shall walk*. The Septuagint added *belly*; but in the Hebrew it has merely *breast*, to reveal the cunning and slyness of its (the serpent's) thoughts; because all its steps were steps of wickedness, and acts of deception. Similar is the case of what follows, *you shall eat earth*: in the place

of *earth* is written *aphar*, which we can express as 'ashes' and 'dust'.

15 *It shall watch your head, and you shall watch its heel.* More correctly, it has in the Hebrew *it will crush your head, and you shall crush its heel.* For our footsteps are indeed shackled by the serpent, and *the Lord shall crush Satan under our feet swiftly.*

16 *Multiplying, I will multiply your sadness and your groanings.* In the place of *sadness* and *groanings*, in the Hebrew it has *sorrows and conception of children. And your turning shall be towards your husband.* Instead of *turning*, Aquila translated as 'companionship', and Symmachus as 'desire' or 'passion'.

17 *Cursed be the earth in [by] your deeds.* 'Deeds' here do not refer to the cultivation of the fields as most people suppose, but to sins, as it stands in the Hebrew. Nor does Aquila disagree when he says: *Cursed be the ground because of you;* and Theodotion has: *Cursed be adama in your transgression.*

20 *And Adam called the name of his wife Life, because she is the mother of all the living.* Scripture shows why she was called Eve, that is, Life, because she is the mother of all the living. For the word Eve is translated as life.

24 *And He cast out Adam, and made him dwell over against the paradise of pleasure. And He set cherubim and a flaming sword which turns to guard the way to the tree of life.* In the Hebrew there is another meaning of quite different import than the one perceived here. For it says: *And He cast out Adam* (there is scarcely any doubt that the Lord is the subject), *and made to dwell in front of the paradise of pleasure the cherubim, and the flaming sword, so that it should turn and guard the way to the tree of life.* It is not the case that God made that same Adam whom He had cast out dwell over against the paradise of pleasure; but rather that God, when Adam had been cast out, placed in front of the gates of paradise cherubim and the flaming sword to guard the forecourt of paradise, so that no one could enter.

4: 1 *And she conceived and bore Cain, and said: I have obtained* (or: *possessed) a man by means of God.* Cain is taken as meaning 'obtaining' or 'possession', that is, *ktēsis.* Therefore in representing its etymology, [Scripture] says *canithi*, that is, 'I have possessed' a man through God's agency.

4–5 *And God had regard for Abel and his offerings; but He did not have regard for Cain and for his sacrifices. And Cain was much overcome with sadness.* How was it that Cain had been able to know that God had received his brother's offerings and had rejected his own, unless that interpretation which Theodotion posited is true: *and the Lord sent forth a flame over Abel and over his sacrifice; but over Cain and over his sacrifice He did not send a flame?* Indeed, we read that fire used to come from heaven to consume the sacrifice, both at the dedication of the Temple in the days of Solomon, and when Elias built the altar on Mount Carmel.

6–7 *And the Lord said to Cain, Why has your countenance fallen? Is it not so, that if you offer sacrifice rightly, but do not apportion [the offering] correctly, you have sinned? Be quiet: its turning will be towards you, and you shall have the dominion over him.* We are compelled of necessity to delay longer over individual details. For in the present verse the meaning in the Hebrew is quite different from that in the Septuagint. *For the Lord said to Cain: Why are you angry, and why has your countenance fallen? If you do well, shall it not be forgiven you? But if you do not do well, your sin shall sit in front of the gates, and its companionship shall be to you. But you, rather, should exercise dominion over it.* Now what it is saying is this. Why are you angry, and why, tortured with jealous spite against your brother, do you lower your countenance to the ground? If you have acted well, shall not all your offence be forgiven you? or, as Theodotion says, shall it not be acceptable? That is, shall I not receive your gift, as I received your brother's? But if you acted badly, sin shall at once sit in front of your porch, and you shall be the companion of such a door-keeper. But because you have free will, I advise that sin should not have dominion over you, but that you should have dominion over sin. Now what has produced the mistake among the Septuagint is the fact that sin, namely *attath*, is of the masculine gender in Hebrew, but of the feminine in Greek; and those who have interpreted it have translated that word with the masculine gender, as it was in Hebrew.

8 *And Cain said to Abel his brother.* What the Lord spoke is understood. So what is found in our scroll, and in that of the Samaritans, namely, *Let us go out into the field,* is unnecessary.

15 *Anyone who kills Cain shall pay seven penalties.* Instead of *seven penalties,* Aquila translated *sevenfold,* Symmachus *seventh,* and Theodotion *through the week.* Our letter to Bishop Damasus about this verse still exists.

16 *And he dwelt in the land of Naid.* What the Septuagint translated as Naid is expressed in Hebrew as *Nod*, and is to be interpreted as *saleuomenos*, that is, unsteady, moving like the waves, and of unfixed abode. The reference is not, therefore, to a land called Naid, as the mass of our people think; but God's decision is discharged in that he wandered hither and thither as a wanderer and a fugitive.

25 *And she called his name Seth: For God has raised up other seed for me instead of Abel, whom Cain slew.* Seth is properly *thesis*, that is, 'placing'. Therefore, because God *had placed* him instead of Abel, he is called Seth, that is 'placing'. Finally, Aquila says: *And she called his name Seth, saying, Because God has placed for me another seed.*

26 *And he called his name Enos: this man hoped to call on the name of the Lord God.* Just as Adam is translated as 'man', so also Enos is to be taken as 'mankind' or 'man', in accordance with the diversity of the Hebrew language. And because he had this name, it is written appropriately concerning him: *Then there was a beginning of calling on the Name of the Lord*; although the majority of the Hebrews think something else, that then, for the first time, idols were constructed in the Name of the Lord and in His likeness.

5: 2 *He made them man and woman, and blessed them, and called their name Adam,* that is, mankind. So the designation 'man' is applicable both to man and to woman.

3 *Then Adam lived 230 years and begat a son in his image and likeness, and called his name Seth.* It is to be understood that up to the story of the Flood, where in our codices it is said that someone aged 200 and however many more years fathered a child, in the Hebrew it has 100 and the remaining years which follow.

4 *Now the days of Adam after he begat Seth were 700 years.* Because the text had made a mistake in the matter of the 200 years, it therefore put here 700 years, while in the Hebrew it has 800, 100 in addition.

25–7 *And Methuselah lived for 167 years and begat Lamech. And Methuselah lived after he had begotten Lamech 802 years, and begat sons and daughters. And all the days of Methuselah which he lived were 969 years, and he died.* This is a celebrated question, and one which has been publicly aired in argument by all the churches, since according to careful calculation it is reported that Methuselah lived for fourteen years after the Flood. For when Methuselah was

167 years old he begat Lamech; then Lamech, when he was 188 years old, begat Noah. Now the years of Methuselah's life, up to the days of Noah's birth, number 355. Then, in the 600th year of Noah's life, the Flood occurred. So by this means it is proved by the usual calculation done by portion after portion [of Scripture], that the Flood took place in the 955th year of Methuselah. Now since he is said above to have lived 969 years, there is no doubt that he continued to live fourteen years after the Flood. How, then, is it true that only eight lives were saved in the ark? Therefore, as in many other instances so also in this, it remains that there is a mistake in the number. However, both in the Hebrew books, and in those of the Samaritans, I have found it written thus: *And Methuselah lived for 187 years and begat Lamech. And after he had begotten Lamech, Methuselah lived for 782 years and he begat sons and daughters. And all the days of Methuselah were 969 years, and he died. And Lamech lived for 182 years, and begat Noah.* Therefore from the day of Methuselah's birth to the day of Noah's birth there are 369 years; add to these Noah's 600 years, since the Flood occurred in the 600th year of his life; and so it turns out that Methuselah died in the 969th year of his life, in the year when the Flood began.

29 *And he called his name Noah, saying, This one will make us rest from our works.* Noah can be explained as meaning 'rest'. Therefore he was called 'rest', because in that man's days all former works ceased as a result of the Flood.

6: 2 So *when the sons of God saw the daughters of men, that they were comely.* The Hebrew word *eloim* is of common number; for both 'God' and 'gods' are designated in the same way. For this reason Aquila dared to say 'sons of *the gods*', in the plural, understanding 'gods' as holy ones or angels. *For God stood up in the assembly of the gods: moreover, in the midst of the gods He gives judgement.* Consequently, Symmachus too follows the sense of this kind of rendering, and says: *The sons of the mighty saw the daughters of men,* and the rest.

3 *And the Lord God said: My Spirit shall not remain in these men for ever, because they are flesh.* In Hebrew is written: *My Spirit shall not judge these men for evermore, since they are flesh.* That is, because a frail condition exists in mankind, I shall not preserve them for everlasting tortures, but shall pay them here what they deserve. Therefore Scripture refers, not to the strictness of God as

is read in our codices, but to the mercy of God when this sinner is visited for his wicked deed. So when God is angry, He speaks to certain people: *I shall not visit* [i.e. *punish*] *their daughters when they commit fornication, nor their wives, when they commit adultery.* And in another place [He says]: *I will visit their iniquities with the rod, and their sins with whips; but I shall not take away My mercy from them.*

Next, lest He might seem to be cruel on the grounds that He had not given a place of repentance for sinners, He added: *But their days shall be 120 years.* This means they shall have 120 years to do penance. So human life is not shortened to 120 years, as many mistakenly suppose; but 120 years were given to that generation for repentance. For indeed we find that after the Flood Abraham lived for 175 years, and others lived more than 200 or 300 years. However, because they made light of doing penance, God was unwilling to wait for the time which He had decreed; but the time was cut short by the space of twenty years, and He brought in the Flood in the hundredth year appointed for their doing penance.

4 *Moreover there were giants on the earth in those days; and after these things, as the sons of God were accustomed to go in to the daughters of men, so they would breed with them. Those were the giants from of old, men called by name.* In the Hebrew, it has the following: *Falling ones* (that is, *annaphilim*) *were on the earth in those days. And after these things, when the sons of the gods used to go in to the daughters of men and breed with them, these were the mighty ones from the beginning, men called by name.* Instead of *falling ones* or giants, Symmachus translated 'violent ones'. The name *falling ones* is indeed fitting both for angels and for the offspring of holy ones.

9 *Noah, a man righteous and perfect in his generation, was pleasing to God.* Scripture says distinctly *in his generation,* to indicate that he was righteous not in respect of the highest degree of righteousness, but relative to the righteousness of his own generation. And this is what is expressed in the Hebrew: *Noah, a righteous man, was perfect in his generations. Noah used to walk with God:* this means that he used to follow His footsteps.

14 *Make for yourself an ark of square wood.* Instead of *square wood,* we read in the Hebrew *wood smeared with pitch.*

16 *You shall make the ark compact in constructing it, and in a cubit you shall finish it above.* Instead of *you shall make the ark*

compact in constructing it, in the Hebrew it has *you shall make a noonday for the ark,* which Symmachus translated more plainly by saying *you shall make diaphanes,* that is, *a clear thing* for the ark, supposing that a window is to be understood.

8: 1–3 *And the water ceased, and the fountains of the abyss and the floodgates of heaven were revealed.* Instead of the fountains having been revealed, all translators have rendered 'closed up' and 'stopped up'. And in place of what follows, *The water diminished upon the earth* and the rest, is written *And the waters turned back from the earth, going and returning.* Observe that, according to Ecclesiastes, all waters and torrents return to the womb of the abyss through hidden channels.

6–7 *After forty days, Noah opened the door of the ark which he had made, and sent out a raven; and it went out, and did not return to him until the water was drying up from the earth.* Instead of *door,* in Hebrew *window* is written; and the matter concerning the raven is differently expressed: *He sent out a raven and it went out, going out and returning until the waters were dried up from the earth.*

9: 18 *And the sons of Noah who went out from the ark were Sem, Cham, and Japheth.* The Septuagint, who were unable to render into the Greek language the letter *heth* which has the sound of a double aspirate, often added the Greek letter *chi* to instruct us that we ought to make an aspiration in words of this sort. So in this verse they translate *Cham* for what is actually Ham—from which the word 'Egyptian' is pronounced as 'Ham' in the language of the Egyptians up to the present day.

27 *May God enlarge Japheth, and dwell in the tents of Sem.* From Sem were born the Hebrews, from Japheth the people of the Gentiles. Therefore because the multitude of believers is wide, he received the name *breadth* because of the breadth which is expressed [in Hebrew] as Japheth. And as for what Scripture says, *May he dwell in the tents of Sem:* this is prophesied about us [Christians], who are engaged in the learning and knowledge of the Scriptures after Israel had been cast forth.

29 *And all the days of Noah were 950 years.* See, after the Flood Noah lived for 350 years. From this it is evident, as we have said above, that the 120 years were given to that generation for repentance, and are not ordained as the period of life for mortal men.

10: 2 *The sons of Japheth were Gomer and Magog and Madai and Javan and Thubal and Mosoch and Thiras.* To Japheth the son of Noah were born seven sons who occupied land in Asia from Amanus and Taurus of Coele-Syria and the mountains of Cilicia as far as the river Don. Then in Europe they occupied land as far as Gadira, leaving behind names for places and peoples, most of which were afterwards changed: others remain as they were. So Gomer actually refers to the Galatians; Magog to the Scythians; Madai to the Medes; Javan to the Ionians who are also the Greeks (from which we get 'the Ionian Sea'); and Thubal to the Iberians who are also the Spaniards from whom derive the Celtiberians, although certain people suppose them to be the Italians. Mosoch refers to the Cappadocians, so that among themselves up to the present day their city is also called Mazeca; but the Septuagint think that Caphthorim are the Cappadocians. Thiras refers to the Thracians, whose name has not been much changed. I know that a certain man has referred Gog and Magog, both as regards the present verse and in Ezekiel, to the account of the Goths who were recently raging in our land: whether this is true is shown by the outcome of the actual battle [recorded in Ezekiel 38–9]. But in fact all learned men in the past had certainly been accustomed to calling the Goths Getae rather than Gog and Magog. So these seven nations, which I have related as coming from the stock of Japheth, live in the region of the north.

3 *The sons of Gomer were Aschenez and Riphath and Thogarma.* The Greeks call Aschenez the Regini, Riphath the Paphlagonians, and Thogarma the Phrygians.

4–5 *The sons of Javan were Elisa and Tharsis, Cethim and Dodanim. From these were divided the islands of the nations in their lands, each according to his language, his family, and his nation.* From the Ionians, that is from the Greeks, were born the Elisaei who are called the descendants of Aeolus; whence also the fifth language of Greece is called *aeolis*, which they themselves call *pemptēn dialekton*. Josephus thinks that Tharsis refers to the Cilicians, alleging that the aspirated letter *theta* has been badly corrupted into the letter *tau* by later individuals: consequently, their mother-city is called Tarsus, famous for the Apostle Paul. Cethim refers to the Citii, from whom the city of Citium in Cyprus is named up to the present. Dodanim are the inhabitants of Rhodes; for so the Septuagint translated it. Let us read the books of Varro *On*

Antiquities, and those of Sisinnius Capito, and the Greek Phlegon and other most learned men; and we shall see that almost all the islands and the sea-coasts of the whole world, and the lands near to the sea, have been filled by Greek settlers who, as we have remarked above, occupied all the places of the sea-coast from the Amanus and Taurus mountains as far as the British Ocean.

6 *The sons of Cham were Chus and Mesraim and Phuth and Chanaan.* Up to the present day, Ethiopia is called Chus by the Hebrews, Egypt is called Mesraim, and the Libyans Phuth. So it is, then, that up to the present day the river of Mauretania is called Phut, and all the Libyan territory round about it is called Phuthensis. Many writers, both Greek and Latin, are witnesses to this fact. However, it is not appropriate to discuss here and now why it is that in only one part of the territory the old name of Libya should remain, and the rest of the land be called Africa. Finally, Chanaan held the land which the Jews later possessed after the Chanaanites had been expelled.

7 *The sons of Chus were Saba and Aevila, Sabatha, Regma, and Sabathaca.* Saba is where the Sabaeans come from, of whom Virgil says: *The incense tree belongs to the Sabaeans alone*, and, elsewhere, *And a hundred altars are warm with Sabaean incense.* Aevila refers to the Gaetuli who are in the more distant parts of Africa and stay close to the desert. Sabatha: from this derive the Sabatheni, who are nowadays called the Astabari. But Regma and Sabathaca have little by little lost their old names, and it is not known what names they now have instead of their ancient ones.

7b *The sons of Regma were Saba and Dadan.* Here Saba is written with the letter *sin*; but above it was written with *samech*, and we have said that because of this the Sabaeans were so called. But in the present verse Saba refers to Arabia. For in the seventy-first Psalm where we have *The kings of the Arabs and Saba shall offer gifts*, there is written in the Hebrew: *The kings of Saba and Saba*, the first word with *sin*, the second with *samech*. Dadan is a people in the western region of Ethiopia.

8, 10 *And Chus begat Nimrod. This man began to be powerful in the earth.* And after a little while, it says: *And the beginning of his kingdom was Babel and Arach and Achad and Chalanne in the land of Senaar.* Nimrod son of Chus was the first to seize despotic rule over the people, which men were not yet accustomed to; and he reigned in Babylon which was called Babel, because the languages

of those building the tower were thrown into confusion there. For
Babel signifies confusion. Then he also reigned in Arach, that is in
Edissa; and in Achad, which is now called Nisibis; and in Chalanne,
which was later called Seleucia after King Seleucus when its name
had been changed, and which is now in actual fact called
Ktēsiphōn, Ctesiphon.

11 *From that land Assur went out and built Ninive and the city
Rooboth.* From this land sprang forth the empire of the Assyrians
who founded Ninus (from the name of Ninus son of Bel), a large
city which the Hebrews called Ninive. The whole prophecy of
Jonah relates both to the destruction and repentance of this city.
Now in so far as Scripture says Ninive and the city Rooboth, we
should not imagine that they were two cities; but because Rooboth
means 'streets', it should be read as follows: *And he built Ninive
and the streets of the city.*

13–14 *And Mesraim begat Ludim and Anamim and Laabim and
Nephtuim and Phetrosim and Chasloim, from whom the Philistines
and Caphthorim went forth.* With the exception of the Laabim,
from whom the Libyans were later given their name (they were at
first called Phuthaei), and the Chasloim, who were later called
Philistines (in debased form we speak of them as Palestinians), the
six other nations are unknown to us, because they were overthrown
in the Ethiopian war, and reached the stage where their former
names were forgotten. They occupied the land from Gaza to the
furthest borders of Egypt.

15 *And Chanaan begat Sidon his first-born, and Chettaeus and
Jebusaeus and Amorrhaeus and Gergesaeus and Evaeus and
Aracaeus and Sinaeus and Aradius and Samaraeus and Amathaeus.*
The first-born son of Chanaan was Sidon, from whom the city in
Phoenicia is named Sidon. Then there was Aracaeus, who founded
Arcas, a town situated over against Tripolis at the foot of Mount
Lebanon. Not far away from this was another city, Sinus by name,
which was overthrown later in various chances of war and pre-
serves the original name only as the name of the place. The
Aradians are those who occupied the island of Aradus, separated by
a narrow strait from the Phoenician shore. To the Samaraeans
belongs Emissa, a noble city of Coele-Syria. Up to our own time
Amath is still called both by Syrians and by Hebrews what it had
been called by the ancients: the Macedonians, who ruled in the east
after Alexander, called this city Epiphania. Some people think that

it was called Antiochia. Others, although not correctly, none the less support their conjecture with a word like the right one and think that it was called Emas, the first stopping-place from Antioch for those continuing the journey to Edessa; and they think that it is the same place which was called Emath by the ancients.

19 *And the boundary of the Chanaanites was from Sidon until you come to Gerar as far as Gaza, as you continue to Sodom and Gomorra and Adama and Seboim as far as Lise.* Because the other cities, namely Sidon and Gerar and Sodom and Gomorra and Adama and Seboim are known to everyone, it seems necessary to observe only that the same Lise is what is now called Callirhoe, where hot waters burst forth and flow down into the Dead Sea.

22 *The sons of Sem were Elam and Assur and Arphaxad and Lud and Aram.* These people occupy the part of Asia from the river Euphrates to the Indian Ocean. Moreover, Elam is the one from whom the Elamite princes of Persia come. It has already been remarked before about Assur that he founded the city of Ninus. Arphaxad is the one from whom derive the Chaldeans, Lud from whom come the Lydians, and Aram from whom come the Syrians, whose mother-city is Damascus.

23 *The sons of Aram were Us and Ul and Gether and Mes.* Us, the founder of Trachonitis and Damascus, held sway between Palestine and Coele-Syria: as a result of this, the Septuagint in the book of Job, where in Hebrew is written *the land of Us*, have translated the territory *Ausitis* or *Usitis*. Ul is the one from whom the Armenians come, and Gether the one from whom derive the Acarnanii or Carians. Finally Mes, instead of which the Septuagint have specified Mosoch, are nowadays called the Maeones.

24–5 *Arphaxad begat Sela, and Sela begat Heber. Two sons were born from Heber: the name of the one was Phaleg, because in his days the earth was divided; and the name of his brother was Jectan.* Heber, from whom the Hebrews descended, because of a prophecy gave his son the name Phaleg which means 'division', on account of the fact that in his days the languages were divided up in Babylon.

26–9 *Jectan begat Helmodad and Saleph and Asermoth and Jare and Aduram and Uzal and Decla, Ebal, Abimael, Seba, Ophir, Evila, and Jobab.* I am unable to find the later names of these thirteen nations; but until the present day, since they are far away from us they are either called as they were before, or, if their names have been changed, they are now unknown. They occupied the whole territory of India from the river Cophene, which is called Hieria.

11: 28 *And Aran died before his father in the land in which he was born in the territory of the Chaldeans.* In place of what we read as *in the territory of the Chaldeans*, in the Hebrew it has *in ur Chesdim*, that is, 'in the fire of the Chaldeans'. Moreover the Hebrews, taking the opportunity afforded by this verse, hand on a story of this sort to the effect that Abraham was put into the fire because he refused to worship fire, which the Chaldeans honour; and that he escaped through God's help, and fled from the fire of idolatry. What is written [in the Septuagint] in the following verses, that Thara with his offspring 'went out from the territory of the Chaldeans' stands in place of what is contained in the Hebrew, *from the fire of the Chaldeans.* And they maintain that this refers to what is said in this verse: *Aran died before the face of Thara his father in the land of his birth in the fire of the Chaldeans;* that is, because, he refused to worship fire he was consumed by fire. Then afterwards the Lord spoke to Abraham: *I am the One Who led you out of the fire of the Chaldeans.*

29 *And Abram and Nachor took wives for themselves: the name of Abram's wife was Sarai, and the name of Nachor's wife was Melcha, the daughter of Aran. And the father of Melcha is the father of Jesca.* Aran was the son of Thara, the brother of Abram and Nachor, and he fathered two daughters, Melcha and Sarai who was surnamed Jesca, *duōnumon* [with two names]. Of these, Nachor took Melcha as wife, and Abraham took Sarai, because marriages between uncles and brothers' daughters had not yet been forbidden by the law; even marriages between brothers and sisters were contracted among the first human beings.

12: 4 *And Abram was 75 years old when he went out from Charra.* A question arises which cannot be answered. For if Thara, Abraham's father, when he was still in the territory of the Chaldeans at 70 years of age fathered Abram, and afterwards died in Charra in the 205th year of his life: how is it that now, after Thara's death, Abram went out from Charra, and is declared to have been 75 years old, when 135 years are shown to have passed from Abram's birth up to his father's death? Therefore that tradition of the Hebrews, which we have related above, is true; that Thara with his sons went out from the fire of the Chaldeans, and that Abram, when surrounded by the Babylonian fire because he refused to worship it, was set free by God's help; and from that time onwards the days of his life and the measure of his age are reckoned for him, namely from that time when he acknowledged the Lord and despised the idols of the Chaldeans. It could, however, be the case, because the Scripture leaves it indefinite, that Thara set out from Chaldea and came into Charra a few years before he met his death; or that he in fact came into Charra immediately after the persecution, and stayed there a little longer. But if anyone is opposed to this explanation, he will seek another solution; and then he will properly reject the things which have been declared by us.

9–10 *And Abram set out and departed into the desert; and there was a famine in the land.* Both in the present place and in several others, *to the south* is written in the Hebrew instead of *desert*. We should therefore take note of this.

15–16 *And the princes of Pharaoh saw her and praised her to Pharaoh and led her into Pharaoh's house; and he treated Abram well because of her. And he had sheep and cattle and asses and servants and handmaidens, mules and camels.* Although it is not force, but voluntary behaviour which stains the body of holy women, and it is possible for Sarai to be freed from blame because in the time of famine she was alone in foreign places and unable to resist the king, and her husband was conniving at the deed; nevertheless, there is another way in which foul necessity can be excused. For according to the Book of Esther, among the ancients whichever woman had pleased the king *was anointed with myrtle oil for six months, and for six months was in different colours and under the care of the women, and only then she went in to the king.* So then it is possible that after Sarai had been pleasing to the king, and while her entry to the king was being prepared throughout that year, Pharaoh gave many things to Abraham; then after that, when Pharaoh was smitten by the Lord, she still remained untouched by sexual intercourse with him.

13: 1–4 *And Abram went up from Egypt, he and his wife, and all that he possessed, and Lot was with him, into the desert. And Abram was very rich in flocks and silver and gold; and he departed into the desert whence he came, as far as Bethel.* After he had been set free from Egypt, it is rightly said that he went up. But what follows clashes with the sense of this verse: for how could he have been very rich when he came out of Egypt? This matter is explained

by that Hebrew truth in which is written 'Abraham was exceedingly heavy', that is, *barus sphodra*; for he had been weighed down
by the weight of Egypt. And although they appear to be riches
consisting of flocks, gold, and silver; for a holy man, however, they
are heavy if they are Egyptian. Finally, he did not (as we read in the
Septuagint) *depart whence he had come into the desert as far as
Bethel*, but, as it is written in the Hebrew, *he went away on his
journey through the south as far as Bethel*. He set out from Egypt
not so as to enter the desert which he had left along with Egypt; but
so as to come through the south, which is opposite the north, to the
house of God where his tent was *in between Bethel and Ai*.

13 *And the men of Sodom were evil, and sinners in the sight of
God exceedingly*. Here *in the sight of God* has been added un-
necessarily by the Septuagint, since in fact the inhabitants of Sodom
were evil and sinners amongst men. Rather, that man is said to be
a sinner in God's sight who can appear as righteous amongst men.
In this way it is said of Zacharia and Elisabeth in their praise that
they were *both righteous in the sight of God*; and in the Psalter it
is said: *No man living shall be justified in Thy sight*.

14–15 *Lift up your eyes and look from the place which you are in
now to the north, and to the south, and to the east, and to the sea:
for all the land which you see, I shall give to you and to your seed.*
He set out the four regions of the world, east and west, north and
south. Now let it be enough to point out here once for all the fact
that in every scriptural passage where 'the sea' is read, it always
does duty for 'the west'. This is because the territory of Palestine is
so situated that it has the sea as its western zone.

14: 2–3 *And the king of Bale, this is Segor. All these conspired
together at the Salt Valley: this is the Sea of Salt*. In the Hebrew
language Bale means *kataposis*, that is, 'swallowing down'. Therefore the Hebrews hand on a tradition that this same place is named
Salisa in another passage of the Scriptures, and the second time is
called *moschon trietizousan*, that is, 'a three-year-old heifer', no
doubt because it was swallowed up in the third earthquake; and
from the time when Sodom and Gomorra, Adama and Seboim were
overthrown by the divine fire, it was called 'The Little One', since
in fact Segor is translated as 'the little one' and is pronounced
Zoara in the Syrian language. And the Vale of Salt Pits (as it is
written in this same book), where formerly there were pits of

bitumen, was turned into the Dead Sea after God's wrath and the raining down of the brimstone. It is called by the Greeks *limnē asphaltitis*, that is, the pool of bitumen.

5 *And they cut in pieces the giants in Astaroth Carnaim, and at the same time the mighty nations with them, and the Ominaei in the city of Save, joined together before they reached Sodom.* The four kings set out from Babylon and killed the giants, that is, the Raphaim: all the strong men of Arabia, and the Zozim in Hom, and the Emim in the city of Save, which is so named up to the present day. Now Zuzim and Emim can be understood as meaning 'dreadful' and 'awesome', in place of which the Septuagint have put 'the mighty nations', conveying the general signification rather than the literal meaning. Finally, they have regarded *bahem*, in place of which they have said *hama autois* (that is, 'with them'), as written with the letter *he*, though in fact it is written with the letter *heth*. They have been led to this conclusion by the resemblance of the elements of the two letters. For *bahem* is written with three letters. If it has *he* as the middle one it translates as 'in them', but if it has *heth* (as in the present instance) it indicates a place, that is, 'in Hom'.

7 *And they returned and came to the fountain of judgement, that is, to Cades.* Because Cades was so named later on, it is specified by way of anticipation; and it refers to a place near Petra, which is called 'The Fountain of Judgement', because God judged the people there.

And they smote the whole territory of the Amalekites and the Amorites who dwelt in Asasonthamar. This is the town which is now called Engaddi, abundant in balsam and palms. Besides, in our language Asasonthamar means 'the city of palms', Because *Thamar* means palm tree. And it should be known that instead of what follows a little later, *and they set in order against them a battle formation in the Vale of Salt Pits*, in the Hebrew is contained *in the Vale of Seddim*, which Aquila translates as *tōn peripedinōn* and Theodotion as *tōn alsōn*, meaning 'pleasant groves'.

11 *And they took all the cavalry of Sodom and Gomorra.* Instead of 'cavalry', in the Hebrew it has *rachus*, that is, property.

13 *And the one who had fled told the news to Abram the passer-by. Now he himself was sitting at the oak of Mambre the Amorite the brother of Eschol and brother of Aunan, who were joined to Abram by oath.* In place of what we have put as *the passer-by* is

written in the Hebrew text *ibri*: for this word means 'passer-by'.
And as regards what Scripture says: *at the oak of Mambre the
Amorite*, we read more appropriately in the Hebrew text *at the oak
of Mambre the Amorite the brother of Eschol and brother* (not *of
Aunan*, as the Septuagint translated, but) *of Aner*, to show that
Mambre, Eschol, and Aner were Amorites and true allies of
Abraham.

14 *And he pursued them as far as Dan.* To a town of Phoenicia
which is now called Paneas. Dan is one of the sources of the Jordan.
For the other source is indeed called Jor, which means *rheithron*,
that is 'a brook'. So when the two sources which are not very far
distant from one another are joined together into one small river, it
is finally called Jordan.

18–19 *And Melchisedech king of Salem brought forth bread and
wine, and he was priest of the Most High God; and he blessed him.*
Because our little book is, in a word, a collection of Hebrew
questions or traditions, let us therefore introduce what the Hebrews
think about this. They declare that this man is Sem, the son of
Noah, and by calculating the years of his life, they show that he
lived up to the time of Isaac; and they say that all the first-born sons
of Noah were priests before Aaron performed the priestly office.
Next, by 'king of Salem' is meant the king of Jerusalem, which was
formerly called Salem. And the blessed Apostle writing to the
Hebrews makes mention of Melchisedech as *without father or
mother*, and refers him to Christ and, through Christ, to the church
of the Gentiles (for all the glory of the head is assigned to the
members); because, while he was uncircumcised, he blessed
Abraham who had been circumcised; and in Abraham he blessed
Levi; and through Levi he blessed Aaron from whom the priesthood
afterwards descended. For this reason he maintains one should
infer that the priesthood of the church which is uncircumcised
blessed the priesthood of the synagogue which is circumcised. And
as to the Scripture which says: *Thou art a priest for ever according
to the order of Melchisedech*, our mystery is foreshown in the word
'order': not at all, indeed, in the sacrifice of non-rational victims
through Aaron's agency, but when bread and wine, that is, the
Body and Blood of the Lord Jesus, were offered in sacrifice.

15: 2–3 *O Lord God, what wilt Thou give me? And I am going
without children, and the son of Masec my slave-girl is this
Damascus Eliezer. And Abram said: Behold, Thou hast not given*

me seed, and the son of my slave-girl shall be my heir. Where we
have *and the son of Masec my slave-girl*, in the Hebrew is written
uben mesech bethi, which Aquila translated as *ho huios tou
potizontos oikian mou*, that is, the son of the one who gives drink
to my household; and Theodotion as *kai huios tou epi tēs oikias
mou*, that is, and the son of the one who is over my household.
Now what he is saying is this: I am dying without children, and the
son of my steward and bailiff who distributes everything and
apportions rations for my household, and who is called Damascus
Eliezer, shall be my heir. Furthermore, Eliezer can be explained
as meaning 'God is my helper'. From this episode they say that
Damascus was founded and so named.

7 *I am God who brought you forth from the country of the
Chaldeans.* This refers to what we have already said a little earlier,
that in the Hebrew is contained *I who led you forth from ur
Chesdim*, that is, from the fire of the Chaldeans.

10–11 *And he placed them opposite one another; but he did not
divide the birds. Then birds came down on the carcases and on their
portions, and Abram sat with them.* Explanation of this solemn
agreement is not relevant to the present little work: we say only
this, that instead of what we have set forth, in the Hebrew it has
*then birds came down on the carcases, and Abram drove them
away.* For through the merit of that man Israel was often freed from
trials.

12 Moreover at sunset *ecstasis* fell upon Abram. In the Hebrew
instead of *extasis* is read *thardema*, that is, *kataphora*, which above
we have translated as 'heavy sleep'.

16 *Then in the fourth generation they shall return hither.* There is
no doubt that these are the ones who are of the seed of Abraham.
People ask why in the Book of Exodus it is written *Then in the fifth
generation the children of Israel came out of the land of Egypt.* We
have produced a small book about this verse.

16: 2 *Behold, the Lord has shut me up that I may not bear
children: therefore go in to my handmaid, that I may have sons
through her.* Observe carefully that the procreation of sons is
written in Hebrew as 'building up'. For in this verse one reads: *Go
in to my handmaid, if in that manner I might be built up from her.*
And maybe this is what is meant in Exodus, that *God blessed the
midwives, and they built themselves houses.*

7 *And the angel of the Lord found her by the spring of water in the desert on the road to Sur.* Quite logically, the Egyptian woman was hurrying to go on the road to Sur, which leads to Egypt by way of the desert.

11 *And she called his name Ishmael, because God has heard my humiliation.* Ishmael is interpreted as 'the listening of God'.

12 *And he shall be a boorish man; his hand shall be upon all, and the hands of all men shall be upon him. And he shall dwell over against the face of all his brothers.* Instead of *boorish man* stands written in the Hebrew *phara*, which means 'wild ass'. Now it means that his descendants would dwell in the desert, and refers to the Saracens who wander with no fixed abode and often invade all the nations who border on the desert; and they are attacked by all.

17: 4–5 *And the Lord spoke to him, saying: Behold, my covenant is with you, and you shall be the father of a great number of nations; neither from now on shall your name be called Abram, but your name shall be Abraam, because I have made you the father of many nations.* It is to be observed that wherever in Greek we read *testament*, in the Hebrew language there is 'treaty' or 'covenant', that is, *berith*. Now the Hebrews say that God added the letter *he* from His own Name which among themselves is written with four letters, to the names of Abraam and Sarah. For at first he was called Abram, which means 'high father'; and afterwards he was called Abraam, which is translated as 'father of many': for 'nations', which follows, is not specifically contained in the name, but is understood. Nor should anyone wonder why we have said that the Hebrew letter *he* has been added, when it appears to the Greeks and to ourselves that the letter A has been added. For a characteristic of that language is actually to write the letter *he*, but to read it as the letter A. In similar fashion, contrariwise they often pronounce the letter A by means of *he*.

15 *And God said to Abraam: As for Sarai, your wife, you shall not call her Sarai, but Sara shall be her name.* Those people are mistaken who think that the name Sara was written first with one R and that another R was afterwards added to it; and because among the Greeks R represents the number 100, they surmise many absurd things about her name. At any rate, in whatever way they maintain that her name was altered, it ought not to have a Greek but a Hebrew explanation, since the name itself is Hebrew. And no one

who calls someone by a name in one language takes the etymology of that word from another language. Therefore Sarai was at first named with the letters *sin, res, iod*; then *iod*, that is, the element I, was taken away; letter *he*, which is read as A, was added; so she was called Sara. Now this is the reason why her name was changed in this way: formerly she was called 'my ruler', the mother of a household of one house only; thereafter she was called 'ruler' absolutely, that is, *archousa*.

16 For there follows: *I shall give you a son from her, and I shall bless him: and he shall become nations, and kings of the peoples shall come forth from him.* In the Hebrew is found distinctly: *You shall not call her name Sarai* and not, as we read in the Greek: *God said to Abraham, As for Sarai your wife, her name shall not be called Sarai.* That is, you shall not say to her, 'You are my ruler', because she is already the future ruler of all the nations. Some people quite wrongly suppose that she had formerly been named 'leprosy', and later 'ruler', on the grounds that leprosy is called *sarath*, which in our language seems to bear at least some similarity [to Sarai]; but in Hebrew it is utterly different. For it is written with *sade* and *res* and *ain* and *thau*, which is clearly very different from the three letters above, that is, *sin, res,* and *he*, with which Saraa is written.

17 *And Abraam fell on his face and laughed, and said in his heart: Shall a son be born to a man one hundred years old, and shall Sara aged ninety bear children?* Then, after a little while, *And you shall call his name Isaac.* There is a difference of opinion why he was called Isaac, but only one etymology of the name; for Isaac means 'laughter'. Some people say that because Saraa had laughed, he was therefore called 'laughter'; but this is incorrect. Others, however, say that it was because Abraham laughed; and this is what we approve. For it was in consequence of Abraham's laughter that his son was called Isaac; only then do we read that Saraa also laughed. But it should be known that four persons in the Old Testament were called by their names without any concealment before they were born: Ishmael, Isaac, Solomon, and Josias. Read the Scriptures.

18: 6 *And he said to her: Hurry, mix three measures of fine flour.* Because the three measures seem to be spoken of here without further qualification and a measure is not a definite amount, I have added *three sata* which stands in the Hebrew, that is, three amphorae; so that we may recognize the same mystery both here and in the Gospel where the woman is said to leaven *three sata* of meal.

10 *Moreover He said: I shall return and come to you at this time and hour, and Sara shall have a son.* Instead of *hour* in the Hebrew we read *life*, so that the order and meaning is: 'I shall return to you in the time of life', as if He had said: 'If I live, if life attend me'. Now these things are said *anthrōpopathōs* in the same way also as other matters.

12 *And Sara laughed within herself, saying: It has not yet happened to me until now, and my lord is an old man.* In the Hebrew this is read in quite another manner: *And Sara laughed within herself, saying: Since I have become old* [lit. *worn away*], *has pleasure happened for me?* At the same time, observe that where we have put *pleasure*, in the Hebrew is written *eden*. Symmachus translated this verse as follows: *After I have become enfeebled through old age, has youth happened for me?*

32 *And he said: Is there anything, O Lord, if I speak?* This is written in Greek as *mēti kurie ean lalēsō.* Abraham spoke to the Lord in this way a second time: it does not seem clearly to express what he means. Therefore in the Hebrew is written with greater clarity: *I beseech Thee, O Lord, do not be angry if I should speak.* For since he seemed in asking the question to be restricting the Lord in His response, he moderates what he requests with words of introduction.

19: 14–15 *And he spoke to his sons-in-law who had taken his daughters in marriage.* Because Lot's two daughters are later said to have been virgins (he himself had also recently said about them to the Sodomites, *Behold my two daughters, who have not known a man*), and Scripture now recounts that he had sons-in-law, some people think that the ones who took husbands remained in Sodom, and that those who were virgins left with their father. Since Scripture does not say this, the Hebrew truth must be set forth, in which it is written: *Lot went out and spoke to the betrothed men who were about to take his daughters in marriage.* Thus the virgin daughters had not yet been joined in marriage.

21 *And He said to him: Behold, I have wondered at your countenance.* In the Hebrew it has: *Behold, I have lifted up your countenance,* that is, I have pleasure in your prayers. Symmachus interprets this in accordance with its meaning when he says: *horasei edusōpēthēn to prosōpon sou.*

28 *And behold, the flame was going up from the ground like the steam of a kiln.* Instead of this, we read in the Hebrew: *Behold, citor was going up like the anathumiasis of a kiln,* which we can express as 'steam', 'smoke', or 'ashes'.

30 *So Lot went up from Segor, and dwelt on the mountain, and his two daughters were with him: for he was afraid to dwell in Segor.* People ask why, since at first he preferred Segor rather than flight to the mountain and wished it to be spared for his dwelling place, he should now again move from Segor to the mountain? We shall reply that that inference of the Hebrews concerning Segor is true: that it was often undermined by earthquake and was first called Bale, and then Salisa. And Lot was afraid and said: If this city was often overthrown when the other cities were still standing, how much more impossible that it be spared in the present general catastrophe? They also say that this time of faithlessness provided the opportunity for his intercourse with his daughters. For he who had seen the other cities undermined while this one stood, and who himself had been plucked out by God's help, ought not to have been in doubt, especially concerning what he had heard granted to him as a favour. So what is said by way of excuse for his daughters— that they thought that the human race had come to an end and therefore they slept with their father—does not exonerate the father.

35 Consequently, the Hebrews put dots above what follows, *And he did not know when he slept with her and when she rose up from him,* as if it were unbelievable, and because nature does not allow any man to have sexual intercourse without knowing it.

36–8 *And Lot's two daughters conceived from their father, and the first-born bore a son, and called his name Moab. He is the father of the Moabites, up to this day. And the younger also bore a son, and called his name Ammon, that is, the Son of My People. He is the father of the sons of Ammon.* Moab can be explained as meaning 'from the father', and the name as a whole has an etymology. But Ammon, the explanation of whose name is, as it were, rendered as 'the son of my nation' or (as is more appropriate in the light of the Hebrew) 'the son of my people', is so derived as to consist partly in the meaning of the name and partly in the word itself, because Ammi, from which the Ammonites are named, means 'my people'.

20: 12 *For truly she is my sister by my father, but not my mother.* That is, she is the daughter of Aran his brother, not of his

sister. But because in the Hebrew it has: *Truly she is my sister, my
father's daughter, and not my mother's daughter,* and it states
rather more clearly that she was Abraham's sister, we say by way of
excuse for her that at that time such marriages had not yet been
forbidden by the Law.

21: 9 *And Sara saw the son of Agar the Egyptian woman, whom
she had borne to Abraham, playing.* In the Hebrew it does not have
what follows: *with Isaac her son.* So this verse is explained by the
Hebrews in two ways, either to mean that he made game of idols,
in line with what is written elsewhere: *the people sat down to eat
and drink, and rose up to play*; or to mean that he arrogated to
himself by means of a jest and a game the rights of the first-born in
opposition to Isaac, on the grounds that he was the elder. Indeed,
when Sara heard this, she would not tolerate it; and this is proved
by her own words when she says: *Cast out this handmaid with her
son. For the son of the handmaid shall not be heir with my son
Isaac.*

14 *So he took bread and a skin of water and gave it to Agar, and
he placed it on her shoulder, and the little boy, and he sent her
away.* When Isaac was born, Ishmael was 13 years old. And after
his weaning, he was banished from the house along with his
mother. But among the Hebrews there is a difference of opinion.
Some declare that the event happened in the fifth year of his
weaning, while others assign it to the twelfth year. So as to select
the shorter period of time, we have calculated that Ishmael was
banished with his mother after eighteen years: consequently, it
makes no sense to say that he sat on his mother's neck when he was
already a youth. So it is truly a characteristic expression of the
Hebrew language that every son in comparison with his parents is
called 'infant' or 'little child'. Nor should we be amazed that a
barbarian language has its own distinctive characteristics, when
even in Rome today all sons are called infants. Therefore Abraham
put bread and a skin on Agar's shoulder; and when he had done
this, *he gave the boy* to his mother, that is, he entrusted him to her
hands; and in this way he sent him forth from the house.

15–17 Now what follows—*And she cast the boy down under a fir
tree, went away, and sat down opposite him about a bow shot's
distance away. For she said: I shall not see the death of my little
child. And she sat over against him,* then immediately there is
added: *The boy cried out and wept; and God heard the boy's voice*

from the place where he was, and the angel of God spoke to Agar from heaven—and the rest, would disturb no one. But in the Hebrew, after what is written as *I shall not see the death of my little child*, we read as follows: that Agar herself sat opposite the boy, lifted up her voice, and wept; and God heard the little child's voice. For because the mother was weeping and in pitiful fashion waiting for the death of her son, God heard the boy, about whom He had made a promise to Abraham when He said, *But I shall also make the son of your handmaid into a great nation.* Besides, the mother lamented not her own death, but the death of her son. Therefore God spared the one for whom tears had indeed been shed.

18 Finally, in what follows it is said: *Rise, and take the boy, and hold his hand.* From this it is clear that the one who is to be held was not a burden to his mother, but her companion. And in so far as he is held by his mother's hand, her anxious tenderness is displayed.

22 *Then said Abimelech, and Ochozath his groomsman, and Phicol, the leader of his army.* Leaving aside Abimelech and Phicol, the third name which is read here is not contained in the Hebrew book.

30–1 And he said: *You shall take these seven sheep from me, that they may be a witness to me that I have dug this well. He named the name of that place The Well of the Oath, because they both swore oaths in that place.* Where 'The Well of the Oath' is read here, in the Hebrew it has *bersabee*. Now the reason why it was so called is twofold. First, because Abimelech received seven she-lambs from the hand of Abraham (for seven is expressed as *sabee*); second, because there they swore oaths (for an oath is also similarly pronounced called *sabee*). And if we read this place-name earlier [in the text of Genesis] before this explanation has been given, we should recognize that it is said by way of anticipation; as in the cases of Bethel and Gilgal, which were called something different until the time when they were so named. It should also be observed, both from earlier verses and from the present place, that Isaac was not born at the oak of Mambre or, as is contained in the Hebrew, *in aulone Mambre*, but in Gerar, where Bersabee exists as a town even to the present day. Not a long time ago this province was called Palaestina Salutaris, as a result of division of territory made by the rulers. Scripture is a witness to this matter when it says: *And Abraham dwelt in the land of the Philistines.*

22: 2 *And God said to him: Take your only-begotten son whom
you love, Isaac, and go into a high land, and offer him there as a
whole burnt offering upon one of the mountains which I shall tell
you.* It is hard to turn the characteristic expression of the Hebrew
language into Latin words. Where in the present verse is said: *Go
into a high land*, in the Hebrew it has *moria*, which Aquila translated as *tēn kataphanē*, that is, 'the clear land', and Symmachus as
tēs optasias, that is, 'the land of the vision'. Therefore the Hebrews
say that this is the mountain on which the Temple was later
founded on the threshing-floor of Orna the Jebusite, as it is also
written in the Chronicles: *And they began to build the Temple in
the second month, on the second day of the month, on Mount
Moria.* This word is understood as 'enlightening' and 'shining'
because the *dabir*, that is, the oracle of God, is there, and the Law
and the Holy Ghost who teaches men the truth and inspires the
prophets.

3–4 *And he departed to the place which God told him, on the third
day.* It is to be observed that from Gerar to Mount Moria, that is,
the site of the Temple, it is a three days' journey; and so it is said
that he arrived there on the third day. Certain people who suppose
that Abraham at that time lived at the oak of Mambre are therefore
incorrect; since from there to Mount Moria is scarcely a full day's
journey.

13 *And Abraham lifted up his eyes and behold, a ram behind his
back was caught by its horns in the thicket sabech.* Eusebius of
Emesa has spoken an absurd thing in respect of this verse, saying
*sabech means a goat which, with its horns straight out, is standing
erect to graze the leaves of the tree.* Then Aquila interpreted it as
suchneōna, which we can express as 'a thorn bush' or 'a thorn
hedge' and, to explain the actual force of the word, 'a very dense
thicket entwined in itself'. From this, Symmachus too is led to the
same opinion and says: *And after this there appeared a ram caught
by its horns in a net.* But the Septuagint and Theodotion seem to
certain people to have a better interpretation, at least in this place:
they presented the word *sabech* as it stands and say: *by its horns
in the thicket sabech.* For *suchneōn* or 'net', which Aquila and
Symmachus put, is written with the letter *sin*; but here the letter
samech is used, from which it is clear that the word *sabech* is not an
explanation of very dense woods and thicket entwined in itself in
the manner of a net, but represents the name of the thicket which

is pronounced in this way in the Hebrew. But by searching carefully I have found that *suchneōn* is often written with the letter *samech*. 14 *And Abraham called the name of that place The Lord sees, so that they say today: 'On the mountain the Lord sees'.* Instead of what is written here as 'sees', in the Hebrew is written *will be seen*. Indeed, among the Hebrews this has passed into a proverbial saying, so that whenever they are in distress and desire to be supported by the Lord's help they say: 'The Lord will be seen on the mountain', that is, just as He had pity on Abraham, He will also have pity on us. So it is that even nowadays they are accustomed to sound the horn as a sign of the ram which was provided.

20–2 *And they told the news to Abraham and said: Behold Melcha, even she has borne sons to your brother Nachor: Us his first-born, and Buz his brother, and Camuel the father of the Syrians, and Cased.* The first-born of Nachor, Abraham's brother, was Us, born of Melcha his wife, Aran's daughter; from whose stock Job descended, as it is written in the introduction to his book: *There was a man in the land of Us whose name was Job.* Certain people, therefore, are mistaken in thinking that Job was of Esau's family: for what is contained in the conclusion of his book, namely, that it was translated from the Syrian language; that he was fourth in descent from Esau; and the rest of the things which are included, are not contained in the Hebrew books. The second son born from Melcha was Buz, whom the Septuagint have preferred to transcribe as Bauz. Now from this man's family comes Balaam the soothsayer (so the Hebrews hand on the tradition) who in the Book of Job is called Eliu. At first he was a holy man and a prophet of God; but later, because of his disobedience and lust for rewards, in that he was eager to curse Israel, he was dubbed with the description 'soothsayer'. And he is spoken of in the same book: *And Eliu the son of Barachiel the Buzite was angry.* Evidently, he descends from the stock of this Buz. Camuel is the father of Damascus. For what is written here in the place of Syria is called Aran; and by that same name it is read in Isaiah. And Chased is the fourth son, from whom the Chasdim, that is, the Chaldeans, were later named.

23: 2 *And Sara died in the city of Arboc, which is in the valley: this is Chebron in the land of Chanaan.* What is put here, namely, *which is in the valley*, is not contained in the authentic codices. The name of the city Arboc has also been gradually corrupted by writers and readers. And it should not be thought that the Septuagint rendered the name of the Hebrew city in a solecistic and corrupt manner, nor otherwise than it is pronounced in itself. For Arboc actually signifies nothing at all. But it is pronounced *arbee*, that is, 'four'; because in that place Abraham and Isaac and Jacob and the head of the human race himself, Adam, were buried, as will be shown more clearly in the Book of Joshua.

6 *Hear us, lord: you are a king from God to us. Bury your dead in our choice sepulchre.* Instead of *king*, it has in the Hebrew 'prince' or 'leader', for *nasi* means not 'king', but 'leader'.

16 *And Abraham hearkened to Ephron; and Abraham weighed the silver for Ephran, as he had spoken in the hearing of the sons of Heth.* In the Hebrew as we have set it out here, his name is written first as Ephron, then as Ephran. For after he had been persuaded for a price to sell the sepulchre and to take the money, although Abraham was compelling him, the letter *vau*, which among themselves is read as o was taken away from his name, and he was called Ephran instead of Ephron, the Scripture indicating by this means that he was not a man of complete and perfect moral virtue, in as much as he had brought himself to sell the memorials of the dead. Therefore let those who sell sepulchres without compulsion in order to receive money, and even extort it from those who are unwilling to pay, know that their name is to be changed and that some of their good name will perish. For even that man [i.e. Ephran] who received the money unwillingly is tacitly held to blame.

24: 9 *And the servant put his hand beneath the thigh of Abraham his master, and swore to him concerning this matter.* The Hebrews hand on a tradition that he swore the oath on his sanctification, that is, on the mark of his circumcision. But we say that he swore by the seed of Abraham, that is, by Christ who was destined to be born from him according to Matthew the Evangelist, who says: *The book of the generation of Jesus Christ, the son of David, the son of Abraham.*

22 *And the man took the golden earring: its weight was a didrachm.* Bace, which in this verse is written for didrachm, is a half-ounce (one twenty-fourth of an *as*); but *secel*, which in the Latin language is called in corrupt fashion a *siclus*, has the weight of an ounce (one-twelfth of an *as*).

43 *Behold, I am standing by the well of water, and the daughters of the men of the city shall go out to draw water: and it shall be that*

the virgin to whom I say, Give me a little water to drink from your water-pot, and the rest. In the Hebrew is written: *Behold, I am standing beside the well of water; and it shall be that the young woman who shall come out to draw water, and I shall say to her, Give me a little water to drink from your water-pot,* and the rest. Instead of *young woman,* which in the Greek language is pronounced *neanis,* we read in that verse *alma,* which is also indeed contained in Isaiah. For in the place where it is written in our codices: *Behold, a virgin shall conceive and bear a child,* Aquila rendered: *Behold, a young woman shall conceive and bear a child.* In the Hebrew is written: *Behold alma shall conceive and bear a child.* Now it should be observed that the word *alma* is never written except in respect of a virgin; and it has an etymology, *apokruphos,* that is, 'hidden'. For it is written in Job: *Where shall Wisdom be found? And which is the place of understanding? And it shall be hidden from the eyes of all the living.* Where just now we said 'shall be hidden', in Hebrew is said *naalma* (the same word as *alma*), formed differently because of the inflexion of the word. Something similar to this, although it is inflected in the masculine gender, is also written in the Book of Reigns in the person of Elisha who says to Gehazi: *And the Lord has hidden it from me.* Therefore *alma,* which means 'hidden girl', that is, a virgin guarded with very great care, seems to me to be worthy of greater praise than a mere virgin. Because according to the Apostle, a girl can be a virgin in body, but not in spirit. But the 'hidden one' who is a virgin has an *epitasis* (extension) of virginity so that she is both 'virgin' and 'hidden one'. And she who is hidden, according to the idiom of the Hebrew language, is consequently also a virgin. But it does not immediately follow that she who is a virgin is a 'hidden one'. In Exodus, too, we read this same word of Mary the virgin sister of Moses. So let the Jews show elsewhere in the Scriptures *alma* put where it means simply 'young woman' and not 'virgin'; then we may allow them that what is said in Isaiah among us, *Behold, a virgin shall conceive and bear a child,* indicates not a 'hidden virgin', but a young woman already married.

59 *And they sent away Rebecca their sister, and her property, and Abraham's servant, and the men who were with him.* In the Hebrew it has: *And they sent away Rebecca their sister, and her nurse, and Abraham's servant, and his men.* For it was proper that the

virgin, setting out to her marriage without her parents, should be attended by the comfort of her nurse.

62–3 *And he himself was dwelling in the land of the south: and Isaac went out to busy himself in the field at evening.* The land of the south means Gerar, from where he had once been led away by his father to be sacrificed. And what Scripture says: *And he went out in the field to busy himself*, which is said in Greek as *adoleschēsai*, is read in the Hebrew as: *And Isaac went out to speak in the field when the evening was already declining.* Now it means that even Isaac, who was a type of the Lord, went out from his house to prayer as would a righteous man, in accord with the fact that the Lord used to pray alone on the mountain; and that at the ninth hour and before sunset he offered spiritual victims to God.

65 *And she took a theristrum and covered herself. Theristrum* means a mantle, a kind of Arab garment found even today, with which the women of that province veil themselves.

25: 1–6 *And Abraham again took a wife, and her name was Cetura: and she bore for him Zamram and Jecsan and Madan and Madian and Jesboc and Sue. And Jecsan begat Saba and Dadan. And the sons of Dadan were Asurim and Latusim and Laomim. And the sons of Madian were Jephar and Apher and Enoch and Abida and Aledea. All these were the sons of Cetura. And Abraham gave all that he had to Isaac; also to the sons of the concubines which he had he gave gifts, and he sent them away from Isaac his son towards the eastern land, since he was still living in the east.* In the Hebrew language Cetura means 'joined' or 'bound'. For this reason the Hebrews suppose that the same woman is Agar with her name changed, who, when Sara was dead, transferred from being concubine to wife. And the age of Abraham, who was already enfeebled, appears to be exempted from blame, lest the old man be charged with having been wanton in new marriages after the death of his aged wife. We leave aside what is uncertain and say this: that the sons born to Abraham from Cetura, according to the historians of the Hebrews, possessed *trōglodutis* and Arabia which is now called *eudaimōn* as far as the limits of the Red Sea. Moreover one of the descendants of Abraham, who was called Apher, is said to have led an army against Libya and to have settled there after he had conquered his enemies; and his descendants named it Africa after the name of their ancestor. A witness of this matter is Alexander who is called Polyhistor, as is Cleodemus surnamed Malchus: they rehearse the barbarian record in the Greek language. And as regards what Scripture says—*And the sons of Dadan were Asurim and Latusim and Laomin*—they think Asurim should be translated as traders; Latusim as forgers of metals of bronze and iron; Laomin as *phularchoi*, that is, chiefs of many tribes and peoples. Others maintain from this verse that the Syrians are called Asurim, and that the provinces of India were occupied by most of Abraham's sons from Cetura.

8 *And Abraham died in a good old age, an old man and full, and he was gathered to his people.* In the Septuagint is incorrectly added: *And Abraham grew weak and died*; for it is not fitting for Abraham to grow weak and be impaired. And what we have set out as *in a good old age, an old man and full,* in the Greek codices is put as full of days. Although this appears to state the meaning, in that he died full of light and of the works of the day, it none the less makes for greater *anagōgē* [spiritual meaning] if *full* is put simply on its own.

13–18 *And these are the names of the sons of Ishmael according to their names and their generations. The first-born of Ishmael, Nebajoth; and Cedar,* and the rest up to that place where it says: *And they dwelt from Evila as far as Sur, which is opposite the frontier of Egypt for those who are coming to the Assyrians; in the sight of all his brethren he fell.* To Ishmael were born twelve sons, and of these the first-born was Nebajoth, from whom the whole area from the Euphrates as far as the Red Sea is named Nabathena, which is part of Arabia, to this very day. For their households, towns, villages, and little forts, and their tribes are widely known by this designation. From one of these sons of Ishmael, the area is called Cedar in the desert; and Duma is another region; and it is called Theman towards the south; and Cedema towards the eastern district. And what we read at the end of this verse in the Septuagint, *Over against the face of all his brethren he dwelt,* is more correctly what we ourselves have put as *In the sight of all his brethren he lay down.* That is, he died in the hands of all his sons, with his children surviving him, and none previously snatched away by death. Now Jacob shows to Laban that brothers may be spoken of as sons when he says: *What is my sin, that you have pursued me and pried into all my baggage? What have you found, out of all the baggage, that belongs to your house? Let it be set in front of my brothers and*

your brothers, and let them pass judgement between us. For as
Scripture recounts it, we cannot believe that Jacob had with him
some of his brothers, unless they were his children.

21–2 *And Rebecca his wife conceived, and her sons were moving
about within her.* Instead of moving about, the Septuagint put
eskirtōn, that is, 'they were playing' or 'they were being boisterous',
which Aquila translated as: *Her sons were broken in her womb*; but
Symmachus as *diepleon*, that is, they were carried in the manner of
a ship on the surface of the sea.

25 *And the first came out all red, like an hairy skin.* Where we have
put *hairy* it has *seir* in the Hebrew. Therefore Esau is also called
Seir, that is hairy, as we also read elsewhere.

30 *And Esau said to Jacob: Give me a taste of this red cooked dish,
for I am growing weak. Therefore his name was called Edom.* Red,
or reddish-brown, is called *edom* in the Hebrew language. Therefore because he sold his rights as first-born for red food, he received
the name of Reddish-brown, that is, Edom.

26: 12 *So Isaac sowed corn in that land, and found in that year
an hundredfold of barley.* Although Isaac had sowed in a foreign
land, I do not think that the fruitfulness of the barley would have
been so great for him. I consequently consider more appropriate
what is contained in the Hebrew and what Aquila translated as
well: *And in that year he found an hundredfold valued,* that is
hekaton eikasmenon. For although both *valuation* and *barley* are
written with the same consonants, *valuations,* however, is read as
saarim; but barley as *sorim.* Now since Scripture is silent about the
actual sort of corn which grew one hundredfold, it seems to me to
have indicated the increase of all the virtues in that man. Then
follows:

13 *And the Lord blessed him, and the man became great and
walked about, going on his way; and he was highly esteemed while
he became very great.* But I am not aware that prosperity in increased barley stocks can make a man renowned.

17 *And Isaac departed from there, and came into the valley of
Gerar and dwelt there.* In the Hebrew it has *torrent* instead of
valley. For Isaac could not dwell in a valley after he had become
highly esteemed. So he dwelt in a torrent, of which it is written: *He
shall drink of the torrent on the way,* from which Elijah also drank
in the time of the famine. But because Elijah was not perfect like
Christ, so then for him the torrent dried up. But our Lord was

handed over in the torrent as well, thereby consecrating our rebirth and the sacrament of Baptism.

19 *And the servants of Isaac dug in the valley of Gerar, and found there a well of living water.* Here also *torrent* is written instead of *valley.* For a well of living water is never found in a valley.

21 *And they dug another well, and disputed about that one also. And he called its name Enmities.* For *enmities,* which Aquila and Symmachus have translated as *tēn antikeimenēn* and *enantiōsin,* that is, 'the adverse' and 'the contrary', it has *satana* in the Hebrew. From this we perceive that Satan is to be interpreted as 'the contrary one'.

22 *And they dug another well, and they did not quarrel with them: and he called its name Breadth.* For *breadth* in the Hebrew it has *rooboth,* by way of demonstrating what we have said above: *He himself built Ninive the city and Rooboth,* that is, its streets.

26 *And Abimelech went to him from Gerar, and Ochozath his groomsman, and Phichol the chief of his soldiers.* Instead of *Ochozath his groomsman,* in the Hebrew it has *the association of his friends* so as to signify not so much an individual as a group of friends who had come with the king, among whom was also Phichol, the chief of his army.

32–3 *And the servants of Isaac came and told him about the well which they had dug, and they said to him: We have found water. And he called its name Abundance.* I do not know why in the Septuagint it has *And the servants of Isaac came and told him about the well which they had dug, and they said to him: We have not found water. And he called its name Oath.* For on that account, what etymology is there that it be called Oath on the grounds that they had not found water? By contrast in the Hebrew, with whose meaning Aquila and Symmachus agree, this verse indicates that they found water and therefore that well was called Abundance; and the city was called Bersabee, that is, The Well of Abundance. For although we have stated above that Bersabee was named after either the word of the oath or the number seven (which is pronounced as *sabee*) referring to the sheep, in this instance, however, in view of the fact that water was found, Isaac punned on the name of the city which was so called. He deviated a little in the pronunciation of one letter, and instead of the hissing *sin* of the Hebrew with which *sabee* begins, he put the Greek *sigma* that corresponds to the Hebrew *samech.* Besides, according to the rule of allegory as well, it is in no way consistent that Isaac should not have discovered water, after so many wells in the regions of the virtues.

27: 11 *Behold, Esau my brother is an hairy man, and I am a smooth man.* Where we read *hairy*, in the Hebrew is written *seir*. Consequently the mountains and the area in which he was later residing were called Seir: of this too we have spoken above.

15 *And Rebecca took with her in the house the garments of Esau her elder son, which were most desirable.* Now in respect of this verse the Hebrews hand on a tradition that first-born sons performed the duty of the priests and possessed the priestly raiment, in which they were clothed as they were offering the victims to God, before Aaron was chosen for the priestly office.

36 *And Esau said: Rightly is his name called Jacob, for he has tripped me up: see! a second time.* Jacob means 'One who Trips Up'. Therefore because he had deceived his brother by cunning, he alluded to the name. He was formerly called Jacob, because at birth he had caught hold of his brother's heel.

40 *And you shall serve your brother; and it shall come to pass, that when you lay down his yoke and break it from off your neck . . .* He indicates that the Idumeans are to be subject to the Jews and that the time will come when they shall cast off the yoke of servitude from their neck and reject their dominion. But according to the Septuagint, who said: *Moreover it shall come to pass when you lay down his yoke and break it from off your neck*, the sentence seems to hang in the air and not to be complete.

28: 19 *And Jacob called the name of that place Bethel; and Ulammaus was formerly the name of the city.* Because he had said above: *How dreadful is this place: this is none other than the house of God, and this is the gate of heaven*, he now put a name on the place: *and he called it Bethel*, that is, the house of God. This place was formerly called Luza, which means 'nut' or *amugdalon*. As a result it is an absurdity that some people suppose the Hebrew word *ulam* to be the name of the city, since *ulam* means 'formerly'. So this is the proper arrangement of the text: *And he called the name of that place Bethel, and formerly Luza was the name of the city.* All the ancient Scriptures are full of the word *ulam* or *elam*, which indicates nothing other than 'before', or 'formerly', or 'forecourt', or 'lintel', or 'doorpost'.

29: 27 *Complete, then, her time of seven days, and I will give her also to you.* After Jacob had been deceived by a trick and had received Lia instead of Rachel for a wife, it is said to him by his father-in-law Laban that he should complete seven days after his marriage to the elder sister, and so he should receive Rachel for whom he should work again as a servant for seven more years. He did not, then, as certain people wrongly suppose, receive Rachel as his wife after another seven years; but seven days after his marriage to his first wife. For what follows is: *And he went in to Rachel, and he loved Rachel more than Lia, and worked as a slave for her for seven more years.*

32 *And she conceived, and bore a son, and she called his name Ruben.* I want to say something about the etymologies of the names of all the Patriarchs all together to shorten my account. It says: *And she called his name Ruben, saying, Because the Lord has seen my humiliation.* Ruben means 'the son of vision'.

33 It says: *And she conceived another son, and said: For the Lord has heard me on account of the hatred which my husband had for me, and He has given me this one also: and she called his name Simeon.* Because of the fact that she had been heard, she put on him the name Simeon. For Simeon means 'hearing'.

34 Now there follows concerning the third son: *And she conceived again and bore a son, and said: Now my husband shall be with me, because I have borne three sons to him: therefore she called his name Levi.* Where we read: *My husband will be in my presence,* Aquila explained it as meaning: *My husband will be united to me.* This is expressed in Hebrew as *illave* and rendered by the Hebrew teachers in another fashion, such that they say: *My husband will accompany me.* That is, I do not doubt the love of my husband for me; he shall be my companion in this life and his love will lead me down and accompany me even to death, since I have borne three sons for him.

35 *She conceived and gave birth to a son, and said: Now I shall give acknowledgement to the Lord over this one; and because of this she called his name Juda.* Juda means 'acknowledgement'. So the name of the acknowledger has been given from his acknowledgement. But in fact acknowledgement is here accepted either for thanksgiving or for praise, as often in the Psalms and in the Gospel: *I shall acknowledge you O Lord, father of heaven and earth*; that is, 'I give thanks to you' or 'I glorify you'.

30: 5–6 *And Bala conceived and bore Jacob a son; and Rachel said: The Lord has judged me, and has heard my voice and has given me a son. Therefore she called his name Dan.* She represents the reason for the name as being the fact that, because the Lord had judged her, she put on the son of her handmaid the name of 'judgement': for Dan is explained as meaning 'judgement'.

7–8 *And Bala, Rachel's servant, conceived again and bore for Jacob a second son. And Rachel said: The Lord has made me dwell in a dwelling-place with my sister, and I have become stronger. And she called his name Nephthalim.* The reason for the name Nephthali given here is quite different from the one written in the *Book of Hebrew Names.* Consequently Aquila also says *sunanestrepsen me ho theos kai sunanestraphēn* for what is written in the Hebrew as *nephthule eloim nephthalethi.* Therefore she put the name Nephthalim on her son from 'a turning around' or 'a bringing together', for it means both bringing together or turning around.

10–11 Then follows this statement: *And Zelpha the handmaid of Lia bore a son to Jacob; and Lia said: In fortune. And she called his name Gad.* Where we have put *in fortune* and in Greek is said *en tuchēi,* which can mean 'by fate', in the Hebrew it has *bagad,* which Aquila explained as meaning *a troop comes;* but we can take it as *under* [lit. *in*] *arms.* For *ba* can signify the preposition 'in' as well as 'he comes'. Therefore the son of Zelpha was called Gad either from 'chance' or from 'under arms', which is pronounced as *gad.*

12–13 There follows: *And Zelpha the handmaid of Lia bore a second son to Jacob. And Lia said: Blessed am I, for women bless me; and she called his name Aser, riches.* Riches, that is *ploutos,* has been incorrectly added since the etymology of the name Aser is revealed by the authority of Scripture when it says: *Blessed am I, and women bless me;* and from the fact that since she is called blessed by human beings, she called her son 'blessed'. Therefore Aser means not *riches* but *blessed one,* at least in the present verse; for in other verses riches can also be spoken of in this way because of the word's ambiguity.

17–18 *And God heard Lia, and she conceived and bore a fifth son for Jacob; and Lia said: God has given me my reward, because I gave my handmaid to my husband. And she called his name Issachar.* The Septuagint have set forth the etymology of this name as *there is a reward.* Now it is not to be supposed (in the way that several people read by incorrectly adding a pronoun) that what is written means *He is a reward;* rather, the whole name signifies *there is a reward*. For *Is* means 'there is' and *sachar* means 'reward'. And this was so because she had purchased for herself access to her husband, which was Rachel's due, by means of her son Ruben's mandrakes.

19–20 There follows: *And Lia again conceived and bore a sixth son to Jacob; and Lia said: God has endowed me with a good endowment. Behold, my husband shall dwell with me at this time, because I have borne him six sons. And she called his name Zabulon.* Where we have put *shall dwell with me*, and the Septuagint have translated *shall choose me*, it has in the Hebrew *iezbuleni*. And this is the import of it. Because I have borne six sons to Jacob I am therefore now free of care, for my husband will dwell with me. So, then, my son is called *The dwelling-place*. In the *Book of Names*, therefore, Zabulon is incorrectly and wilfully explained as meaning *nocturnal emission*.

21 *And after this she bore a daughter and called her name Dina.* This is translated as *lawsuit*, which the Greeks more graphically call *dikēn*. For she was the cause of the altercation in Sicem. After the children the names of the parents must also be set forth. Lia means 'working', Rachel 'an ewe', whose son Joseph is called 'increase' because his mother had desired that another be added to her.

32–3 *I shall pass over upon all your flock today: separate from there every striped and variegated animal, and every animal of single colour among the lambs, and the striped and variegated among the goats, and it shall be my wages. And my righteousness shall answer for me on the following day, when my wages shall come before you. Every animal on which there shall not be striped or variegated [colour] on the goats and on the lambs shall be stolen along with me,* and the rest. The meaning is greatly disordered by the Septuagint, and up to the present I have been unable to find any of our own people who can explain clearly what is being said in this place. You wish me, says Jacob, to serve you again for another seven years: do what I ask. Separate all the variegated and striped, both sheep and goats, and give them into the hands of your sons; and then from both flocks give to me the white and black animals, that is, those of a single colour. Then if any animal be born variegated from the white and black ones which are of a single colour, it shall belong to me; but if any of a single colour be born to them, it shall be yours. I am not asking a difficult thing. You have on your side the nature of flocks, that white be born from white and black from black; on my side will be my righteousness, while God looks upon my lowliness and labour.

Laban eagerly seized the choice which was given and so, doing as Jacob asked him, put a distance of three days' journey between Jacob and his own sons, lest any trickery arise through the proximity of the flocks. So Jacob devised a new artifice, and fought against the nature of the white and the black flock with a cunning produced by nature herself. For three rods, of poplar, almond, and pomegranate (although the Septuagint have storax, nut tree, and plane tree), he partly stripped of their bark and he made a variegated colour of the rods, such that wherever he had left bark on a rod, its old colour remained; but wherever he had removed the bark, white colour was revealed.

Now Jacob used to watch closely; and at the time when the flocks were accustomed to mate and were going eagerly to drink after the heat of the day he would place the variegated rods in the water-troughs. Then the rams and he-goats were admitted, and by means of that same eagerness for drinking he would make the ewes and she-goats be mated; so that out of twofold desire while they were eagerly drinking and being mounted by the male animals, they might conceive such kind of offspring they were viewing in the mirror of the waters as the shadows of the rams and he-goats mounting them from above. For because of the rods placed in the drinking-troughs, even the colour of the mirror-images was variegated.

Now it is not astonishing that this is the nature of female creatures in the act of conception: the offspring they produce are of such a kind as the things they observe or perceive in their minds during the most intense heat of sexual pleasure. For this very thing is reported by the Spaniards to happen even among herds of horses; and Quintilian, in that lawsuit in which a married woman was accused of having given birth to an Ethiopian, brought as evidence in her defence that what we have been describing above is a natural process in the conception of offspring.

Then, after striped and variegated she-goats and lambs had been born of the flocks which were white and of a single colour, Jacob separated them and took them away from the original flock; but if any of a single colour, that is, white or black, were born, he handed them over to the hands of Laban's sons. And he would place the rods which he had stripped of bark in the drinking-troughs where the waters were poured out; and the flocks would come to drink opposite them, so that they should conceive when they came to drink.

41–2 *And the flocks conceived opposite Jacob's rods, the rods which he had placed before the flocks in the water-troughs so that they might conceive by means of them; but he did not put them in with the late-born sheep. And the ones born later became Laban's, and the ones born early were Jacob's.* This is not contained in the Septuagint; but instead of *late-born* and *ones born early* they have translated in some other way which has no relevance for the meaning. Now what Scripture is saying is this: Jacob was circumspect and cunning, and retained justice and fairness even in his new artifice. For if the flocks had produced all variegated lambs and goats, there would have been some suspicion of a trick and Laban in jealousy would have engaged in open opposition to this business. Therefore he so regulated everything that both he himself might receive the fruit of his labour, and Laban might not be robbed completely. Whenever the sheep and goats were mounted for the first time, because the progeny of springtime is better, he would lay the rods before them so that offspring of variegated colour might be born. But as for whichever sheep or goats sought a sire at a later time, he would not put the rods in front of these so that flocks of a single colour might be born. And whatever was born first was his because it was variegated and of different colours; whatever was born later was Laban's. For the flock would rise of a single colour, be it black or white. Now where in this place is written *that they might conceive by means of the rods,* it has in the Hebrew *ieamena*: I cannot express the force of the Hebrew word except by circumlocution. For *ieamena* strictly speaking refers to the last moment of passion in sexual intercourse, when the whole body is convulsed and the final moment for pleasure in the deed is near.

31: 7–8 *And your father has lied to me, and has changed my wages ten times; but God has not allowed him to harm me. If he said: This variegated flock shall be your wages, the whole flock was born variegated. And if he said: The flocks of a single colour shall be your wages, the whole flock was born of one colour.* Instead of what we have put: *he has changed my wages ten times,* the Septuagint, led on by some conjecture or other, (since the Hebrew word *moni* signifies a number rather than lambs) have put *with ten lambs.* In short, this meaning is shown to be the more acceptable by what follows, in that Laban always changed the agreement in respect of individual offspring. If he saw that the flock had been born variegated, he would say after they had brought forth: 'I wish in future that the ones born for me should be variegated'. Contrariwise, when he saw the flocks of a single colour being born, (because Jacob, when he heard of the above, would not put the rods into the drinking-troughs), he would say that the flocks in future should produce offspring of a single colour for himself. And what more? Up to ten times the contract was changed, always by Laban, in respect of his own flock, or that of Jacob. And whatever he had stipulated should be born for him, he changed into the opposite colour. And lest ten times of giving birth in six years should seem incredible to anyone, read Virgil, in which it is said: *Flocks twice in the year great with young.* So it is taught that the nature of Italian sheep and those of Mesopotamia is of the same kind.

19 *And Rachel stole her father's idols.* Where in the present verse we read *idols*, in Hebrew is written *theraphim*, which Aquila understands as *morphōmata*, that is, figures or images. This was to enable us to know what *theraphim* means in the Book of Judges.

21 *And he crossed the river and came to Mount Galaad.* Not that the mountain was called Galaad at that time; rather, as we have often pointed out, by anticipation it was invested with the name by which it was called later on.

41 *And you have changed my wages by ten lambs.* This is the same mistake as above. *Times* should be read instead of *lambs*.

46-7 *And Jacob said to his brothers, Let us gather stones. And when they had gathered the stones, they made a heap and ate upon it; and Laban called it The Heap of Testimony, and Jacob called it The Heap is a Witness.* In the Hebrew language heap is pronounced *gal*, and testimony as *aad*. Then in the Syrian language heap is called *igar*, and evidence *sedutha*. Therefore Jacob called it the Heap of Testimony, that is, Galaad, in the Hebrew language; but Laban called it the very same thing, that is, the Heap of Testimony, *igar sedutha*, in the language of his own people. For he was a Syrian, and he had exchanged the ancient language of his ancestors for the tongue of the province in which he was dwelling.

32: 2-3 *And the angels of God met him, And Jacob said when he saw them: These are the camps of God; and he called the name of that place Encampments.* Where *camps* are written in this verse, it has *manaim* in the Hebrew, so that we may know which site it refers to whenever it is set out in another place without further interpretation. And it is a noble thing that he is received by choirs of angels accompanying him, as he is about to go to his brother who is his enemy.

10–11 *And Jacob said: O God of my father Isaac, O Lord, who said to me, Return to your land, and I shall bless you, I am less than all your mercy and all your truth which you have performed for your servant.* Instead of what we have presented as *I am less*, something else which confuses the meaning is contained in the Greek and Latin books.

28–9 *And he said to him: What is your name? And he said: Jacob. Moreover he said to him: Your name shall no longer be called Jacob, but your name shall be called Israel, because you have prevailed with God, and with men you shall be strong.* Josephus, in the first book of the *Antiquities*, thinks that Israel is so called because he stood against the angel: after careful and wide research I have not been able to find this in the Hebrew. And why should I have to seek the conjectures of individuals when the One who imposed the name Himself explains the etymology: *Your name*, He says, *shall not be called Jacob, but Israel shall be your name.* Why? Aquila explains it as *hoti ērxas meta theou*; Symmachus as *hoti ērxō pros theon*; and the Septuagint and Theodotion as *hoti enischusas meta theou*. For *sarith*, which is derived from the word Israel, means *prince*. So the significance is as follows: your name shall not be called 'One who Trips Up', that is, Jacob; but your name shall be called 'Prince with God', that is, Israel. For just as I am a prince, so you also shall be called a prince in that you have been able to wrestle with Me. Now if you have been able to fight with Me, who am God or an angel (for many people interpret this in different ways), how much more will you be able to fight with men, that is, with Esau, whom you ought not to dread?

Now in the *Book of Names*, the statement which explains Israel as meaning 'a man seeing God' or 'a mind seeing God', a cliché of almost everybody's speech, seems to me to explain the word not so much accurately as in a manner that is forced. For Israel in this verse is written with these letters, *iod, sin, res, aleph, lamed,* which means 'prince of God', or, 'directed one of God', that is, *euthutatos theou.* But 'a man seeing God' is written with these letters: 'man' is written with the three letters *aleph, iod, sin* (so that it is pronounced *is*), and 'seeing' with three, *res, aleph, he,* and is pronounced *raa.*

Then *el* is written with two letters, *aleph* and *lamed*, and means 'God' or 'strong one'. So although those men are of powerful influence and eloquence, and the shadow of those who have understood Israel as 'man or mind seeing God' weighs down upon us, we are led rather by the authority of Scripture and of the angel or God who called him Israel, than by the authority of any secular eloquence.

30–1 Then what follows afterwards is this: *And He blessed him there, and Jacob called the name of that place the Face of God: for I have seen God face to face, and my life has been saved.* In the Hebrew is said Phanuel, so that we may know that it is the place which in other books of Holy Scripture is so written in Hebrew as it is read in the Greek, Phanuel.

33: 1–3 *And he divided his children between Lia and Rachel and the two handmaids, and he put the handmaids and their children first, then Lia and her children last, and Rachel and Joseph last; and he himself crossed over in front of them.* He did not make three groups, as most people reckon, but two. In short, where we have *he divided,* Aquila put *hēmiseusen,* that is, *he halved,* so as to make one column of the handmaids with their little ones and another of Lia and Rachel, who were freewomen, with their sons; and so as to make the handmaids go first, the freewomen next; and so that he himself might meet his brother and entreat him before either group [lit. flock].

17 *And Jacob built a house there, and tents for his flocks. So he called the name of that place Tabernacles.* Where we have *Tabernacles, sochoth* is read in the Hebrew. Indeed to this day there is a city across the Jordan with this name, in the territory of Scythopolis, about which we have written in the *Book of Places.*

18 *And Jacob came to Salem, a city of Sichem in the land of Chanaan, when he had come from Mesopotamia of Syria.* A mistake arises about the way in which Salem is called a city of Sichem, since Jerusalem where Melchisedech reigned as king was called Salem in an earlier verse. Either each city has the same name (which we can also find in the case of other places in Judaea, such that the name of city and place is the same in one tribe and in another); or we may say that this Salem which is here designated as belonging to Sichem is to be taken as meaning in this verse 'perfect' and 'complete'; and that that city which was later called Jerusalem is to be rendered into our language as 'peaceable'. For this word means

both things, if the accentuation is altered a little. The Hebrews hand on a tradition that the thigh of Jacob, who was lame, grew strong again and was healed in that place; therefore the same city adopted the name of 'cared for' and 'complete'.

34: 20–1 *And Emor and Sichem his son came to the gate of the city, and spoke to the men of the city, saying, These men are peaceable towards us.* Where in the present instance the Septuagint translated as *peaceable*, Aquila translated as *apērtismenous*, that is, 'perfect' and 'complete'. In the Hebrew, *salamim* is read for this, from which it is clear that what we have said above about Salem is correct.

25 *And they went into the city with care, and killed every male.* Instead of what is read in the Greek as *asphalōs*, that is, 'carefully', in Hebrew is written *bete*, that is, 'boldly' and 'with confidence'.

35: 6 *And Jacob came into Luz, which is Bethel, in the land of Chanaan.* Here, as has been stated above, it is most clearly established that Bethel was formerly called not Ulammaus but Luz, that is, *amugdalon.*

8 *And Debbora, the wet-nurse of Rebecca, died, and was buried close to Bethel.* If Rebecca's wet-nurse, Debbora by name, died—as the Septuagint have translated here as well—and that word is the Hebrew *meneceth*, we cannot understand why they should have put 'property' in that verse and 'wet-nurse' in this.

10 *And God said to him: Your name shall no longer be called Jacob, but your name shall be Israel. And He called his name Israel.* In the preceding narrative the name was not laid upon him by the angel at all; rather, what was to be imposed by God was foretold. So in this verse it is taught that what was promised in that narrative as something yet to happen was fulfilled.

16 *And it happened that, while he was drawing near to Chabratha in the land of Chanaan to come to Ephratha, Rachel gave birth.* The Septuagint translated the Hebrew word *chabratha* as *hippodrome* (on what grounds I do not know) in the following, where Jacob speaks to Joseph: *As for me, when I came from Mesopotamia to Syria so as to come to Ephratha, your mother Rachel died in the land of Chanaan, on the road of the hippodrome.* And then immediately in that verse where it says in Hebrew: *and they buried her on the way to Ephratha, that is Bethlehem,* the Septuagint put *hippodrome* instead of Ephratha. But at any rate if *chabratha* means *hippodrome*, Ephratha cannot mean *hippodrome*. Now

Aquila translated this word as follows: *And it happened kath hodon tēs gēs*, that is, *on the journey of the land, as he was going into Ephratha.* But it is better if it is translated: *in the choice time of the land, when he was going into Ephratha.* Now this indicates springtime, when everything bursts into flower and the time of the year is 'choice'; and when people walk along the road they pluck and 'pick' from the neighbouring fields whatever might come to hand, being drawn by the different sorts of flowers. In fact, Ephratha or Bethlehem is the name of one particular city with a similar interpretation. For it can indeed be rendered as 'fruitful' and as 'house of bread', on account of that Bread who said that He had come down from heaven.

18 *And it came to pass, that when her life departed from her, for she died, that she called his name The Son of My Sorrow; but his father called his name Benjamin.* In the Hebrew, the sounds of the names are clearly similar since 'the son of my sorrow', the name which the dying mother placed upon her son, is pronounced Benoni; while 'the son of the right hand', that is, 'the son of strength', which Jacob changed it to, is pronounced as Benjamin. So then those who suppose that Benjamin should be understood as meaning 'the son of the days' are mistaken. For while 'right hand' is pronounced *iamin* and ends in letter N, 'days' are in fact also pronounced as *iamim*, but are concluded with letter M.

21 *And Israel went forth, and stretched his tent beyond the tower Ader.* The Hebrews maintain that this is the place where the Temple was later built and that the tower Ader means 'the tower of the flock', that is, the tower of the congregation or company; that the prophet Michaeas also witnesses to this when he says: *And thou, O cloudy tower of the flock, daughter of Sion,* and the rest; and that Jacob at that time had been in possession of tents across the place where later the Temple was built. But if we follow the order of the journey which they took, the place of the shepherds is near to Bethlehem where the flock of angels sang at the Lord's birth, and where Jacob pastured his flocks and gave a name to the place, and (what is more genuinely the case) where, as a result of some prophecy, a mystery which at that time was already destined to come about was displayed.

27 *And Jacob came to Isaac his father in Mambre, the city of Arbee: this is Chebron.* Instead of *arbee* in the Septuagint it has *plain,* although Chebron is situated on a mountain. The same city

is also called Mambre, and was so named in ancient times after a friend of Abraham.

36: 4 *And Ada bore Eliphaz for Esau.* This is the Eliphaz whose writing is recalled in the Book of Job.

19 *These are the sons of Esau, and these are their princes. He himself is Edom, and these are the sons of Seir.* Esau and Edom and Seir are the names of one man; and it has been related above why he is named in different ways.

20 Now as for what follows: *And of the Chorraean who inhabited the land,* and the rest—after Scripture has recounted the sons of Esau, it goes back further and explains who were the chiefs before Esau in the land of Edom from the family of the Chorraei, who, in our language, are to be interpreted as *free men.* Let us carefully read Deuteronomy, where it is written the more explicitly how the sons of Esau came and killed the Chorraei and took possession of their land as an inheritance.

22 *And the sons of Lothan were Chorri and Aemam, and the sister of Lothan was Thamna.* This is the Thamna about whom it was said above: *and Thamna was the concubine of Eliphaz, Esau's first-born son; and from her was born Amalech.* So this is why he recalled the Chorraei, because Esau's first-born son had taken a concubine from among their daughters. Now as for what is said: *Theman and Cenez and Amalech,* and the rest—we should recognize that names were later given to the territories of the Idumeans, after the names of these men.

24 *This is Ana, who found Jamin in the wilderness, when he was pasturing the asses of Zebeon his father.* Among the Hebrews there are many differing discussions about this verse; among the Greeks and ourselves, however, there is silence about it. Some people think that *aiamim* refer to 'seas', because 'seas' are written with the same letters as this word is in the present verse. And they maintain that while he was pasturing his father's asses in the wilderness, he discovered gatherings of waters which are called 'seas' according to the idiom of the Hebrew language: that is to say, he discovered a pool. The discovery of such a thing in the desert is difficult. Some think that this word means 'hot waters', in accord with the near likeness of [a similar word in] the Carthaginian language which is closely related to Hebrew. There are those who think that wild asses were admitted by this man to she-asses, and that he discovered this manner of mating, so that from them were born very

swift asses which are called *iamim*. Most people think that he was the first who made herds of mares in the desert be mounted by asses so that new animals, called mules, should be born from this mating, contrary to nature. Aquila translated this verse as follows: *This is Ana, who found sun tous ēmim*. And Symmachus does likewise, *tous ēmim*, and this translation indicates the plural number. But the Septuagint and Theodotion both translated by saying *ton iamim*, which indicates the singular number.

33 *And Jobab the son of Zara from Bozra reigned in his stead.* Some suppose that this is Job, as is appended at the end of his own book. But the Hebrews claim that he was begotten from the stock of Nachor, as has already been related above.

37: 3 *And Israel loved Joseph more than all his sons, because he was the son of his old age; and he made for him a tunic of many colours.* Instead of *a tunic of many colours*, Aquila translated *an astragaleion tunic*, that is, a tunic reaching to the ankles. Symmachus translated as *a tunic with long sleeves*. The one did so because it reached to the ankles and was wonderful in its variety of colours because of the craftsman's handiwork, the other because it had sleeves; for the ancients used to make more use of the *colobium* than we.

28 *And they sold Joseph to the Ishmaelites for twenty golden pieces.* Instead of *golden pieces* it has *silver* in the Hebrew; for the Lord ought not to have been sold for a cheaper metal than was Joseph.

36 *So the Madianites sold Joseph in Egypt to Phutiphar the eunuch, the chief cook of Pharaoh.* In most places, Scripture speaks of *archimagiros* (that is, chiefs of the cooks) instead of *masters of the army*, because *mageireuein* in Greek means 'to kill'. Therefore Joseph was sold to the chief of the army and the fighting men, not to Petephre as is written in Latin, but to Phutiphar the eunuch. Then people ask how it is that later on he is said to have a wife. The Hebrews hand on a tradition that Joseph was bought by this man for base use because of his very great beauty, and that his genital organs were withered by the Lord; and afterwards he was chosen in accordance with the custom of hierophants for the office of high priest of Heliopolis; and the daughter of this man was Aseneth, whom Joseph later took as wife.

38: 5 *And she again bore a son, and called his name Selom: moreover she was in Chazbi when she bore him.* The Hebrew word [*chazbi*] is put in this verse instead of the name of the place, which Aquila explained as referring to an event when he translated: *and she called his name Selom. And it came to pass that she lied in giving birth, after she had given birth to Selom.* For after she had given birth to Selom, her giving birth to children ceased. Therefore Chazbi is not the name of a place, but signifies 'a lie'. Consequently it is written in another place as well, *The work of the olive tree shall lie*; that is, the olive tree shall not produce fruit.

12 *And Judas was comforted and went up to those who were shearing his sheep, he and Hiras the Odollamite, his shepherd.* Instead of *shepherd, friend* is read [in the Hebrew]. But the word is ambiguous because both nouns are written with the same letters: but *friend* is read as *ree, shepherd* as *roe.*

14 *And she sat at the gate of Enam, which is by the crossing of Thamna.* The Hebrew word *enaim* is translated as *eyes.* Therefore it is not the name of a place. Rather, the meaning is this: she sat at a place where two roads met, or at a crossroads, where a traveller has to look more carefully which road he should take to walk upon.

26 *And Judas recognized them, and said: She is more righteous than I, because I did not give her to Selom my son.* In the Hebrew it has: *She is justified from me*, not because she was righteous, but because by comparison she had done less evil than he. The disgrace in no way arose out of promiscuity, but because she needed children.

29 *And behold, his brother came forth, and she said: Why has the wall been divided because of you? and she called his name Phares.* Instead of *wall*, Aquila and Symmachus translated *division*, which in Hebrew is pronounced *Phares.* Therefore because he divided the afterbirth he received the name of 'division'. In consequence the Pharisees, who had separated themselves from the people as if they were righteous, were also called 'divided ones'.

30 *After this his brother came forth, in whose hand was the scarlet; and she called his name Zara.* This name means 'the east'. Therefore he was called Zara, that is, 'the east', either because he appeared first, or because very many righteous men were born from him (as is contained in the Book of Chronicles).

40: 1 *After these things the chief of the vintners of the king of Egypt sinned.* Where we put *the chief of the vintners*, what is written in the Hebrew is *masec*, that same word which we have just recently read as the title of Abraham's servant, whom in the manner of ordinary folk we may call a cupbearer. Nor should it be considered a lowly duty, since among barbarian kings, even to this day, it is considered of the very greatest merit to have offered the cup to the king. And the poets habitually write about Ganymede and Jupiter that the god made over his lover to this duty.

9–10 *And behold, a vine was in my sight, and on the vine three clusters; and it was flowering with three clusters.* The Hebrew word which is pronounced by them as *sarigim* means three vine-shoots, and three branches or shoots.

16 *And I seemed to be carrying on my head three baskets of meal-cakes.* Instead of *three baskets of meal-cakes* it has in the Hebrew *three baskets of flour.*

41: 2 *And behold, seven cows were coming up from the river, fine to see and choice of flesh, and they pastured in achi.* Twice *achi* is written in Genesis, and it is neither a Greek nor a Latin word. But the Hebrew itself has also been corrupted, for it is pronounced as *in ahu,* that is, *in the marsh.* But because among the Hebrews the letters *vau* and *iod* are similar and differ only in size, the Septuagint translated *ahu* as *achi,* and added the Greek letter *chi* according to their custom, to represent the double aspiration of the Hebrew letter *heth.*

16 *And Joseph answered Pharaoh and said: Without God an answer of safety shall not be given to Pharaoh.* In the Hebrew it has something different: *Without me, God shall answer the peace of Pharaoh.* Finally, Symmachus after his fashion translated more clearly: *Not I, but God shall answer the peace of Pharaoh.*

29 *Behold, seven years of great plenty shall come in all the land of Egypt.* I wonder how we are to interpret the Hebrew word *sabee,* which we have taken above as meaning *plenty* or *overabundance* with respect to the well which Isaac's servants dug last of all. The Septuagint translated most correctly in that place and took it to mean *an oath;* since it can be understood as 'oath', and 'seven', and 'overabundance', and 'plenty', according as place and context may demand. But also in what follows, the same word is written in the Hebrew wherever *plenty* is read.

43 *And a crier shouted before him; and he set him up over all the land of Egypt.* Instead of what Aquila translated as: *And he called for the bowing of the knee before him,* Symmachus takes up the Hebrew word itself and says: *And he called before him abrech.* Consequently it seems to me that neither 'crier' nor 'bowing the

knee', which can be taken as a greeting or entreating of Joseph, should be understood, so much as what the Hebrews hand on by tradition when they say that from this word *tender father* is in fact to be translated. For *ab* means 'father', and *rech* 'soft' or 'most tender'; and the Scripture indicates that he was indeed father of all in respect of sound judgement, but a very tender young man, even a boy, in respect of his age.

45 *And Pharaoh called Joseph's name Saphaneth Phanee, and he gave him Aseneth the daughter of Phutiphar the priest of Heliopolis as wife.* Although in Hebrew this name means *a discoverer of hidden things*, none the less, because it was put on him by an Egyptian, it ought to have a meaning proper to that same language. Therefore by the Egyptian word Saphaneth Phanee or, as the Septuagint wished to transcribe it, Psomthom-Phanech, is meant *the saviour of the world*, because he had rescued the world from impending destruction by famine. Now it must be observed that he had taken as wife the daughter of his former lord and purchaser, who was hitherto the priest of Heliopolis. For it was not lawful to be high priest of that idol without being a eunuch: consequently, that notion of the Hebrews about him, which we have already related earlier, is proved to be true.

50–2 *And to Joseph were born two sons before the years of famine came, whom Aseneth the daughter of Phutiphar the priest of Heliopolis bore for him. And Joseph called the name of the first-born Manasse, because God has made me forget all my toils and all my father's house. And he called the name of the second Ephraim, because God has made me increase in the land of my lowliness.* Because of the question which is to be put forward a little later about the sons of Joseph, take note of the fact that before the time of the famine, when Jacob entered into Egypt, Joseph had only two sons, Manasse and Ephraim. He named Manasse (for in Hebrew *forgetfulness* is spoken of in this manner) because he *forgot* his toils, and Ephraim because God *increased* him. For from this name *increase* is taken across into our language.

43: 11 *And take down gifts to the man, some resin and honey, incense, and stacte, and terebinth, and nuts*, or, as Aquila and Symmachus translated, *almonds.* We have set out this verse, therefore, so as to know that where in our codices *incense* is contained, in the Hebrew is *necotha*, which Aquila translated as *storax.* Therefore the house of *nechota* which is read in Isaiah is to be understood most clearly as a store-room for incense or storax, because different kinds of aromatics were stored in it.

34 *And they drank and became drunk with him.* It is a characteristic feature of the Hebrew language that it puts drunkenness in place of abundance, as in that verse where it says: *In its drops the budding shoot will become drunk*, there is no doubt that it refers to the earth watered with the rains.

44: 1–2 *And put each man's silver in the mouth of his sack, and put my silver condy in the youngest's sack.* Instead of *sack* the Hebrew has *boot* or *money-bag*. For *condy*, that is, *cup*, which we also read in Isaiah, Aquila translated *goblet*, and Symmachus *a broad drinking-vessel*.

45: 9–10 *Therefore come down to me; do not stay; and you shall dwell in the land of Gesen of Arabia.* Of *Arabia* has been added here, for it is not contained in the Hebrew books. As a result a mistaken notion has spread abroad, that the land of Gesen is in Arabia. Besides, if as it stands in our codices it is written as *gesem* with a final M (which does not seem at all good to me), it means *a land which has been rained on*. For *gesem* is to be translated as *shower of rain*.

17 *Then Pharaoh said to Joseph: Tell your brothers, Do this: load your carriages, and go into the land of Chanaan.* In place of *carriages*, which the Septuagint and Theodotion have understood as *ta phoreia*, the rest translated as *beasts*.

21 *And he gave them rations for the journey.* The word *seda*, which in this verse all with one voice have understood as *episitismos*, that is, *rations* or *provisions for a journey*, is contained also in the Psalter. For where our people read: *Blessing, I will bless her widows* (although in most codices instead of widow, that is, *chēra*, some read *thēran*), in the Hebrew it has *seda*, that is: *Blessing, I will bless her rations*. Besides, *thēra* can mean hunting rather than produce of the land, even though it is the custom of the Egyptians to call grain *thēra*, which nowadays in lax fashion they call *athera*.

46: 26–7 *Therefore all the souls who went with Jacob into Egypt and who came forth from his loins, apart from the wives of Jacob's sons, were sixty-six souls; and the sons of Joseph, who were born to him in Egypt, were nine souls. Thus all the souls which went with Jacob into Egypt were seventy-five.* There is no uncertainty about the fact that, except for Joseph and his sons, sixty-six souls who came forth from Jacob's loins went into Egypt. For the number is added up gradually through individual persons in such a way that it wins approval, and it is found in the Hebrew books.

However, this is what we read in the Septuagint: *And the sons of Joseph, who were born to him in Egypt, were nine souls.* Let us realize that in the Hebrew instead of *nine* there is *two*. For Ephraim and Manasse, before Jacob went into Egypt and the time of the famine assailed them, were born of Aseneth the daughter of Phutiphar in Egypt. But furthermore, what we read above, namely, *And the sons of Manasse which the Aramaean concubine bore for him, were Machir; and Machir begat Galaad; and the sons of Ephraim the brother of Manasse were Suthalaam and Thaam; and the sons of Suthalaam were Edem,* has been added, since what we read later on is described as if it had been done by anticipation. For at that time when Jacob entered Egypt, Ephraim and Manasse were not of an age to be able to beget children. As a result it is clear that all the souls who entered into Egypt and who came forth from Jacob's loins were seventy, while sixty-six entered later and found in Egypt three souls, namely, Joseph with his two sons; and Jacob himself was the seventieth.

Lest we should appear to be speaking against the authority of Scripture, even the Septuagint translated in Deuteronomy that *Jacob went into Egypt with seventy souls.* If, then, anyone contradicts our opinion, he will make Scripture opposed to itself. For the Septuagint themselves who said here by anticipation that seventy-five souls with Joseph and his descendants entered Egypt, in Deuteronomy recorded that only seventy entered. But if, on the contrary, it be set against us how, in the Acts of the Apostles in Stephen's speech, it is said to the people that seventy-five souls entered Egypt, there is an easy defence. For Saint Luke, who is the writer of this very history, when he published among the Gentiles the book of the Acts of the Apostles, was under no obligation to write some contrary opinion which was opposed to the same Scripture which had already been disseminated among the Gentiles. And in any case, the Septuagint (at that time, at least) possessed a greater authority in reputation than Luke, who was unknown and of low esteem and not regarded among the nations as being of great trustworthiness. And this is generally to be observed, that whenever the Holy Apostles or apostolic men speak to the people, they make use for the most part of those witnesses which had already been dissemi-

nated among the Gentiles; although most people have it as a tradition that Luke the Evangelist, being a proselyte, was ignorant of
Hebrew letters.

28 *Therefore he sent Judah before him to Joseph, to meet him at
the city of heroes in the land of Ramesse.* In the Hebrew it has
neither *the city of heroes*, nor *the land of Ramesse*, but only *Gesen*.
Some of the Jews claim that Gesen is now called the Thebaid. And
what follows later—*he allowed them to occupy the best land of
Egypt in Ramesse*—they believe refers to the village of Arsinoë, as
it was once called.

47: 31 *And he said to him: Swear to me. So he swore to him; and
Israel worshipped over against the top of his staff.* Now in respect
of this verse certain people pretend to no purpose that Jacob had
worshipped the top of Joseph's staff, namely because he honoured
his son and adored his power; although in the Hebrew it is read in
quite another fashion and says: *And Israel worshipped at the head
of his bed.* This was because, after his son had sworn to him, he was
free of care with regard to the request he had made and worshipped
God over against the head of his bed. Because he was a holy man
and dedicated to God and was weighed down with old age, he used
to have his bed placed in such a way that he was ready for prayer
without difficulty, even when he was in the condition of one lying
down.

48: 1 *And it was told to Joseph, Behold, your father is sick. And
he took with him his two sons Manasse and Ephraim.* From this
verse is proved that very thing which we said above, that Joseph
hitherto had only two sons, Ephraim and Manasse. For if, many
years later, when Jacob his father was dying he led only two sons to
the blessing (at that time when his sons were not able to father
children since they were little ones and sucklings), he could not
have had grandsons from them when his father and brothers entered Egypt.

2 *And Israel was consoled, and sat upon his bed.* I do not know the
reason why the Septuagint produced the same word now in one
way, now in another: this one thing I say boldly, that the very word
metta which they have translated in this verse as *bed* they have
taken as *staff* rather than *bed* in the verse above, where we said that
Jacob worshipped.

5–6 *And now, behold, your sons who were born to you in the land
of Egypt, before I came to you in Egypt, are mine. Ephraim and*

Manasse shall be to me like Ruben and Simeon. And those whom you have begotten after these things shall be yours and shall be called by the name of their brothers. If anyone was in doubt that seventy souls of the sons of Israel entered into Egypt, and that Joseph, at the time when Jacob entered, had not nine, but only two sons, it is corroborated by the present verse, since Jacob himself says that he had two sons, not nine. Now in that he says, *Ephraim and Manasse shall be to me like Ruben and Simeon,* he means this. Just as Ruben and Simeon shall be two tribes and shall be called after their own names, so Ephraim and Manasse shall be two tribes; and they shall produce two peoples, and so they shall inherit the land of promise just as my own sons shall also do. Moreover, he says, *the remaining sons whom you shall beget after my death* (and thereby he proves that they had not yet at that time been produced) *shall be yours, and shall be called by the name of their brothers in their inheritance.* He says that they shall not receive land individually, nor shall they possess their own allotted portions like the rest of the tribes; but they shall be mingled together in the tribes of Ephraim and Manasse as if they were additions to the people.

22 *And I have given to you Sicima in particular above your brethren (more than your brethren), which I took from the hands of the Amorites with my sword and arrow.* According to Greek and Latin usage, [the noun] Sicima is declined. But in Hebrew it is pronounced Sichem, as also the Evangelist John bears witness, although an error has grown up and it is read in a defective manner as Sichar. And today it is Neapolis, the city of the Samaritans. Therefore because Sichem in the Hebrew language is rendered as 'shoulder', he played skilfully with the word, and said: *And I shall give to you one shoulder.* For instead of 'particular', that is, *exairetōi,* 'one' is written in the Hebrew.

Now in that he says that he took possession of it by his bow and sword, he here refers the bow and the sword to righteousness by means of which he, a pilgrim and stranger, was worthy to be freed from danger after he had killed Sichem and Emor. For as we read above, he was afraid that neighbouring towns and forts would rise up against him because he had overthrown an allied city; but the Lord did not permit them to harm him. Or, if you wish, it can be understood as follows: I shall give to you Sicima which I purchased by my bravery, that is, which I procured with money rather than with much toil and sweat. Then as for what he says: *above your brethren*, he shows that he had given it to the tribe of Joseph without [the process of casting] lots. For in fact Joseph was buried in that same place and his tomb is seen there even today.

49: 3–4 *Ruben my first-born: you are my strength and the beginning of my sons. Hard to be borne, and hard in boldness and injustice, may you not bubble forth like water. For you went up on to your father's bed; then you violated my couch, when you went up.* In the Hebrew it is written as follows: *Ruben, my first-born, my strength and the head among my children: the one greater to be borne and greater in strength. You have been poured out like water; may you not increase. For you went up to your father's couch, and defiled the couch in your going up.* Now the meaning is as follows: you are my first-born, the greater among my children; and according to the rank of your birth you ought to have received the inheritance which by right was due to the first-born son, both the priesthood and the kingship. This is shown, indeed, by the phrases 'burden to be borne' and 'very powerful strength'. But because you sinned and were poured out in an attack of lust, like water which cannot be contained in a vessel, so I order that you should not sin again, and that you should be among the number of your brethren and pay the penalty for sin; because you have lost the rank of first-born son.

5–6 *Simeon and Levi, brothers, completed the wickedness of their invention. May my soul not enter into their deliberation, and may my liver not be a rival in their assembly; for in their anger they slew men, and in their passion they hamstrung a bull.* We are necessarily compelled in accord with the plan of our work to repeat at greater length things which are at variance with the Hebrew truth. For there it is read: *Simeon and Levi are brothers: vessels of iniquity are their armaments. Let not my soul enter into their secret plan and in their assembly, lest my glory be laid waste; for in their anger they killed a man, and in their lust they dug underneath the wall.* So he indicates that it had not been the result of his own plan that they killed Sichem and Emor, men allied to him by covenant; and that they had shed innocent blood contrary to the law of peace and friendship; and that they, so seized by cruelty as if by some fury, had overturned the walls of a friendly city.

7 Therefore he continues, and says: *Cursed be their fury, for it is insistent; and their wrath, for it is harsh. I shall divide them in Jacob, and scatter them in Israel.* For Levi did not receive his own

inheritance, but possessed a few cities among all the tribes to dwell in; and in fact it is written about Simeon in the Book of Joshua that he, too, did not attain to his own allotted territory, but received something from the tribe of Judah. Further, in Chronicles it is written more clearly that when he had been increased and did not have a place to occupy, he went out into the wilderness. Some people in a prophetic manner interpret the men who were killed as the Apostles, and the bull which had been hamstrung by the Pharisees as Christ.

8–9 *Judah, your brethren shall praise you.* Because Judah means 'acknowledgement' or 'praise', it is consequently written: *Judah, your brethren shall acknowledge you,* or, *your brethren shall praise you. The sons of your father shall praise you. Judah is a lion's cub; from the tender shoot, my son, you have gone up. He crouches like a lion and like a lion's cub: who shall rouse him?* Although the mystery concerning Christ is vast, none the less it is prophesied according to the letter of Scripture that kings out of Judah should be begotten through David's stock, and that all the tribes should pay homage to him. For he does not say: *the sons of your mother,* but *the sons of your father.* And where it goes on and says: *from the tender shoot, my son,* it has in the Hebrew *from the captivity, my son, you have gone up,* in order to show that he is to lead the peoples captive and (in accordance with a more holy understanding) that he has gone up on high and has led captivity captive. Or it may be the case, as I consider preferable, that the captivity refers to the Passion, and the going up to the Resurrection.

11 *Tying his colt to the vine, and the foal of his ass to the rope.* In the Hebrew it has as follows: *Tying his colt to the vine, and his ass, my son, to the sorec,* because evidently the foal of the ass on which Jesus sat (this refers to the people of the Gentiles) he bound to the vine of the Apostles, who are of the Jews; and to the *sorec,* that is, the choice vine, he tied the ass on which He sat, the Church gathered out of the nations. Furthermore, in that he says *my son,* he makes an *apostrophē* (direct address) to Judah himself, because Christ is the One who is to do all these things. But this also should be known. Where we read: *binding his colt to the vine,* it is possible in the Hebrew for *his city* to be read instead of *colt:* with the same meaning in other words the Church is shown forth, concerning which is written elsewhere: *A city set on a mountain cannot be hidden;* and *The rush of the river makes glad the City of God.*

14–15 Issachar desired a good thing, resting between the midst of the inheritances; and he saw the rest, that it was good, and the land, that it was fruitful: he placed his shoulder to the work, and became a farmer. In the Hebrew it is written as follows: *Issachar is a bony ass, lying down between the boundaries; and he saw the rest, that it was good, and the land, that it was beautiful: and he bent his shoulder to carrying burdens, and became one who served for an allotted payment.* Because he had said above concerning Zabulon that he should occupy the shores of the Great Sea and should also border on Sidon and the rest of the cities of Phoenicia, he now returns to the inland province, and makes Issachar its inhabitant with his blessing, in that he is to occupy the most beautiful area in Galilee in close proximity to Zabulon. So he calls him a bony ass and a shoulder dedicated to carrying, because he most of all was labouring in the labour of the land, carrying to the sea-shore those burdens which were produced from his own regions, bearing also tribute to kings. The Hebrews say that it is signified metaphorically that he meditated on the Holy Scriptures day and night, and gave his zeal to labouring; and that therefore all the tribes should serve him, as if bringing gifts to a master.

16–18 Dan shall judge his people, as one of the tribes of Israel. Dan shall become a serpent on the road, a prince upon the path, biting the hooves of horses; that the one who goes up upon him shall fall backwards. I shall await Thy saviour, O Lord. Samson the judge of Israel was from the tribe of Dan. Therefore he says as follows: Now I see by means of the Spirit that Samson your nazirite tends his locks of hair and triumphs over enemies cut to pieces; for in the likeness of a serpent and a prince besieging the roads he allows none to cross through the land of Israel. And even if anyone is rash and trusts in his strength as if in the swiftness of an horse, and wishes to plunder it in the manner of a robber, he will not be strong enough to flee. Now he speaks the whole thing in the form of a metaphor about serpent and horseman. 'So I saw your nazirite who was so strong; and because he died on account of an harlot, and by dying killed our enemies, I thought, O God, that he himself was Christ your Son. But because he died and did not rise again and Israel was once more led away captive, another saviour of the world and of my people is to be expected by me, so that he *for whom it is laid up* may come, *and he himself shall be the One whom the nations await*'.

19 *Gad, a brigand shall rob him; and he himself shall rob the sole of the foot.* We have translated according to the Hebrew. But where we have put *brigand*, *gedud* is written in that place, so as to pun on the name Gad: this can be expressed more clearly as *euzōnos*, that is, 'armed' or 'ready for military action'. Now all this refers to the fact that he had formerly sent away Ruben and the half-tribe of Manasse to sons who were in occupation of the land across the Jordan, and returning after fourteen years he found a great battle in progress against them waged by the neighbouring peoples; and, when the enemies had been defeated, he strove bravely. Read the Book of Joshua the son of Nave and the Chronicles. I am not unaware that further mysteries exist in the blessings of the Patriarchs; but this is not relevant to the present work.

21 *Nephthalim is an unbound thicket, which yields beauty in what it produces.* In the Hebrew it is written as follows: *Nephthalim is a watered field, yielding eloquence of beauty.* It means that hot waters originate in that tribal territory and that it is watered above Lake Genesareth by the stream of the Jordan. Furthermore, the Hebrews maintain that the *watered field* and *eloquence of beauty* are prophetic statements on account of Tiberias, which seemed to have acquaintance with the Law. Then, where we have put *watered field*, and the Septuagint have put *stelechos aneimenon*, that is, 'unbound thicket', *aiala sluaa* is read in the Hebrew, which can be translated as 'a hart sent forth', to show how the more fertile land is swift to produce early fruits. But it is preferable if we assign everything to the teaching of the Saviour, particularly with regard to what he taught in that place [at Genesareth], as it is also written in the Gospel.

22–6 *A son increased is Joseph, a son increased upon the fountain; daughters with ordered step parade upon the wall. And they made him angry, and strove; and those that had arrows were enraged against him. He sits in the strength of his bow; and the chains of his hands were burst asunder, by the hands of the Mighty One of Jacob; whence the Rock of Israel is fed by the God of your father,* and the rest. Because the Septuagint disagree [with the Hebrew] over most things [in this verse], instead of their translation we have represented [the verse] as it is contained in the Hebrew. And this is the meaning of the verse: O Joseph, you are named in this way because the Lord has increased you for me, and since you are destined to be greater among your brethren (because in fact the tribe of Ephraim was the most powerful, as we read in the Books of Reigns and Chronicles), O my son Joseph, I declare, you are so handsome that the whole host of the maidens of Egypt looks forth at you from the walls and the towers and the windows. Your brothers were jealous of you and provoked you to anger; for they had arrows of envy and were wounded by the darts of jealousy. Truly you placed in God, Who is the strong warrior, your bow and your arms for fighting; and your chains with which your brothers bound you were unbound and broken asunder by Him, so that the tribe of Ephraim might be born of your seed. Mighty and firm and invincible as hardest stone, you also have dominion over ten tribes of Israel.

27 *Benjamin is a ravening wolf: in the morning he shall still eat, and in the evening he shall give food.* Although this is a most clear prophecy of Paul the Apostle, in that he persecuted the Church in his youth and in his old age was a preacher of the Gospel, none the less in the Hebrew it is read as follows: *Benjamin is a ravening wolf*, or, *a wolf which captures: in the morning he shall eat the booty, and in the evening he shall divide the spoil.* The Hebrews have explained this as follows: the altar on which the sacrifices were offered and at whose foot the blood of victims was poured out was in the territory of the tribe of Benjamin. So they say this means that the priests offer the victims in the morning, and in the evening divide those things which are by the law ascribed to themselves from the people; and they set forth 'the bloodthirsty wolf', 'the ravening wolf' as an interpretation of the altar, and the 'dividing of booty' as an interpretation of the priests who serve the altar and who live from the altar.

COMMENTARY

PREFACE

At the beginning ... public treasury Jerome's opening broadside against his detractors is at once cryptic and revealing. The identity of the person or persons whom he attacks under the 'code-name' Luscius is uncertain; what is not in doubt, however, is the serious nature of the charges levelled against him. His direct appeal to the comic dramatist Terence (*c*. 190–*c*. 159 BC), whose public defence of his work against the critic Luscius Lanuvinus is most evident in the prologue of the play *Andria*, is especially illuminating; and a short explanation of Terence's circumstances may help to clarify matters further, not least because Jerome's tutor for a time was Aelius Donatus, who commented on Terence's works, and to whom we owe almost all our knowledge of Lanuvinus and his attacks on the poet.[1]

Like the other great comic poets Caecilius (*c*. 219–*c*. 166 BC) and Plautus (*c*. 254–184 BC), Terence had taken Greek plays, especially those of the Athenian dramatist Menander (*c*. 342–292 BC), and had rendered them into Latin for Roman audiences. Other, less talented writers, such as Luscius Lanuvinus, followed the same practice, for no stigma attached to the 'translation' of these Greek plays into Latin verse. But in the prologue of the *Andria* (line 16), itself originally a work by Menander, Terence admits that he has incorporated into his 'translation' parts of the *Perinthia*, yet another of Menander's plays. In other plays, he might also mingle stock characters and situations belonging to one Greek original into an entirely different play which he was 'translating'. His critics, therefore, accused him of 'contaminating' original works with foreign matter; and he used the prologue of the *Andria* (lines 9–21) in particular to try to refute them.[2]

---

[1] On Jerome and Donatus, see F. Cavallera, *Saint Jérôme: Sa vie et son œuvre* (Paris, 1922), i. 7–9; J. N. D. Kelly, *Jerome: His Life, Writings, and Controversies* (London, 1975), 10–14.

[2] For modern definitions and discussions of *contaminatio*, and critical evaluation

Terence was not only charged with violating the integrity of original works by introducing foreign material into them: he was also called a plagiarist. By this, Lanuvinus and other critics meant that he had taken for his own use material from Greek plays already translated by other Latin authors. From the prologue to the *Adelphoi* (lines 6–14), a 'translation' of a play by Menander, we learn that others might have *regarded him as a thief*, because he had inserted into it material from the Greek play *Synapothnēskontes* of Diphilus, already translated into Latin by Plautus.[3] Lanuvinus also belittled Terence, born a slave and of African origin, by ascribing his success and fame to the help and influence of his aristocratic friends, and by denigrating the content and style of his plays.[4] Terence, however, seems to have defended himself to good effect; whereas of Luscius Lanuvinus and his writings virtually nothing is known. Even the latter's name is uncertain, and is sometimes given as Luscius Lavinius.[5]

In all this, Jerome singles out the accusation of *theft* which Lanuvinus brought against Terence. From what has been said above, it may be possible to define more closely what Jerome means. It seems that someone had accused him of making use of material already translated by others, incorporating it into his translation work; adding a few original matters, and passing it off as his own. This might have been valid as criticism of Jerome's *De Situ et Nominibus Locorum Hebraicorum*, which comprises of his translation of a well-known monograph by Eusebius, slightly altered by Jerome, enriched with information of his own, and published not long before the release of *QHG*.[6] But a Latin translation of this text already existed, which Jerome had publicly acknowledged and denigrated in his preface to this work: given this, it is easy to see how he could be called a 'thief', and accused specifically of plagiarism as Terence had been.[7]

of them, see G. E. Duckworth, *The Nature of Roman Comedy* (Princeton, NJ, 1952), 202–8.

[3] Ibid. 64. The relevant lines read: 'Eam nos acturi sumus novam: pernoscite | Furtumne factum existumetis, an locum | Reprehensum, qui praeteritus neclegentiast.'   [4] Ibid. 64–5.

[5] See the entry under his name in *The Oxford Classical Dictionary*[2], ed. N. G. L. Hammond and H. H. Scullard (Oxford, 1970), 626.

[6] See Cavallera, *Saint Jérôme*, i. 145–6, ii. 27–8; and P. Jay, *L'Exégèse de saint Jérôme d'après son 'Commentaire sur Isaïe'* (Paris, 1985), 184–5.

[7] For the note in the preface, see PL 23: 122 (cols. 904–5); and for further information on Jerome's detractors, see Cavallera, *Saint Jérôme*, ii. 105–6.

In the eyes of his critics, however, Terence's most serious misdemeanour lay in his having 'contaminated' one play with material from another. Jerome therefore may imply that 'his Luscius' had likewise accused him of mixing up various Greek sources on which he was dependent, an opinion sometimes voiced by modern scholars.[8] Given Jerome's reputation as one who had translated Greek works, such a charge would not, in itself, be surprising; and his constant use of the Greek Bible translations of Aquila, Symmachus, and Theodotion in his own exegetical work, sometimes without acknowledgement, might have provided some support for the allegation.

The Mantuan bard . . . extortion But 'contamination' is nowhere explicit in this preface. Rather, Jerome at once speaks of Virgil, the 'Mantuan bard', suffering the same thing as Terence and accused of plunder. He is speaking of reactions to the *Aeneid*, which owed so much to Homer's *Odyssey* and *Iliad* that early critics of the work accused Virgil of plagiarism. According to a work ascribed to Suetonius, Virgil had taunted these critics, urging them to try the same thefts, *furta*: then they would understand that it is easier to purloin Hercules' club than a line from Homer.[9] Virgil may here imply that he had been charged with theft; and this is not unlikely, when it is recalled that the *Aeneid* owed much to the epic poems *Annales* and *Bellum Poenicum* of his Latin predecessors Ennius (239–169 BC) and Naevius (?–201 BC) respectively. These men had consciously modelled their work on that of Homer, and the first book of Ennius's *Annales* had treated of the sack of Troy and events down to the founding of Rome.

[8] In the case of the *QHG*, this point has been argued most forcefully and influentially by P. Nautin, s.v. 'Hieronymus', in *Theologische Realenzyklopädie*, xv (Berlin, 1986), 306. Nautin's opinion, to which others before him subscribed, has been convincingly challenged by Adam Kamesar: see his 'Studies in Jerome's *Quaestiones Hebraicae in Genesim*: The Work as seen in the context of Greek scholarship', unpublished D.Phil. thesis (Oxford, 1987), 84–6 (hereafter Kamesar, 'Thesis'). In some other writings, however, Jerome may have borrowed Jewish tradition from Greek authors whom he does not bother to quote: see G. Bardy, 'Saint Jérôme et ses maîtres hébreux', *RB* 46 (1934), 145–64.

[9] See Suetonius, *De Viris Illustribus. De Poetis: Virgil* 46, end, where Virgil is quoted: 'cur non illi quoque eadem furta temptarent? Verum intellecturos facilius esse Herculi clavam quam Homero versum subripere.' I am indebted to my colleague Dr David Hunt of van Mildert College, Durham for the reference. It is not certain that Suetonius wrote this Life. Jerome's tutor Donatus, however, had written a commentary on Virgil which is unfortunately no longer extant: it may be the source of Jerome's information.

As for Cicero, Greek attacks on him were only to be expected, not least since his philosophical writings were highly derivative. In particular, his moral philosophy as expressed in the *Tusculan Disputations* and the *De Officiis* owed much to the Stoics; and his dependence on Greek sources for his philosophical and rhetorical opinions helped earn him the contempt of men like L. Cestius Pius, who were scarcely temperate in their criticisms of him.[10]

So it is not astonishing . . . to overcome jealousy with renown The exact identity of the 'filthy swine' who grunt against Jerome is unclear. After the quarrel with Rufinus, Jerome would often refer to his erstwhile friend in the guise of a pig as *Grunnius*, 'the grunter'; and if *QHG* was composed around 392–3, as seems most probable (see above, Introduction, pp. 23–6), then tensions between the two men over Origen's theology, which erupted into the public arena in 393, may have already existed between them in private when *QHG* was being composed. Indeed, this preface culminates in a mordant critique of Origen's methods. Rufinus, in any case, had misgivings about Jerome's emphasis on the Hebrew text as opposed to the LXX.[11] But the words indicate more than one critic of Jerome, among whom we should probably include the enigmatic Luscius Lanvinus who, as we have already seen, gave vent to his hatred of Terence in a personal attack on the poet. So incensed is Jerome that he alludes to these 'pigs' in the words of Matt. 7: 6, where Jesus warns his disciples not to cast their pearls before swine, lest they trample them under their feet, and turn and tear the disciples. That Luscius may still be in mind here is suggested by the appearance of his name again in Jerome's Preface to Book 12 of his *Comm. in Esa.* in tandem with mention of the *Testamentum Grunii Corocottae Porcelli*.[12]

and lightning . . . mountains Jerome here quotes Horace, *Odes* 2. 10. 10–11: 'But I am far away . . . view'. While writing *QHG*, Jerome was in the seclusion of his monastery at Bethlehem, as he had been since 385. The quotation from Quintilian comes from a work no longer extant.

Wherefore . . . riches of the world Beginning with a quotation

[10] For L. Cestius Pius, see H. Bornecque, *Les Déclamations et les déclamateurs d'après Sénèque le Père* (Hildesheim, 1967), 160–2.
[11] See Kelly, *Jerome*, 195–6.
[12] See Cavallera, *Saint Jérôme*, i. 13. Luscius features again in *Contra Rufinum* 1. 30, along with Asinius Pollio, the arch-critic of Cicero.

from Virgil's *Eclogue* 6, lines 9–10, Jerome begs for acceptance of his work. His intention, stated here, of treating the whole of Scripture in the manner of QHG was never realized. He had already spoken of *books* of Hebrew Questions in the Preface of his *Liber de Nominibus Hebraicis*, and continued to speak of books of Hebrew Questions years later, when he was writing his commentary *In Esaiam* between 408 and 410: see *In Esa.* 5 on 15: 5, even though in the same work (*In Esa.* 15 on 54: 1) he refers only to 'the book of Hebrew Questions which we have written on Genesis'.[13]

It is thus often suggested that, having used QHG to demonstrate the superiority of the Hebrew over LXX's translation, Jerome resorted entirely to his Vg rendering, which thereafter took the place of further 'Hebrew Questions'.[14] But in truth Jerome nowhere says why he did not continue the project, which seemed still to be in his mind while he was working on the early part of his Isaiah commentary. Furthermore, underlying this suggestion is the notion that work on QHG led Jerome finally to abandon attempts at 'improving' VL on the basis of LXX, and to have direct recourse to the Hebrew for his Vg translation.[15] But this notion is unproven and, as will presently be seen, may even be seriously flawed.[16]

Therefore it shall be my concern . . . or different   Incomprehension of, and hostility to, Jerome's translation of the Bible direct from the Hebrew original are well known, and were to be voiced with some force as versions of the individual books appeared.[17] So the purpose of QHG, stated here, is first and foremost to make clear the fundamental value of the Hebrew text for proper understanding of

---

[13] '. . . de quo in Hebraicarum Quaestionum libro quem in Genesim scripsimus'.

[14] See Cavallera, *Saint Jérôme*, i. 146–7; G. Grützmacher, *Hieronymus: Eine biographische Studie zur alten Kirchengeschichte*, ii (Berlin, 1906), 62; the comments of Kelly, *Jerome*, 156–7; and Kamesar, 'Thesis', 61.

[15] See especially L. Schade, *Die Inspirationslehre des heiligen Hieronymus* (Freiburg i.B., 1910), 149–53; W. Schwarz, *Principles and Problems of Biblical Translation* (Cambridge, 1955), 26–34; J. Gribomont, 'Jerome', in A. di Berardino (ed.), *Patrology*, iv, trans. P. Solari (Westminster, Md., 1991), 224–5.

[16] A. Kamesar, *Jerome, Greek Scholarship, and the Hebrew Bible* (Oxford, 1993), 41–3, shows how Jerome, while still in Rome c.382–5, had already become convinced that the Hebrew, not the LXX, was the key to understanding the Old Testament: he cites *Eps.* 20, 28, 34, 36, and 37. Jerome's 'conversion' to Hebrew thus pre-dates work on QHG; and such writings of his as seem to suggest he still 'had faith in' LXX at that time in fact, on close inspection, reveal his misgivings about its superfluities and crass errors, ibid., pp. 49–54.

[17] See e.g. Augustine, *Ep.* 71. 3–5; Rufinus, *Apologia* 2. 24–37, cited by H. F. D. Sparks, 'Jerome as Bible Translator', in P. R. Ackroyd and C. F. Evans (eds.), *The Cambridge History of the Bible*, i (Cambridge, 1970), 521.

the Scriptures. This task includes the refutation of those who made mistaken conjectures about the Hebrew: Jerome possibly has in mind Antiochene scholars like Eusebius of Emesa and Diodore of Tarsus, who often cited as authorities 'the Hebrew' or 'the Syrian', but not in such a way as to come to grips with the reality of the Hebrew text itself.[18] And to ensure that no one should miss the point, Jerome brings into play for the first time a phrase for which he has justly become famous: at the end of this preface, he speaks of 'Hebraica veritas' ('the Hebrew truth'; see also 13: 1–4; 19: 14; 49: 5–6), as he condemns the shortcomings of Origen's attitude to the original language of the Old Testament.[19]

For Jerome, the importance of the Hebrew is manifest first of all in those places where the LXX and VL 'burst forth in abundance', including in their renderings material not found in the Hebrew. Jerome's negative opinion of such 'superfluities' is well known, and appears in his comments on (e.g.) Gen. 4: 8; 13: 13; 25: 8; 30: 12–13. He will also insist on Hebrew, not spurious Greek etymologies for Hebrew words, as in the case of Gen. 17: 15. Consistent with this approach are his remarks on the Egyptian etymology of the name Zaphenath-Paneah given to Joseph in Gen. 41: 45. Etymology is, indeed, one of his most pressing concerns: the term itself is used no fewer than four times in Greek (2: 23 twice; 17: 15; 26: 32–3) and nine in Latin (4: 1; 17: 19; 19: 36–8; 24: 43; 29: 32; 30: 12–13, 17–18; 32: 28–9; 43: 34) in the course of the book. His Christian predecessors, notably Origen and Didymus of Alexandria, and contemporaries like Gregory of Nazianzus, were wont to discover in the etymologies of words, and names of people and places, spiritual meanings which were otherwise hidden from view. Jerome's preoccupation with correct Hebrew etymology was, therefore, to some degree dictated by the activity of earlier Christian scholars; and it was no accident that the composition of *QHG* was accomplished almost simultaneously with his writing of the monographs on Hebrew personal names and place-names. These expound the meanings of Hebrew terms, and Jerome uses *QHG* to modify and improve his interpretations in the earlier works (e.g. 30:

---

[18] See Kamesar, *Jerome*, 128–51.

[19] Probably slightly earlier than *QHG* is *In Ecclesiasten* (PL 23: 445B), which has the phrase 'according to the truth of the Hebrew meaning': for this, and for full discussion of what Jerome means by 'the Hebrew truth' and its relationship to the literal meaning of the text, see Jay, *L'Exégèse de saint Jérôme*, 89–102, 142–7. The similar expression *Hebraea veritas* is found in the body of the text at 19: 14–15.

19–20). The extended treatments of the Table of Nations in Gen.
10, and of the names of the Patriarchs in Gen. 29: 32–30: 21, are
of a piece with those monographs in their careful explanation of
words according to their Hebrew roots.[20]

The sense of what he does in *QHG* is revealed most clearly
through comparison of texts: the LXX in a Latin translation, or
very occasionally the VL itself, is set forth for most of the verses
under scrutiny, and the Hebrew original is then held open to view.
In this way, Jerome is able to demonstrate the differences between
the Hebrew original and the versions, and to evaluate them. Careful
reading of *QHG* with the commentary provided here will, in our
view, confirm Kamesar's conclusion, that throughout this book
Jerome is entirely partial to the Hebrew text of Scripture.[21]

But we neither charge . . . worship one God The Hebrew text,
therefore, is of supreme importance for Jerome, a fact corroborated
by his candid admission that LXX made mistakes (e.g. Gen. 4: 6–
7; 5: 4; 17: 15) and failed to understand the Hebrew correctly (e.g.
13: 1; 17: 6; 27: 40—see particularly the commentary on 4: 6–7).
He thus expresses reservations about LXX from the start and
continually throughout *QHG*: there is nothing in this treatise to
suggest that, having begun work with a favourable appraisal of the
version, he became progressively disillusioned about its value as his
writing gathered pace.[22]

Why, then, does Jerome apparently contradict himself, by stating
here that he is not accusing the Septuagint of errors? Properly to
appreciate his stance, we must understand that he is defending
himself against 'jealous people' who 'slander' his work; and that the
defence which he mounts here is repeated later, with amplifications,
in the Preface to his Vg translation of the Pentateuch, and in his
Apologia adversus Libros Rufini 2. 518–21. The LXX translators,
he declares, in reality altered certain texts of Scripture.[23] Two of
their reasons for doing so are set out already in *QHG*: they wished
to conceal the mysteries of the coming of Christ; and they did not
wish to lead King Ptolemy to the erroneous conclusion that Jews
might believe in two divine powers. In other words, the translations

---

[20] On the importance of etymology in Jerome's commentaries, see most recently
Jay, *L'Exégèse de saint Jérôme*, 292–7; and on the *Book of Names* and the *Book of
Places*, see Gribomont, 'Jerome', 228.

[21] See Kamesar, *Jerome*, 77–80.

[22] See also Kamesar, ibid. against Schade, *Die Inspirationslehre*, 143–9.

[23] See Kamesar, 'Thesis', 61–2; and Jay, *L'Exégèse de saint Jérôme*, 121.

set forth by LXX were not conceived in error: they were *deliberate*, and were dictated by theological and political considerations.

Jerome's apparent defence of LXX proves, on closer inspection, to be nothing of the kind. For if the translators effectively concealed and obscured the Christian message in their version, what possible justification can Jerome's detractors bring forward for their continuing adulation of LXX as the Christian Bible *par excellence*? Indeed, Jerome makes plain in the course of *QHG* that it is the Hebrew text of the Bible, and not the LXX translation, which properly contains and expresses the Christian mysteries (see e.g. 9: 27; 18: 6; 26: 17; 35: 21; 49: 8, 11, and comment on these verses). In his Preface to the translation of the Pentateuch he also remarks that the LXX translators were imprecise, because they were ignorant of what they were really announcing: the Hebrew text is thus of correspondingly greater importance.[24]

Throughout this section of the preface, Jerome assumes that his readers will know the story of LXX's origins in the request of King Ptolemy II Philadelphos (282–246 BC) that the Jewish Torah be made available for his library in Greek translation. The episode is described in the *Epistle of Aristeas*, and was widely known.[25] *Aristeas* also insisted that LXX was officially authorized and entirely accurate, and recorded that Ptolemy held the Jewish God to be supreme, his devotion to the God of the Jews being acknowledged even by the high priest Eleazar (*Ep. Ar.* 37, 42). But the notion that the LXX translators hid certain things from the king derives, not from *Aristeas*, but from Rabbinic tradition, according to which the original Hebrew of certain verses was either altered or given a particular nuance, in the Greek version. A list of Rabbinic texts which set out these alterations is given in our comments on 2: 2 below. Jerome almost certainly knew this Rabbinic tradition.[26] He used it in much the same way as the Rabbis, in so far as it enabled him to prove two things. It showed, first, that knowledge of

---

[24] Cf. Kamesar, *Jerome*, 68, who notes how Jerome thus challenges an argument used by Fathers like Irenaeus and Hilary, that LXX's pre-Christian origins somehow guarantee the impartiality of the version.

[25] For a convenient account of recent scholarly opinions on the origins of LXX, see E. Schürer, *The History of the Jewish People in the Age of Jesus Christ*, iii/1, rev. and ed. G. Vermes, F. Millar, and M. Goodman (Edinburgh, 1986), 475–93; and ibid. 677–87 for recent work on *Aristeas*. Jerome's attitude to the latter is discussed by Kamesar, 'Thesis', 53–4.

[26] Justin Martyr was aware of it: see *Dial.* 68. 7, 71. 1, 84. 3, and D. Barthélemy, *Les Devanciers d'Aquila* (SVT 10; Leiden, 1963), 203–4.

the original Hebrew text is an absolute *sine qua non* for knowing
what Scripture actually says; and second, that the traditions of the
Jews themselves are of immense value in determining where and
why LXX have made 'alterations'. For it is not only the Hebrew
Scripture which is true. A prominent characteristic of *QHG* is
Jerome's positive assessment of Hebrew *tradition*, sometimes with
the explicit assertion that it is 'true': (see e.g. 12: 4; 14: 2–3; 19: 30,
33; 22: 20–2; 36: 33; 29: 34; 41: 43; 41: 45; 37: 36; 49: 27).

Yet it may be significant that Jerome neither in the preface, nor
in *QHG* itself, specifies which verses the LXX translators altered.
The Rabbis listed nine verses in Genesis, three of which (1: 26; 11:
7; 15: 13) Jerome does not discuss. In the case of the remaining six
(1: 1; 2: 2; 5: 2; 15: 16; 18: 12; and 49: 6) he notes the differences
between LXX and the Hebrew without referring to the tradition of
alterations for King Ptolemy. This silence over details may suggest
that, although Jerome knew the Rabbinic tradition about the
changes, and partly accepted its rationale, he none the less dissented
from the Rabbinic view that the changes were perfectly in order.[27]
Yet even the Evangelists . . . from what we read   Should any doubt
remain over Jerome's view of LXX, what follows is designed to
dispel it once and for all. In the New Testament, both Our Lord and
St Paul often quote the Scriptures in a form not attested by LXX,
but agreeing, suggests Jerome, with the original Hebrew. The evidence of the New Testament was, for obvious reasons, crucial to his
argument; and when it does not help to prove his case, his arguments can become laboured, as in his comments on 46: 26–7. But
it is one of his recurring arguments in favouring the Hebrew text
over LXX, and goes back at least to the time when he was revising
the Latin translation of the Gospels (*Ep.* 20. 2). As such, it forms
part of Jerome's sustained questioning of the widely held view that
LXX represented a special divine revelation specifically intended
for Gentile Christians.[28]

To what should have proved to be a decisive argument for all his
Christian readers, he adds the evidence of Josephus, who retold the
story of Aristeas in *Ant.* 12. 11–119. Josephus, however, had made
it clear that the Pentateuch alone had been translated at Ptolemy's
command by the seventy translators (*Ant.* 12. 11, 107–9; *Contra*

[27] According to Kamesar, *Jerome*, 66, *b. Meg.* 9a may even suggest that the
changes were divinely inspired.
[28] See Kamesar, *Jerome*, 51, 63–5.

Apionem 2. 46). Thus even if the Torah had been accurately rendered into Greek, the same need not necessarily hold good for the rest of the Hebrew Bible. Jerome does, indeed, suggest that there are fewer discrepancies between LXX and the Hebrew in the case of the Torah than in the case of the remaining books; but even this is of little weight. For later generations had found it necessary to produce not one, but at least three new Greek translations of the Torah, as well as of the rest of Scripture. These new renderings, very different in kind from LXX, at the very least and for whatever reason implied that the LXX could not be entirely relied upon for accuracy. And it is clear from the Preface to his translation of the *Chronicon* of Eusebius that he had been aware of the differences between the LXX and the Three for many years before he came to compose *QHG*.[29]

Aquila is spoken of traditionally as a convert to Judaism (*jer. Meg.* 1: 11), Jerome himself testifying as much in *Ep.* 57. 11. His version, which kept as close as possible to the Hebrew original, appeared in the first half of the second century AD. It is characterized by a literalism which suggests that those who had no knowledge of Hebrew may have found it difficult to follow.[30] Symmachus is a shadowy figure. Some, including Jerome (*Comm. in Hab.* 3: 11–13; *De Vir. Illust.* 54), believed him to have been an Ebionite; others a Samaritan who later converted to Judaism. His version is dated variously in the late second and early third centuries AD. His Greek is much more polished than Aquila's, and the most recent study of his work suggests that he was well versed in Jewish exegetical traditions.[31] Theodotion may also have been an Ebionite, and Jerome refers to him as such in the places listed above where he refers to Symmachus. But he may none the less have been a Jew (see Jerome's Prologue to his *Comm. in Dan.*, and *Ep.* 112. 19) who produced a Greek version of the Bible around the middle of the second century AD. He was fond of transliterating Hebrew words,

[29] For the *Chronicon*, see Kelly, *Jerome*, 72–5; it was produced around 380. See further Kamesar, *Jerome*, 44.

[30] For a comprehensive survey of modern critical study of Aquila's version, see Schürer, *History of the Jewish People*, iii/1. 493–9.

[31] See A. Salvesen, *Symmachus in the Pentateuch* (Manchester, 1992): she discusses his identity at length (pp. 283–97), and concludes that there are no grounds for regarding him as an Ebionite. Rather, he was a Jew, possibly even R. Meir's disciple Sumkhos, and his translation was made between AD 193 and 211 (pp. 295–6). For general discussion, see L. J. Greenspoon, s.v. 'Symmachus, Symmachus's Version', in *The Anchor Bible Dictionary*, vi (New York, 1992), 251.

and his translation often attempts to render individual Hebrew
words by standard Greek equivalents.[32] In one way or another,
each of the Three had some sort of intimate connection with
Judaism, and might be counted as representatives of the Jewish
tradition of translation and exegesis of Scripture. Origen had collected the versions of these three translators, and had transcribed
them along with the Hebrew into his Hexapla, itself part of a
sustained attempt on his part to determine the correct text of the
Septuagint. It is no doubt with this fact in mind that Jerome ends
his preface with an attack on Origen's scholarly procedures.

Finally, . . . dark corners The common folk, the unlettered
Christian, need not be troubled with all this, says Jerome: only
those who especially have the ability to know the intricate details of
scriptural exegesis would wish to busy themselves in the complexities of Hebrew learning. The latter he speaks of metaphorically
as exotic foreign merchandise made up of Oriental luxuries, balsam, pepper, and dates. Those who disparage him will be pleaséd
with this, since he here suggests that the majority of Christian folk
may rest content with the LXX as their Bible. His words give
support to Kamesar's argument that Jerome was realistic in his
appraisal of the Church's continuing adherence to the LXX as Holy
Scripture: he accepted an emended Hexaplaric-LXX as the most
that the Christian public might tolerate for use in church, but
encouraged his Latin readers the while to progress from that starting-point first to his own Vulgate and the Three, and finally to the
Hebrew text itself.[33]

But the case of Origen presented difficulties. Jerome here calls
him Adamantius, 'the man of steel', as he had done earlier when
commenting on the *Ep. to Titus* 3: 9 and approving his work on the
Hexapla. He even interrupted work on *QHG* to translate Origen's
Homilies on Saint Luke for Paula and Eustochium, who had been
so deeply disappointed with Ambrose's endeavours. In this preface,
however, his attitude to Origen has changed for the worse. Quoting
Virgil, *Georgics* 4. 176, he compares himself with this man, who

---

[32] See further Schürer, *History of the Jewish People*, iii/1. 499–504. The versions
of Aquila, Symmachus, and Theodotion present particularly complex problems to
modern scholars as regards their relation to LXX, their origins, dates, purposes, and
antecedents. For the classic discussion of these and other matters, in the light of
manuscript discoveries at Qumran, see Barthélemy, *Les Devanciers*, and, most
recently E. Tov, *Textual Criticism of the Hebrew Bible* (Assen, 1992), 143–8.

[33] See Kamesar, *Jerome*, 63–72.

had also acquired a knowledge of Hebrew language and tradition. But, says Jerome, he preaches to the people using the common edition of LXX, the Lucianic recension, with all its defects, even though in his exegetical writings he clearly shows understanding of the Hebrew, and knowledge of the Three. He therefore knows full well the discrepancies which exist between the original and the translation, but continues to employ a flawed and inadequate rendering. He was also in a position to know the reading of the 'authentic codices' of LXX (see 23: 2) better than anyone else. Jerome's words here suggest that Origen was not, in the last resort, concerned with the Hebrew text in and of itself; indeed, the evidence suggests that his use of it was ultimately confined to explication of the LXX.[34]

The military language which Jerome employs is intended to depict Origen as a man defeated by the evidence: he is 'overcome by the Hebrew truth', but does not dare admit this. Such is Jerome's consequent contempt for Origen's name that his hatred for him is equalled only by his love of the Scriptures; and his final remarks may be taken as a scathing dismissal of Origen's endeavours. These he regards as 'images and shadows of ghosts'. The phraseology is superficially reminiscent of Heb. 10: 1, which speaks of the Torah as a shadow (*umbra*) of the image (*imago*), the Christian dispensation. But Jerome is unlikely to have borrowed these words from Hebrews, since he here uses both 'shadow' and 'image' in a pejorative sense. His expression more likely harks back to his old master Cicero, with the intention of representing the insubstantial and derivative nature of all that is based on the LXX, as contrasted with the Hebrew truth which is the substance, source, and reality.[35]

---

[34] So, convincingly, Kamesar, *Jerome*, 6–28, arguing against the notions that Origen's work was directed towards promoting the Hebrew text (so P. Nautin, *Origène*, i: *Sa vie et son œuvre* (Paris, 1977), 344–53, esp. 351–3), or towards viewing the Hebrew text on an equal footing with the LXX in the Church (so D. Barthélemy, 'Origène et le texte de l'Ancien Testament', in J. Fontaine and C. Kannengiesser (eds.), *Epektasis: Mélanges patristiques offerts au Cardinal Jean Daniélou* (Paris, 1972), 258–60; id., 'La Place de la Septante dans l'église', in *Aux grands carrefours de la révélation et de l'exégèse de l'Ancien Testament: Journées du Colloque Biblique de Louvain* (Recherches Bibliques, 8; Louvain, 1967), 13–28.

[35] See Jay, *L'Exégèse de saint Jérôme*, 257–8, quoting Cicero, *De Republica* 2. 30. 52; *De Officiis* 3. 17. 69; *Tusc.* 3. 3; *Pro Rab. Post.* 15. 41. In Jerome's writings, 'shadow' and 'image' seem to mean much the same thing; they are used of the old Law and its types, which contrast with the reality of the New Covenant.

CHAPTER 1

verse 1 Throughout this book, Jerome assumes on the part of his
readers knowledge and understanding of both the Old and the New
Testament. So here, commenting on one of the best known verses of
Scripture, he presumes that they will know the teaching of the New
Testament, that God the Father created the universe through the
agency of His Son, Jesus Christ. This is made plain by the opening
verses of St John's Gospel (see especially John 1: 1–3, 10), and by
statements in the Epistles like that in Heb. 1: 2, which asserts that
the Son was the One through Whom God created *tous aiōnas*, the
ages or the *worlds*. The New Testament seems to go even further,
and to forge a direct link between the Son's activity in creation and
the opening words of Genesis; indeed, Col. 1: 13–20 speaks of the
Son as the One in whom and through whom all things, in heaven
and on earth, were created. These same verses declare that the Son
was before all things, which themselves consist in Him. Such thinking may, indeed, have arisen from the author's meditation on the
first words of Gen. 1: 1, and his elaboration of them in the manner
of a Jew expounding Scripture according to midrashic rules of
exegesis.[1]

Whatever the exegetical bedrock underlying Col. 1: 13–20, this
text is a very early example of something which, in the writings of
the Fathers, became quite widely accepted; namely, the perception
that Gen. 1: 1 refers to the creation of the Universe through the
agency of God the Son.[2] Jerome's remarks can best be interpreted
by considering the two strands of thinking which appear in his own
comments, the Christian and the Jewish. The Fathers were so
convinced that God the Son was the agent in creation, that the first
words of Genesis were, by some of them, understood as 'by means
of the Son God created heaven and earth'. Since the Son was agent
of creation, he must therefore have preceded it in time. Hence
Jerome quotes three authorities. The work of the first, Aristo of
Pella in the *Dialogue of Jason and Papiscus*, has not come down to

[1] See C. F. Burney, 'Christ as the *APXH* of the Creation', *JTS* 27 (1926), 175–6;
and W. D. Davies, *Paul and Rabbinic Judaism* (London, 1965), 151–2.

[2] For example, in addition to those authors cited by Jerome on this verse, see the
extended discussion in Theophilus, *Ad Autolycum* 2. 10; Irenaeus, *Demonstratio* 43;
Origen, *Comm. in Joh.* 1. 16–18; Methodius, *On Created Beings* 11; Gregory of
Tours, *Historia* 1. 1 (35: 6); Tertullian, *Adversus Hermogenem* 19–20; Serapion of
Thmuis cited in Petit, *La Chaîne*, 7.

us complete: this reference in *QHG* is the only indication that Aristo so understood the opening of Genesis.[3] Tertullian (*Adv. Prax.* 5. 1) notes a translation of the Hebrew by unnamed persons as 'In the beginning, God became a son'; and Hilary of Poitiers (*Tractatus in Ps.* 2: 2) lists three meanings of the Hebrew *bᵉrēʾšīt*: 'in the beginning; in (or:by means of) the head; and in (or: by means of) the Son'.[4] The Greek translation of *bᵉrēʾšīt* into *en archē* was itself an incentive to the Fathers to find reference to Christ in the opening word of Scripture, since *archē* may mean 'source', 'principle', 'beginning', 'head', or even résumé. So much was clear to Origen, *Comm. in Joh.* 1. 90–124, who lists no fewer than six meanings of the word, and who in *Hom. in Gen.* 1. 1 states that God created the world by means of *archē*.

When he turns to consider the Jewish evidence, however, Jerome does not hesitate to assert that *bᵉrēʾšīt* means 'in the beginning'; and he clearly points out, by way of contrast, what the Hebrew equivalent of 'in the Son' might be. He records the translations of Septuagint, Symmachus, and Theodotion as representing the obvious sense of the Hebrew; but he also notes Aquila's understanding of the word as *in capitulo*, that is, 'in the chapter' or, more literally, 'in/by means of the little head, the capital point, the résumé'. There is thus some overlap in semantic range between *bᵉrēʾšīt* and *en archē*; but it is notable that Jerome's whole exegesis from now on is dominated not by the Greek, but by the Hebrew expression. Ambrose, *Hexaemeron* 1. 16 (13. 23) also knows of this rendering of the Hebrew, although he does not name Aquila as its author. Governing Aquila's translation is the fact that *bᵉrēʾšīt* contains the consonants *rʾš*, which may be vocalized as *rōʾš*, 'head'. This perception of a Jewish translator, who here represents the 'Hebrew truth' for which Jerome so often strives, provides a direct lead to the rest of the comment, in that it is the sense of the verse, rather than its literal meaning, which may be applied to Christ. So Jerome remarks that Christ is referred to '*in ipsa fronte*' of Genesis,

[3] See M. J. Routh, *Reliquiae Sacrae*, i (Oxford, 1846), 95. L. Ginzberg, 'Die Haggada bei den Kirchenvätern und in der apokryphischen Literatur', *MGWJ* NS 6 (1898), 539–40, suggests that the Christian sources which Jerome quotes here may represent a Christianized form of exegesis found in the Palestinian Targums.

[4] For further discussion of early Christian renderings of 'beginning' as 'Son', see A. Díez Macho, 'Targum y Nuevo Testament', in *Mélanges Eugène Tisserant* (Studi e Testi, 231. i; Rome, 1964), 173–4; J. Daniélou, *Théologie du Judéo-Christianisme*, i (Tournai, 1958), 219–22.

that is, literally, 'on the very forehead' of Genesis, the head of all the biblical books.

Aquila's translation also makes it possible for Jerome to link his comments to Ps. 40: 8, which refers to 'the chapter of the book'. This Psalm had already been applied to Christ by the author of Heb. 10: 7; and Jerome develops the application further by his perception that the book of which the Psalm is speaking is Genesis, and its 'chapter' or 'little head' the opening word. Thus, by a somewhat circuitous route, he is able to establish the true sense of the opening word of Genesis, as distinct from its literal signification: it alludes to the Son of God. And to remove the possibility of any remaining doubt in the matter, he lets his readers know that the Jews name the individual books of Scripture from their opening words, *ex principiis*: thus it was 'in principio' ('in the beginning') that God created heaven and earth. According to Eusebius (*HE* 6. 25. 2), Origen had recorded the Hebrew names of the biblical books in order; but there is no indication that he put these titles to theological use.[5]

It is noticeable that Jerome here avoids any suggestion that the opening word of Gen. 1: 1 should be interpreted in the light of Prov. 8: 22, which states that the Lord created Wisdom as the *rēʾšīth*, the 'beginning', of His way. By expounding the two verses in the light of one another, some Jewish authorities concluded that *rēʾšīth* was the equivalent of Wisdom; and that therefore the *bᵉrēʾšīth* of Gen. 1: 1 meant that the Lord had created the world by means of Wisdom. Verses like Jer. 10: 12; Prov. 3: 19; and Ps. 104: 24 would confirm such exegesis. Consequently, we find FTP and FTV rendering the Hebrew of Gen. 1: 1 as 'by means of Wisdom the Lord created . . .'.[6] See also the comments of R. Banai in *Gen. Rab.* 1: 1. The single extant MS of TN of Gen. 1: 1 reads: 'From of old, by Wisdom, the son of the Lord completed the heavens and the earth.' The MS shows signs of having been tampered with; and the present reading was probably manufactured by a Christian censor.[7]

---

[5] See further N. R. M. de Lange, *Origen and the Jews: Studies in Jewish–Christian Relations in mid-third-century Palestine* (Cambridge, 1976), 52–3, 176; and Petit, *La Chaîne*, 7.

[6] For the text, see M. L. Klein, *The Fragment-Targums of the Pentateuch According to their Extant Sources*, 2 vols. (Rome, 1980). Translations are ours, except where stated. The margin of FTP has a variant reading, 'from the beginning the Lord created . . .'.

[7] For the text of TN, see the *editio princeps* of A. Díez Macho, *Ms. Neophyti I*, 5 vols. (Madrid and Barcelona, 1968–78); translations are ours, unless stated. Díez

verse 2 In this verse, Jerome had to deal with a very rare Hebrew word, which the Masoretes vocalized as *mᵉraḥepet*: the VL translated it as *superferebatur*, 'moved, was carried above', a rendering which Jerome himself in essence accepted for his Vg translation *ferebatur*, 'moved, was carried'. See also his commentaries *In Hab.* 2: 3; *In Jon.* 2; *In Esa.* 2. 4: 1; and *Ep.* 69. 6. LXX translated in the same way. Jerome's explanation of the word here, however, seems to be based on Deut. 32: 11, describing an eagle which *hovers* or *broods* over its young; such, at any rate, is the most probable meaning of the Hebrew verb *yᵉraḥēp*. The only other occurrence of the verbal root *rḥp* in biblical Hebrew, at Jer. 23: 9, has the sense of 'tremble' or 'shake'.

But Jerome gives the word a very precise significance which is largely shared by Ambrose, *Hexaemeron* 1. 29 (28. 24). According to the latter, God warmed the waters, that is, gave life to them; and he cites 'the Syrian' as his authority for interpreting the verse in this way. Basil, too, quotes the Syrian: the word refers to a bird warming and giving life to its eggs.[8] The same understanding is found in Diodore (see the Catena fragment in Petit, ii. 32) and possibly in the writing of Eusebius of Emesa.[9] In earlier times, it seems likely that Origen, too, had understood the word to refer to a bird brooding, since the Latin translation of his *In Isa. Homilia* 4. 1 speaks of the

Macho himself considers TN's version of Gen. 1: 1 the result of Christian scribal activity: see vol. i, p. 3. The scribal peculiarities of TN are discussed by M. F. Martin, 'The Palaeographical Character of Codex Neofiti I', *Textus*, 3 (1963), 1–35. For further comments on the reading of this Targum, see Díez Macho, 'Targum y Nuevo Testamento', 174.

[8] See F. Field, *Origenis Hexaplorum Quae Supersunt*, 2 vols. (Oxford, 1875): Basil's quotation of the Syrian is found in the list of readings for Gen. 1: 2 in vol. i, p. 8; and see now the Catena fragment at Petit ii. 30–1. Basil's 'Syrian' seems to have been either Eusebius of Emesa or Diodore, according to Petit, ibid., note (b). On the identity of the Syrian in general, see Field, i, pp. lxxvii–lxxxii; H. B. Swete, *Introduction to the Old Testament in Greek* (Cambridge, 1902), 56, 116; A. Rahlfs, 'Quis Sit Ho Suros', in *Kleine Mitteilungen: Mitteilungen des Septuaginta-Unternehmens der Akademie der Wissenschaft in Göttingen*, i/7 (Berlin, 1915), 404–12; and S. Jellicoe, *The Septuagint and Modern Study* (Oxford, 1968), 248. The Syrian is not here related to any of the extant Targums, all of which put 'was blowing'. Pesh uses the same root as the Hebrew which, however, in Syriac has the sense of 'hover, wave, cherish, brood (of a hen)'; and the sense of 'cherish' is certainly included in the Latin *confovebat* used by Jerome, which we have translated above as 'was keeping warm'. With this in mind, it is worth noting that de Montfaucon regarded the Syrian as the Peshitta: see his *Hexapla*, i (Paris, 1713), Introduction, pp. 20 ff. Most recent scholarship accepts that the 'Syrian' in the writings of Theodore of Mopsuestia at least represents an Old Syriac version or the Peshitta itself: see Kamesar, *Jerome*, 38–9, and bibliography there cited.

[9] For Eusebius and Diodore here, see Kamesar, *Jerome*, 129–32.

waters over which the Spirit of God *incubabat*, 'was brooding', the very word used by Jerome in his comment. Origen, then, may be the ultimate source for Jerome's rendering; but it is equally possible that they both owe something to Jewish tradition. This possibility is strengthened when the remark of Ambrose and Basil is noted, that 'the Syrian' is very closely related to the Hebrew.[10]

There is, indeed, a famous story about the mystical speculations of Simeon ben Zoma told by R. Joshua ben Hananiah (*c*. AD 90–120), in the course of which ben Zoma expounds *merahepet* as meaning 'like a dove which hovers over her chicks, but does not touch them': such is the version recorded in *b. Ḥag.* 15a. The same story is found in other texts, although the Babylonian Talmud alone offers this particular explanation of *merahepet*.[11] The mystical reveries of ben Zoma were well known: he was one of the four Rabbis who were said to have entered paradise, where he gazed and lost his reason.[12] His understanding of *merahepet* may once have been more widespread than extant Rabbinic sources suggest: the Rabbis tended to be reserved about mystical experiences, and the rendering by the Targums of *merahepet* as 'was blowing' may reflect such a reserve. According to *Gen. Rab.* 2: 4, ben Zoma was adamant that 'was blowing' was not written in Scripture, but *merahepet*. Even so, the Babylonian Talmud is witness that ben Zoma's interpretation of the word was widely known; and Jerome may have heard it from Jews of his own day. Origen, too, may have encountered it among his Jewish contemporaries, if the Latin translation of his work faithfully reflects what he originally wrote; and he may be yet another channel leading to Jerome's comment.[13]

The Hebrew here speaks of the 'Spirit of God', not 'the Spirit of the Lord'. Jerome insists that this verse refers to the Holy Ghost: so

---

[10] Ambrose in particular stresses the linguistic similarities and agreements between the Syrian and the Hebrew: 'denique Syrus, qui vicinus Hebraeo est et sermone consonat in plerisque et congruit . . .'.

[11] See also *jer. Ḥag.* 2: 1 (which quotes Deut. 32: 11 to cast light on *merahepet*); *t. Ḥag.* 2: 6; *Gen. Rab.* 2: 4; the comments of E. E. Urbach, *The Sages: Their Concepts and Beliefs*, i (Jerusalem, 1979), 189–90; and S. Lieberman, 'How Much Greek in Jewish Palestine?', in Biblical and Other Studies (P. W. Lown Institute of Advanced Judaic Studies; Cambridge, Mass., 1963), 135–9.

[12] See *t. Ḥag.* 2: 3, 4; *b. Ḥag.* 14b–15b; *jer. Ḥag.* 2: 1 ff.; and I. Gruenwald, *Apocalyptic and Merkavah Mysticism* (Leiden, 1980), 86–95.

[13] For Origen's knowledge of Jewish teachings on creation, see de Lange, *Origen and the Jews*, 124–7.

does Origen, *De Princ.* 1. 3. 3. He specifies this against people who refer it to the 'spirit of the world', an expression used by St Paul in 1 Cor. 2: 12; but it is hard to know precisely what is meant by the phrase, since he does not identify those who interpret the verse in this way. Ambrose states (*Hexaemeron* 1. 29) that some think the spirit in this verse means the air (see especially Diodore in a Catena fragment, Petit, ii. 32; Theodoret, *QG* 8), or the breath of life: with the latter, compare Theophilus *Ad Autolycum* 2. 13, and the views of some Rabbis in later Midrashim such as *Midrash Pss.* 139 that the spirit refers to the soul or spirit of the First Man. But Ambrose follows 'the opinion of the saints and the faithful' in taking it to mean the Holy Spirit.

In 1 Cor. 2: 12, the spirit of the world is opposed to the Spirit from God; and Ambrose's reference to the air is redolent of Eph. 2: 2, which speaks of the prince of the power of the air, opposed to God. Possibly Jerome is rebutting groups who saw in Gen. 1: 2 some hint of a hostile and malignant spiritual adversary of God at the time of creation; and the Aramaic Targums, except Targum Onkelos (TO), may be similarly motivated when they expound the words as 'the spirit of mercy (or: love) from before the Lord (or: God)'. For many Gnostics, the created order was an evil thing, and had been brought into existence by a wicked power: see, for example, the Valentinian account of creation involving Achamoth, Spirit, and the Demiurge described by Irenaeus, *Adv. Haer.* 1. 1. 10–11. On the other hand, Jerome may have in mind the doctrines of the Stoics, and such Christians as had been influenced by them into thinking of the Spirit of God as a reference to the *anima mundi*, or 'world soul'. His emphasis on the Holy Ghost as the life-giver and creator would be consistent with attacks on the Stoics; or on those who regarded all created objects as possessed of some life-force, whom he also attacks in his commentary on St Matthew's Gospel; or on the Pneumatomachians, who denied the divinity of the Holy Ghost.[14] Like Ambrose in the *Hexaemeron*, he concludes his argument by quoting Ps. 104: 30.

verse 10 Jerome's comment on this verse is found elsewhere in his

---

[14] See *Commentariorum in Mattheum Libri IV*, ed. D. Hurst and M. Adriaen (CCSL 77; Tournai, 1969), 52, on Matt. 8: 26. The Pneumatomachians are the object of Basil's attack in his exegesis of the verse: see Kamesar, *Jerome*, 130–1; and Ginzberg, 'Die Haggada' (*MGWJ* ns 7), 17–18, for other authorities who regarded spirit in this verse as a reference to wind.

writings: see, for example, his remarks on Gen. 36: 24 in the
present work; and *In Esa.* 5. 19: 5–7; 6. 13: 10. For the miracle of
Christ walking on the water, see Matt. 14: 22–33; Mark 6: 45–52;
John 6: 16–21. Porphyry (*c.* AD 232–*c.*305) wrote a work against
the Christians in fifteen books, which was burned in 448, and now
survives only in fragments and stray quotations in works such as
this, which seek to refute his arguments.[15]

CHAPTER 2

verse 2   Jerome follows the Hebrew text of this verse in his Vg, as
do also the Aramaic Targums. But LXX put the completion of
creation on the sixth day; the same reading is found in the Samaritan Pentateuch, the Pesh, and *Jub.* 2: 16. The reason for the
change is obvious: the original Hebrew might be taken to imply
that God worked on the Sabbath, which He Himself declares a day
of rest. God, therefore, must be made to observe the first Sabbath
by not working. Jewish tradition lists this alteration as one of a
number made for King Ptolemy when the Torah was translated into
Greek.[1] The contents of these traditional lists differ somewhat, as
can be seen from *b. Meg.* 9ab; *jer. Meg.* 1. 1. 4; *Masseketh Soferim*
1: 7–9; *Mekh. de R. Ishmael Pisḥa* 14: 64–77; *ARNb* 37; *Yalquṭ
Shim'oni* 3; *Midrash Tannaim* on Exod. 22; and *MHG* on Exod.
4: 20.
   Rabbinic authority, however, preferred not to use this means of
removing a potential difficulty from the text, emphasizing instead
either the completion of creation before the seventh day, or pointing to the Sabbath itself as the completion of creation (*Gen. Rab.*
10: 9). The Targums also translated the verse literally, with the
exception of one manuscript of TO and the main text of FTP,
which state that God was 'filled with desire for' his work on the
seventh day. TO, however, seems to have addressed the problem by

---

[15] See A. von Harnack, *Porphyrius, 'Gegen Die Christen' 15 Bücher: Zeugnisse,
Fragmente und Referate* (Abhandlungen der königlich preussischen Akademie der
Wissenschaften, 1; Berlin, 1916), 80–1. On Jerome's knowledge and refutations of
Porphyry, see P. Courcelle, *Late Latin Writers and their Greek Sources*, trans. H. E.
Wedeck (Cambridge, Mass., 1969), 72–8.
   [1] See further A. Geiger, *Urschrift und Uebersetzung der Bibel* (Breslau, 1857),
439–42; J. Bowker, *The Targums and Rabbinic Literature* (Cambridge, 1969), 319–
20; and Kamesar, *Jerome*, 66–7.

stating that God *šyẓy*, that is, 'finished' his work, in the sense of ceasing from it.[2]

Yet the possibility that God might have worked on the first Sabbath was matter for debate between Jews and Christ in John 5: 2–18. Jerome's words have close affinities with sentiments expressed in that Gospel. His attitude towards work on the Sabbath reflects the general stance of his Christian contemporaries; but moderate Christian defence of the Sabbath was not unknown: see, for example, Ignatius, *Ad Magnesios* 9; and Tertullian, *Adv. Marc.* 2. 21, 4. 12.

verse 8 LXX took the Hebrew expression *gan b^e\u02bdēden* in this verse to mean 'a paradise in Edem'. In 2: 15, however, as Jerome notes, they translated Eden as 'pleasure' or 'delight': the Hebrew root *'dn* does, indeed, signify 'delight'. Jerome here omits the preposition 'in', and uses the word *deliciae*, the second of three meanings he gives to it in *Lib. Heb. Nom.* (p. 65) as his rendering of Eden. It has the sense of delights, allurements, or enticements, and may have about it an air of the evanescent (cf. *Ep.* 100. 3); but he uses it elsewhere to speak of this garden: see *Comm. in Hiez.* 9. 28: 11–19; *Comm. in Hier.* 5. 63, 6. 21.

He also has a comment on Gen. 2: 15, where LXX take Eden to mean 'pleasure', and which he renders into Latin as *voluptas*: this same word he puts in his Vg to interpret Eden here and at 2: 15; 3: 23. It is his first choice for the meaning of the word in *Lib. Heb. Nom.* (p. 65). Vg only once in these early chapters of Genesis (at 4: 16) regards Eden as the name of a place. This may possibly result from Jerome's knowledge and apparent approval of Symmachus' translation 'a flowering paradise', which seems to regard Eden as a qualification of the preceding word 'garden'. Indeed, another reading of Symmachus extant for this verse, preserved by Ishodad of Merv and one Greek MS., renders 'a garden in Eden' as 'the luxury (Greek: *truphē*) of the world': cf. LXX of Gen. 3: 23 , 24, 'the paradise of luxury, *truphēs*'; and Philo, *Leg. All.* 1. 45.[3] Both Symmachus and Jerome's Vg indicate that Eden might not necessarily be understood as a place: this seems to have been known to

---

[2] See B. Grossfeld, 'Targum Onkelos and Rabbinic Interpretation to Genesis 2: 1, 2', *JJS* 24 (1973), 176–8.

[3] See A. Salvesen, *Symmachus in the Pentateuch* (Manchester, 1991), 7–9, for full discussion of these readings of Symmachus and their affinities with Ephrem's interpretation of Eden in *Hymni de Paradiso* 5. 14. 6.

Origen, *Sel. in Gen.* 2: 8, who quotes a Jewish tradition confirming that Eden was indeed a location, the middle of the world. Eusebius of Emesa (Devreesse, p. 59) is much clearer, asking directly whether Eden is the place where paradise was located, or paradise itself? He does not answer the question, preferring to remain ambiguous.[4] While Jerome does not explicitly tackle this question, either here or in Vg, the works of Origen, Symmachus, and Eusebius may have played their parts in his thinking and, in particular, in his choice of wording in Vg verses cited above. Neither does he discuss the opinion that the Garden of Eden was a purely heavenly reality, which many Greek Fathers felt it necessary to refute (see Petit, *La Chaîne*, 160–5).

What the LXX translated as 'over against the east' is the word *miqqedem*, which one witness to QHG (Codex Monacensis 6311) reads as *meccedem*: Kamesar, *Jerome*, 143, warms to Field's suggestion (vol. i, p. 13) that the original reading was '*meccedem* non *mimizra*', '*meccedem*, not *mimizra*'. There is ambiguity in *miqqedem*, which may mean either 'from the east' or 'from of old': LXX takes the first option, as do Josephus, *Ant.* 1. 37, Philo, *Leg. All.* 1. 49, and some Syriac sources listed by Salvesen.[5] Other sources, however, translated as 'from of old': Jerome lists Aquila, Symmachus, and Theodotion among them, and they also include his own Vg, Pesh, and all extant Targums. Indeed, it was commonly held by Jews of Jerome's time that the Garden of Eden had been one of a number of items created before the universe existed: see *IV Esdras* 3: 6 (cf. *Syr. Bar.* 4: 3); PJ of Gen. 2: 8; *b. Pes.* 54a; *Ned.* 39b; *PRE* 3: 2; and *Yalquṭ Shim'oni* 20. An equally ancient tradition attested by *Jub.* 2: 7 and *Gen. Rab.* 11: 9; 15: 3; 21: 9 puts the creation of Eden on the third day of the first week. It was known to Eusebius of Emesa (Devreesse, p. 59); but Jerome does not follow this, preferring a solution like the Talmud's.[6]

Kamesar believes that Jerome's comments are directed against

---

[4] See de Lange, *Origen and the Jews,* 25, quoting Origen's *Sel. in Gen.* 2: 8. For Eusebius of Emesa, see Devreese, p. 59, and cf. Diodore's statement of the two opinions in a Catena fragment, Petit, ii. 88. There is no hint in QHG of the debate in *Gen. Rab.* 15: 2, noted by de Lange, whether Eden was in the garden, or the garden located in Eden. Theodoret, *QG* 25, records the view that certain people located the paradise in heaven.

[5] See Salvesen, *Symmachus*, 7–8, for this and for what follows.

[6] Cf. M. Rahmer, *Die hebräischen Traditionen in den Werken des Hieronymus durch einen Vergleichung mit den jüdischen Quellen,* i: *Die 'Quaestiones in Genesin'* (Breslau, 1861), 17.

the opinion of Eusebius of Emesa (Devreesse, p. 59), that God created Eden after He had made Adam.[7] This is probable; but the opinion was not restricted to Eusebius, since Theophilus, *Ad Autolycum* 2. 24, seems also to regard Adam as created before Eden by understanding Gen. 1 to refer simply to the creation of Adam, and Gen. 2: 8 to the subsequent creation of the garden.

verse 11　The river Pishon, which according to this verse encompasses the land of Havilah, is identified with the Ganges by Josephus, *Ant.* 1. 38. He also equates the 'land of Havilah' with India, where Jerome locates this river in agreement with the Targums PJ and TN. Pishon as the Ganges was well known; Jerome refers to it again in *In Esa.* 6. 13: 12, and *Eps.* 51. 5. 5, 125. 3. 2; and it features also in Ambrose, *De Paradiso* 14; Eusebius, *Onomasticon* (ed. Klostermann) 80. 24; Acacius, in a Catena fragment (Petit, ii. 101); and Augustine, *De Gen. ad Litt.* 8. 7. Kamesar is thus almost certainly correct in suggesting that Jerome did not borrow this information from Acacius.[8] His agreement with the Jewish Targums, against the tradition of the Samaritan Targum that Pishon is the Nile and the note in *Gen. Rab.* 16: 4 that it stands for Babylon, is particularly noteworthy.[9]

verse 12　The identity of the precious stones in this verse was of interest, given that the second of them features as part of the high priest's vestments, according to Exod. 25: 7; 28: 9; 39: 13. VL translated in the same manner as LXX, whereas other ancient versions referred to different types of stone. So the Hebrew *habbᵉdōlaḥ* is taken as 'bdellium' by Pesh, TO, PJ, and TN: Jerome follows this in Vg. Pesh, TO, and PJ understood *'eben haššōham* as 'beryl stone', TN as 'precious stones and pearls'. The 'others' whom Jerome refers to are Aquila, Symmachus, and Theodotion, whom he follows here and in Vg by translating 'bdellion and onyx': so much is clear from his *Ep.* 64. 15 (*ad Fabiolam*), where he discusses the high priestly robes and transliterates the Hebrew of the second stone as *SOOM*. He notes that Josephus, by translating it as 'sardonyx', agrees with the Hebrew and Aquila.[10] His reference is to Josephus, *Ant.* 3. 165, 168, part of an extended discussion of the

---

[7] See Kamesar, *Jerome*, 141–5.

[8] See Kamesar, 'Thesis', 116.

[9] The medieval commentators Rashi, Saʿadia, and Naḥmanides, and the *Zohar* and *Midrash Aggadah* also identified Pishon with the Nile. Cf. *b. Ber.* 59a.

[10] For identification of the 'others' as Aquila, Symmachus, and Theodotion, see Field, i. 14, 131, 157–8.

priestly vestments and their precious stones of a kind common from Second Temple times onward: see also *ben Sira* 45: 11; 50: 9; *Wisdom* 18: 24; Philo, *De Vita Mosis* 2. 122–3, *Quis Rerum* 176, *QE* 2. 109, 114–15; pseudo-Philo, *LAB* 11: 15; 12: 9; 13: 1; and 25: 11, which refers specifically to this verse of Genesis. PJ of Exod. 35: 27 says that the precious beryl (= onyx) stones for the high priest's garments came from Pishon; cf. *b. Yoma* 75a; *Exod. Rab.* 25: 2; *Num. Rab.* 12: 16; *Sifre Naśo'* 45; *Tanḥ Naśo'* 27.

verse 15 LXX read: 'And the Lord God took the man whom He had formed, and placed him in the paradise to work it and to guard it', adding the words 'whom He had formed' which occur also in 2: 8. See comments on 2: 8 above. Here, however, the reading which Jerome attributes to Symmachus is problematic. Some witnesses to *QHG* read *alsēs*, not *aktēs*: the former being an otherwise unattested and unknown word, suspicion arises that *aktēs* may be a valiant attempt by scribes to make sense of it; and so it has consequently been the object of conjectural emendations in plenty.[11] Of these, the reading *akmēs*, 'of youth', may have a certain appeal, in that Symmachus at Gen. 18: 12 translated Hebrew *'ednāh* as *akmē*.[12] Jerome's comments are purely philological: he offers no explanation why Adam was put in the paradise.

verse 17 LXX attempted, as far as was possible, a literal translation of the Hebrew *mōt tāmūt*, an infinitive absolute and finite verb which mean 'you shall certainly die'. The same sort of translation is offered by Aquila, Theodotion, TO, TN, Pesh ('you shall die a death'), VL, and Jerome's Vg. The Hebrew verb 'you shall die' is singular, but LXX, Theodotion, and most witnesses to the VL translated as a plural, no doubt wishing to emphasize that the warning applied to Eve as well as to Adam. Jerome prefers the singular in *Eps.* 22. 18. 2, 140. 7. 2.

Jerome here expresses approval of Symmachus' rendering, although he does not make use of it in Vg.[13] It would have been

---

[11] See Field, i. 14.

[12] See Salvesen, *Symmachus*, 8–9.

[13] Jerome explicitly quotes Symmachus approximately twenty-seven times in *QHG*, approving his translation as being 'plainer' (e.g. 6: 16; cf. 41: 16) and 'according to the meaning' (e.g. 19: 21). His high regard for this version is evident in his commentary *In Esaiam*, where he uses it more frequently than either Aquila's or Theodotion's precisely because of its customary clarity: see Jay, *L'Exégèse de saint Jérôme*, 105–6. Salvesen, *Symmachus*, 10, suggests that in Vg, Jerome's rendering of this verse is only superficially literal, and is intended to show that death has been brought into the world from outside; the same may apply to the translations of

evident to the earliest students of Scripture that Adam and Eve did not die on the selfsame day that they ate from the tree.[14] It would therefore be natural to interpret the words of 2: 17, not in a strictly literal fashion, but to show that death was likely to confront the couple from that day on. Symmachus' interpretation is not far removed from that of PJ, which reads: 'you shall be liable to death', although the latter includes notions of death as a judicial penalty which are not necessarily implicit in Symmachus' version. Jerome indicates that the Hebrew may properly be understood in the manner of Symmachus: if it is, then the problem of interpretation is eliminated. There is no need to invoke the scriptural notion that one day in God's sight is as a thousand years (Ps. 90: 4), and, since Adam did not survive for that length of time (Gen. 5: 5), his death might be deemed to have occurred on the day he sinned. Such a solution is found in *Gen. Rab.* 19: 8, and Justin, *Dial.* 81. 2. Neither need the verse be referred to the death of the soul rather than the body, which is the solution advocated by Philo, *Leg. All.* 1. 105–8, *QG* 1. 16, and Origen, *Hom. in Gen.* 15. 2.

verse 21 Lying behind Jerome's comment is a detailed discussion within Judaism of the meaning of *tardēmāh*, summarized conveniently by Rab (*Gen. Rab.* 17: 5) to the effect that the word may mean either sleep (as in Adam's case); or a prophetic state (as in Abraham's case, described in Gen. 15: 12); or a sleep of terror. The Greek word *ekstasis* may include all these, and more besides; so Jerome and other translators sought for a more precise rendering. Thus Philo discoursed on *ekstasis* at length (*Quis Heres* 249–66), distinguishing four different types, namely madness, consternation, calmness, and possession of a prophetic sort. Like Rab, he defined Adam's in this verse as 'a stillness and calmness of the mind' in sleep (257), while Abraham's was prophetic, inspired by God (258). *Sekel Ṭov* on Gen. 15: 12 also lists four types of *tardēmāh*, and describes as sleep the one listed here.

The Targums, too, largely agree with Rab and Philo on this verse: TO and the marginal gloss of TN speak of 'sleep'(so also Pesh),

LXX, Aquila, Theodotion, and Pesh. She also lists other Jewish and Christian interpretations of this verse which attempt, by implication, to explain why Adam did not die that very day.

[14] Kamesar, *Jerome*, 90, cites Theodoret, *QG* 38, as asking the question directly. He, too, quotes Symmachus. See further Ginzberg, 'Die Haggada' (*MGWJ* NS 7), 154–5.

while PJ and TN specify 'deep sleep', an idea which Aquila and
Symmachus wish to convey by their use of two rare Greek words.[15]
A variant of this understanding is the reading 'pleasant sleep' found
in a fragmentary MS of Targum from the Cairo Geniza.[16] This
latter may be related to the view of *b. Sanh.* 39a, that Adam would
have despised Eve if his rib had been removed while he was conscious, and he had seen the flesh from which she was made. Jerome
supports his understanding of the word as 'deep sleep' with reference to Jonah 1: 5, which states that Jonah lay down and 'went into
a deep sleep', *wayyērādam*, during the course of a storm at sea: this
is a form of the verbal root *rdm*, from which *tardēmāh* derives.

   It is not accidental that Jerome chose a verse from Jonah, a
prophetical book, to prove his case. Kamesar has indicated that he
was concerned to refute the claims of the Montanists, that true
prophecy depended on *ekstasis* in the sense of *mentis excessus*, the
departure of the mind from bodily control. The Montanists set
great store by ecstasy, believing that the age of the Spirit had now
arrived: they opposed this ecstatic-prophetic dispensation to that of
the Catholic Church. But the Fathers, in their several ways, were
adamant that ecstasy was not necessary for true prophecy. Their
case might appear a strong one, in that Origen himself (*De Princ.* 1.
7; *In Cant. Cant.* 2, on Song 1: 11–12) had spoken of Adam as a
prophet, predicting the mystery of Christ and His Church at Gen.
2: 24. Jerome, in his prologues to his commentaries on Isaiah and
Nahum, makes this very point; and he never used the phrase *mentis
excessus* in the Vg. For him, the true meaning of the Hebrew
tardēmāh undermines the claims of the Montanists, who had used
this verse and Gen. 15: 2 as proof of their doctrines.[17] It should be
noted, however, that Augustine, *De Gen. ad Litt.* 9. 19, retains the
notion of Adam's ecstasy as described by LXX, and says that
through it, one becomes *as if* he were a member of the angelic court,
entering God's sanctuary. Adam awoke *as if* he were full of

---

[15] On Symmachus' word *karos* as meaning stupor, or some kind of anaesthetic
state, see further Salvesen, *Symmachus*, 11–12. For other Jewish sources which refer
to Adam's sleep or deep sleep, see Josephus, *Ant.* 1. 35; *Jub.* 3: 5; *II Enoch* 30: 17.

[16] See Klein, i. 2.

[17] See Kamesar, 'Thesis', 169–72. As opponents of the Montanist view of ecstasy
he cites Epiphanius, *Adv. Haer.* 48. 4. 4.–48. 6, 48. 7. 8–9; Eusebius, *HE* 5. 17. 1;
Jerome's prologues to the commentaries on Isaiah and Nahum, and his *Ep.* 106. 18;
Didymus the Blind, *Comm. in Gen.* 230. 7–10, and comments on Acts 10: 11–12,
2 Cor. 5: 12–13. Jay, *L'Exégèse de saint Jérôme*, 183–4, discusses Jerome's continuing concern with Montanism as expressed in the *In Esaiam*.

prophecy, and gave voice to the significance of marriage which St Paul describes in Eph. 5: 31–2 as a 'great mystery'. It was ecstasy which had made Adam *as it were* a prophet.

verse 23 LXX, Vg, and VL read: 'because she was taken from her man, husband': Jerome seems to follow the Hebrew in his translation of this clause. His comment recalls *Gen. Rab.* 18: 4, where R. Pinchas and R. Hilqiah in the name of R. Simon state the impossibility of reproducing the Hebrew play on the words *'îš* and *'iššāh* in any other language. They cite Greek and Aramaic as examples, and consequently set forth this verse as a proof that the creation of the world took place by means of the Hebrew language. The Targums, indeed, carefully avoid any endeavour to transfer the pun into Aramaic; but Jerome praises Symmachus for his attempt to reproduce it in Greek, and tries to emulate him by using the forms *virago* and *vir* in Vg.[18] He is not entirely successful in this, since the most common meaning of *virago* is 'female warrior' or 'heroic woman'; but he does use the pun on other occasions (e.g. in his *Comm. in Osee* 1. 2: 16–17). Origen, *Comm. in Matt.* 14. 16 (on Matt. 19: 4), also records the difficulty of reproducing in Greek what is a pun in Hebrew: he resorts to transliteration of the latter and, like Jerome, notes the renderings of both Symmachus and Theodotion. See also his *Ep. ad Afr.* 18 (12). Further, he uses the Hebrew text of Gen. 2: 23 to illustrate the force of the Lord's ruling that a man should marry only one wife, and not divorce her; only one woman was created from the original single man. But Jerome himself, in commenting on the same New Testament passage, makes no allusion to the Hebrew Bible (*Comm. in Matt.* 3 on 19: 4).

Theodotion evidently derived the Hebrew word for 'woman', *'iššāh*, from the root *nāśā'*, 'to bear, carry, take up', by understanding the words 'because she was taken (up) from Man' as providing the actual grounds for the etymology. Theodotion's procedure would have derived support from a Greek transliteration of the Hebrew *'iššāh* as *essa*: in this form, it is indistinguishable in pronunciation from Hebrew *'eśśā'*, meaning 'I shall take up'. The transliteration is preserved as a reading of 'the Hebrew' and is

[18] See Salvesen, *Symmachus*, 13. Theodor and Albeck, in their edition of *Bereschit Rabbah*, pt. 1 (Berlin, 1912), 165, note Symmachus' reading, and post-Talmudic comments on this verse. For Symmachus, see further Petit, *La Chaîne*, 210 and notes. Augustine, *De Gen. contra Manichaeos* 2. 18, also notes the difficulties inherent in any Latin translation of this verse.

noted by Field, who quotes Origen (*De Hist. Susannae* 12) as witness that the etymology of 'woman' had already been connected with the verb 'take up'.[19]

CHAPTER 3

verse 1　Most witnesses of LXX state that the serpent was 'wisest', *phronimōtatos*, of all the beasts; but a variant 'wiser' is attested (see Wevers, p. 89). The Hebrew has *'ārūm*, which means 'crafty, shrewd' or, in a good sense, 'prudent', the latter most often in the Book of Proverbs. LXX were not alone in translating it with a word meaning 'wise': this rendering is found in TN, some witnesses to TO, and in PJ, where, however, it is glossed by the addition of 'in respect of evil'. VL and Jerome in his Latin rendering here and in *Ep.* 22. 29 have *sapientior*.

Jerome's sense that the word means *calliditas*, 'slyness', finds expression in his Vg, where *'ārūm* is rendered as *callidior*, 'more sly'. He knew that the word presented difficulties, witnessed, for example, by Augustine, *De Gen. ad Litt.* 9. 1–2; *De Gen. contra Manichaeos* 2. 20. For the LXX's word *phronimos* usually has good connotations; thus attempts were made to argue that it must, in this verse, have a bad sense, since the serpent is the cause of Eve's sin. See especially Origen, *Comm. in Ep. ad Rom.* 9. 2; Diodore in Catena fragment, Petit, ii. 106, who says that it is a *façon de parler*; Theodoret, *QG* 31; and Clement of Alexandria, *Stromateis* 6. 154. 4. There was also the threat of the Ophites, a Gnostic group who worshipped the serpent as a god embodying supreme wisdom, and who drew on this text for support (see Irenaeus, *Adv. Haer.* 1. 30; Origen, *Contra Celsum* 6. 24). They were still active in Jerome's day, as his *Ep.* 14. 9 makes plain. It was therefore essential to show that Scripture presented the serpent in a bad light. Jerome's predecessors had done this by resorting to homonymy, to show that *phronimos* might mean 'sly' as well as 'wise': Jerome, by contrast, went directly to the Hebrew word which, he remarks, clearly describes the serpent's cunning.[1]

---

[19] See Field, i. 15.

[1] For this, see Kamesar, *Jerome*, 159–67, who defines and discusses homonymy, polysemy, and katachresis in Greek scholarship as means of solving literary and textual problems: they were readily applied by Christians in biblical study. Hebrew *'ārūm* itself has both good and bad senses.

verse 8 The Hebrew text of this verse has the expression *lᵉrúaḥ hayyōm*, which is reproduced in garbled form as *laroeaiom* by Codex Monacensis 6299; otherwise, the other witnesses to *QHG* transliterate it as *barua haium*. Hebrew *rúaḥ* may mean 'spirit' or 'wind': hence the different renderings of Aquila, Symmachus, and Theodotion. Jerome evidently approves the translation of Theodotion, whom he quotes by name some 15 times in *QHG*, less frequently than Aquila (approximately 32 times) and Symmachus (approximately 27 times).[2] The Targums also reflect the problem in translating these words: TN has 'in the breeze of the day'; the marginal gloss of TN, FTP, and FTV have 'in the strength of the day', possibly taking 'spirit' as implying power; and TO and PJ have 'at the decline of the day'. This last translation is not far removed from the 'afternoon' of LXX; while Pesh has 'towards the end of the day'. In Vg, Jerome put 'at the breeze after noon', striving to incorporate the insights of the Greek translators and, possibly, the Jewish understanding preserved in TO and PJ.

verse 14 Jerome notes the precise reading of the Hebrew here, no doubt because he sees in it further support for his view of the serpent as a sly and cunning beast, expressed in his comment on 3: 1 above. The breast is the seat of thought; and it is entirely appropriate that the deceitful serpent should have its breast close to the dust. He makes no attempt, however, to explain the addition of LXX, who may be groping for the range of meanings implicit in the Hebrew, or who may obliquely refer to an ancient legend about the serpent. PJ of this verse and of Exod. 7: 9, *Gen. Rab.* 20: 5, *ARNa* 1, *PRE* 14: 3, and other sources record a tradition that the serpent originally had feet, which God cut off when He cursed the beast. Josephus, *Ant.* 1. 50, knew this story as already established in the first century AD; and LXX may have hinted at it in their translation. See also the anonymous authors of Catena fragments in Petit, *La Chaîne*, 258–9.

verse 15 Jerome's comment conceals a good deal, since he clearly prefers his understanding of the Hebrew as speaking of the *crushing* of the serpent. This, he notes, agrees with St Paul's statement in Rom 16: 20. There seems little doubt that his rendering of the Hebrew has involved him in selecting meanings from many possibilities, and has been directly influenced by the New Testament.

---

[2] Of the Three, Theodotion is least quoted also in Jerome's *In Esaiam*. For discussion of Jerome's attitude to Theodotion, see Jay, *L'Exégèse de saint Jérôme*, 106–8.

The Targums PJ, TN, FTP, and FTV offer multiple translations, and indicate that the uncommon root *šūp* could be understood as 'keep' or 'observe', a sense which they share with LXX and TO. They also point to a meaning 'crush', 'grind', or 'bruise': so Aquila, Symmachus, Pesh, and Vg. Finally, they also give it the sense of 'heal', as does R. Levi in *Gen. Rab.* 20: 5. The extended Haggadah which the Palestinian Targums offer here is, therefore, a careful exegesis of this unusual verbal root. Jerome does not refer to Aquila's rendering *prostripsei*, which is very close to his own: he seems more concerned to provide Hebrew support for Paul's remark in Romans.[3]

In so doing, he indicates on the strength of the Hebrew text that it is the Lord, Christ, who shall crush Satan. This verse had, indeed, been invoked by other Fathers to the same end; see, for example, Irenaeus, *Adv. Haer.* 4. 66. 2, 5. 21. 1; Cyprian, *Testimonia* 2. 9; Augustine, *De Gen. ad Litt.* 11. 36. But their exegesis had been restricted by LXX's rendering of *šūp* as 'keep', and by that version's lack of clarity regarding the subject of the first verb.[4] For Jerome, the Hebrew text dissolves all difficulties, and accords with Christian understanding.

verse 16 In his comment on the first part of this verse, Jerome once more sets the reading of the Hebrew against the LXX which reads 'your groaning', the plural being a widely attested variant (Wevers, p. 93). The other ancient versions agree with the Hebrew at this point: LXX may have read *hegyōnēk*, 'your groaning', instead of Hebrew *ḥērōnēk*, 'your conception'.

The Hebrew which LXX rendered as 'turning' (cf. Pesh: 'you shall turn') is *tᵉšūqātēk*, a rare word which elicited different interpretations. LXX and Pesh seem to have read or understood it as *tᵉšūbātēk*, from root *šūb*, 'return': so also TO and TN, who stand very close to LXX here. The meaning 'desire' is shared by Symmachus and PJ. It is similarly interpreted by R. Joshua ben

---

[3] See Salvesen, *Symmachus*, 14–15 for a summary of interpretations of this verb; further Rabbinic references are given in M. Kasher, *Torah Shelemah* (Jerusalem, 1936–1976), ii. 274.

[4] See M. Harl, *La Bible d'Alexandrie*, i: *La Genèse* (Paris, 1986), 109: the subject is *autos*, a masculine form which can only with difficulty refer to the 'seed' (neuter in Greek) of the woman spoken of immediately beforehand. Is it, then, to be understood as an undefined man? Some witnesses to VL even read *ipsa*, 'she' (see Fischer, pp. 68–9). Jerome's solution to this morass of difficulties seems simplicity itself.

Levi, according to *b. Yeb.* 62b; and it is clear from *Gen. Rab.* 20: 7 that both explanations of the word were known and used by the Amoraim. Aquila's derivation of the word possibly arises from root *nšq*, 'to kiss'.[5] Jerome follows none of the above for Vg, however, where he has 'and you shall be under your husband's power'. His *Comm. in Eph.* 3 reinforces the idea that the wife is subject to the husband as lord; see also Augustine, *De Civ. Dei* 15. 7.

verse 17 The Hebrew text here reads 'cursed be the earth *ba'ªbūrekhā*': the last word is a preposition with suffix, meaning 'because of you', and Aquila, like TO, TN, FTP, *Jub.* 3: 25, and Pesh, translated it accordingly. But LXX understood it as deriving from Hebrew root *'bd*, 'to serve, to work'. In Hebrew script, the letters *r* and *d* may easily be confused; and, while LXX may have translated from a Hebrew MS which contained the consonants *b'bdk* (meaning 'through your deed') rather than *b'brk*, it may also be the case that the translators misread a MS which used the word of our present Hebrew text. Jerome certainly read *ba'ªbūrekhā*, but followed Theodotion in deriving it from the verbal root *'br* meaning 'to transgress, to sin'. PJ had the same notion, translating 'cursed by the land because it did not declare *your sin* to you': Jerome's comments thus reflect a genuinely Jewish understanding of the verse.[6] In Vg, however, he has the singular 'in your deed', although his remarks here make it plain that he took that deed as a reference to Adam's transgression. In *Ep.* 129. 2, he simply retains the LXX translation.

verse 20 Jerome follows the Hebrew Bible in deriving the name *Ḥawwāh*, Eve, from root *ḥyh*, 'to live'. In labouring the point somewhat, he recalls the translations to TO and PJ, which state that Eve was mother of all human beings (literally, all 'the sons of men'): see also R. Simon's remark in *Gen. Rab.* 20: 11. The original Hebrew may imply that Eve was mother of living things other than human beings; indeed, some witnesses of Josephus, *Ant.* 1. 36, explain Eve simply as 'mother of all', while the rest add to this 'the living'. It is therefore as mother of humanity alone that her name properly means 'life', and Jerome suggests that LXX's translation as *Zōē* should be understood in this manner. All this may be deliberate, given that *Zōē* was a favourite character in Gnostic

---

[5] See Salvesen, *Symmachus*, 15.
[6] See further Geiger, *Urschrift*, 456–7; and C. T. R. Hayward, 'Pirqe de Rabbi Eliezer and Targum Pseudo-Jonathan', *JJS* 42 (1991), 224.

accounts of the origins of things. Thus in the system of Valentinus she is part of a second tetrad emerging from the first dyad of Father and Truth.[7] Jerome may also be concerned to show that the Hebrew form of the word Eve does not permit any association between her name and *Evoe*, the exclamation of the Bacchantes, as some had postulated: see Clement of Alexandria, *Protrep.* 2. 12. 2; Theophilus, *Ad Autolycum* 2. 28. And elsewhere he is concerned to point out that Eve alone was mother of all humanity, just as the Church whom she foreshadows is the one parent of all Christians, redeemed humanity (*Ep.* 123. 12). In all this, he may be concerned to correct the explanations of Eve given in *Lib. Heb. Nom.* (p. 65) as 'calamity or woe' as well as 'life'.

verse 24 Scriptural proof of Adam's complete expulsion from paradise is important for Jerome: he insists on it elsewhere (e.g. *Ep.* 39. 3; *In Hier.* 8. 28. 11–19), and is possibly concerned to oppose the notion, espoused by Eusebius of Emesa, that God had placed Adam close to paradise to punish him (Devreesse, pp. 61–2). Kamesar regards this as likely, noting also that Theodore of Mopsuestia used the LXX reading of this verse to show how God left Adam near the garden as a sign of His mercy.[8] Jerome rules out both these possibilities. In this, he closely resembles the readings of all the Aramaic Targums, which unambiguously state that Adam was banished from the garden; PJ specifies that God drove Adam out from His very Presence, 'from the place where He had made the Glory of His Shekhina dwell from the beginning, between the two cherubim'. *Jub.* 3: 32 is also clear that Adam went from Eden to another land after his expulsion; cf. Josephus, *Ant.* 1. 51.

In speaking of the gates and forecourt of paradise, however, Jerome departs from the language of Scripture and the Targums, and alludes to Jewish tradition extant in works like *The Apocalypse of Moses* 19, 28. Later Jewish authorities, such as Resh Lakish in *b. Sanh.* 98a, and R. Joshua ben Levi in *b. 'Erub.* 19a, discuss the geographical location of the gates of the Garden of Eden: *b. Tamid* 32b even reports that Alexander the Great found them! Emphasis on Adam's expulsion from paradise and the supernatural watch set to its gates and forecourt, however, has a particular Christian significance. For Jerome (see *Eps.* 39. 3, 70. 3) and other early

---

[7] See Irenaeus, *Adv. Haer.* 1. 1.   [8] See Kamesar, *Jerome*, 157–8.

Fathers, Christ's death was the momentous act which reversed Adam's transgression, reopened the gates of paradise, and allowed the baptized once more to enter its courts: see also Origen, *Sel. in Gen.* 2: 16–17, Cyril of Jerusalem, *Procatechesis* 15, and Catena fragment in Petit, *La Chaîne*, 180. The pious Fathers of the Jews are also restored to paradise by Christ's blood: see especially Jerome, *Ep.* 70. 3. For entry into the Church as a re-entering of paradise, see especially Cyprian, *Eps.* 73. 10, 75. 15, and Cyril of Jerusalem, *Procatechesis* 33, *Mystagogic Catecheses* 1. 1.

CHAPTER 4

verse 1 Jerome is concerned only with the derivation and meaning of the name Cain, and is content to follow LXX's understanding, refining it somewhat to incorporate two senses of the verb *qnh*, which he also recorded in *Lib. Heb. Nom.* (p. 63). In Vg, he translates as 'I have possessed'. He is silent about the exegetical problems which Jewish commentators found in this verse.[1]

verses 4–5 The question was how Cain and Abel could have recognized God's response to their offerings. Theodotion and Jerome testify that the tradition of fire from heaven was known in antiquity, as does John Chrysostom. *Hom. in Ep. Heb.* 23 (on 11: 4); but extant Jewish writings which refer to it date mostly from the Middle Ages. Rashi (1040–1105) states without reserve that fire devoured Abel's sacrifice, indicating that God had accepted it, but gives no source for his exegesis. R. David Qimḥi, *Midrash Aggadah*, *Sefer Ha-Yashar*, *Yalquṭ Shimʿoni* 524, and *MHG* likewise record it. Rahmer, however, may be mistaken in assuming that Rashi found the tradition in an ancient collection of Midrashim which is now lost, if Ginzberg was correct in stating that the Haggadah is found in the *Sifra Shemini* and *Lev. Rab.* 7: 3.[2]

---

[1] See Salvesen, *Symmachus*, 19 for a summary of the problems, and Kamesar, *Jerome*, 106, for his use of *Lib. Heb. Nom.* and the explanation of Cain's name among other Fathers.

[2] See Rahmer, *Die hebräischen Traditionen*, 18, and Ginzberg, 'Die Haggada' (*MGWJ* ns 7), 228; but I cannot trace Ginzberg's references in modern editions of *Sifra* and *Lev. Rab.* For Rashi's comment, see M. Rosenbaum and A. M. Silbermann, *Pentateuch with Targum Onkelos, Haphtaroth and Rashi's Commentary*, i (New York, n.d.), 17. The other sources are quoted in Hebrew by M. Kasher, *Torah Shelemah*, Genesis vol. (Jerusalem, 1934), 311–12.

Fire from heaven consumed Solomon's and Elijah's sacrifices (2 Chron. 7: 1; 1 Kgs. 18: 38). Jerome specifies that Elijah built an altar. Solomon's offering took place, of course, on the great altar in the Temple (2 Chron. 4: 1). Jerome may, therefore, imply that Cain and Abel had access to an altar, and such a tradition is attested in PJ of Gen. 8: 2 when it tells of Noah's rebuilding the altar which Adam had constructed on his departure from Eden. On that same altar, Cain and Abel offered sacrifice. Other sources, too, tell of Adam's altar (e.g. *b. AZ* 8a; *Gen. Rab.* 34: 9; *Num. Rab.* 20: 18; *PRE* 23: 5; 31: 3; 35: 3): its existence is at least implied by *Jub.* 3: 27, which says that Adam offered up incense on the day he left paradise.

verses 6–7 LXX read: 'And the Lord God said to Cain, Why are you sorrowful, and why has your countenance fallen . . .?' The difference between LXX of these verses and the original Hebrew is striking, and Jerome does his best to explain how it came about. He states that LXX have made a mistake (see also 5: 4; 17: 15), and concentrates on his own translation and exposition of the Hebrew.[3] On many occasions in *QHG* his criticism of LXX is trenchant, and it is worth listing some of his more negative comments, such as 13: 1, where he flatly contradicts their reasoning; 13: 3; 14: 3; 17: 16; 21: 15; 25: 8; 26: 32; 27: 40; 28: 19; 30: 32, 41; 31: 7; 32: 10; 35: 8, 16; 48: 2; and 49: 5–6, 22. Some of these passages use language critical of LXX which Jerome was to employ some twenty years later in his commentary on Isaiah, produced between 408 and 410. Thus he records LXX's errors at *In Esa.* 9. 28: 9–13, and admits that he is at a loss to know why LXX have translated in a certain way (*In Esa.* 1. 1: 24 and 2: 1; 2. 5: 17; 4. 9: 14–21; 5. 21: 6–10), sentiments expressed also in *QHG* 26: 32; 35: 8, 16; and 48: 2. The last of these references encapsulates his amazement, when he frankly admits: 'I do not know the reason why LXX have produced the word now in one way, now in another'.[4]

He first elucidates his translation 'will it not be forgiven you?', which represents the original Hebrew *hᵃlōʾ . . . śeʾēt*. The last of this pair of words derives from the root *nśʾ*, 'to lift up, bear, accept': hence Theodotion's rendering. Jerome understands it first as par-

---

[3] The factors which led to LXX's strange rendering are discussed by Harl, *Bible d'Alexandrie*, i. 114 ff.

[4] For Jerome's attitude to LXX at the time when he composed *In Esaiam*, see Jay, *L'Exégèse de saint Jérôme*, 119–22.

don or forgiveness. He probably has in mind the common scriptural expression *nāśāʾ ʿāwōn*, 'to forgive iniquity'. This would then imply, second, the subsequent acceptance of Cain's sacrifice. Jerome might well recall here another scriptural expression *nāśāʾ pānīm*, 'to lift up (someone's) face', that is, 'to accept, receive', and thus approve of that person. Jewish exegetes did indeed take *śᵉʾēt* here to mean 'pardon', as can be seen from *Gen. Rab.* 22: 6; *Midrash Aggadah*; the version of Symmachus; and PJ of this verse, 'is it not the case that, if you perform your deeds well, your sin will be forgiven you?' It would seem that Jerome tried not only to set out the original Hebrew clearly, but also to convey a sense which had wide currency among Jews.

But Jews recognized that *śᵉʾēt* in this verse might also have the sense of 'accept' or 'receive', as the translations of Aquila (*arsin*, 'lifting up') and Theodotion show in their separate ways. In Vg, Jerome followed the latter and translated with *recipies*. He is silent, however, about the reappearance of the word *tᵉšūqāh*, which had featured in 3: 16 and which is discussed there. He translates it here as *societas*, 'companionship', which is Aquila's rendering of it in 3: 16; in Vg, however, he follows Symmachus, who here and at 3: 16 put *appetitus*, 'desire'.[5]

He turns his attention instead to a problem in the Hebrew, which he solves by stating clearly that Cain, since he has free will, is to have dominion over *sin*. The Hebrew had God tell Cain that he shall have the dominion *bō*, either 'over it', that is, sin; or 'over him', that is, over Abel his brother. In Hebrew, 'sin' (*ḥaṭṭāʾt*) is normally a feminine noun. In this verse, however, its use is peculiar, since, as Jerome notes, it appears to be construed as a masculine form, in that the participle which immediately follows it, and which it appears to govern, is the masculine singular *rōbēẓ*, 'crouching'. The preposition *b*, 'over', is given a *masculine* suffix to produce *bō*, 'over him'; and it is this which led LXX and Theodotion to refer the preposition not to 'sin', which is a feminine noun in Greek, but to the masculine Abel. Jerome's understanding, that Cain is to have dominion over sin, is also the clearly expressed view of the Targums PJ, TN, FTP, FTV, GM, the version of Symmachus, *b. Sanh.* 91b, *ARN* 16, and *Gen. Rab.* 22: 6 (R. Haninah). All these Jewish sources are also clear that Cain is to have dominion of his evil

---

[5] See above, notes on 3: 16, and Salvesen, *Symmachus*, 20–2.

inclination (Hebrew: *yeẓer*), which seems to be reflected in what Jerome has written. Indeed, the whole of his comment on this verse appears to be indebted to contemporary Jewish understanding of its grammar, syntax, and exegesis.

verse 8   Jerome here, and on other occasions, criticizes the 'super-fluity' of LXX. But he himself adds the words 'let us go forth outside' in Vg and *Ep.* 36. 6, and thus follows the general sense not only of LXX, but also of PJ, TN, Ngl, FTP, FTV, and Pesh. Origen, *Sel. in Gen.* 4: 8, notes what Cain said, and that the Hebrews regarded it as based on apocryphal material: Jerome may be arguing here that the latter affords no proof of authenticity.[6]

verse 15   The last two Hebrew words of this verse, *šibʿātayim yuqqām*, are particularly problematic: LXX have translated as 'he shall pay seven penalties', which is followed by VL; see also *Test. Ben.* 7: 3–4. As he remarks, Jerome had written a letter to Pope Damasus (*Ep.* 36. 2–9) about this verse, in which almost each word is patient of several different interpretations.[7] Here, however, Jerome concentrates solely on the meaning of *šbʿtym*. He may imply that his readers should consult his letter to Damasus; indeed, without fuller information about the verse, his comments lack a general setting and can only be related to the LXX. In Vg, Jerome translated with the words 'septuplum punietur', 'he (or: it) shall be punished sevenfold': this approximates to Pesh and to Aquila's rendering recorded here and more fully in *Ep.* 36. 2 as 'septempliciter ulciscetur'. The latter puts into Latin an original Greek (Wevers, p. 99) *heptaplasiōs ekdikēthēsetai*, 'he (or: it) shall be punished (or: avenged) sevenfold'. The general sense of LXX is not too far removed from this understanding.

The renderings of the Hebrew noted so far are fairly easy to determine; but quite how Symmachus translated *šbʿtym* is by no means clear. Jerome here reports him as having put 'seventh'; Procopius records in his name the translation *hebdomōs ekdikēsin dōsei*, 'he shall give satisfaction seven times'; while Jerome in *Ep.* 36. 2 has 'ebdomatos sive septimus vindicabitur'. The word *ebdomatos* presents a textual difficulty which Salvesen has dis-

---

[6] Origen may also refer to circles associated with Aquila as knowing this addition: see de Lange, *Origen and the Jews*, 51–2. But this is not certain: see Kamesar, *Jerome*, 100–1, and the note in the second apparatus of Wevers, p. 97.

[7] For discussion of the whole verse and the *Epistle* 36 to Damasus, see Rahmer, *Die hebräischen Traditionen*, 18–20; Ginzberg (*MGWJ* NS 7), 293–8; Harl, *Bible d'Alexandrie*, i. 116–18; and Salvesen, *Symmachus*, 24–6.

cussed in detail.[8] She concludes that Symmachus may originally have translated *šbʿtym* into Greek as *hebdomaios*, Latin *septimus*, 'seventh', making the Hebrew mean 'Cain will be punished the seventh': he would then be close to Theodotion, as Jerome reports him here, who has 'per hebdomaden' ('through, until seven'). This translation most likely refers to a well-known Jewish Haggadah, according to which Cain's punishment was either extended through seven generations because he had not repented (so TO of this verse; *Test. Ben.* 7: 3–4; *Gen. Rab.* 22: 12; 32: 5), or was to be suspended up to the seventh generation after him because he had done penance (so TN and GM of this verse, and PJ of Gen. 4: 24).

Jerome's *Ep.* 36 shows how the ambiguity of the Hebrew could lead to widely differing interpretations. The exegesis selected here is directly related to his cryptic note in *QHG*. Jerome took LXX (and presumably Theodotion) to mean that God told Cain that he would not die, but live to the seventh generation suffering tortures of conscience; and that whoever killed Cain, either in the seventh generation or as the seventh, would thereby free Cain from the torture. So it was not Cain's killer who would receive seven penalties; rather, the killer would release Cain from the seven punishments he was to endure (*Ep.* 36. 2). He next took Aquila and Symmachus to mean that Cain would be killed by Lamech, reckoned as living in the seventh generation from Adam: Gen. 4: 23–4 is taken to signify he had been destined to kill Cain in the seventh generation (*Ep.* 36. 4). Some people, he says, explain the words with reference to seven particular sins of Cain, which he lists in order (*Ep.* 36. 6): it is interesting to compare a list of seven sins attributed to Diodore in the Catena (Petit, ii. 132), along with seven corresponding punishments Cain endured. Jerome adds that Cain was thus entrusted to God's mercy through seven generations in the hope that, driven by the evils that befell him and the duration of his misery, he might repent and deserve absolution.

verse 16 Jerome's comment, reflected in Vg translation of Hebrew *Nod* as 'fugitive', is found often among Jewish exegetes. Thus *saleuomenos* is Theodotion's translation here; in *LAB* 2: 1, Cain dwells in the land 'quaking'; according to TN, he dwelt as 'an exile

---

[8] The matter is thoroughly discussed by Salvesen, *Symmachus*, 25–6, esp. notes 95, 99; and by G. Vermes, 'The Targumic Versions of Genesis 4: 3–16', *Annual of the Leeds University Oriental Society*, 3 (1961–2) (Leiden, 1963), 81–114, repr. in *Post-Biblical Jewish Studies* (Leiden, 1975), 92–126, esp. 118–19.

and wanderer'; as also in later sources cited by Kasher.[9] But LXX's notion that Nod is a place was shared also by Josephus, *Ant.* 1. 60, *Lib. Loc.* 959, and FTP, which gives a second translation of the word in the same way as TN, 'an exile and a wanderer'; TO, PJ, and FTV speak of 'a land of exile and wandering'.[10] Jerome's initial understanding of Nod as 'unsteady' is shared by Rashi (ad loc.), who applies the description to the land rather than to Cain. He does, however, retain the notion of Nod as a place in *Eps.* 21. 8, 147. 9, and *Comm. in Hab.* 2; and in *Lib. Heb. Nom.* (p. 69) he lists it as a proper noun meaning 'motion or moving like the waves'.

verse 25 Jerome's comment, as Kamesar has noted,[11] is directed against the seemingly fanciful explanations of Philo, at *QG* 1. 78 and *De Post.* 10, 124, 170, and of Didymus the Blind, at *Comm. in Gen.* 144. 9. The former in *QG* derives the name from Hebrew root *šth*, 'to drink', and regards Seth as one who drinks water, like plants, and who symbolizes thereby the growth of spiritual fruit within the soul. In *De Post.* he explains the name as 'watering', and is followed by Didymus. Jerome is very down-to-earth, invoking Aquila's support in his derivation of the name from root *šyt*, 'to put, place'. He thus translates the verb here and in Vg as *posuit*, 'placed': VL had *suscitavit*, 'raised up', which could lend support to the idea that the murdered Abel had been resurrected in the person of Seth, a notion attacked by Origen, *Comm. in Joh.* 6. 70. But *Lib. Heb. Nom.* (p. 71) had given 'resurrection' as a meaning of Seth, along with 'grass', 'seed', and 'cup': these Jerome here dismisses.

verse 26 Jerome opens with the observation that Enosh, like Adam, may mean both human individual or mankind as a whole. Most Christian exegetes took this verse positively to mean that in the days of Enosh people began to invoke the true God: see, for example, Augustine, *De Civ. Dei* 15. 18. Jerome apparently suggests that the Hebrew of this verse, *'āz hūḥal liqrō' bᵉšēm YHWH*, of which he offers a translation, supports such an understanding. He says nothing of LXX's divergence from the Hebrew.[12] Rather, he

    [9] See Kasher, *Torah Shelemah*, 326, 332. The same understanding is attributed to Symmachus by some witnesses: see Wevers, p. 99.

    [10] On TO's translation, see J. Bowker, 'Haggadah in the Targum Onqelos', *JSS* 12 (1967), 54–6.

    [11] See Kamesar, *Jerome*, 107–8.

    [12] For the origins and meaning of the LXX translation, see S. D. Fraade, *Enosh and his Generation: Pre-Israelite Hero and History in Postbiblical Interpretation* (Chico, Calif., 1984), 5–11; Harl, *Bible d'Alexandrie*, i. 119; Kamesar, *Jerome*, 145–9.

records instead a Jewish tradition that idolatry began at this time: it is well known, being found, for example, in *Gen. Rab.* 23: 7, where occurrences of the word 'begin' in other parts of Scripture are related to acts of rebellion against God.[13] The generation of Enosh was full of idolaters, according to *b. Shabb.* 118b, a point taken up by the Targums. This tradition may be reflected in the interpretation of the name Enosh as 'man or desperate or impetuous' in *Lib. Heb. Nom.* (p. 65). Like Jerome, the Targums specify that idols were dubbed with the Lord's name: so PJ, TN, and FTP, and similarly *Mekh. de R. Ishmael Baḥodesh* 6: 30–4. They have interpreted the verb *hūḥal* by deriving it from one or other of two roots *ḥll*, the first meaning 'to begin', the second 'to profane', i.e. to profane the Name of God by applying it to idols. All these interpretations of the verse remove an apparent contradiction in Scripture, since Exod. 6: 3 states that it was only in the days of Moses that the name *YHWH* was revealed.[14] That the manufacture of idols began in primeval times is an ancient idea, attested by *LAB* 2: 9; but the latter places their origin in the days of Thubal rather than those of Enosh.

LXX, Theodotion, 'the Hebrew', and *Jub.* 4: 12 have rendered the Hebrew '*āz*, 'then', as if it were *zeh*, 'this man'; and in Vg Jerome follows suit with 'this man began to call on the Name of the Lord', doubtless because it suited the Christian understanding of the verse. He does not join LXX in translating *hūḥal* as 'hoped', but uses 'began'. LXX probably derived the word from root *yhl*, 'to hope'; but the understanding of it as 'began' is very strongly attested. Jerome's translation here, 'then there was a beginning of calling', closely resembles that of Symmachus, 'then there was a beginning . . .'; while his Vg rendering, 'this man began . . .,' is identical with the first of Aquila's translations recorded by Wevers.[15]

Despite Jerome's silence about the matter, a complex problem arising out of patristic use of LXX and Aquila may be concealed in his comment on this verse.[16] The LXX note that Enosh hoped

---

[13] See Rahmer, *Die hebräischen Traditionen*, 20.

[14] On the meaning of the name Enosh, see also Fraade, *Enosh*, 58. For the revelation of the Divine Name, cf. le Déaut, *Targum du Pentateuque*, 5 vols. (Paris, 1978–81), i. 108; and J. Bowker, *The Targums and Rabbinic Literature* (Cambridge, 1969), 140–1.

[15] See the second apparatus of Wevers, p. 101; and Kamesar, *Jerome*, 145, 149. The second reading given in Aquila's name, 'then it was begun to call on the Name . . .', may be compared with that of Symmachus.

[16] For what follows, see further Fraade, *Enosh*, 63–90, and Kamesar, *Jerome*, 146–50.

epikaleisthai the Name of the Lord: the verb here would normally be taken as in the middle voice, and translated 'to call on the Name of the Lord'. The expression, in fact, is a stock LXX rendering of the common Hebrew *qārā' bᵉšem YHWH*, 'to invoke the Name of the Lord'. But Julius Africanus took the verb as a passive, to yield 'this man hoped to be called by the Name of God'; and other Fathers, among them Eusebius of Emesa (Devreesse, p. 62) felt they had good reason to follow his translation. First, the reference to mysterious and hitherto unmentioned 'sons of God' in Gen. 6: 2 might now be easily and reasonably explained as descendants of Enosh and Seth. Next, the way was open to understand Aquila's first and very literal rendering of the Hebrew as *houtos ērxato tou kaleisthai en onomati kuriou* as meaning 'this man began to be called by the Name of the Lord', thus showing the piety of Enosh and his sons. But in reality Aquila's *kaleisthai en onomati* stands for the common Hebrew *liqrō' bᵉšem*, 'to call on the Name'; this was evidently obscure to the Greeks who followed Julius Africanus, but was immediately apparent to Jerome with his knowledge of the original Hebrew.

CHAPTER 5

verse 2 Rabbi Huna in *Gen. Rab.* 21: 2 notes that Eve may properly be called Adam: see also *Midrash Aggadah* 20, and later Midrashim listed by Kasher.[1] The brevity of the comment conceals a problem, as is often the case in *QHG*. Jerome presumably intends to rule out the suspicion that God created an androgynous being: LXX could be taken to imply such a creation by stating of Adam in 5: 1 that God created *him*, and continuing in 5: 2 with the words 'male and female He made them'. Thus speculation might arise that God had created one being which was male 'and female', i.e. having female parts. Jewish interpreters knew this, and in *Gen. Rab.* 8: 1 R. Jeremiah ben Lazar actually states that God created Adam as androgynous. Accordingly, this was yet another verse which the Rabbis record as having been altered in the Greek translation prepared for King Ptolemy.[2]

---

[1] See Kasher, *Torah Shelemah*, 351.
[2] See above, comment and notes on 2: 2. TO and PJ are a little vague in their

verse 3 Eusebius of Emesa (Devreesse, p. 62) had also noted the one hundred years' discrepancy, and indeed 'the rest,' according to the Syrohexaplar, read 130 years. Augustine, *De Civ. Dei* 15. 10–11, treated the matter systematically. See notes to verses 25–7 below, which explain why Jerome was concerned with this long-standing problem of chronology.[3] As often, Origen, *Sel. in Gen.* 5: 3, displays concerns entirely different from Jerome's: he comments on the meaning of Adam's image and likeness which Seth bears.

verse 4 The difference between Hebrew and LXX numbers amounts exactly to one hundred years. Augustine, *De Civ. Dei* 15. 10, notes and comments on these and other discrepancies.[4]

verses 25–7 For discussion among Christian writers, see especially Ambrose, *Expositio Evangelii secundum Lucam* 3. 48; and Augustine, *De Civ. Dei* 15. 10–11, and *QG* 2. Jerome reiterates the LXX chronology to show the embarrassing result in the case of Methuselah, whose life extended beyond the Flood. But only eight persons survived that disaster (Gen. 6: 18; 1 Peter 3: 20), and all were Noah's immediate family. Once more, as in his comment on 4: 6–7, Jerome admits that LXX are in error; and he demonstrates that the chronology of the Hebrew and Samaritan texts is entirely consonant with other parts of Scripture. He felt it necessary to prove his point in detail, and the message is clear: the Hebrew preserves the truth, while LXX actually create a major chronological and theological problem with their translation. In Vg, therefore, he adopts his version of the Hebrew as set out here.

Jerome's approach to this matter is unique among his contemporaries and predecessors. He notes that if the Hebrew text is adopted, the problem fades away. By contrast, those who held to the LXX were compelled to adopt desperate measures. So Josephus,

renderings of 5: 2, and may admit the notion of an androgyne: see Bowker, *The Targums*, 143.

[3] For studies of the differences in chronology between LXX and the Hebrew in this chapter of Genesis, see B. Z. Wacholder, *Essays on Jewish Chronology and Chronography* (New York, 1976), pp. 106–35; G. Larsson, 'The Chronology of the Pentateuch: A Comparison of the MT and LXX', *JBL* 102 (1983), 401–9.

[4] There was suspicion among Jews that Christians had falsified the text of Scripture: see Rahmer, *Die hebräischen Traditionen*, 21–3. But the Samaritan Pentateuch, to which Jerome will allude in his commentary on 5: 25–7, also differs from Hebrew and LXX, which Josephus follows in *Ant.* 1. 82, in the chronology of the period before the Flood. For a convenient, comprehensive display of these discrepancies in tabular form, and detailed discussion of them, see J. Skinner, *A Critical and Exegetical Commentary on Genesis* (Edinburgh, 1912), 134–9.

Ant. 1. 86, whom Julius Africanus appears to follow (see the fragment preserved in PG 10: 68), and a scribal correction in Codex Alexandrinus altered the text of LXX to make Methuselah 187 when Lamech was born, such that he could die six years before the Flood![5] Augustine approved a solution along these lines, and argued that it could be supported by the best manuscripts, three Greek, one Latin, and one Syrian: his support for LXX is unwavering, and he even suggests that the Hebrew text has been falsified by the Jews.[6] Ambrose made a virtue of necessity, seeing in Methuselah's survival of the Flood a type of the Resurrection of Christ.

Now all this is astonishing, considering that Eusebius of Caesarea had made available to the Christian world full details of the Hebrew, Samaritan, and LXX texts of this chapter in his *Chronicon* (PG 19: 147–54). As Kamesar has noted, a glance at Eusebius's work would reveal that the figures given by the Hebrew text eliminate all difficulties. But this information was not used. Kamesar indicates that for earlier Christian authors such as Theophilus (*Ad Autolycum* 3. 24), and Hippolytus (*Chronicon* 8. 21, 9. 1, 4–5) there seemed to be no difficulty; but Eusebius himself had suggested that the Jews had altered the Hebrew text in the matter of Methuselah, and from the fourth century onwards the problem came to exercise the minds of scholars, as Jerome asserts. Their solution, as we have seen, often involved tampering with the text of LXX: Jerome's approach, by contrast, is evidence of his originality.[7] In saying that Methuselah died in the year the Flood began, he agrees with PJ, TN, FTP of Gen. 7: 10, and *Gen. Rab.* 32: 10 that the waters came down after the seven days of mourning for the Patriarch were ended.

verse 29   The name Noah, Hebrew *nōaḥ*, suggested to exegetes two Hebrew roots for its origins, first *nwḥ*, 'to rest'; and *nḥm*, 'to console oneself', the latter because the Hebrew text differs from LXX, and explains the name as 'this one will comfort us, *ynḥmnw*', not 'this one will give us rest'. While Jerome, like LXX and Origen, *Hom. in Gen.* 2. 3, invokes the first root here and in *Lib. Heb. Nom.* (pp. 69, 132, 141, 151, 157), he translated the Hebrew in Vg

---

[5] See Wevers, p. 106, first apparatus, and Harl, *Bible d'Alexandrie*, i. 123–4.

[6] Augustine, *De Civ. Dei* 15. 10–11; *QG* 2. His special pleading for the integrity of LXX in *De Civ. Dei* 15. 13 is striking.

[7] On this, see Kamesar, 'Thesis', 178–82.

with *consolabitur*, 'will comfort', apparently following Aquila. *LAB* 1: 20 has an explanation very close to that of *QHG*: Noah is so called because 'this man will give rest to us and to the earth, from those which are upon it; on whom punishment shall come because of the wickedness of their evil deeds'. See also John Chrysostom, *Hom. in Gen.* 21. PJ, however, explains the name in a manner which encompasses both of Jerome's understandings: 'this man will console us from our work which does not prosper (i.e. rests, is inactive)... because of the sins of mankind'. The fact that the Hebrew provides an explanation of the name through root *nḥm* rather than *nwḥ* is remarked by R. Yohanan in *Gen. Rab.* 25: 2.

CHAPTER 6

verse 2 This verse presented obvious problems for orthodox Jewish believers, since it might be interpreted in an anti-monotheistic sense. Hence, from early post-biblical times, these 'sons of God' were understood as 'angels', as a variant reading of LXX testifies: see also VL of this verse; *Jub.* 4: 15; *I Enoch* 6: 2; *Test. Reuben* 5: 6–7; *Test. Naph.* 3: 5; *Damascus Document* 2: 16–21; *Genesis Apocryphon* 2: 1; Philo, *De Gig.* 6; Josephus, *Ant.* 1. 73; 2 Peter 2: 4; Jude 6; gloss of TN on Gen. 6: 2; Justin, *Apology* 1. 5; Clement of Alexandria, *Stromateis* 5. 1. 10; Tertullian, *Apologeticum* 22. 3, *De Virginibus Velandis* 7, *Adv. Marc.* 5. 18; *PRE* 22: 2. Jerome cites Ps. 82: 1 as a proof text for this exegesis.

Literal renderings of the Hebrew, however, were known and used from the first century AD onwards, as *LAB* 3: 1 makes clear: hence Aquila's version which Jerome cites here, that of Theodotion, and the transliteration of Pesh, which are equally 'literal'. Augustine, *De Civ. Dei* 15. 23, quotes Aquila with approval; and it is 'the sons of God' which Jerome himself uses in this verse of his Vg.

The reading of Symmachus, however, betrays a shift of understanding towards a Rabbinic view of the phrase revealed in TO, PJ, and *Gen. Rab.* 26: 5 (R. Simeon bar Yoḥai), which also interpret the phrase as 'sons of the mighty'. This may be compared with TN's rendering 'sons of the judges', found also in *Sifre Num.* 6; *Sifre Zuṭṭa* 11: 4; *'elōhīm* was taken as 'rulers' or 'judges', the sense which it apparently has in Exod. 22: 28. All these interpretations seem designed to avoid any notion of angels or supernatural beings;

indeed, R. Simeon bar Yoḥai put a curse on those who spoke of
'sons of God' in this verse. But Jerome appears to view Symmachus'
reading as generally consonant with that of Aquila.[1]

verse 3   Jerome is concerned to remedy a possible misunderstand-
ing of God's character which the LXX might imply, and demonstrates from two other biblical passages, Hos. 4: 14 and Ps. 89:
32–3, that God's punishment is inextricably linked with His mercy.
The Hebrew verb concerned is *ydwn*, found in this form only here
in the whole Hebrew Bible, which LXX took as if it were *ylwn* or
ydwr 'dwell, remain', the sense which it is given also by *Jub.* 5: 8,
TO, Pesh, Vg, *jer. Sanh.* 10: 3, and *Gen. Rab.* 26: 6. Indeed, a
Hebrew text actually reading *ydwr* is now attested by the Dead Sea
Scroll 4Q252, whose original text may be conveniently consulted in
the article by T. H. Lim, 'The Chronology of the Flood Story in a
Qumran Text (4Q252)', *JJS* 43 (1992), 289. But *ydwn* more likely
means 'will judge', and is rendered as such by *LAB* 3: 2, Josephus,
Ant. 1. 75, PJ, TN, Ngl, FTP, FTV, and Symmachus. Origen, *De
Princ.* 1. 3. 7 had used the LXX of this verse to argue that the Holy
Ghost is taken away from all who are unworthy, and that he dwells
not with those who are flesh, but in those whose land has been
renewed: cf. *Contra Celsum* 7. 38. Jerome's exegesis of the verb
here as 'will not judge' would rule out Origen's interpretation.

In fact, however, Jerome appears to countenance both understandings of the verb as 'judge' and 'dwell': in this, he is not alone,
for *Jub.*, having translated the verb as 'dwell' in 5: 8, goes on to
deliver a sustained homily on judgement, 5: 11–18. So also *Gen.
Rab.* 26: 6 plays with both readings of the verb as 'judge' and
'dwell'; and in *jer. Sanh.* 10: 3, R. Simeon interprets the words as
'My Spirit shall not judge him, because I will not put my Spirit in
them when I pay to the righteous their recompense'. Jerome was
evidently aware of the two different senses traditionally attributed
to *ydwn*, and has combined them to express a theology of Divine
justice tempered with Divine mercy.[2]

While Jerome makes LXX speak of God's activity with these men
'in aeternum', 'for ever', he understands the Hebrew to speak of 'in

---

[1] See P. S. Alexander, 'The Targumim and Early Exegesis of "Sons of God" in
Genesis', *JJS* 23 (1972), 60–71; Salvesen, *Symmachus*, 31–2.

[2] See further Bowker, *The Targums*, 154–7; J. P. Lewis, *A Study of the Interpretation of Noah and the Flood in Jewish and Christian Literature* (Leiden, 1968),
90 ff.

sempiternum', 'for evermore' or 'for everlasting', and remarks that God will not reserve them for everlasting tortures. He thus appears to be aware of the famous statement of *m. Sanh.* 10: 3 that the Generation of the Flood have no portion in the World to Come, nor shall they stand in the Judgement, which the Rabbis supported with reference to this very verse. They, however, understood *m. Sanh.* 10: 3 to mean that the Generation of the Flood were amongst the most despicable of God's enemies: they are listed along with those who deny the resurrection of the dead and the divine origin of the Torah, the 'Epicurean', readers of non-canonical books, sorcerers, blasphemers, the kings Jeroboam son of Nebat, Ahab, Manasseh, and other violent and deceitful persons. In other words, their particular punishment betokens not God's mercy, but his severity, as the later explanations of this Mishnah in *t. Sanh.* 13: 6, *jer. Sanh.* 10: 3, and *b. Sanh.* 108a make clear. If Jerome is dependent on this Mishnah, he has certainly altered it to suit his own exegetical purposes.[3] His remarks about the future leniency of God towards sinners rather reflect the Targumic tradition, which admits the completeness of God's judgement on the Generation of the Flood, but tempers it for the future: 'None of the wicked generations who are destined to arise shall be judged with the standard of judgement of the Generation of the Flood' (PJ, cf. TN of Gen. 6: 3). What follows is a statement of Jewish exegesis of the verse,[4] that the men of that generation were given 120 years in which to repent: their lives were not limited to 120 years, a point which Augustine makes (*De Civ. Dei* 15. 24) in words similar to Jerome's here, and with similar scriptural proof examples. See also his comment on 9: 29. There were those who, like Josephus, *Ant.* 1. 75, 152, used this verse to argue that 120 years was the span of human life: see, for example, Clement of Alexandria, *Stromateis* 6. 11; and compare Hippolytus, *Comm. in Psalm.* fr. 4 (PG 10: 714-15). But customary Jewish exegesis took the 120 years as space for repentance: see especially TO, PJ, FTP, FTV, *Mekh. de R. Ishmael Shirta* 5: 37-40, *Tanḥ. Beshallaḥ* 15, and *Seder 'Olam Rabbah* 28. The antiquity of the interpretation is now confirmed by its presence in the Qumran document 4Q252; see further Lim, 'Chronology of

---

[3] See Kamesar, *Jerome*, 183-5, who suggests (p. 183) that Jerome's reading of the verse was influenced by Symmachus, 'my Spirit shall not judge the men everlastingly, *aiōniōs*'.

[4] See Rahmer, *Die hebräischen Traditionen*, 23.

the Flood', 289–90, 292; and H. Jackson, '4Q252: Addenda', *JJS* 44 (1993), 118.

Finally, Jerome's exposition of this verse is close to the rendering of FTP, which includes the notions of 'doing repentance', the Divine 'decree', God's 'giving' that generation a 'duration' for repentance, and a creative elaboration of Hebrew *yādōn* as 'judge' on the one hand and 'remain, endure' on the other:

And the Word of the Lord said: The generations who are destined to arise after the Generation of the Flood will not be so *judged*. The *decree* of judgement of the Generation of the Flood is sealed, to perish and be destroyed in complete destruction. Have I not *put my Spirit upon* the sons of men, that they should do good deeds? But because they are flesh, their deeds are evil. Behold, I have *given them the duration* of 120 years that they should *do repentance*, and they have not done it.

This Targum may, in fact, throw light on Jerome's comments in *QHG* and may also explain his decision to translate *yādōn* in Vg as 'remain': all the senses of the word which he notes have Jewish pedigrees.

verse 4   The Hebrew *nᵉpilīm*, which derives from the root *npl*, 'to fall', was rendered as 'giants' by LXX, and Jerome followed this in Vg: it is a common translation, found in Theodotion, TO, and TN, owing much to the appearance of *nᵉpilīm* in Num. 13: 33(34). There they are huge individuals, making Israel seem like grasshoppers. So they are seen as part of an ancient giant-band which has many names: *Gen. Rab.* 26: 7 gives seven. Not entirely out of kilter with this interpretation is Symmachus, whose translation 'violent ones' emphasizes their character without commenting on their physical stature.

But the second occurrence of 'giants' in the LXX represents a different Hebrew word, *gibbōrīm*; Symmachus again represented this as 'violent ones', while 'giants' remains the rendering of TO, TN, and PJ. Aquila translated as 'the powerful', and Jerome followed this interpretation for his Vg, *potentes*.[5] Jerome's point seems to be that Symmachus translated both *nᵉpilīm* and *gibbōrīm* as 'violent ones'; and that the supernatural beings and their offspring can rightly be understood as equally sharing in the character of 'falling ones'.

---

[5] See further Salvesen, *Symmachus*, 34–5.

verse 9 In qualifying the degree of Noah's righteousness, Jerome follows closely a well-known Jewish tradition summed up by R. Yohanan in *b. Sanh.* 108a: Noah was righteous in his own deeply corrupt generation, but not by the standards of other generations. The same opinion is found in *Tanh. Noah* 5; *Lekh* 26; *Gen. Rab.* 30: 9; *Midrash Aggadah* 34. Indeed, Jerome's comment about Noah's following God's footsteps may recall R. Judah's view stated in *Gen. Rab.* 30: 10, that Abraham was able to walk *before* God (Gen. 17: 1), whereas Noah could only walk with Him, since he had formerly been sunk in deep mire (i.e. sins).

His recording of this Jewish tradition, although unacknowledged, is striking, in that Christians tended to regard Noah as a model of righteousness. There were representatives of this school of thought within Judaism also, most particularly the Aramaic Targums PJ and TN. Even within the sources we have quoted, we find voices raised in favour of Noah: Resh Lakish in *b. Sanh.* 108a asks if Noah were righteous in his particularly wicked generation, how much more righteous would he have been in any other time? See also *Gen. Rab.* 30: 9, for similar sentiments expressed by R. Nehemiah.[6]

However, Jerome may owe something to Origen, who speaks of Noah's relative righteousness in *Hom. in Num.* 9. 1; or both he and Jerome may have derived their interpretation from Philo, who in *De Abr.* 36 states that Noah was not good in the absolute sense, but only compared with others of his day.[7]

verse 14 The Hebrew calls the wood *gōper*, a word found nowhere else in the Bible. Jerome's explanation of it may be related to the requirement that the ark be smeared with pitch, Hebrew *kōper*, set out later in this verse: see also Vg. Its meaning was quite uncertain. TO has 'cedar wood', in common with *LAB* 3: 4, *Gen. Rab.* 31: 8, PJ, TN, FTP, FTV, *Tanh. Noah* 5; but Pesh has 'juniper wood', and in Vg Jerome translated it as 'smoothed wood'.

verse 16 The Hebrew says that Noah should make *ṣōhar*, 'light', for the ark. The word is unexpected, and caused uncertainty. LXX

---

[6] See Rahmer, *Die hebräischen Traditionen*, 24. On the Jewish tendency to denigrate Noah, and on Christian praise of his character, see Lewis, *Noah and the Flood*, 159 ff.

[7] See also *Quod Deus Immutabilis Sit* 117; *QG* 1. 97, where a similar understanding may be implied; and de Lange, *Origen and the Jews*, 127.

translated it as *episunagōn*, 'gathering together' or 'compacting', which Jerome translates here literally. Presumably LXX meant that the ark was to be made compactly, or narrowed as it was built from the keel upwards. The notion that it was to be made of two or three stories, found in Origen, *Hom. in Gen.* 2. 1; Ambrose, *Hexaemeron* 6. 72; and Augustine, *QG* 6, depended on the LXX rendering of *sōhar*.[8] Jerome's understanding, however, is based on the common Hebrew word *ṣhrym*, 'noonday', which is Aquila's rendering in the verse. He evidently regards Symmachus, however, as having captured the true sense of the word, for in Vg he translates as 'window'. This understanding is shared by TN, and by R. Abba bar Kahana in *Gen. Rab.* 31: 11 (against the view discussed below), and could claim support from Gen. 8: 6 with its reference to a window (Hebrew: *ḥallōn*). Jerome alludes to this below in his translation of 8: 6–7.

It is possible that Jerome deliberately opted for the meaning 'window', like Symmachus, to rule out a tradition that *sōhar* signified a precious stone as the source of light.[9] This last is found in *Gen. Rab.* 31: 11 (R. Levi), where the stone is called *mrglyt*, as also in PJ of this verse; *b. Sanh.* 108b; *jer. Pes.* 1: 1; and *PRE* 23: 1. TO is tantalizingly ambiguous, rendering the word as 'light': in all probability, it refers to the Haggadah of the precious stone.[10]

But this view needs modification, since Kamesar observes that the word used by Symmachus, *diaphanes*, may also refer to a mineral: he cites Galen, to show that *diaphanes* is like the Roman *lapis specularis*, that is the mica or moonstone, and Pliny *Nat. Hist.* 9. 13, to indicate that there was a pearl, *margarita*, similar to the *lapis specularis*. Indeed, *margarita* appears in Hebraized form as a loanword in *Gen. Rab.* 31: 11 defining the *sōhar*, the precious stone illuminating the ark. He suggests that Jerome has taken Symmachus' translation, but has accommodated it to his own use by making it mean 'window': it should, however, be noted that *diaphanes* does primarily mean 'that which is clear, translucent'. Kamesar also accounts for Jerome's interest in this verse. By rendering *sōhar* here as they have done, and by rendering the 'window' of

---

[8] See further Harl, *Bible d'Alexandrie*, i. 132.
[9] Rahmer, *Die hebräischen Traditionen*, 24.
[10] See also B. Grossfeld, *The Targum Onqelos to Genesis*, The Aramaic Bible, vi (Edinburgh, 1988), 55.

8: 6 as 'door', LXX created a difficulty: how could Noah be said to open the door (8: 6), when God had shut the ark completely (7: 16)? The heretic Apelles had heavily emphasized this problem, as Origen shows in *Hom. in Gen.* 2. 1–2. Jerome unravels the confusion by careful attention to the Hebrew text, where no such difficulty exists.[11]

CHAPTER 8

verses 1–3   LXX's 'revealed' represents Hebrew *wayyissāk^erū*, 'shut up, stopped'. Hence in Vg Jerome put 'were shut up', 'clausi sunt': some witnesses to VL read this also, but most have the similar 'conclusi sunt'. The translators to whom Jerome refers are first Symmachus, who reads 'were closed'; then Aquila, who has 'were sealed'. He may also have in mind the Targums: TO, Ngl, and GM (cf. Pesh) have 'were shut', TN 'were sealed, stopped', and PJ 'were locked'.

He sets the Hebrew 'turned back' against LXX 'subsided' (Greek: *enedidou*), translating the latter with *cessavit*, 'stopped', the very word which VL had used to render LXX's verb *ekopasen* in verse 1, describing the ceasing of the water. He brings proof from Eccles. 1: 7 that the Hebrew Bible is consistent in its usage. He makes this point elsewhere: see, for example, his comments on 1: 10; 12: 9–10. Thus for Jerome the Flood disappeared naturally, its waters going back to the sea: in this, he differs from some other authorities, who assume that their abatement was miraculous.[1]

verses 6–7   Codex Alexandrinus here reads of his sending out the raven 'to see if the water had ceased'. On the window, see 6: 16. In introducing the raven, Jerome again (cf. his comment on 4: 15) alludes obliquely to a matter he had discussed in another work. Here, he says that the Hebrew expresses 'differently' what is found in LXX. He means that in the LXX the raven is said not to return (*ouk anestrepsen*), while in the Hebrew we read that it used to go out and then come back (*wayyēẓē' yāṣō' wāšōb*).[2] The importance of

---

[11] See Kamesar, 'Thesis', 183–7, who also discusses Origen's attempts to deal with the door and window on LXX evidence without recourse to the Hebrew.

[1] Thus John Chrysostom, *Hom. in Gen.* 26. 3; Didymus, *Comm. in Gen.* 194. 22–195. 1, cited by Kamesar, 'Thesis', 139–40.

[2] Pesh has 'and did not return'. In the Hexapla, the reading of 'the Syrian' (see

this verse is clear from his *Dialogus adversus Luciferianos* 22, where he follows LXX (as do also some witnesses to Vg): the raven does not return. It symbolizes evil and the devil: once sent out, it should never return. He has probably derived this allegorical interpretation from Philo, *QG* 2. 35–6. He then contrasts the raven with the dove which Noah also sent out (8: 8–12), the symbol of the Holy Ghost which Christians receive in baptism, when the devil is exorcized and takes his leave.[3] Augustine, *QG* 13, candidly states the problem raised by LXX: the raven did not return, whereas the dove did, finding no rest for its feet. Did the raven, therefore, die? Or did it stay alive by other means? If it had rested on dry land, the dove could surely have done the same. Thus, he tells us, some suppose that the raven settled on a corpse, which the dove would naturally avoid. Such explanations of LXX are forced; and Jerome's setting forth of the Hebrew text makes clear that they are also unnecessary.

CHAPTER 9

verse 18   Having noted that LXX often use letter *chi* to represent Hebrew *ḥeth*, Jerome seems keen to point to his knowledge of the Egyptian language: see also 41: 2, 45; 45: 21.

verse 27   The Hebrew root *pth* means 'be spacious, wide'; and the text of Genesis itself implies that the name Japheth is related to this verb. The name is explained as 'width' in *Lib. Heb. Nom.* (p. 67). Jerome, for reasons of Christian theology which he states, accepts the etymology, no doubt regarding the name as an imperfect *hiph'il* form of the verb. In one of the most overtly Christian comments in the book, Jerome envisages the Gentile Christians taking over scriptural knowledge and learning from the Jews, the children of Shem.

LXX of the second part of the verse speaks of the 'houses' of Shem, but there are witnesses to a variant reading 'tents', as in VL. Jerome either took up this variant, or translated the Hebrew with

above, ch. 1 n. 7) is recorded as being not like the Greek, since it says 'and it returned', as also 'the Hebrew': see Field, i. 26. In this case, 'the Syrian' cannot be the Peshitta. TN of this verse repeats the point that the raven went out and returned, perhaps in conscious opposition to the renderings of LXX and Pesh.

[3] See also Rahmer, *Die hebräischen Traditionen*, 68–9, and Jerome, *Ep.* 69. 6.

its reference to Shem's 'tents'.[1] He seems aware that the 'tents' of Shem were interpreted by Jews as referring to a Study House, a Beth Ha-Midrash, which Shem, and later Eber, had headed. His comment sounds suspiciously like a Christianized version of PJ of this verse, which reads: 'May God make beautiful the boundaries of Japheth. May his sons become converts, and dwell in the Study House of Shem.'[2] Jerome's language strengthens the suspicion. He speaks of Christians 'who are engaged in' (Latin, *versamur*) Scripture learning; the verb may equally be translated 'who are turned to', suggesting a conversion from former paganism to Christianity.

The Targum, too, naturally took the sons of Japheth as Gentiles, and foresaw their conversion to Judaism. We should recall *m. Meg.* 1: 8, which permits the writing of Scripture in Greek; indeed, Rabban Simeon ben Gamaliel permits such writing for Greek alone, and the translation of the Scriptures into Greek is further discussed in *jer. Meg.* 1: 9. 10, *b. Meg.* 9b, *b. Yoma* 9b. The Study House of Shem, where Scripture could be studied and God's instruction sought, is often referred to in Targum and Midrash.[3] Most striking is a midrashic interpretation of Gen. 25: 27, which describes Jacob as a man 'dwelling in tents'. A marginal gloss of TN (cf. PJ) interprets: 'Jacob was a man perfect in good work, dwelling and ministering in the Study House of Shem and Eber, and seeking *instruction* from before the Lord.' In this last instance, Jacob is contrasted with his wicked brother Esau, who later became a symbol of the Roman Empire in much Rabbinic writing.[4] Jerome knew that the Rabbis had equated Esau with Rome;[5] and his commentary on Gen. 9: 27 may consequently have been influenced by the Jewish interpretation noted here, which he turns on its head.

[1] See Wevers, p. 132, and Fischer, pp. 132–3.

[2] PJ has understood Japheth as if it derived from the Hebrew root *yph*, 'be beautiful': see further le Déaut, *Targum du Pentateuque*, i. 133. Shem's Beth Ha-Midrash features also in the two marginal glosses of TN of this verse.

[3] See PJ of Gen. 22: 19; PJ, TN, FTP, Ngl, FTV of Gen. 25: 22; PJ, TN, Ngl, TO, of Gen. 25: 27; *Gen. Rab.* 63: 6; *b. Ber.* 16a; *PRE* 32: 4; and G. ben-Ami Sarfati, 'The Tent = The House of Study', *Tarbiz* 38 (1968), 87–9.

[4] See Gerson D. Cohen, 'Esau as Symbol in Early Medieval Thought', in A. Altmann (ed.), *Jewish Medieval and Renaissance Studies* (Cambridge, Mass., 1967), 19–48; H. Hunzinger, 'Babylon als Deckname für Rom und die Datierung des I. Petrusbriefes', in H. Reventlow (ed.), *Gottes Wort und Gottes Land: Festschrift für H.-W. Hertzberg* (Göttingen, 1965), 67–77; S. Zeitlin, 'The Origin of the Term Edom for Rome and the Christian Church', *JQR* 60 (1969), 262–3; L. H. Feldman, 'Josephus' Portrait of Jacob', *JQR* 79 (1988–9), 130–3.

[5] Jerome, *In Esa.* 7. 21. 1–12.

Thus he could make the converted Gentiles, mostly under the sway of Rome's imperial power, 'dwell in the tents of Shem'. All this was made easier because his Christian predecessors had come to regard Japheth as a type of the Church: see, for example, Justin, *Dial.* 139. 2–3; Irenaeus, *Demonstratio* 21, *Adv. Haer.* 3. 5. 3, 5. 34. 2.[6]

verse 29   See Jerome's comment on 6: 3.

CHAPTER 10

The following studies are particularly valuable for proper appreciation of Jerome's opinions here: A. Neubauer, *La Géographie du Talmud* (Paris, 1868); P. S. Alexander, 'The Toponymy of the Targumim, with Special reference to the Table of Nations and the Boundaries of the land of Israel', D. Phil. thesis (Oxford, 1974); M. McNamara, *Targum and Testament* (Shannon, 1972), 190–205; Kamesar, 'Thesis', 88–95; le Déaut, *Targum du Pentateuque*, i. 134–41, and the literature cited there. It should be noted that although Jerome depends on Josephus, *Ant.* 1. 122–47, throughout his commentary on this chapter, he does not slavishly copy this author. He rather modifies the material which Josephus supplied, adds to it, and takes from it, moulding it to his own concerns.

verse 2   Jerome seems to have translated the Hebrew text of this verse: LXX place Elisa between Javan and Thubal. He begins by circumscribing the boundaries of Japheth's sons, for they are Gentiles (see above, 9: 27): he largely follows Josephus, *Ant.* 1. 122. The latter speaks of Taurus and Amanus as mountains: according to some traditions (e.g. *t. Ḥall.* 2: 11), Taurus Amanus formed the extreme northern boundary of the land of Israel. Jerome will refer to them below, in his comments on verses 4–5, given their importance in establishing the boundaries of the Holy Land.[1] Josephus also names the river Don and Gadira as their other boundaries, and notes that the sons of Japheth gave their names to the various lands.

The individual identifications of national groups follow Josephus, *Ant.* 1. 123–5. Specifically, Gomer is equated with the Galatians: so Josephus, *Ant.* 1. 123, and those Rabbinic sources which describe the first eparchy of Gomer as *'pryqy*, which is to be

---

[6] Cf. Harl, *Bible d'Alexandrie*, i. 143.

[1] See McNamara, *Targum and Testament*, 201–2; Alexander, 'Toponymy of the Targumim', 104–6; le Déaut, *Targum du Pentateuque*, iii (*Nombres*), 321.

understood as Phrygia, the home of the Galatians.² For Magog identified with the Scythians, see Josephus, ibid.; but Jerome here stands aside from Rabbinic identifications of this nation as either Germania, Kandya, or the Goths, on whom he has something to say later.³ For Madai as the Medes, we may add to Josephus' evidence in *Ant.* 1. 124 all extant Targums, *Gen. Rab.* 37: 1, and *jer. Meg.* 1: 9. But *b. Yoma* 10a understands the place as Macedonia.

Javan is referred to Ionia and its Greeks, as also in *b. Yoma* 10a; but other Rabbinic sources suggest Macedonia or Ephesus.⁴ Jerome's identification of Thubal with the Iberian Spaniards follows Josephus, and in no way corresponds to Rabbinic sources.⁵ He uses it also in *In Esa.* 18. 66: 18–19, quoting Lucan, *Pharsalia* 4. 10. He is dependent again on Josephus for information about the Cappadocians and their city, pausing to note the LXX reading here: the Rabbinic tradition is quite different.⁶ See also *In Esa.* 18. 66: 18–19. But for Thiras as Thrace, Jerome once more has the support of Josephus, *jer. Meg.* 1: 9, and all the extant Targums.⁷

It was Ambrose, *De Fide* 2. 16, who interpreted Magog here, and Gog and Magog in Ezek. 38–9, as meaning the Goths, and Jerome takes issue with it: see also his commentary on the relevant parts of Ezekiel (Book 11, preface). Josephus has none of this material. Jerome argues that the general equation of Goths with Getae is decisive; so they are not Gog or Magog. The Goths presented Rome with major threats in Thrace and the Balkans in 379 and 381, and on both occasions Theodosius II had managed to keep them at bay. But Jerome's comment seems to have in mind the battle of

---

² On this point, see McNamara, *Targum and Testament*, 198: it is the reading of PJ, TN, FTV, *Gen. Rab.* 37: 1 (R. Samuel ben Ammi). By contrast, *b. Yoma* 10a and *jer. Meg.* 1: 9 have Germania. For further information on Rabbinic identification of the names in this and the following verse, see M. Goshen-Gottstein, *Fragments of Lost Targumim*, ii (Ramat-Gan, 1989), 99–102 (in Hebrew).

³ For Magog as Germania, see PJ, TN, FTV, *Gen. Rab.* 37: 1; as Kandya, see *b. Yoma* 10a; and as Gothia, see *jer. Meg.* 1: 9; Goshen-Gottstein, *Fragments*, ii. 100.

⁴ Macedonia: *Gen. Rab.* 37: 1, and all extant Targums. Ephesus: *jer. Meg.* 1: 9; see Goshen-Gottstein, *Fragments*, ii. 100.

⁵ The extant Targums, *b. Yoma* 10a, and one tradition in *jer. Meg.* 1: 9 identify it with Bithynia; *Gen. Rab.* 37: 1 has 'Isinya, unless this refers to the next item: see Goshen-Gottstein, *Fragments*, ii. 100.

⁶ It is regarded as Mysia by *jer. Meg.* 1: 9 and TN; PJ reads 'asya, which should probably be corrected into Mysia, according to le Déaut, *Targum du Pentateuque*, i. 135. FTV has Moskia, and *b. Yoma* 10a Susya.

⁷ Among Jewish authorities, there was debate whether this last son of Japheth should be identified with Thrace or with Persia: see *b. Yoma* 10a; *Gen. Rab.* 37: 1 (R. Simon); Goshen-Gottstein, *Fragments*, ii. 100–1.

Adrianople (378), whose definitive character may be marked by the fact that it is the last event which he records in his translation of Eusebius's *Chronicon*.[8] He was, however, familiar with the Jewish identification of Magog with the Goths, attested in the Jerusalem Talmud: in *In Esa.* 10. 30: 27–9 and *In Hiez.* 11. 38: 1–23 he notes that they think Gog and Magog come from Scythia, the very region which he and Josephus identify with Magog in this verse!

verse 3 Jerome has taken over these identifications directly from Josephus, *Ant.* 1. 126; but he omits certain details, including the statement that Aschanaxes, Josephus' version of Aschenez, founded the Aschanaxians.[9]

verses 4–5 This information also is largely derived from Josephus, *Ant.* 1. 128, who, however, omits mention of Dodanim in common with some MSS of LXX. Most witnesses of LXX, however, represent Hebrew Dodanim as *Rhodoi*, the Rhodians: Jerome's translation of the verse in *QHG* follows the Hebrew at this point. The Aeolian Greeks spoke their own dialect, and in classical times inhabited the coast of Asia Minor opposite Lesbos, that island itself, Thessaly, and Boeotia. Their speech was distinct from the Dorian spoken in most of the Peloponnese and southern Aegean islands; from Ionian, the dialect of Attica, Euboea, and adjacent islands; from Attic, a distinct form of Ionian; and from Arcadian, spoken in that district and in Cyprus and parts of Pamphylia. Most of the Targums and other Rabbinic sources identified Elisa simply with Hellas, i.e. Greece in general.[10] Tarsus is also equated with Tharsis by the Rabbinic texts we have considered.[11] Jerome effectively quotes Josephus, adding that the city was the Apostle Paul's home (Acts 9: 11; 21: 39; 22: 3). Cethim is variously understood by Jewish tradition as Italy or Achaia. For Dodanim, Jerome

[8] See Kamesar, 'Thesis', 90 n. 26. Augustine, *De Civ. Dei* 20. 11–12, was unhappy with this neat geographical identification, since these peoples symbolize the universal realm of the devil outside the city of God. On Jerome's criticism of Ambrose, see further G. Nauroy, 'Jérôme, lecteur et censeur de l'exégèse d'Ambroise', in Y.-M. Duval (ed.), *Jérôme entre l'Occident et l'Orient* (Paris, 1988), 187–92, who argues that Jerome in *QHG* wrongly supposed that Ambrose had written the *De Fide* before Adrianople, rather than after that battle.

[9] Vallarsi, PL 23 ad loc., believes that Jerome's text should properly include this note from Josephus. The Rabbinic traditions differ greatly from Jerome and Josephus: *jer. Meg.* 1: 9 has Asia Minor, Adiabene, and Germanicia; FTV Asia, Parkevi, and Barbaria. See further Goshen-Gottstein, *Fragments*, ii. 101.

[10] See all extant Targums except FTP; *Gen. Rab.* 37: 1; *jer. Meg.* 1: 9; Goshen-Gottstein, *Fragments*, ii. 101.

[11] That is, the Targums, *Gen. Rab.* 37: 1, and *jer. Meg.* 1: 9.

follows LXX in equating it with Rhodes; but most Jewish authorities knew it as Dardania, a region of Mysia in Asia Minor.[12]

Jerome then refers to Greek and Latin authors as proving his
point, naming Marcus Terentius Varro (*c.* 116–27 BC), author of
forty-one *Books of Antiquities Human and Divine*; Sisinnius
Capito, an author of the Augustan age; and Phlegon of Tralles, who
lived in the time of the Emperor Hadrian and wrote *Olympiades*, a
history dealing with the period from the first Olympiad up to AD
140. It is not certain that Jerome had read these authors; he may,
indeed, have used their names simply to convince his audience of
his great learning and wide range of knowledge.[13]

verse 6 This section abridges Josephus *Ant.* 1. 130–3. Jerome
discusses the question of how Africa got its name in his comment
on 25: 1–6.

verse 7 Josephus, *Ant.* 1. 134 equates Saba with the Sabaeans, to
which Jerome has added quotations from Virgil, *Georgics* 2. 117
and *Aeneid* 1. 416–17. He also knows Aevila as the Gaetuli, and
Sabatha as the Astabari: Astaboras he names later (*Ant.* 2. 249) as
a river joining the Nile at Meroe, capital of Ethiopian Sheba.[14] But
Jerome parts company with Josephus and Rabbinic tradition in
claiming ignorance of Regma and Sabathaca. His commentary *In
Ioelem* 3: 7–8 speaks of Saba, and he quotes the same lines from the
Aeneid as he does here, adding that certain Sabeans are really
Arabians. This point he pursues in his next comment.[15] For
Jerome's Regma, Hebrew *ra'māh*, LXX also have Regma.

verse 7b Jerome's observation, based on Ps. 72: 10 (LXX 71: 10),
is entirely correct: in the preceding section, he had been dealing
with the name *Šᵉbā'*, whereas here we have *Sᵉbā'*. For the identification of the two peoples, he is again indebted to Josephus, *Ant.* 1.
135. See also *In Hiez.* 8. 27: 22 and *In Esa.* 13. 45: 14. It is possible,
as Kamesar argues, that his use of the Psalm text to illustrate his
point depends on Eusebius of Emesa.[16]

---

[12] For Cethim as Italy, see *Gen. Rab.* 37: 1, TN, FTV, FTP, Targum 1 Chron. 1:
7; as Achaia, see *jer. Meg.* 1: 9 and PJ. All these sources identify Dodanim with
Dardania; but some authorities took it as Rhodes: see *Gen. Rab.* 37: 1, and
McNamara, *Targum and Testament*, 193.

[13] See P. Courcelle, *Late Latin Writers*, 78–86.

[14] So H. St J. Thackeray, *Josephus* (Loeb Classical Library), iv (Cambridge, Mass.
and London, 1967), 66.

[15] See Kamesar, 'Thesis', 88–9 for the whole of this section.

[16] See Kamesar, 'Thesis', 89. Jerome differs *toto caelo* from the Targums of this
verse: see le Déaut, *Targum du Pentateuque*, i. 136–7.

verses 8, 10   LXX of verses 8 and 9 call Nimrod a giant, *gigas*, for Hebrew *gibbōr*: Vg has 'powerful' (v. 8) and 'strong' (v. 9). LXX may imply that he was the first of giants on earth, thus contradicting their own translation which had already referred to giants in Gen. 6: 4. This was a problem confronted by Augustine, *QG* 18; but for Jerome, following the Hebrew, it does not arise. Josephus, *Ant.* 1. 113 had already named Nimrod as the first universal tyrant, and had made him responsible for the plan to build the tower of Babel (Gen. 11: 1–9). Jerome certainly implies that Nimrod was wicked: he must have known this generally held Jewish assessment of his character, for it features in Philo, *De Gig.* 66, to say nothing of Rabbinic sources (e.g. *b. ʿErub.* 53a; *b. Ḥag.* 13a; *b. Meg.* 11a). Symmachus translated Hebrew *gibbōr* as 'violent'. It is less clear whether Jerome also implies that Nimrod planned the tower; but this, too, was the opinion of Philo, *QG* 2. 82, of the Rabbis (e.g. *b. Ḥullin* 89b, *b. Pes.* 94b, *PRE* 11: 3), and of Augustine, *De Civ. Dei* 16. 4. Kamesar lists other Christian authors who may have influenced Jerome's comments here.[17]

That Babel signifies 'confusion' is a biblical notion: Gen. 11: 9 seems to derive the word from root *bll*, 'confuse'. The identification of Arach with Edissa is found also in PJ, TN, and *Gen. Rab.* 37: 4. The name was given to it by Seleucus I (312–280 BC).[18] Achad is named as Nisibis also by PJ, TN, FTP, FTV, and *Gen. Rab.* 37: 4. Chalanne, Hebrew Kalneh, is also identified as Ctesiphon on the east bank of the Tigris by all the Targums and *Gen. Rab.*[19]

verse 11   Jerome makes this comment again in *In Osee* 1. 2: 16–17. It is an opportunity for him to introduce the story of Ninus son of Bel (related also by Augustine *De Civ. Dei* 16. 3) about the foundation of the Assyrian Empire. It was very popular: Augustine (*De Civ. Dei* 4. 6) states his sources for the story as Justin and Pompeius Trogus. The Hebrew word *rᵉḥōbōt* can mean 'broad places, streets': see further his comment on 26: 22. His understanding of the word is found also in Vg, where, as here, he uses the word *platea*. This is a Greek word; and it is significant that the Aramaic Targums use the identical Greek loan-word to translate *rᵉḥōbōt*,

---

[17] See Kamesar, 'Thesis', 124, quoting Origen, Epiphanius, *Adv. Haer.* 3. 1–2, and *Clementine Homilies* 9. 4.

[18] See McNamara, *Targum and Testament*, 194.

[19] See ibid. 193, and Goshen-Gottstein, *Fragments*, ii. 104.

rendering it as *plṭyʾt* (PJ), *plṭyʾt* (TN), *plṭyywwt* (gloss of TN), and *plṭyyt* (FTV).

verses 13–14 The forms of the names in LXX are rather different, being Loudieim, Enemetieim, Labieim, Nephthalieim, Patrosōnieim, Chaslōnieim, Phulistieim, and Chaphthorieim. Jerome's source here is once more Josephus, *Ant.* 1. 137; but he has made alterations. Thus he adds to the information about the Laabim, which Josephus provides, the note that the Libyans were first called Phuthaei: this he has derived from 10: 6. He also adds that Chasloim were later called Philistines. He possibly derived this from a Jewish source, which he may have misunderstood; for PJ interprets Chasloim (Hebrew Kasluhim) as 'the people of Pentapolis', and this notion of 'five cities' may have suggested to Jerome the five Philistine cities with their five overlords (1 Sam. 6: 5).[20] The Ethiopian war is recounted by Josephus, *Ant.* 2. 238–53, and refers to an Ethiopian invasion of Egypt in the days of Moses, who was appointed leader of the Egyptian armies by Pharaoh, and successfully repelled and punished the attackers. The story is found also in surviving fragments of the second-century BC Hellenistic-Jewish writer Artapanus.[21]

verse 15 On Sidon, Jerome follows Josephus, *Ant.* 1. 138. Thereafter, however, Josephus (*Ant.* 1. 138–9) does not follow the order of the biblical text, and Jerome himself once more modifies some of Josephus' remarks. They both agree on Aracaeus and the situation of his town. Josephus lists Sinus along with all the others, except Aradius and Amathaeus, as having no record in Scripture but their names, since they were destroyed by the Hebrews; but Jerome singles out its location as near Tripolis. *Gen. Rab.* 37: 6 likewise places it near Mount Lebanon; possibly Jerome knew this, and its corresponding identification in the Targums.[22] He also speaks of Sinus alone as overthrown in war: he entirely omits the rest. The

[20] PJ probably refers to the Pentapolis of Cyrenaica; so le Déaut, *Targum du Pentateuque*, i. 139. Note also that in Ngl and FTV the Kasluhim are dubbed Pentesekinites, the notion of five occurring again.

[21] *Ap.* Eusebius, *Praep. Evang.* 9. 7–10. For a translation of Artapanus' account, and discussion of its relationship to Josephus' work, see J. J. Collins, 'Artapanus', in J. H. Charlesworth (ed.), *The Old Testament Pseudepigrapha*, ii (London, 1985), 894–5; 899.

[22] See further Grossfeld, *Targum Onqelos to Genesis*, 61; Orthosia may be meant, as in PJ and TN.

war he speaks of is probably identical with the Hebrew conquest of
their cities which Josephus relates. He says that they number seven,
the traditional number of the Canaanite peoples conquered by
Israel when she took possession of her land under Joshua; and he
relates their destruction to the cursing of their forefather Canaan
(*Ant.* 1. 140–2).[23]

The island of Aradus features in Josephus, *jer. Meg.* 1: 9, and
Gen. Rab. 37: 6. Samaraeus, Hebrew Zemarites, is identified as
Emissa also in *Gen. Rab.* 37: 4, *jer. Meg.* 1: 9, PJ, and FTV. Finally
Amathaeus, Hebrew 'the Hamathites', stands for the famous city of
Hamath, as Josephus points out: so also *jer. Meg.* 1: 9. Jerome's
remark about the Macedonians naming it Epiphania derives from
Josephus: it is so named in *Gen. Rab.* 37: 6. Its identification with
Antiochia is the view of PJ, TN, FTV. On Emath, see further *In Esa.*
4. 10: 5–11.

verse 19   LXX of this verse read 'and Seboim, as far as Lasa': this
last is Hebrew *Lasha*, and its identification with Callirhoe is attested also by *Gen. Rab.* 37: 6, *Sifre Deut.* 6, *jer. Meg.* 1: 9, PJ of
this verse and Deut. 1: 7.[24] The form Lise is represented variously as
Lece, Leshe, and Leset in the MSS.

verse 22   To the end of this list of sons LXX add Kainan. Jerome
has reproduced the Hebrew text; cf. *LAB* 4: 9. The comment is an
abridged version of Josephus, *Ant.* 1. 143–4. Josephus, however,
says that Elam was ancestor of the Persians, while Jerome speaks of
the Elamite princes of Persia. The latter has no doubt recalled that
Cyrus I, founder of the Persian Empire (ruled 553–528 BC), made
the Elamite city of Susa one of his principal seats, and took as one
of his titles King of Anshan, a district of Elam. On Assur and Ninus,
see above, 10: 11.

verse 23   The sons of Aram are spelled here as in Vg: the last two
are closer to the Hebrew Gether and Mash than LXX, which have
Gather and Mosoch. Josephus, *Ant.* 1. 145, records the material
about Us, to which Jerome has added LXX's interpretation of the
beginning of Job; elsewhere (15: 2–3), Jerome records a different
tradition about the founder of Damascus. The note about Ul and
the Armenians also derives from Josephus. The latter, however,
says that the Bactrians derive from Gether: they lived in the north-

---

[23] It is at this point that Josephus gives his version of Noah's drunkenness and the
cursing of Canaan and his offspring recorded in Gen. 9: 20–7.
[24] See also Goshen-Gottstein, *Fragments*, ii. 105–6.

ern part of Afghanistan, whereas the Carians, whom Jerome places here, were settled in south-west Asia Minor. The identification of Mes-Mosoch with the Maeones, inhabitants of Lydia (?), is made also in *In Esa.* 18. 66: 18–19.

verses 24–5 LXX here read: 'And Arphaxad begot Kainan, and Kainan begot Sala, and Sala begot Eber . . .'. Jerome follows the Hebrew in omitting Kainan; cf. *LAB* 4: 9. Jerome has expanded Josephus' account of Heber and Phaleg (*Ant.* 1. 146), which includes both the statement that the Hebrews descend from Heber, and the meaning of Phaleg as 'division', from root *plg*, 'divide'. He has added a reference to prophecy lacking in Josephus, but found in *Gen. Rab.* 37: 7 and *Seder 'Olam Rabbah* 1 in the name of R. Halafta.[25] While recording the biblical explanation of Phaleg's name as referring to the division of the earth, his comment specifies also the division of the *languages* at the time of the tower of Babel.

What precisely was divided in Phaleg's time is not entirely clear. Was it peoples before Babel as TN and, it would seem, *LAB* 6: 1 understand? or was it simply the territories to which they belonged, as suggested by *Jub.* 8: 8–9, Josephus, *Ant.* 1. 146, and *LAB* 4: 9?[26] Jerome's specific statement that it was the languages agrees with Rashi and with PJ of Deut. 32: 8, which reads: 'When the Most High set the world as an inheritance for the nations who had come forth from Noah's sons, when he separated writings and languages for the sons of men at the generation of the division, *beḏārā deḏalgūṯā* . . .' The generation of the division refers to Phaleg's days, as PJ of Gen. 10: 11; 22: 9 make plain. The tradition is not common in Judaism, and Jerome may be indebted to a Targumic source for his knowledge. Augustine, *QG* 19, seems to approve Jerome's interpretation.

verses 26–9 In verse 28, LXX have omitted Ebal, Hebrew *'ūḇāl*, which Jerome has supplied: so also the VL. The forms of these

[25] Cf. Rahmer, *Die hebräischen Traditionen*, 27. See also Rashi and *MHG* on this verse. Jerome's word for prophecy here is *vaticinium*, which he mostly uses in the quite general sense of 'prediction' or 'foretelling of future events': for the background of the word in pagan thought, and the various nuances in Jerome's use of it, see Jay, *L'Exégèse de saint Jérôme*, 342–3.

[26] *LAB* seems to envisage two divisions of humanity, the first in the time of Phaleg (4: 9) which includes the division of the earth and, by implication, the people on it: see further 6: 1. This last says of the period *before* Babel: 'Then those inhabiting the earth, who had been divided, afterwards gathered together and lived as one.' This initial division must surely refer to Phaleg's days, for 6: 1 then goes on to tell of the divisions *following* the Tower of Babel's collapse.

names in LXX are: Elmōdad, Saleph, Hasarmōth, Iarach,
Hoddorra, Aizēl, Dekla, Abimeēl, Sabeu, Ouphir, Heuila, and
Iōbab. See Josephus, *Ant.* 1. 146–7, for the territories of these
nations. The disclaimer of ignorance is entirely Jerome's own. For
Hieria, Josephus has Seria.

CHAPTER 11

verse 28   The Hebrew word '*wr*, which is the place-name Ur, also
means 'light, fire', and provided the starting-point for the widely
disseminated tradition that Abraham had been thrown into a fiery
furnace. Jerome accepts the truth of it: see his comments below on
12: 4; *In Esa.* 18. 65: 8; *In Osee* 3. 14: 5–9; *In Zech.* 2. 9: 13; and
his Vg translation of Neh. (2 Esdras) 9: 7. For the first time in this
book, Jerome uses the expression 'tradunt Hebraei' ('the Hebrews
hand on a teaching, tradition') to introduce an Haggadic paraphrase of a verse.[1]

He gives an abbreviated outline of a story found in many sources,
which often differ among themselves in describing the circumstances, personnel, and events surrounding Abraham's suffering.[2] It
originated in pre-Rabbinic times, as is clear from *LAB* 6: 15–18,
and received many embellishments: see, for example, *Gen. Rab.* 38:
13, where a parallel is drawn between Abraham's experiences and
those of Daniel at Nebuchadnezzar's court. But the essential story
was so well known that the Aramaic Targums often simply alluded
to 'the furnace of fire of the Chaldeans' in shorthand style: see PJ
and TN of Gen. 11: 31; 15: 7; 16: 5. Indeed, the beginning of PJ's
version of this verse is similar to Jerome's comment: 'Now it
happened, when Nimrod threw Abram into the furnace of fire
because he would not worship his idols, that no authority was given
to the fire to burn him'. Jerome says nothing of Nimrod's activity,
although he appears also in *Gen. Rab.* and other accounts; and the
extent of his abridgement of the Jewish tradition is apparent only in
the second part of his comment. Giving another translation of the

---

[1] See Introduction, pp. 4–5.

[2] For a survey and detailed discussion of the sources, see especially G. Vermes,
'The Life of Abraham (1)', in *Scripture and Tradition in Judaism*[2] (Leiden, 1973),
67–95. Cf. also Bowker, *The Targums*, 187–9; and C. T. R. Hayward, 'Inconsistencies and Contradictions in Targum Pseudo-Jonathan: The Case of Eliezer and
Nimrod', *JSS* 37 (1992), 49–52.

scriptural verse, this time of the Hebrew text, he notes that Aran died by fire, having refused to worship fire. The note becomes clear when set alongside the account in *Gen. Rab.*, that Aran was undecided whether to support Abram or the idolaters; that he finally sided with Abram when he saw that the fire did not harm him; and that he was consumed by the flames because of his doublemindedness. But Jerome does make clear that Jewish tradition linked Aran's death with the story of Abraham in the furnace.[3] Such is the meaning of his words: 'And they maintain that this (i.e. Abraham's being cast into the fire) refers to what is said' in the verse about Aran's death.

A chronological problem is involved here, which Jerome regarded as solved by these Jewish traditions: this he addresses in commenting on 12: 4. But there is covert allusion to it here, without explanation. The Hebrew says that Aran died *'al p'nē* his father. The words may mean 'before' in the temporal sense, as the first translation given by Jerome allows; or they may mean 'before the face of', as in the second translation. It is the first possible meaning which leads to the chronological difficulty discussed in 12: 4, and the second which supplies Jerome with the resolution.

verse 29 LXX give the name of Abram's wife as Sara, and describe Aran as 'father of Melcha and father of Iesca'; Jerome's rendering makes explicit that Melcha and Iesca have one and the same father. For Thara's three sons Abram, Nachor, and Aran, see Gen. 11: 27. This verse states that Aran had two daughters, Melcha and Iesca; and Jerome identifies Iesca with Sarai, the wife of Abraham.[4] He follows established Jewish tradition, set out in *b. Sanh.* 69b; *b. Meg.* 14a; *Sifre Num.* 24; *Midrash Pss.* 118; *Seder 'Olam Rabbah* 2; PJ of this verse; and Josephus, *Ant.* 1. 151; so also Augustine, *De Civ. Dei* 16. 12. The effect of this is to make Sarai Abraham's niece, even though Gen. 20: 12 and *Jub.* 12: 9 speak of her as his (half-)sister.

As Jerome remarks, the law forbidding marriages within degrees of kindred had not yet been given to Moses: Lev. 18: 9; 20: 17 forbid marriage of brother and sister, and marriage of aunt and nephew is ruled out by Lev. 18: 13. But from Second Temple times onwards, Jews believed that the Patriarchs had kept many of the commandments of the Torah before it was given to Moses; *Jub.*

---

[3] See also Rahmer, *Die hebräischen Traditionen*, 24–5.
[4] See Rahmer, ibid. 27.

took this for granted. The tradition that Abram married his niece began as an attempt to absolve him from a charge of having broken the Law; for while Lev. 18: 13 forbids nephews to marry aunts, it is silent about marriages of uncles and nieces.[5] But of these legal concerns which led to Iesca's identification with Sarai, Jerome says nothing.[6]

CHAPTER 12

verse 4 Jerome neatly states the difficulty in terms very similar to those in a Catena fragment variously attributed to Diodore, Theodoret, or Theodore of Mopsuestia (Petit, ii. 168–70). For Thara's age at Abraham's birth, and his age when he died, see Gen. 11: 26, 32. On the 'fire of the Chaldeans', see above on 11: 28. The author of the Catena fragment tries to resolve the problem by invoking the peculiarities of biblical expression: he insists that Abram, Nachor, and Aran were no more triplets whom Thara fathered in his seventieth year, than Shem, Ham, and Japheth were triplets sired by Noah in his 500th (Gen. 5: 32). Rather, all these sons were born to their respective fathers at different times, such that the three named in each case had been born by the time the father was of the age given in the biblical text.

Jerome's solution of the chronological problem differs entirely from the one just given, and appears unique. It rests on a Jewish tradition which he describes quite simply as true. He suggests that Abraham came out of the fire of the Chaldeans as it were new-born. There is nothing in extant Jewish lore precisely to compare with the tradition which Jerome gives, although he may have known Jewish calculations no longer available to us. The usual Jewish solution was to postulate Abraham's having left Chaldea before Thara's death.[1] The other options which Jerome records do not coincide

---

[5] See further Vermes, 'Bible and Midrash', in P. R. Ackroyd and C. F. Evans (eds.), *The Cambridge History of the Bible*, i (Cambridge, 1970), 218–19; id. 'The Life of Abraham', 75–6.

[6] Compare also with Jerome's remarks here PJ of Lev. 20: 17, which specifically points out that God permitted marriage of brother and sister in the case of the first human beings so that the world might be populated, *before the giving of the Torah*; but that since the Torah has been given, such liaisons are forbidden. See also *b. Sanh.* 58b; *jer. Yeb.* 11: 1; *Sifra Qedoshim* Pereq 11: 11; *Midrash Pss.* 89: 3; PRE 21: 1; and B. Grossfeld, *The Targum Onqelos to Leviticus and the Targum Onqelos to Numbers*, The Aramaic Bible, viii (Edinburgh, 1988), 43.

[1] See further Rahmer, *Die hebräischen Traditionen*, 25–6. Rashi commenting on

with Jewish thinking either, and may be of his own devising. But his recourse to Jewish tradition is clear and exegetically simple; and it seems that some Christian exegetes accepted Jerome's opinion: see Augustine, *De Civ. Dei.* 16. 15, *QG* 25.

verses 9–10 LXX have: 'And Abram went away, and journeyed, and encamped in the desert'. The Hebrew has, literally, 'to the Negeb', which is desert. But Hebrew often uses Negeb to refer to the south; cf. TO of this verse, and of 13: 1, 3. Hence Jerome's comment, translating as 'ad austrum'; similar is Vg, reading 'ad meridiem'.[2] He will use this understanding to comment on 13: 1–4, below. The effect of his translation, however, is to diminish the theological significance of the verse: Philo, *De Abr.* 87, perceived in Abraham's departure from the crowd a love of the desert solitude which is dear to God. Similarly, Christ went into the desert alone to pray (Matt. 14: 13).

verses 15–16 LXX and Vg read: 'and they treated Abram well . . .'. The Bible is speaking of Sarai, Abraham's wife, who was brought into Pharaoh's harem during Abraham's first visit to Egypt (Gen. 12: 10–15). This may imply that she became Pharaoh's concubine, and Jerome seeks to defend her by suggesting that she acted under duress, and then to show that possibly she may not have had time to be taken to Pharaoh's bed. As Theodoret, *QG* 63, also points out, there were those who believed that Pharaoh had actually had intercourse with Sarah, and Jerome is concerned to counter this idea. In support of his second argument he brings Est. 2: 12–13; and Augustine, *QG* 26, makes approving mention of it.

CHAPTER 13

verses 1–4 It is customary to speak of 'going up' to the land of Israel: see *Sifre Deut.* 23, 37, 113. Jerome presents Abraham as now freed from Egyptian bonds, just as his descendants were to be freed later: like them, he should immediately 'go up' to the land of

---

11: 32 offers the classical solution, that Abraham left Haran and came to Canaan sixty years or more before his father's death. Scripture, however, recorded Thara's death before noting Abraham's departure, lest the latter should seem to have deserted his aged father. He assumes, with *Gen. Rab.* 39, that Thara was a wicked man, and therefore effectively dead while actually still alive. See also Ibn Ezra's comments ad loc. in *Miqra'oth Gedoloth.*

[2] Jerome may be following Aquila and Symmachus, who at Gen. 13: 1, 3; Num. 2: 10 render Negeb as 'south'. See Salvesen, *Symmachus*, 238.

Israel. See Exod. 3: 16–17, where Moses is to announce the coming
Exodus with the news that God will make Israel 'go up' to the land
flowing with milk and honey. Rahmer's suggestion that Jerome's
comment may depend on otherwise unknown Jewish exegesis derives some support from what follows.[1]

Jerome sets against the perfectly proper LXX translation that
Abraham was very rich (*plousios*) the Hebrew *kābēd m^e'ōd*, literally
'very heavy'. Rashi also comments at this point that Abraham was
heavily laden with burdens. So Jerome can suggest that Abraham
was encumbered by the seeming riches of Egypt, a place symbolizing all that is worldly. His particular love of asceticism has evidently coloured interpretation of this verse, for which he invokes
the support of the 'Hebrew truth'. Abraham is a 'holy man', the
prototype of the Christian monk. But other commentators understood the riches as entirely proper for a pious man who had obeyed
God: see *jer. Qidd.* 4: 13; *Aggadath Bere'shith* 16, 34; and
Ambrose, *De Abr.* 2. 20, following the LXX.

The interpretation of Abraham's journey to Bethel (VL renders as
'whence he *had* come') uses the explanation of the Negeb, which
LXX have translated 'desert', as meaning 'south': see Symmachus
and above, comment on 12: 9–10. TO, PJ, and TN of this verse do
likewise, even though Abraham is clearly journeying northwards
from Egypt to get to Bethel.[2] Jerome makes Abraham return to
Bethel, here expounded as 'house of God': he had left Egypt and the
desert entirely, on this view, to go at once to the place of God's
presence. Again, we should recall Exod. 3: 12, saying that Israel set
free from Egyptian slavery should at once 'worship God on this
mountain'. PJ of Gen. 13: 3 also insists on Abraham's immediate
journey to Bethel, adding to the Hebrew that he *returned* to the
place where he had pitched his tent and had first built an altar to
God.[3]

verse 13 LXX have: 'But the men who were in Sodom . . .' The
Hebrew describes them, literally, as 'evil, and sinners to the Lord
exceedingly'. Jerome's comment is very close to TN: 'And the
people of Sodom were evil one towards another, and sinners in

[1] See Rahmer, *Die hebräischen Traditionen*, 28–9.
[2] See further Aberbach and Grossfeld, *Targum Onkelos to Genesis*, 80–1.
[3] Hebrew: 'And he went on his journeys from the south, even as far as Bethel, to
the place where his tent had been . . .' TN, TO, and PJ have: 'to the place where he
had *spread*, *pitched*, his tent . . .': Cf. Vg, 'where he had formerly made (*fixerat*) his
tent'.

respect of incest and shedding of blood and idolatry before the Lord exceedingly.' A similar interpretation is found in *b. Sanh.* 109a; *jer. Sanh.* 10: 3; *t. Sanh.* 13: 8; *Gen. Rab.* 40(41): 7. This last reads: ' "Evil" means that they were evil to one another; "sinners" in the matter of incest; "to the Lord" refers to idolatry; "exceedingly" refers to the shedding of blood.' Perhaps TO is closest to Jerome's rather terse comment, remarking that they were 'evil in matters concerning their wealth, and sinners with regard to their bodies'; PJ provides a longer explanation along the same lines, including the crimes listed in *Gen. Rab.* and TN. For the description of Zacharia and Elisabeth, see Luke 1: 6. Jerome ends by quoting Ps. 143: 2.

verses 14–15 Another geographical note, similar to that in 12: 9, is given here. Like Jerome, TO, TN, PJ, and Pesh define the sea as the west.[4]

CHAPTER 14

For further discussion, and analysis of Jerome's general principles in *QHG* which this chapter reveals, see my article 'Some Observations on Saint Jerome's "Hebrew Questions on Genesis" and the Rabbinic Tradition', *PIBA* 13 (1990), 58–76.

verses 2–3 The Hebrew has: 'and the king of Bela: this is Zoar. All these were confederate together in the Vale of Siddim: this is the Sea of Salt.' The town Bela, LXX Bale, is regularly understood as 'swallowing up', in line with the meaning of the Hebrew root *bl*ʿ: see *Gen. Rab.* 42: 5, *Tanḥ Lekh* 8, *Midrash Aggadah* of this verse, PJ, and TN. All these sources hold that its inhabitants were 'swallowed up', presumably in the earthquake to which Jerome next alludes.

Salisa, Hebrew Shalishah, is named at 1 Sam. 9: 4; 2 Kgs. 4: 42; but what follows is best explained by Isa. 15: 5, where Zoar appears in one possible reading of the text to be identified with a place called Eglath-shelishiya: this latter means, literally, 'three-year-old heifer'.[1] Extant Jewish sources do not, however, record a tradition exactly like the one Jerome sets out here; although they do

---

[4] For the distinctiveness of this comment, as opposed to Origen's remarks in *Sel. in Gen.* 13: 3, see Kamesar, *Jerome*, 99.

[1] See also *In Esa.* 5. 15: 5, 6. 15: 3–9. For discussion of these passages, see Jay, *L'Exégèse de saint Jérôme*, 187; and Hayward, 'Some Observations', 60–1.

note that Zoar was spared while earthquakes were happening elsewhere (*Gen. Rab.* 49: 6) and remained standing for a year after the destruction of the other cities (*b. Shabb.* 10b).

LXX had used Segor to represent Hebrew Ṣoʿar, which means 'small': in Aramaic, called here by Jerome 'the Syrian language', it is *zwʿr*, and so PJ represents this place-name, as does TN on most occasions (although not in this verse, where it reproduces the Hebrew form of the name). See also Josephus, *Ant.* 1. 204. Jerome often uses this exegesis of Zoar and its smallness: see, for example, his comment on 19: 30; *In Soph.* 2: 8–11; *Eps.* 108. 11, 122. 1. He clearly regards the matter as of some significance, possibly because the exegesis of this verse affects a number of other biblical passages.[2] Furthermore, Zoar was a place visited by Christian pilgrims (see *Itinerarium Egeriae* 12. 5–6), and for that reason would have been of interest. For the note about the Vale of Salt Pits (Vg: 'the wooded vale'—see further on 14: 7) and the Dead Sea, he depends without acknowledgement on Josephus, *Ant.* 1. 174; *War* 4. 455–6, 476–85.

verse 5 LXX have: 'And they cut in pieces the giants who were in Astaroth Karnain, and strong nations at the same time as them, and the Ommaioi who were in Saue the city'. The words 'before they reached Sodom' are not represented either in LXX or Hebrew. The Hebrew has: 'And they smote the Rephaim in Ashtaroth-Carnaim, and the Zuzim in Ham, and the Emim in Shaveh-Kiriathaim.' Jerome's comments about this last place are confirmed in *Lib. Loc.* 966, where he records it as an ancient city in which the Amorites, a powerful people, once dwelt: it was destroyed by Cherdolaomer.

Jerome agrees with LXX and extant Targums that the Raphaim are giants. He seems to identify the mysterious Ashtaroth-Carnaim with Arabia, for which I can find no precedent. On the Zuzim and Emim (Hebrew *ʾēmāh* means 'fear') he is very close to TO and PJ, and seems to set traditional Hebrew interpretation of these names against the LXX. He excuses the latter, however, because they convey the general sense of the Hebrew.

But in their translation of Hebrew *bhm* as 'at the same time as them', LXX have made a mistake, and he points out the cause of confusion. It appears that Jerome's Hebrew text read *bhm* (*bᵉhōm*), 'in Hom', like some MSS of the Samaritan Pentateuch: TO and PJ

---

[2] See Introd., p. 17; and Hayward, 'Some Observations', 61–2, where the relationship of Jerome's comments to Targumic material is discussed.

follow this reading. But *bhm* (*bāhem*), 'among them', is read not only by LXX, but also TN, FTV, *Gen. Rab.* 41(42): 4, and Pesh. The MT reads *bᵉhām*, which looks like a compromise between the two readings set out here. All this indicates that the textual problem is more complex than Jerome will admit: what is significant is that he opts here for the 'official' Jewish solution represented by TO and PJ, while in Vg he retains the LXX translation of 'among, with them'.[3]

verse 7 Cades was not so called at the time of Abraham, but is here given its later, more familiar name 'by anticipation', a principle noted by Jerome at 31: 21; 46: 26–7, and described on two other occasions (21: 30–1; 46: 47) by the Greek word *prolēpsis*. Rabbinic exegesis knows the same device: see, for example, *Gen. Rab.* 42: 7, *Tanḥ Lekh* 8, *Ḥuqqat* 11, *Num. Rab.* 19: 6. Cades is identified with Petra by TO and PJ, the latter, like *Gen. Rab.* 42: 7, adding reference to Moses judging the people; cf. *Num. Rab.* 19: 14.

Jerome has, in essence, quoted the Hebrew text concerning the smiting of the Amalekites and Amorites. LXX have: 'and they smote all the princes of Amalek and the Amorites who were dwelling in Asasonthamar'. For Asasonthamar as Engaddi, see PJ, TO, TN, *Gen. Rab.* 42: 7.

The final part of the comment refers to verse 8, and notes the translations given by Aquila and Theodotion of the Hebrew word *hsdym*, 'Siddim'. Above, on verse 3, Jerome has rendered this word as 'salt pits'; here, he apparently agrees with Aquila and Theodotion that the word means 'pleasant groves'.[4] Hence, presumably, his Vg rendering here and in verse 3 as 'wooded valley'. While what Jerome perceived the Greek of these translators to mean is clear, great doubt attends the words they actually used. The versions of Aquila and Theodotion reproduced here are problematic.[5] Jerome's understanding of these two translators, however,

---

[3] See further *Gen. Rab.* 42: 6; McNamara, *Targum and Testament*, 203–4; Hayward, 'Some Observations', 62–3; and for PJ's renderings Geiger, *Urschrift*, 457.

[4] See Wevers, p. 161, who gives Aquila's reading as *tōn irineōnōn*: the codices read *prineōēn* and *aprineainon*. None of these words is found in the Greek lexicons (so CCSL 72 (*S. Hieronymi Presbyteri Opera*, i: *Opera Exegetica*), p. 18). Field, (i. 31) gives *prineōnōn*, likewise not found in the lexicons; see also Hayward, 'Some Observations', 64.

[5] Since we know what sense Jerome made of the two translations, the textual problem of the Greek words in not properly our concern. But the matter is of

may be influenced by Jewish tradition now found in Targums PJ, TN (and v. 3), both of which took Siddim here as *pardēs*, park or pleasure garden.[6]

verse 11   Here and in Vg Jerome translated Hebrew *rkš* as 'property', vocalizing the word as *rᵉkūš* rather than *rekeš*, 'steeds', as LXX had done.

verse 13   Jerome understands that the word Hebrew derives from the root *'br*, 'to pass by'. We may compare *Gen. Rab.* 42: 8; Philo, *De Mig. Abr.* 20; and the Christian interpreters listed by Kamesar.[7] Note carefully, however, the discussion in *Mekh. de R. Ishmael Nezikin* 1: 31–43 about the ambiguity of the term *'bry* as meaning either an Israelite, or merely one who had come from across the river Euphrates: this text strives to show that 'Hebrew' equals 'Israelite'. Jerome's comment does not resolve the ambiguity, and makes no attempt to do so. This is because Christians had long seen the 'Hebrews' as their spiritual ancestors, who had 'passed over' from darkness to light, from Egypt to the promised land, from the life of the world to the contemplation of God. Origen, in particular, had spoken of the Church as Hebrews who 'have crossed over', and his influence was sufficient to ensure widespread knowledge of the exegesis.[8] See also *Ep.* 71. 2.

The comment about the oak of Mambre is obscure. Kamesar argues that Jerome is trying to deal with a problem, more apparent in VL than in LXX, which emerges if we read (with one MS of *QHG* noted by Vallarsi ad loc.) *Amorris* for *Amorrhaei* in Jerome's citation of the scriptural verse and his succeeding comment. The latter might then mean: 'But the Amorite himself was sitting at the oak of Mambre the brother of Eschol.' Thus in VL the subject of

---

intrinsic interest, and for discussion of the words and suggested emendations, see Field, i. 31; Vallarsi, PL 23: 1009; CCSL 72, p. 18; Salvesen, *Symmachus*, 9; Hayward, 'Some Observations', 74.

[6] Aquila and Targum often share interpretations of Hebrew expressions: see A. E. Silverstone, *Aquila and Onkelos* (Manchester, 1931), and C. T. R. Hayward, *The Targum of Jeremiah*, The Aramaic Bible, xii (Wilmington, 1987), index under 'Aquila'.

[7] See Kamesar, 'Thesis', 116–17 for Julius Africanus, *Chronicon* (*Julii Africani quae supersunt ex quinque libris Chronographiae*), PG 10: 69; Eusebius, *Praep. Evang.* 7. 8. 21; Jerome, *Lib. Heb. Nom.* (p. 155); and see Petit, ii. 166 for the comments of Gennadius and Acacius.

[8] See Origen, *Sel. in Gen.* 14: 13, *Hom. in Gen.* 20. 4, *Mart. Exhort.* 33, *Hom. in Num.* 19. 4, among other references collected and discussed by de Lange, *Origen and the Jews*, 31–2.

the verb 'was sitting' is unclear; no less an authority than Augustine took 'the Amorite', rather than Abraham himself, to be the subject of the verb. Jerome, arguing from the original Hebrew, took 'the Amorite' as an adjective qualifying Mamre.[9] Jerome's reading, however, goes further: it means that Mam(b)re must be a person, not a place, a point made by R. Nehemiah in *Gen. Rab.* 41(42): 8. Abraham, then, has three allies who are *germanos*, that is, both 'genuine ones' and 'brothers'.[10]

R. Judah, however, in *Gen. Rab.* 42: 8, takes Mamre not as a person, but as a place, specifically a plain. This understanding is partially reflected in TN, 'in the plain of the vision of Mamre the Amorite', and TO, 'the plain of Mamre the Amorite', which last corresponds to Jerome's Vg translation in this verse, 'in convalle Mambre Amorrhaei'. Yet all these Targums appear to regard Mamre as a person. The effect of TO's rendering in particular is to bridge the dispute between R. Judah and R. Nehemiah; Jerome seems to have been aware of this dispute, his comments in *QHG* showing sympathy and support for R. Nehemiah's viewpoint, while his Vg seems to adopt an Onkelos-like compromise with the opposing opinion of R. Judah.

Jerome also notes that the third ally of Abraham is in the Hebrew called Aner, and not Aunan as LXX and VL have it. He records this, no doubt, since Aunan is the form which LXX and VL use to transcribe the name of Onan (Gen. 38: 4, 8, 9), who was adjudged guilty of sexual sin.

verse 14   See *In Hiez.* 8. 27: 29; *In Hier.* 1. 80 on 4: 15. For Dan as Paneas, see also *PRE* 27: 2, and Jerome's *Ep.* 73. 8. His remarks about the sources of the Jordan may ultimately be based on his own observation, for they coincide neither with Rabbinic notions nor with the somewhat uneven information provided by Josephus. The former (*b. Bekhoroth* 55a) speaks of one source only for the river, which is interpreted as coming down (Hebrew *yrd*) from Dan. Josephus speaks of two sources, but with some confusion of expression. In *Ant.* 1. 177 he names Dan as one of them, and in *Ant.* 18. 28 he says that Paneas is near the sources (plural) of the Jordan.

[9] See Kamesar, *Jerome*, 173–4. The original reading of LXX was almost certainly *ho Amoris*: see Wevers, p. 163, where the apparatus records the confusion which the word engendered in the tradition.

[10] Kamesar, *Jerome*, 174, notes also that Jerome may have adopted the reading of Symmachus here, and that Eusebius, *Onomasticon* 124. 5–7 also understood that Mambre might be either a person or a place.

In *War* 3. 509–13, however, he says it rises apparently at Panion, but actually in the pool Phiale, whence it flows underground to Panion. This information strongly implies only one source. Jerome also disagrees with Origen, *Comm. in Joh.* 6. 25, who derives Jordan from root *yrd*, 'to go down'; indeed, in *Lib. Heb. Nom.* (p. 67) he gives the meaning as 'their descending', to which he adds (p. 140) 'their laying hold upon, or one who sees judgement'. Jerome's etymology in *QHG* is based presumably on Hebrew $y^{e^{\flat}}\bar{o}r$ (his Ior), a biblical word which refers to the river Nile (as in Gen. 41: 1–3; 17–18) and to watercourses in general, and the place-name Dan. He may even be trying to make sense of Josephus' garbled information. See also *Ep.* 78, *mansio* 41.

verses 18–19 LXX use the plural form of 'bread' in this verse, and record that God blessed *Abram*. On Jerome's description of his work as a collection of Hebrew *quaestiones* and *traditiones*, see the Introduction, pp. 2–7. He summarizes four Jewish traditions about Melchizedech, all of which are extant in Jewish sources.

First, Melchizedech is identified with Shem: this is assumed by *b. Ned.* 32b; *Gen. Rab.* 43: 6; *Lev. Rab.* 25: 6; *Num. Rab.* 4: 8; *ARNa* 2; *PRE* 8: 2. The Targums PJ, TN, FTV, and FTP of Gen. 14: 18 all repeat the tradition, as do *Midrash Pss.* 76: 3; *Midrash Aggadah* 1: 23; *MHG* 1. 187; *Tanḥ Lekh* 15. Epiphanius, *Adv. Haer.* 2. 1. 55. 6 (*Contra Melchizedecianos*) relates it as a Samaritan belief. There is no indication in Jerome's comment that the Jews have invented this tradition as an anti-Christian device. On the contrary, in *Ep.* 73. 9 he is keen, for Christological reasons, to stress the Jewish opinion that Melchizedech was a real human being, and not the Holy Ghost or an angel as some Christian authorities had argued.[11] The indications are that the tradition is old: Philo emphasized the priestly character of Shem in *De Sob.* 65–6, and *Jub.* 8: 12–21 had spoken of Shem's territory as the site of the Garden of Eden and the Holy of Holies. Since the Bible supplies no genealogy for Melchizedech, it would be natural to search for a priestly character contemporary with him, and to identify the two. Shem seems to

---

[11] *Ep.* 73 *Ad Evangelum (Evagrium) Presbyterum*, PL 22: 679, tries to refute the contention of an anonymous author that Melchizedech was the Holy Spirit. At the same time, Jerome argues against Origen, Didymus the Blind, Hippolytus, Irenaeus, Eusebius of Caesarea, Eusebius of Emesa, Apollinaris, and Eustathius, who seem to have regarded Melchizedech as an angel. He insists that the Christian use of the Melchizedech as a figure of Christ would be without foundation, unless he had been really and truly a human being who was both priest and king (*Ep.* 73. 3, 9).

have fitted the bill, as the notice about Melchizedech's life may indicate.[12]

Second, he is said to have lived until the days of Isaac. PJ of Gen. 22: 19 notes that Isaac went to study in the Beth Ha-Midrash of the great Shem for three years: without specifying the time-span, R. Berekhiah reports the same tradition in the name of the Rabbis at *Gen. Rab.* 56: 11. PJ, FTP, and FTV of Gen. 24: 62 agree that Isaac came from Shem's Beth Ha-Midrash just before he met Rebecca for the first time; and in PJ of Gen. 38: 6 and *Gen. Rab.* 85: 10 in the name of R. Meir we hear that Tamar was Shem's daughter. All this agrees with what Jerome tells us were Jewish traditions, which he sets out more fully in *Ep.* 73.[13]

Third, the Targums stress that Melchizedech-Shem was the priest acting at that time (PJ), ministering before God Most High (TO) in the high priesthood (TN, FTP). For Melchizedech as high priest in Christian tradition, see the Canon of the Roman Mass (Traditional Rite) in the prayer *Supra Quae*.[14] Before Aaron was appointed high priest, the first-born had exercised priestly functions: such is implied by Exod. 24: 5, and spelled out by PJ and Ngl of this verse; *m. Zeb.* 14: 4; *b. Zeb.* 115b; *b. Bekhoroth* 4b; and *Exod. Rab.* 28: 3. Since Genesis speaks of sacrifices to God in those days, it was natural that the question of who might legitimately have ministered as priests at that time should arise. Philo, too, seems to have approached the Rabbinic view that the first-born acted in this way.[15] Jerome specifies that these were first-born sons of Noah: in *Ep.* 73 he gives further details, and says that their succession and order has been copied out by the Jews.[16] Such a listing of priests in order from the ancestor Noah is found in *Num. Rab.* 4: 8, which tells why unsuitable persons like Esau were excluded from office.

Finally, identification of Salem in this verse with Jerusalem is a Jewish tradition found in *Genesis Apocryphon* 22: 13; Josephus *War* 6. 10; *Ant.* 1. 180; and the Targums PJ, TN, TO, FTP, FTV.

---

[12] On Shem and Melchizedech, see Bowker, *The Targums*, 196–9; le Déaut, *Targum du Pentateuque*, i. 163–5, and literature cited there.

[13] See *Ep.* 73 *Ad Evangelum* (*Evagrium*) *Presbyterum*, PL 22: 679; and Rahmer, *Die hebräischen Traditionen*, 72.

[14] See R. le Déaut, 'Le Titre de Summus Sacerdos donné à Melchisédech est-il d'origine juive?' *RSR* 50 (1962), 222–9.

[15] See *De Congr.* 98; *De Sac.* 118–20, commenting on Num. 3: 12–13; 8: 16–18; and the Targums of those verses. On the priesthood of the first-born, see also R. le Déaut, *La Nuit pascale* (Rome, 1963), 85 n. 43.

[16] The Latin has: 'cuius series et ordo describitur'.

It is assumed in the Rabbinic literature generally, and is strongly implied by Scripture in Ps. 76: 2. Among Christian writers, Clement of Alexandria, *Stromateis* 1. 5, refers to it. There were other places called Salem, as Jerome admits in his comment on 33: 18, where he appears to accept the view that Melchizedech was priest-king of Jerusalem; but Eusebius of Emesa (Devreesse, p. 67) denied the identification of Salem with Jerusalem in this chapter.

It is remarkable that Jerome does not dismiss all this as Jewish fable. Rather, he contents himself with juxtaposing to it Christian exegesis of Melchizedech without further comment. What follows is based on Heb. 7: 1–10, in the course of which Christ is compared with Melchizedech. But Jerome goes further, seeing in this man not a Jewish high priest, but a Gentile who is uncircumcised: here he follows earlier writers like Justin Martyr and Tertullian, who had strongly emphasized that Melchizedech was a type of the true priestly Christian race.[17] Jerome develops this along the lines of Heb., not noting that Abraham was in fact uncircumcised when Melchizedech blessed him! The whole emphasis, as might be expected, is on the superiority of Melchizedech's priesthood, and its power to bless the later Aaronic line. Perhaps to counter this view of things, R. Isaac the Babylonian stated that Melchizedech was born circumcised (*Gen. Rab.* 43: 6; *ARNa* 2), but of this possibly polemical statement Jerome appears happily ignorant. For Jerome, Melchizedech's priesthood constitutes a *mystery* (see also 18: 6; 35: 21; 49: 9, 19), a truth about Christ's saving work, and its historical and eternal significance, which is concealed in the text of the Scriptures.[18]

Jerome at last quotes Ps. 110. 4 on the order of Melchizedech's priesthood: this verse is the subject of attention in Heb. 5: 6; 6: 20; 7: 17, where it is applied to Christ. Melchizedech had brought forth bread and wine, which encapsulate the order of his priesthood. Christ had declared that bread and wine were his body and blood, to be offered in sacrifice by the Church as his memorial. But the Christian sacrifice is unbloody, and Jerome, like his predecessors, can contrast it with the bloody, non-rational victims of Aaron's

[17] See Justin, *Dial.* 19. 2–4, 28. 2–5; Tertullian, *Adv. Jud.* 2; Jerome, *Ep.* 73; and Hayward, 'Pirqe de Rabbi Eliezer and Targum Pseudo-Jonathan', 228–9.
[18] On *mysterium* and its significance in Jerome's commentaries, see Jay, *L'Exégèse de saint Jérôme*, 266–9.

order of priesthood: for the Body and Blood of the Lord are the rational and unbloody offerings of the Church's Eucharist.[19]

CHAPTER 15

verses 2–3 LXX read: 'Master, what shall you give me? and I am departing without a child; but the son of Masek my home-born female slave is this Damascus Eliezer.' The Hebrew phrase *mešeq bētī* which Jerome reproduces is difficult, in that the form *mešeq* occurs only here in Scripture. LXX understood it as the name of Eliezer's mother, described as a home-born slave (*oikogenēs*); but Aquila saw in it the root *šqh* in the *hiph'il* form, which has the sense 'to cause to drink'. Jerome reproduced this possibly because he thought it had Christian overtones: in *In Esa.* 7. 17: 1 he alludes to Eliezer as a drinker of the blood, i.e. of the Eucharist. Theodotion's translation of the word is very similar to TO, which reads 'this administrator who is over (or: in) my house'.[1] PJ's rendering speaks of Eliezer 'the administrator of my house', adding 'by whose hands miracles were performed for me in Damascus'. Jerome's comment, too, alludes to Damascus, and interprets the words 'I am going without children' as 'I shall die without children': so also PJ, which has 'I am going forth *from the world*, who am without sons'.[2] LXX may have the same sense. The word 'steward', *procurator*, is chosen by Jerome as a translation of *mšq* in Vg. In *Lib. Heb. Nom.* (p. 65) he explains Eliezer as meaning 'God's help'.

The final sentence of Jerome's comment is ambiguous. It may also be translated: 'By this man they say that Damascus was

---

[19] See also *Ep.* 46. 2. Cyril of Jerusalem, *Mystagogic Catecheses* 23. 8, 10, speaks of the 'unbloody sacrifice'. For discussion of Melchizedek and his bread and wine as a type of Christ and the Eucharist, see J. Daniélou, *The Bible and the Liturgy* (Notre Dame, Ind., 1956), 143–7, noting particularly his exegesis of Eusebius, *Dem.* 1. 10, 5. 3; and for further use of the typology by Jerome, see Jay, *L'Exégèse de saint Jérôme*, 283.

[1] On this rendering, see Aberbach and Grossfeld, *Targum Onkelos*, 92–3; Grossfeld, *Targum Onqelos to Genesis*, 69–70. Cf. also Hayward, 'Inconsistencies', 36–7. According to Kamesar, *Jerome*, 151–3, Eusebius of Emesa may have combined a Targumic-like exposition of the phrase with LXX's reading, and Jerome may be disputing this exegetical mixture.

[2] See FTP and FTV of this verse: LXX's *apoluomai*, 'I am departing', and Aquila's *aperchomai*, 'I am going away', may imply death. See also Geiger, *Urschrift*, 457.

founded and so named.' Jewish tradition associates Eliezer with Damascus, as the note in PJ quoted earlier tells. PJ of Gen. 14: 14 notes how Abraham pursued the foreign kings who captured his brother and chose Eliezer to go with him. According to *Gen. Rab.* 42(43): 2 and *PRE* 27: 2, Eliezer alone accompanied Abraham to Damascus on the expedition to defeat the kings; cf. also *Gen. Rab.* 44: 9, which recalls Abraham's pursuit of the kings with Eliezer to Damascus. What none of these Jewish sources relate is the founding and naming of Damascus; and it is possible that Jerome has once more handed on a scrap of information from his Jewish sources, to the effect that Eliezer's successful raid with Abraham led him to found the famous city, named in the Bible for the first time in Gen. 14: 15. But the foundation of Damascus by Eliezer contradicts information given by Jerome in 10: 23, and his source in this present verse may not, indeed, be Jewish at all.[3]

verse 7   See comments on 11: 28 and 12: 4.

verses 10–11   For Jerome's treatment of the covenant (which he terms *sacramentum*, a 'solemn agreement'[4]) 'between the pieces', see *In Esa.* 6. 15: 3–9. He declines to discuss it here. The difference between LXX and the Hebrew lies in the vocalization of the verb *wysb*, which LXX have understood as *wayyēšeb* from root *yšb*, 'and he sat'. The present Hebrew text, which Jerome assumes, is vocalized *wayyaššēb*, from root *nšb* in *hiphʿil*, 'and he scared away'. Aquila's translation uses *aposobein*, 'scare away'; and such a meaning may also have been known to Philo, who in *QG* 3. 8 says that Abraham 'stopped and sat over' the birds, and interprets the verse allegorically to refer both to Abraham's sitting and his restraining wrongdoing and greed. He has a similar comment in *Quis Heres* 243–7. But Abraham's driving away the birds was known to Christians, as the Catena fragment G23 (Petit, i. p. 26) and Theodoret *QG* 67 show: according to the latter, the birds represent the Egyptians who held Israel in bondage.

Jewish sources often remark that this event symbolizes Israel's protection from trouble by Abraham's merit: thus PJ states that 'the Gentiles, who are likened to the unclean bird, came down to

---

[3] See Kamesar, *Jerome*, 153 n. 202, who does not, however, record the Jewish associations of Eliezer with Damascus.

[4] At 26: 17, *sacramentum* occurs with reference to baptism. But the word also forms part of Jerome's exegetical vocabulary: he uses it alongside *mystery*, sometimes with a meaning almost identical to type. It seems to stress the sacral aspect of a mystery: see Jay, *L'Exégèse de saint Jérôme*, 269–70.

plunder Israel's possessions; but the merit of Abraham was protecting them'; cf. *Gen. Rab.* 44: 16 (R. Azaraiah). See also TN for a more complex presentation of the same idea, and Ngl, FTP, and FTV, which speak of Abraham's merit protecting Israel from the depredations of the four world empires.[5]

verse 12 See commentary on 2: 21. VL, Ambrose (*Ps.* 8. 1. 1) and Augustine (*QG* 30) use *pavor*, 'terror', to describe Abraham's state, to which *LAB* 23: 6 adds 'sleep'.

verse 16 The apparent contradiction between this verse and Exod. 13: 18 in the LXX was one of the questions Jerome addressed in his *Ep.* 36. 10–13 to Pope Damasus, to which he refers his readers. There, after careful computation of the biblical genealogies, he notes Aquila's rendering of Exod. 13: 18, that Israel came up from Egypt 'armed', explaining how the Hebrew so rendered is *ḥmšym*. This word, says Jerome, was also taken by the synagogue of his day to mean 'armed' (*Ep.* 36. 13); but he remarks how the sense of 'five' or 'fifth' may also be derived from it if its root is taken as the numeral *ḥmš*, 'five'. In this, his interpretation resembles *Mekh. de R. Ishmael Beshallaḥ* 1: 70–85. Jerome follows Aquila and TO in his rendering of Exod. 13: 18.

CHAPTER 16

verse 2 Jerome does not here quote LXX, which reads 'that *you* may produce children through her' (so also VL), but comes close to translating the Hebrew.[1] This he quotes, understanding the form *'bnh* as *niphʿal* of root *bnh*, 'to build' in the same manner as the MT, TO, PJ, TN, *Gen. Rab.* 45: 2; 71: 7. Scripture uses this word to describe the raising up of children: see, most clearly, 2 Sam. 7: 11–12. In post-biblical tradition, we find the word used in the same sense: TN of Lev. 20: 17 speaks of God having given to the first human beings a favour to marry within forbidden degrees so that the world might be built up.[2] See Jerome's comments above on 11: 29, and below on 19: 30.

---

[5] See further Geiger, *Urschrift*, 457–8; Rahmer, *Die hebräischen Traditionen*, 29; le Déaut, *Targum du Pentateuque*, i. 171; id. *La Nuit pascale*, 147–8.

[1] For the readings of VL, see Fischer, p. 180; and for LXX's translation, see Harl, *Bible d'Alexandrie*, i. 164.

[2] The Hebrew of this verse says: 'If a man takes his sister . . . and sees her

In quoting Exod. 1: 20–1, he seems to agree with the Jewish tradition that God had rewarded with progeny the midwives Shiphrah and Puah, who delivered Israelite babies in Egypt under Pharaoh's oppression. These were royal and priestly offspring, according to PJ, TN, FTV of this verse, and *b. Soṭ* 11b, *Sifre Num.* 78, *Exod. Rab.* 1: 17, *Tanḥ. Wayyaqhel* 4. Yet what he quotes from Exodus does not agree with the Hebrew text, which reads: 'And God did good to the midwives, and the people multiplied and became very mighty. And because the midwives feared God, He made houses for them'. LXX, however, with FTP and FTV translated the final words as 'they made houses for themselves'. In Vg Jerome translated the last clause as 'and He built houses for them', even though the verb used in Hebrew is 'made'; he may have been influenced by a text like Gen. 33: 17, where 'build' and 'make' appear as equivalents. Thus in the Hebrew Jacob is said to have 'built a house for himself, and he made booths for his cattle'. LXX rendered both verbs here as 'made'.

verse 7 The woman concerned is Hagar, Sarai's handmaid, who had been evicted from Abraham's household.

verse 11 Jerome's translation of this verse corresponds with neither the Hebrew nor LXX, which have: 'And you shall call his name Ishmael, because the Lord has heard your humiliation.' The speaker of these words is an angel: Jerome may have altered the text to present it as a description of what happened in the naming of Ishmael. For this meaning of the name, compare also Aquila; Philo, *De Mut. Nom.* 202, *De Fuga* 208; *Lib. Heb. Nom.* (p. 67); *PRE* 30: 5; 32: 1. The Hebrew *yišmā'ē'l* probably means 'May God hear', or, 'God shall hear'; but one does not listen to suffering or humiliation, hence TO translates 'the Lord has accepted your prayer'.

verse 12 'Boorish', *rusticus*, is used also by VL. Jerome attempts to reproduce the sound of the Hebrew *pere'* in Vg with *ferus*, 'wild, savage', following Aquila's translation as *agrios*, 'wild', especially used of wild animals. He refers elsewhere to the descendants of

nakedness, it is a shameful thing [*ḥesed*], and they shall be cut off . . .'. TN tells of God's allowing, by a special favour (*ḥesed* in Hebrew, *ḥisda'* in Aramaic), the world to be built up by these incestuous unions, which, since the giving of the Law, are a disgrace (also *ḥesed* in Hebrew, *ḥisda'* in Aramaic). See also *Sifra Qedoshim* Pereq 11: 11; *b. Sanh.* 58b; *jer. Yeb.* 11: 11, *PRE* 21: 1; *Midrash Pss.* 89: 3 on the verse 'the world shall be built up through *ḥesed*'; and Grossfeld, *The Targum Onqelos to Leviticus*, 43.

Ishmael as Saracens, and describes some of their customs and beliefs. Their lack of fixed dwellings, and their raids on settled peoples, often feature in these descriptions: see, for example, 25: 13–18; *In Esa.* 5. 21: 13–17, 17. 60: 6–7; *In Hier.* 1. 21, 2. 84; *In Hiez.* 8. 25: 1–7; *In Gal.* 2. 4: 25–6; *Eps.* 123. 13, 129. 4. He says they may be found in the region of Jerusalem, and some of his information tallies quite remarkably with details of Ishmael's descendants found in PJ and other Targums.[3]

CHAPTER 17

verses 4–5 LXX have: 'And God spoke to him saying, Even I, behold, my covenant is with you . . .'. LXX almost invariably translated Hebrew *b^erit* as *diathēkē*, which may indeed mean 'covenant', but whose primary sense is 'will, testament'.[1] Jerome gives its meaning as either *foedus*, 'treaty', which he uses in Vg of this verse; or *pactum*, 'covenant'. A Jewish tradition that God took one letter *he*, ה, from His own Name *YHWH* and added it to the name of Abram may be found in *Midrash Aggadah* (ed. S. Buber, Vienna, 1894) ii. 79; but a quite different statement is found in the name of R. Joshua b. Qorha in *Gen. Rab.* 47: 1, that God took the letter *yodh* from the name of Sarai (Hebrew *śry*) and divided it: half was given to Abraham, the other half to Sarah. *Yodh* represents the number ten, and letter *he* represents five, half that number. Thus *'brm* became *'brhm*, and *śry* became *śrh*. Rahmer thinks that the tradition which Jerome records is inaccurate; but he was unaware of the passage in *Midrash Aggadah*, which had not then been published.[2]

---

[3] See also *Gen. Rab.* 45: 9, and the picture of Ishmael and his descendants as thieves, who would not accept the Torah because it contained the command not to steal: *Sifre Deut.* 343; PJ of Deut. 33: 2; *Mekh. de R. Ishmael Baḥodesh* 5: 74–8; *Pes. Rab.* 21. On agreements between Jerome and PJ in descriptions of the Saracens, see C. T. R. Hayward, 'Targum Pseudo-Jonathan and Anti-Islamic Polemic', *JSS* 34 (1989), 77–93.

[1] For discussion of *b^erit* and detailed bibliography, see M. Weinfeld, s.v. '*berīth*', in *TDOT* ii. 253–79.

[2] See Rahmer, *Die hebräischen Traditionen*, 28, and Kamesar, *Jerome*, 112 n. 53. The latter also ('Thesis', 108) notes and contrasts Philo's interpretation of the change of Abram's name from 'uplifted father' to Abraham, 'elect father of sound'; *De Cher.* 7; *De Mut. Nom.* 66–76; *De Gig.* 62–4; *De Abr.* 82; *QG* 3. 43; and Ambrose, *De Abr.* 1. 27.

Jerome understands Abram here and in *Lib. Heb. Nom.* (p. 61)
as 'high father', from *'āb* 'father' and *rām* 'high', a view not so far
removed from that of Philo.[3] He then follows biblical etymology in
explaining the addition of the extra letter, and noting that 'nations'
is not actually expressed in the new form of the name. But the new
name Abraham ends in the consonants *h* and *m*, which suggest to
Jerome the word *hᵃmōn*, 'multitude', itself part of the biblical
explanation of the name.[4] The Hebrew and LXX state clearly that
Abraham is thus constituted father of a multitude of peoples. See
also *In Esa.* 17. 62: 4. In this comment, therefore, he modifies the
interpretation of Abraham's name given previously in *Lib. Heb.
Nom.* (pp. 61, 134, 150, 151, 154, 155, 156, 161) as 'father seeing
the people' and 'father seeing the multitude'.

His comments about the letter *he* are not, perhaps, crystal clear.
The LXX had expressed the change of name as from *Abram* to
Abraam, necessarily so, since the Greek alphabet has no letter H as
such. Rather than pointing this out, Jerome records that letter *he*
(H) may be written in Hebrew, but pronounced as A. This can,
indeed, be the case; for this letter, although standing for the consonant H, may be used conventionally to represent the vowel long
A (especially at the end of a word), or even the vowel E. And his
final remark would seem to mean that the letter *'aleph*, the first
letter of the Hebrew alphabet, may be used conventionally and
occasionally to indicate the presence of vowel E. In the beginning of
his *Lib. Heb. Nom.* (p. 60), he sets out rather more clearly the
problems arising from transliteration of Hebrew words which begin with guttural letters *'aleph, he, ḥeth*, and *'ayin*. These letters do
not exist in the Latin alphabet, and especially at the beginnings of
words carry vowels, which are the sounds actually heard and
reproduced. But they do not represent vowels: they may carry
different vowel sounds both in initial and medial positions in
words. Hence problems of transliteration into Greek and Latin
would be inevitable.

verse 15 LXX have: 'And God said to Abraam, As for Sara your
wife, her name shall not be called Sara, but Sarra shall be her
name.' Jerome's translation seems to follow the Hebrew: he re-
serves quotation of LXX for later in his comment. Sarai became
Sarah, but LXX, once more faced with the fact that the Greek

---

[3] See Philo's works quoted in n. 2 above. For modern discussions of the names
and bibliography, see R. E. Clements, s.v. *''abhrāhām'* in *TDOT* i. 52–8.

[4] See Kamesar, *Jerome*, 117.

alphabet has no letter H, represented the changed name as *SARRA*. Their procedure was not as arbitrary as it may seem, since in Greek the letter R is often aspirated as RH, especially at the beginnings of words. But Jerome was concerned about the exegesis of this changed name on the basis of R representing one hundred in Greek: it was used to suggest that Sarah now achieves a higher level of virtue. See Ambrose, *De Abr.* 2. 85; Justin, *Dial.* 113; and Didymus the Blind, *Comm. in Gen.* 114. 3–6. He insists that it is only proper that a Hebrew change of name should have a Hebrew explanation. He gives this, noting first, and quite correctly, the change of consonants from the old to the new name: in his comments on the preceding section he has already explained how Hebrew *he* may represent vowel A.

Regarding the sense of the names, however, Jerome has affinity with Philo, who naturally followed LXX in representing the change from Sara to Sarra. Philo gives to Sara (Hebrew Sarai) the sense of 'my ruler' (see also *Lib. Heb. Nom.*, p. 71); and to Sarra (Hebrew Sarah) 'ruler' absolutely: see *De Cher.* 5, 7, 41; *De Mut. Nom.* 77; *QG* 3. 53; *De Abr.* 99; *De Congr.* 2. It seems odd that Jerome should agree with these explanations, based on the LXX which he has just criticized, until we note that they correspond in some degree with Rabbinic interpretations very likely current in his own day. Thus in *b. Ber.* 13a we are told: 'At the beginning she was only Sarai, lady of a people; but at the end she was lady of the whole world.'[5] Kamesar suggests that he may have used such a Rabbinic source. He notes Jerome's strong objection to the LXX account of the name change, because it is misleading philologically and leaves the new name without explanation, a point taken up by Augustine, *De Civ. Dei* 16. 28. Jerome is concerned to explain why she is 'ruler absolutely': and this the LXX form of her name cannot comprehend.[6]

verse 16 Jerome quotes part of this verse, but then reverts to verse 15, which LXX rendered as: 'And God said to Abraam, As for Sara your wife, her name shall not be called Sara, but Sarra shall be her name.' He then gives the original Hebrew and repeats part of his comment already made on that verse. Abraham himself is forbidden to address his wife any longer as Sara: he must use her new name, which Jerome takes to mean 'ruler' of all the nations.

[5] Quoted by Rahmer, *Die hebräischen Traditionen*, 27. See also *t. Ber.* 1, *Sekhel Tov* on Gen. 17: 16, and *Gen. Rab.* 47: 2.
[6] See Kamesar, 'Thesis', 105–9.

What Jerome does not explicitly discuss is the Hebrew of this verse, which refers all the promises to Sarah: 'And I shall bless *her*, and shall also give to you from *her* a son; and I shall bless *her*, and *she* shall become nations; kings of peoples shall come forth from *her*.' His failure to tell of this is strange, given that it could only give powerful support to the comment he has just made about the meaning of Sarah's *sara*, and that it constitutes further evidence that LXX have not properly appreciated the significance of that name.[7]

Indeed, LXX's translation is ambiguous: 'And I shall bless *her* and give to you a son from *her*; and I shall bless *her* [variant: *him*], and he [or: *she*] shall become nations, and kings of nations shall come forth from *him*.' There are even MSS of the version which render the Hebrew straightforwardly:[8] Philo seems to have been aware of both LXX readings, following the first for his *QG* 3. 54, and the second for his comments in *De Mut. Nom.* 148–51. Since this verse was taken by Christians as prophesying the Church, its interpretation was of some moment for them. If the promises are taken as referring to Sarah herself, then she may be regarded as a type of Mother Church, foreshadowing Mary the Mother of Christ; if, however, they are referred to her son Isaac, then the verse speaks of that 'seed of Abraham' (Gal. 3: 16; Rom. 4: 13) which is typical of Christ Himself. Jerome's comments seem to favour the first interpretation: but see also Theodoret, *Qu. in 1 Reg.* 3; Origen, *Hom. 1 Reg.* 1. 18.

Some etymologists had evidently derived her first name from Hebrew *ṣāraʿat*, 'leprosy', and Jerome refutes this. Although in Latin the words Sarah and *ṣāraʿat* may sound similar, the resulting bogus etymology is hardly valid for explanation of Hebrew names.[9]

---

[7] Kamesar, *Jerome*, 115–16, argues on the basis of a variant in de Lagarde's apparatus of *QHG* that Jerome may in fact have read 'kings of peoples shall come forth from *her*', rather than 'from *him*', as all other witnesses read. Sarah will thus be 'ruler' absolutely as in the Hebrew of verse 16, and as in those MSS of LXX of this verse which read likewise: 'and I shall bless her, and she shall become nations, and kings of nations shall come forth from her': see Wevers, p. 180. Although Jerome makes no explicit reference to any differences between LXX and Hebrew on this point, the fact that he so much stresses the Hebrew text throughout this discussion gives force to Kamesar's argument.

[8] See further Harl, *Bible d'Alexandrie*, i. 171, citing the sources which follow.

[9] E. Burstein ('La Compétence de Jérôme en hébreu: Explication de certaines erreurs', *REA* 21 (1975), 5–6), following the text of *QHG* presented in CCSL 72, pp. 21–2, believes that Jerome reproduced the Hebrew word for 'leprosy' incorrectly as *sʿrt* rather than *srʿt*. The text given in PL, however, has Jerome spell the word

verse 17 The question whether Isaac was named because of Abraham's or Sarah's laughter is addressed again in *In Gal.* 2. *MHG* on this verse links Isaac's name to the laughter of both Abraham and Sarah, suggesting that there may have been debate in Jewish circles on the question raised by Jerome. Certainly Josephus, *Ant.* 1. 198, 213, says that he was named because Sarah had laughed: Jerome rejects this outright, possibly because he knew the tradition still extant in Rashi's commentary on this verse that Sarah's laugh was in fact a derisive sneer. Sarah's laughter is related in Gen. 18: 12. For the same four men whose names were given before birth, see *jer. Ber.* 1: 6; Isaac is named in this verse, Ishmael in Gen. 16: 11; Solomon in 1 Chron. 22: 9; and Josiah in 1 Kgs. 13: 2. See also *Mekh. de R. Ishmael Pisḥa* 16: 82–91 and *Sekhel Ṭov* on Gen. 16: 11 for the three whose names were given by God, to whom Ishmael among the Gentiles may be added. Similar are *Gen. Rab.* 45: 8 and *PRE* 32: 1, but in the latter source the number of persons has increased to six.

CHAPTER 18

verse 6 For the word translated by LXX as 'measures', the Hebrew has *s⁽ᵉ⁾īm*: Aquila and Symmachus rendered it as *sata*, the word used in Matt. 13: 33 in the parable of the leaven. The 'mystery' (see above, 14: 18) to which Jerome refers is the doctrine of the Trinity, as he explains in his *Comm. in Matt.* on this verse. His understanding of the Hebrew word as *saton* is presumably mediated either through Aquila and Symmachus, or through Josephus, *Ant.* 9. 71, 85–6, who states that this measure equals one and a half Italian *modii*. Jerome is thus stating that this *Hebrew* word speaks of the 'mystery' of the Trinity, since it prefigures the three 'measures' which feature in Christ's own teaching. In this comment, he undermines any claim that LXX alone holds 'mysteries'; it is the Hebrew itself which contains these things. LXX state that the flour is to be made into cakes, *egkruphias*, a word which derives from the verb *kruptō*, 'hide': it was therefore possible to apply the cakes to some 'hidden thing' or mystery. Philo had done

correctly, and records no variant MS readings: in view of the numerous mistakes in Greek and Hebrew orthography to be found in the CCSL edition of *QHG*, we may suggest that Burstein may be mistaken in this matter.

that very thing, the 'mysteries' being God Himself and His two
'powers' (*QG* 4. 8, where the matter is discussed at length; *De Sac.*
59–60). So this interpretation was ripe for exploitation by Clement
of Alexandria, *Stromateis* 5. 80. 3; Origen, *Hom. in Gen.* 4. 1,
Hom. in Lev. 13. 3; and others.[1] Jerome, however, uncovers the
mystery of the Trinity by quite different means.

verse 10   The Hebrew has: 'I shall surely return to you at about the
time of life', an obscure expression which occurs again in verse 14;
cf. 2. Kgs. 4: 16. Jerome's explanation of it, which he includes in Vg
here and in the other two verses quoted, does not correspond
precisely to other ancient versions; but see TO, 'as at this time when
you are alive', and *Sekhel Ṭov* on this verse, 'at about this time next
year, when all of you are alive and enduring'. Perhaps Jerome has
adapted this Jewish explanation, which is found also in PJ and
FTV. He notes that the angel is using human terminology to address human beings, employing a Greek technical term to describe
the manner of speech.[2]

verse 12   Symmachus seems to have translated Hebrew *bᵉlōtī*, 'I
have become worn out,' euphemistically in the manner of TO, PJ,
TN, FTV, Pesh, and Vg which put 'I have become old'. Aquila had
no such qualms, and translated quite literally. LXX seem to have
taken the Hebrew as *biltī*, and the following *ᶜednāh* as *ᶜadēnāh* for
ᶜad hēnāh, 'up until now'.[3] On the sense of *ᶜednāh*, 'pleasure', see the
comments on *ᶜeden* 2: 8 and 2: 15, and the discussion in *Gen. Rab.*
48: 17, where one of the five meanings there listed is 'youth',
preferred by Symmachus, TO, TN, FTV, and Pesh. Rab Ḥisda in *b.*
BM 87a records that Sarah's flesh became young again when she
conceived.[4] Jerome's rendering of the word as 'pleasure' here and in
Vg is reminiscent of Aquila's 'luxury'.

[1] See also Ambrose, *De Abr.* 1. 37; Rufinus, *In Gen.* 4. 1; *In Lev.* 13. 3; Harl,
Bible d'Alexandrie, i. 174, and W. T. Miller, *Mysterious Encounters at Mamre and
Jabbok* (Brown Judaic Studies, 50; Chico, Calif., 1984), 66, 187.
[2] For discussion of *anthrōpopathōs*, see Jay, *L'Exégèse de saint Jérôme*, 162–3,
whose observations are confirmed by Jerome's use of the word in this verse.
[3] This verse is another of those traditionally said to have been altered in LXX for
King Ptolemy: see above, comments on 2: 2. Quite what constituted the change from
the Hebrew in LXX translation is difficult to determine, unless it is the matter
discussed here, a view which is commonly held today: see E. Tov, 'The Rabbinic
Tradition concerning the "Alterations" inserted into the Greek Pentateuch and their
Relation to the Original Text of the LXX', *JSJ* 15 (1984), 65–89, esp. 78–9.
[4] See Miller, *Mysterious Encounters*, 34.

verse 32 Abraham had used this expression in verse 30, asking God to spare the inhabitants of Sodom and Gomorrah if righteous persons were to be found in the towns; thus, says Jerome, like all competent orators, he begins his address with a *praefatio*, a formula of introduction supplied with respectful and solemn terms of address to gain the hearer's favourable response. The LXX translation of the words, like the Targums, may be designed to lessen the rather anthropomorphic expression put into Abraham's mouth.

CHAPTER 19

verses 14–15 The difficulty is inherent in Scripture, which speaks in 19: 8 of two daughters of Lot who have not known a man, then in 19: 14 of his *ḥᵃtānāyw*, sons-in-law, the *lqḥy* of his daughters. Two daughters are also reported in 19: 15. How many daughters were there? *Gen. Rab.* 49: 13 speaks of four, and four sons-in-law, which *Gen. Rab.* 50: 9 explains as two daughters already married (hence the *ḥᵃtānāyw* of 19: 14) and two betrothed, a separate group referred to in the expression 'the *lqḥy* of his daughters'. It was natural, then, to suppose that the two married daughters had stayed in Sodom, while the unmarried had left with their father: see also Rashi's comment on these verses. Although what 'some people think' superficially accords with this Haggadah, Jerome is really reporting something quite different: these people speak of married daughters and unmarried daughters, not daughters engaged to be married. In other words, 'some people' did not understand 'the *lqḥy* of his daughters' as a reference to betrothed persons, which is a vital part of the Midrash.

By contrast Josephus, *Ant.* 1. 202, carefully skates over these difficulties: he says that Lot took from Sodom his wife 'and his daughters, *duo de ēsan eti parthenoï*', which last may mean either 'and there were two of them, still virgins', or 'and two of them were still virgins'. That is to say, Josephus may give the impression that there were only two of them, but his language allows, and perhaps even invites the conclusion that other daughters existed who may not have been virgins, and by implication therefore remained in Sodom. That the married daughters remained in Sodom is a tra-

dition certainly found in later Midrashim, such as *MHG* on Gen.
19: 26 and *PRE* 25: 5.

Jerome may have taken his cue from Josephus, a suspicion
strengthened when it is noted that the latter appears to have understood the 'sons-in-law' as 'suitors', which is very close to Jerome's
description of them as *sponsos*, which in this setting, given what
Jerome is saying, must mean 'betrothed men'. While Josephus is
the most likely Hebrew source for Jerome's interpretation of
ḥᵃtānāyw, the LXX translation of it as 'his sons-in-law' proved
difficult. Kamesar has shown how Eusebius of Emesa appealed to
biblical idiom, and John Chrysostom to the customs of ancient
peoples, to show that the term 'sons-in-law' in this place refers to
men who are not yet married; but their concern is solely for the
LXX text.

In translating the 'Hebrew truth', however, Jerome vocalizes the
word *lqḥy* in a way approved by *Gen. Rab.* 50: 9, which, as we
have seen, includes other traditions which he has earlier discarded.
Rather than reading *lᵉqūḥē*, meaning 'the ones taken by, i.e. married
to' his daughters, both Jerome and the Midrash adopt the form
lōqᵉḥē, 'the ones about to take' his daughters in marriage: see also
Vg. Thus the *ḥᵃtānāyw* cannot yet be sons-in-law: they must be
engaged to the daughters, or suitors. It may be that this way of
reading *lqḥy* allowed Jerome to seek in this instance another meaning for the root *ḥtn*, which otherwise always refers to a relationship
determined by marriage.[1]

verse 21 The Hebrew *nāśā' pānīm* means, literally, 'lift up the
face', that is 'show respect for'. LXX translated the phrase with
thaumazō, 'wonder at', which in classical Greek has also the sense
of 'honour'.[2] For the interpretation of the Hebrew here as referring
to prayer, see *Sifre Num.* 42, *Num. Rab.* 11: 7, Vg, and the general
understanding of TO in this verse. But Symmachus presents a
textual problem. Lagarde's reading is reproduced here, and means
literally: 'in seeing, I was abashed at [later meaning: respected] your
countenance'. Salvesen reads the first word as *hora ei*, and comments on the development of meaning of the verb *dusōpeō* from

---

[1] On the meaning of *ḥtn* in biblical Hebrew, see E. Kutsch, s.v. '*ḥtn*', in *TDOT* v.
273–6. For Eusebius's and John Chrysostom's approaches to the LXX rendering of
the word as *gambros*, see Kamesar, *Jerome*, 168–9, who also correctly points out the
differences between *Gen. Rab.* 50: 9 and Jerome's interpretation; Rahmer, *Die
hebräischen Traditionen*, 30, overlooks their significance.

[2] See Harl, *Bible d'Alexandrie*, i. 182.

'put out of countenance' to 'win over, respect'. The sense of the
words given her reading of Symmachus would be 'Lo! Did I revere
your countenance?'[3]

verse 28 The Hebrew says that *qīṭōr* was going up like *qīṭōr* of a
kiln: Jerome translates the second occurrence of the word into
Greek (here reproduced) as 'a rising of vapour, an exhalation'. In
Vg, he renders the first occurrence as 'ashes', the second as 'smoke'.
The word is rare, being found twice in this verse and in Ps. 119: 83;
148: 8. Jerome's understanding is close to TO, which on both
occasions here took it as *tᵉnānā*, that is, 'smoke', 'vapour', 'reek-
ing'. More striking still is his retention of the Hebrew word *citor* in
transliteration: this is the procedure followed by PJ and TN, who
virtually reproduce the Hebrew with *qwṭr'* and *qyṭwr* respectively.
The only Talmud passage to deal with the word, *b. Menaḥoth* 26b,
seems to assume that everyone knows what *qyṭr* is, noting only that
it is sent up from a furnace only when fire has kindled most of the
fuel. Rashi repeats this comment, noting that such vapour is given
off in furnaces where stones are burnt into lime; so also *Sekhel Ṭov*
on this verse. It is most probable that Jerome is indebted to Jewish
understandings of the sort found in TO for his explanation of this
rare word.

verse 30 On Segor and Salisa, see comments on 14: 2–3, and
Philo, *QG* 4. 55, who says that Abraham did not think it safe to be
near cities which had been burned up; and *Sekhel Ṭov* on this verse.
According to *Gen. Rab.* 51: 8, Lot's two daughters thought that the
world had been completely destroyed, as in the Flood; see also
Aggadath Bere'shith and *MHG* on this verse, and Jerome, *Ep.* 22.
8.[4] But Philo exonerates only the younger, *De Ebr.* 165. Lot had no
such excuse, says Jerome, and thus flatly contradicts Origen,
Contra Celsum 4. 45, *Hom. in Gen.* 5. 3–4, *Comm. in Ep. ad Rom.*
4. 9. Origen defended both Lot and his daughters on the grounds
that they were partly to blame and partly excusable. Echoing the
Stoic notion that actions may be either morally good, bad, or
indifferent, he urges that the incest was morally indifferent, had
been undertaken in good faith to populate a world in which they
believed they were the only human beings left, and was not clearly

---

[3] See Salvesen, *Symmachus*, 235, 246, 252. She has followed the reading of the
majority of witnesses: see Wevers, p. 197, who himself follows Lagarde and reads
horasei.
[4] See Rahmer, *Die hebräischen Traditionen*, 30.

condemned by Scripture. Lot could be excused since he did not act out of lust or concupiscence, and was the victim of his daughters' cunning; but he might be blamed for his ability to be deceived, and his drunkenness. Eusebius of Emesa (Devreesse, p. 72) excused Lot on the grounds that he became drunk with fear. Irenaeus, *Adv. Haer.* 4. 48. 1, earlier had also stressed that Lot acted without lust, consent, or knowledge, and treats his two daughters as types of the two 'synagogues' of Jews and Christians.

verse 35 LXX have: 'So they made their father drink wine on that night; and the younger went in and slept with her father on that night. And he did not know when she lay down, or when (she) rose up.'[5] The Hebrew has: 'And on that night they made their father drink wine. And the first-born went and slept with her father; and he did not know when she lay down nor when she rose up.' In the MT, a dot is written above the letter *waw* of *wbqmh*, 'nor when she rose up'. Midrashically, this is to signify that while Lot did not know when she slept with him, he none the less knew when she rose up to go from him: so *Gen. Rab.* 51: 8; *Sifre Num.* 9–10; *b. Nazir* 23a; *ARNa* 34; and PJ of this verse. There are other examples of such dotted words in the Hebrew Bible, the work of scribes who may, as in cases such as this one, have preceded the Masoretes.[6] The Hebrew tradition which Jerome expounds in this and the preceding verse accords with the observable facts of everyday life, and is thus to be preferred: Lot must have known what was happening, and attempts to exempt him from blame are both futile and senseless.

verses 36–8 Jerome has followed the Hebrew, omitting LXX's explanation of Moab as 'out of my father'; but this is essentially how he himself interprets the name here, as if it were *mēʾāb*, 'from the father': see also *Lib. Heb. Nom.* (pp. 69, 76). It bears clear hints of the incestuous union spoken of in the preceding verses: the fact that the mother names her son in this way is scandalous, according to *Gen. Rab.* 51: 11. The younger daughter is modest in her choice

[5] There is also ambiguity in LXX, which may be reflected in the textual tradition of *QHG*: 'and he did not know when she slept (with him), nor when he rose up from her.' See Wevers, p. 200.

[6] For Rabbinic lists of such words and phrases, see Rahmer, *Die hebräischen Traditionen*, 30–1. There are ten instances of dotted words and phrases in the Pentateuch, according to the list in *ARNa* 34. The verses which *ARN* lists for Genesis are conveniently translated by Bowker, *The Targums*, 321.

of name: according to the Hebrew, she called him *ben ʿAmmi*. Here, as Jerome points out, we do not have an etymology, since the name Ammon is partly derived from *ʿam*, 'people', and the name Ammon itself partly contributes to its own meaning. See TO, where she calls him Bar-Ammi, 'son of my kin', a description of the lad rather than a proper name.[7] *Lib. Heb. Nom.* gives the meaning as 'son of my people or people of sorrow' (pp. 61, 78, 90); Jerome presumably has discarded the latter interpretation in *QHG*.

CHAPTER 20

verse 12 See comments on 11: 29. Jerome translated the Hebrew of this verse in Vg as he does here: it is a rendering very close to Theodotion's. The emphasis is only slightly different from what is said in 11: 29. But see PJ of this verse, which makes Sarah the daughter of Abraham's uncle, i.e. his cousin. Jerome was well aware that the words sister and brother in Hebrew may have the broader meanings of cousin, or even extended family; but he makes no use of such an excuse for Abraham in this verse. See *Adv. Helvidium* 1–12. For the difference between the laws of marriage before and after the Flood, and before the giving of the Torah, see Augustine, *De Civ. Dei* 15. 16.

CHAPTER 21

verse 9 Jerome notes the absence of words in the Hebrew, which none the less are retained in some MSS of Vg. The Jewish exegesis which he records is strikingly similar to the interpretation of *Gen. Rab.* 53: 11, where R. Ishmael understands the word *mᵉṣaḥēq*, 'playing', in the bad sense of idol worship, and uses the same text as Jerome (Exod. 32: 6) to prove his point. On the other hand, R. Simeon bar Yohai refers it to Ishmael's jesting and taunting of Isaac about the inheritance, such that Sarah was determined to evict Hagar and Ishmael, the proof for which is found in the words 'Cast out this handmaid . . .' (Gen. 21: 10). The Midrash explains that Ishmael was building altars and offering up 'pretend' sacri-

---

[7] See Aberbach and Grossfeld, *Targum Onkelos*, 118. TN has the same reading.

fices.[1] Jerome alludes to this tradition again at *In Gal.* 2 on Gal. 4: 29–30.[2] His use of Jewish tradition to explain the word 'playing' is quite different from Diodore's claim (Petit, ii. 195–6, 197) that the Hebrew word can be explained by homonymy, 'play' being used to express 'fight' or 'persecution' on the basis of LXX of 2 Reigns 2: 14. Diodore's case can only be based on LXX, since the Hebrew root used in 2 Sam. 2: 14 is *śḥq*, not *ṣḥq* as in Gen. 21: 9.

As regards the rights of the first-born, an extended paraphrase of Gen. 22: 1 in PJ has Ishmael insist that he was destined to be Abraham's heir since he was the eldest son of his father. Other Jewish texts refer this verse to Ishmael's idolatry: so PJ, TN, FTV, and FTP; *t. Soṭ.* 6: 6–11; some witnesses to *Sifre Deut.* 31; *Exod. Rab.* 1: 1; *Tanḥ. Toledot* 5; *Shemoth* 1, 14; and the *MHG* on this verse. The late tradition that Ishmael was trying to kill Isaac, found in *PRE* 30: 1, *Tanḥ. B. Shemoth* 24, does not feature in Jerome's report.

verse 14 For the age of Ishmael at Isaac's birth, see Gen. 16: 16; 17: 25; 21: 5. Rahmer's discussion of Jewish opinions on Ishmael's age clearly sets out the evidence of Talmud and Midrash, which indeed bears some close resemblances to Jerome's remarks.[3] He states first the opinion that Ishmael was banished in the fifth year of Isaac's weaning. Ishmael would then have been 18, and this is the view which Jerome approves: see also *Ep.* 36. 10. It effectively corresponds with the view of *Yalquṭ Shim'oni* and *Sekhel Ṭov* on this verse, and with some witnesses of *PRE* 30: 2, that he was 17 (*Yalquṭ* and *Sekhel Ṭov*) or 18 (*PRE*), the former source being understood to mean that he had completed his seventeenth year. It is not in tune with Diodore's (or Eusebius of Emesa's?) view that Ishmael was 15 years old (Petit, ii. 196–7).

If Ishmael had been expelled in the twelfth year of Isaac's weaning, it would mean that Ishmael would be 25 years old, and would approximate to the view of *Gen. Rab.* 53: 13. There, however, his age is given as 27; the Midrash assumes that Isaac's weaning means that he has reached the age of bar mitzvah, i.e. 13, to which we add

[1] See Rahmer, *Die hebräischen Traditionen*, 31–2, who also comments on the remarkable parallels between Jerome and the Midrash.
[2] See R. le Déaut, 'Traditions targumiques dans le Corpus paulinien? (Hebr 11, 4 et 12, 24; Gal 4, 29–30; II Cor 3, 16)', *Biblica*, 42 (1961), 37–43.
[3] See Rahmer, *Die hebräischen Traditionen*, 32–3.

Ishmael's age at Isaac's birth, to yield the sense that Ishmael was in his twenty-seventh year at his expulsion. These are not the only computations: for example, some witnesses of *PRE* 30: 2 give Ishmael's age as 24.[4]

Given all this, it is evident that Ishmael was a grown child. Thus the Hebrew text, which reads literally: 'and he took bread and a skin of water and gave them to Hagar and placed them on her shoulder and the boy, and he sent them away', cannot mean that Abraham put Ishmael on Hagar's neck or shoulder: this point is made by *Gen. Rab.* 53: 13. Jerome understands 'the boy' as object of the verb 'he gave', taking the latter in the sense of 'he entrusted': he translates similarly in Vg, 'he entrusted (*tradidit*) him to her'. This is also the interpretation of Ibn Ezra, Naḥmanides, and Augustine, *QG* 53. Although Diodore (or Eusebius?) alludes to this reasoning, he prefers the suggestion that the conditions of those days, in which people married at the age of 40 or 50 years, conspired to ensure that 15-year-old people were still properly children (Petit, ii. 197).

verses 15–17   The information which LXX fail to supply allows Jerome to point to the superiority of the Hebrew. He comes close to suggesting that the LXX version makes little sense, since it is Hagar's tears which serve to recall to God the promise He had made in Gen. 17: 20. The vicarious element, much to the fore in his comment, perhaps betrays a Christian understanding of the Hebrew text as well as concern for the latter's superiority. That LXX posed problems for Christian interpreters is evident from the lengths to which some of them went to try to justify the version: see, for example, Augustine, *QG* 54.

verse 18   LXX have: 'Rise up and take the child, and hold him in your hand.' See comments on 21: 14, above.

verse 22   The Hebrew has: 'Then said Abimelech and Phicol, the captain of his army'. LXX have introduced Ochozath, Hebrew Ahuzzath, from 26: 26, where he is apparently listed along with the other two men. The word translated 'groomsman', *numphagōgos*, is uncommon, and means either one who leads the bride from her house to the groom's, or one who acts as matchmaker for another person. See further on 26: 26.

---

[4] As Rahmer, ibid. 33, notes, the age of weaning in the narrow sense of getting a child to eat solid rather than liquid food is given in *b. Giṭṭ.* 75b as either eighteen months or two years (so also *b. Ket.* 60b).

verses 30–1 LXX state that Abraham said these words. The explanation of Beer-Sheba notes the word-play which is possible with the unvocalized Hebrew word *šbʿ*. First, it may be articulated as *šebaʿ*, 'seven', which has obvious reference to the seven sheep. Second, it may be vocalized as *šᵉbūʿā*, 'oath', an allusion to the pact sworn between Abraham and Abimelech. See also PJ of this verse: 'Therefore he called that well The Well of the Seven Young Lambs because there the two of them swore an oath.' The name Beer-Sheba is found earlier in this chapter at verse 14, and Jerome explains it by means of the 'principle of anticipation', on which see above, 14: 7. He gives two other examples of this: Bethel, formerly Luz, received its name in Gen. 28: 19, but was earlier named as such at Gen. 12: 8; 13: 3; while Gilgal, formerly Gibeath Ha-ʿaraloth (Josh. 5: 3) received its name in Josh. 5: 9, but was so called earlier, in Josh. 4: 19–20.

Isaac's birth is recorded in Gen. 21: 2–3, and follows immediately an account of Abraham's stay in Gerar. The present chapter also ends (21: 34) with references to Abraham in the land of the Philistines. Jerome places Gerar twenty-five miles south of Eleutheropolis, on the very southern edge of Palestine.[5] Beer-Sheba, in fact, traditionally marks the southern boundary of the land of Israel, and Jerome notes its existence in his day. As he will explain in his comment on 22: 3–4, this area is three days' journey from Jerusalem, as he may have known from personal experience.[6] There is no scriptural evidence to suppose that Abraham had changed his place of residence; the journey which he undertook to go to Mount Moriah lasted three days (22: 3–4); and the location of Beer-Sheba is known: hence we know also that Isaac's birthplace was not the oak of Mamre. See further on 22: 3–4. Palaestina Salutaris, also known as Palaestina Tertia, is recorded in AD 429 as one of three provinces into which Roman Palestine was divided: it comprised of the Negeb and southern Transjordan.[7] Jerome knew of it before this time, and a law of AD 396 referring to a *praesides* of Hygia Palaestina, that is, Palaestina Salutaris, may be the earliest reference to it.[8]

---

[5] See *Lib. Loc.* 945.
[6] For Jerome's journeys in the land of Israel during 385–6, see Kelly, *Jerome*, 117–20.
[7] See M. Avi-Yonah, *The Jews of Palestine* (Oxford, 1976), 228.
[8] See the note in PL 23: 1019.

CHAPTER 22

verse 2 The versions and ancient interpreters discovered in the word Moriah, which appears at first merely to be the name of a place, a remarkable range of meanings. LXX seem to have derived it from root *rwm*, 'to be high'; Aquila may have related it to *'ōr*, 'light'; and Symmachus takes it from root *r'h*, 'to see'. In Vg, Jerome follows Symmachus, and translates 'the land of vision'. The identification of Moriah with the Temple Mount in Jerusalem is as old as 2 Chron. 3: 1, as Jerome notes:[1] see also Josephus, *Ant.* 1. 226; TO and PJ, 'the land of worship'; Ngl, 'Moriah, where the House of the Sanctuary is to be built'; *jer. Ber.* 4: 5; *Gen. Rab.* 55: 7; *Song Rab.* 4: 11; *Tanḥ. Wayyera'* 45; *Pes. Rabb.* 40. These sources ultimately associate Moriah with root *yārē'*, 'to fear, worship'. Other sources note that *mōr*, 'myrrh', was a prime ingredient of the incense and oil used in the Temple service.[2]

Jerome seems to stress the sense of 'enlightening', linking Moriah with *'ōr* and *'ōrāh*, 'light': the Torah is a light (Ps. 119: 105), and the usual translation of Torah in the Aramaic Targums is *'wryyt'*, 'illumination'. Hebrew has also the word *hōrā'āh*, meaning 'legal decision, instruction'. Hence from this mount Law and teaching go forth: see also Isa. 2: 3, and Jerome's comment on that verse in *In Esa.* 1. 2: 3. He refers to the *d*ᵉ*bīr*, the Holy of Holies in Solomon's Temple (1 Kgs. 6: 5, 16, etc.), perceiving in that word the root *dbr*, 'speak': hence his comment about the oracle. It was in this room that the Ark (*'rwn*) of the Covenant was kept, with the tables of the Law. Origen explains the meaning of it in *Comm. in Joh.* 1. 23; but it should be noted that, unlike Jerome, he enumerates its contents as the Ark, the tablets, and the two cherubim. Jerome's words are more in line with Jewish tradition, especially the Aramaic Targum, which speaks of God's oracular Word as a *Dibbur* spoken from between the cherubim (PJ and TN of Num. 7: 89), and of the Holy

---

[1] Jerome may have quoted this verse from memory: it actually reads: 'Then Solomon began to build the house of the Lord on Mount Moriah ... on the threshing-floor of Ornan the Jebusite. He began to build in the second month of the fourth year of his reign.' See also Eusebius of Emesa, Devreesse, p. 73.

[2] See Aberbach and Grossfeld, *Targum Onkelos*, 128–9, citing *b. Keritoth* 6a; and Rashi. While it is possible that some of these interpretations may presuppose a Hebrew text which reads *hmwr'h*, as Salvesen, *Symmachus*, 44, suggests, this is not a necessary pre-condition for understanding the variety of exegesis before us.

Ghost as 'the Spirit of the Sanctuary' (Fragment Targum, Nürnberg MS, Gen. 37: 33).[3]

All these shades of meaning cluster around the one word Moriah.[4] We should also note that the expression Holy Spirit was sometimes used by Jews to express the Presence of God in the Temple at Jerusalem.[5] Most of them feature in *Gen. Rab.* 55: 7 explaining Moriah. For R. Hiyya Rabbah, it is the place whence 'teaching', *hwryyh*, goes forth for the world; for R. Yannai, the place whence 'fear', *yr'h*, goes forth. Both Rabbis then discuss the Ark, kept in the *d*ᵉ*bir*: one says that from it 'light' goes forth, the other, that it is the place whence 'fear' goes forth. They then turn to discuss the *d*ᵉ*bir* itself: for R. Hiyyah, it is the place whence the *Dibbur*, Oracle, goes forth; for R. Yannai, it is the place whence the Word, *Dabar*, goes forth. R. Joshua ben Levi says that it is from this place that the Lord will pass a decision (*mwrh*) on the nations of the world and bring them down (*wmwrydm*) to Gehenna; R. Simeon bar Yohai that it is a proper *r'wy* place corresponding to the Temple; and R. Judan b. Palyya that there Abraham will have a vision, *mr'h*. R. Pinhas sees it as the place of the dominion *mrwt* of the world, and the Rabbis as the place where the incense will be offered, the proof of which is Song 4: 6, with its reference to myrrh.

verses 3–4 Jerome has earlier established that Isaac was born in Gerar: see 21: 30–1. Here he seems to disagree with Josephus and those who followed him in placing Isaac's birth, and Abraham's residence, at the oak of Mamre in Hebron: see *Ant.* 1. 186. Jerome had himself journeyed from Hebron to Jerusalem (*Ep.* 108. 10–12), and personal experience probably led him to punctuate as he does: 'and he came to the place . . . on the third day'. The Hebrew, however, and LXX as punctuated by Rahlfs, take 'on the third day' with the following words, 'then Abraham lifted up his eyes'. This difference in punctuation was significant for Christian interpreters, in that Isaac's arrival at the appointed place 'on the third day' might

---

[3] See M. McNamara, *The New Testament and the Palestinian Targum to the Pentateuch* (Rome, 1966), 182–8; and P. Schäfer, 'Die Termini "Heilger Geist" und "Geist der Prophetie" in den Targumim und das Verhältnis der Targumim zu einander', *VT* 20 (1970), 307.

[4] See also Rahmer, *Die hebräischen Traditionen*, 34–5. Kamesar, *Jerome*, 188–9, suggests that Jerome is concerned to substantiate the renderings of Aquila and Symmachus.

[5] See P. Schäfer, *Die Vorstellung vom Heiligen Geist in der Rabbinischen Literatur* (Munich, 1972), esp. 73–88, 135–43.

be regarded as prefiguring the Resurrection of Christ: see Origen, *Hom. in Gen.* 8. 4–5, who assumes the same reading as Jerome here.[6]

verse 13   LXX have: 'And Aoraham lifted his eyes and looked; and behold, one ram caught by its horns in the bush sabek.' For 'one ram' LXX apparently read the Hebrew as *'ayil 'eḥād*, as do the Samaritan Pentateuch, PJ, TN, Symmachus, and some forty Hebrew MSS; but MT has *'ayil 'aḥar*, which Jerome, Vg, and some witnesses to TO have rendered here as 'a ram behind his back'.

The fragment of Eusebius of Emesa on this verse edited by Devreesse (p. 74) does not agree with Jerome's attribution here, but points to the word *sabech* and interprets it as 'forgiveness', doubtless deriving it from the Aramaic root *šbq*, 'forgive'.[7] Many Fathers regarded the ram caught in the thicket as a type of the Lord on the cross: see, for example, Melito of Sardis, fr. 11; Origen, *Hom. in Gen.* 9. 9, 14. 1; Ambrose, *Ep.* 8. 3; Augustine, *De Civ. Dei* 16. 32, *De Trin.* 3. 25; and the imagery of a goat with horns extended, no doubt forming the shape T, is in truth known to us almost as Jerome quotes it. It features as an interpretation of *sabech* in the Greek Catenae (Petit, ii. 202 no. 2), though not in the name of Eusebius. It may, however, derive from Eusebius of Emesa, even though given anonymously in some witnesses or attributed to Gennadius in others.[8] This imagery Jerome demolishes with some asperity on the basis of the Hebrew, which says that Abraham saw the ram caught in *sᵉbak*.

The meaning of *sᵉbak* is 'thicket', the sense given to it by Aquila, by Jerome in Vg (*vepres*), and by R. Levi in *Gen. Rab.* 56: 9. Symmachus translated as *en diktuōi*, 'in a net': both he and Aquila most probably took *sᵉbak* as being related to *śibkāh*, 'lattice-work'. Symmachus may have been determined to avoid the image of an animal destined for sacrifice caught in a tree or bush as part of his general anti-Christian endeavour.[9] But in the minds of some

[6] See Harl, *Bible d'Alexandrie*, i. 193; Wevers, pp. 213–14.

[7] A variant attributed to 'the Syrian and the Hebrew' by Eusebius of Emesa (Devreesse, p. 74; Petit, i. 182) has the ram 'suspended', *kremamenos*, rather than caught, *katechomenos* in the bush, which increases the typological potential of the verse. See also Salvesen, *Symmachus*, 45. *Sabech* is interpreted as 'forgiveness' also by Diodore (Petit, ii. 200) and Gennadius (Petit, ii. 202).

[8] For Eusebius' exegesis, which seems to have taken *sabech* as qualifying either the bush or the ram, see Kamesar, *Jerome*, 134–7.

[9] See Salvesen, *Symmachus*, 45, 293. But F. Nikolasch, 'Zur Ikonographie des Widders von Gen 22', *Vigiliae Christianae*, 23 (1969), 215–17, cited by Kamesar,

exegetes Aquila and Symmachus seemed to be creating a problem
by using *śibkāh*, which begins with letter *sin*, to explain *sᵉbak*,
which begins with letter *samech*. For this reason, Jerome says, they
preferred LXX and Theodotion, who merely transliterated the
Hebrew word as *sabech*. But Jerome is concerned to support the
sense of the word given by Aquila and Symmachus, and reports
after careful researches of his own that Hebrew also has a root *sbk*,
'to interweave' which begins with letter *samech* and from which the
noun *sᵉbak* used in this verse in fact derives.[10]

verse 14   The unvocalized Hebrew word *yr'h*, which occurs twice
in this verse, might be read as the form *yir'eh*, 'sees', or as *yērā'eh*,
'will be seen'. LXX opted first for the active, second for the passive
sense, rendering: 'the Lord has seen, so that they say today, The
Lord has been seen'. But in Vg Jerome took the second occurrence
of the verb, vocalized in our MT as a passive form, in an active
sense: 'And he called the name of that place The Lord Sees. Whence
until today it is said, On the mountain the Lord will see'. Here he
also renders the second verb as active, noting that the Hebrew has
a passive form: he does not note the passive as a reading of LXX.
For the passive, see also Augustine, *De Civ. Dei* 16. 32, *QG* 58, *De
Trin.* 3. 25. The Jews speak of the *ʿAqedah*, or Binding, of Isaac as
a sign of God's deliverance of Israel in past, present, and future.[11]
Jerome's words here may be rendered literally as 'whenever they are
set in distress': they are very close to the words of the Targums. See
TN of this verse: 'when his sons are standing in the hour of
distress'; and especially PJ: 'when the sons of Isaac my son enter the
hour of affliction, *ʿᵃnīqē'*. This last Aramaic word is used also by
FTV, while FTP and Ngl have the closely related form *ʿᵃnanqī*:
Jerome here speaks of *angustia*, 'distress'.

The proverbial use of Abraham's words is underlined by the
explanation of them; and we know from *m. Taʿan.* 2: 4, 5 that they
were invoked in solemn liturgies at times of drought, when the
prayer-leader would say: 'May He who answered Abraham our

Jerome, 137–8, relates Symmachus' rendering to the rope which ties the ram to the
tree in paintings of the kind found at Dura-Europos.

   [10] See Kamesar, *Jerome*, 137–8.

   [11] The literature on the Binding of Isaac is extensive; but a good introduction and
detailed discussion can be gained from the following: S. Spiegel, *The Last Trial* (New
York, 1967); le Déaut, *La Nuit pascale*, 132–212; G. Vermes, 'Redemption and
Genesis xxii', in *Scripture and Tradition in Judaism*² (Leiden, 1973), 193–227;
Bowker, *The Targums*, 228–34.

father on Mount Moriah answer you, and hearken to the voice of your crying today.' And the sounding of the *shōfar*, or ram's horn, at New Year's Day services in the synagogue as a memorial of Isaac's Binding (cf. *b. RS* 16a), is designed to invoke the mercy of God by recalling the events on Mount Moriah.[12]

verses 20-2 LXX read: 'And it was told to Abraham . . . Ox the first-born and Baux his brother . . . and Chasad.' For Job as descendant of Us, see above, comment on 10: 23, and the view of R. Simeon ben Lakish in the name of bar Qappara (*Gen. Rab* 57: 4), who dated him to the time of Abraham.[13] But almost all Christian writers thought that he was descended from Esau, including Epiphanius, *Adv. Haer.* 1. 1. 8; Augustine, *De Civ. Dei* 18. 47; John Chrysostom, *Homily* 2 (on Patience); and Theodoret, *QG* 95. Their authority for believing so was a note placed at the end of the LXX version of the Book of Job, which reads:

> This man is explained from the Syrian book as dwelling in the land of Ausitis, on the borders of Idumaea and Arabia. Formerly, his name was Jobab. He took an Arabian wife, and fathered a son whose name was Ennon. Now he himself was son of his father Zare, of the sons of Esau, and of his mother Bosorrha, so that he was fifth from Abraam. Now these are the kings who reigned in Edom, a country which he also ruled: first Balak, the son of Beor . . . and after Balak Jobab, who is called Job . . .

The *Test. Job* 1: 4 and Aristeas the Exegete also record that Job was son of Esau.[14] Jerome notes that this is not contained in the Hebrew, and therefore, by implication, forms no part of the 'Hebrew truth'. In *Ep.* 73 *Ad Evangelum* (*Evagrium*) he stresses Jewish denial of this opinion, doubtless because Esau had already become a code-word in Israel for the Roman Empire and its anti-Jewish law.[15]

The descent of Balaam from Buz, and his identification with the Elihu of the Book of Job (32-7) is a Jewish tradition attested by *jer. Soṭ.* 5. 20d. Other authorities identified him with Bela son of Beor

---

[12] On the ʿAqedah in the Synagogue Liturgy, see Vermes, 'Redemption', 211-18.

[13] The Rabbis were generally agreed that Job was a Gentile, but there were widely differing opinions about his origins. See J. R. Baskin, *Pharaoh's Counsellors: Job, Jethro and Balaam in Rabbinic and Patristic Tradition* (Chico, Calif., 1983), 29-30, 38-9.

[14] Aristeas is preserved *ap.* Eusebius, *Praep. Evang.* 9. 25. 1-4. See R. Doran, 'Aristeas the Exegete', in J. H. Charlesworth (ed.), *The Old Testament Pseudepigrapha*, ii (London, 1985), 859.

[15] Jerome knew of this identification: see *In Esa.* 5. 21: 11-12.

(PJ of Gen. 36: 32), Laban (*b. Sanh.* 105a; PJ of Num. 22: 5), or
Kemuel (*Gen. Rab.* 57: 4). His story is found in Num. 22: 1–24: 25,
according to which he was invited by the Gentile king Balak to
curse Israel. Rabbinic tradition generally regarded Balaam as utterly degenerate, self-seeking, and malicious towards Israel. Even
though at first he had the gift of prophecy, his evil traits soon
became apparent.[16] Jerome refers to Job 32: 2 to show that Elihu
was a Buzite.

The Hebrew refers to Camuel as father of Aram, for which LXX
have put 'the Syrians', since Aram is the usual Hebrew name for the
region of Syria with its capital Damascus. In Isa. 7: 1 Rezin is called
the king of Aram, Syria. Cased stands for Hebrew *kesed*, the
Chaldeans: Jerome makes the same remarks in *Lib. Heb. Nom.* (p.
64), explaining the word as 'like ones who devastate'.[17]

CHAPTER 23

verse 2 Jerome explains that the words 'which is in the valley' are
not represented in the 'authentic codices' of LXX; nor do they
figure in the Hebrew.[1] 'City of Arboc' is an attempt by LXX to
render Hebrew *qiryat 'arba'*, literally, 'city of four'; and the addition
'which is in the valley' is taken up later by LXX Gen. 35: 27,
explaining Kiriath Arba as 'a city of the plain'. Jerome explains here
and in *Lib. Loc.* 906–7 that the Greek 'word' Arboc is corrupt and
meaningless. The tradition that this place was named after four
ancient Patriarchs is represented most generally by TN, which calls
it 'the city of the four fathers'. The Targum's vagueness is probably
deliberate, for when we turn to *Gen. Rab.* 58: 4 we discover that
the element 'four' was variously explained of different persons and
events. Of these, Jerome's explanation that it is the burial place of
Adam, Abraham, Isaac, and Jacob is but one: we are also told that
the place had four different names; that four righteous men lived

[16] For studies of Balaam in pre-Rabbinic and Rabbinic writings, see Baskin,
Pharaoh's Counsellors, 75–113; G. Vermes, 'The Story of Balaam: The Scriptural
Origin of Haggadah', in *Scripture and Tradition*[2], 127–77.

[17] For Jerome's explanation of the name as 'like breasts' and 'like demons' at *In
Esa.* 7. 23: 13, and 12. 43: 14–15, see Jay, *L'Exégèse de saint Jérôme*, 295.

[1] 'Authentic codices' of LXX for Jerome presumably include the version found in
Origen's Hexapla. On the status of the Lucianic recension or 'current edition' in
Jerome's mind, see Jay, *L'Exégèse de saint Jérôme*, 113–14.

there, or were circumcised there; and that the four Matriarchs Eve, Sarah, Rebecca, and Leah were buried there.[2]

He finds scriptural proof for his comments in Josh. 14: 15. Here the Hebrew defines Kiriath Arba as *hā'ādām haggādōl bā'anāqîm*, 'the great man among the Anakim': Arba is thus understood as the name of a person, as also in Josh. 15: 13, rather than a place. But in Vg, Jerome translated Josh. 14: 15 as 'Cariath-Arbe; Adam the greatest Man is placed there, among the Enacim.' Thus, for Jerome, Scripture itself as well as Jewish tradition attests Adam's burial at Kiriath Arba which is Hebron. See also his comments on Arboc in *Lib. Loc.* 906–7, which are very close to what he says in *QHG*. In this, he has apparently altered his earlier belief that Adam was buried at Calvary: in *Ep.* 46. 3 to Marcella, he tells how the blood from Christ's cross dripped directly on to Adam buried below, to wash away his sin. Adam's burial at Calvary had been asserted by earlier writers such as Origen, *Comm. Series in Matt.* 126–7, as also by Ambrose, *Ep.* 71. 10. See further G. Bardy, 'Saint Jérôme et ses maîtres Hébreux', *RB* 46 (1934), 162–3, and T. O'Loughlin, 'Adam's Burial at Hebron: Some Aspects of its Significance in the Latin Tradition', *PIBA* (forthcoming). See also *Ep.* 108. 11. It should be noted how he refers to Adam as *princeps*, 'head' or 'beginning' or 'capital point' of the human race; just as Christ is called *princeps* in his capacity as agent of creation (see comments on 1: 1) and Second Adam.

verse 6   Jerome has not rendered LXX, who have: 'Nay, O lord; but do thou hear us.[3] Thou art a king among us from God. Bury thy dead in our choice tombs.' The Hebrew reads *nāśî'*, 'prince' or 'chief', which Jerome duly explains: it does not have *melek*, 'king'. PL's reading *NASI* is to be preferred to Lagarde's *nasin*, which gives the word the appearance of being an Aramaic plural noun.

verse 16   As Jerome remarks, the proper name Ephron is written fully the first time it occurs, with letter *waw* to represent the long o. In the second occurrence of the name, however, *waw* is lacking; but MT and all the ancient versions (including Vg) still vocalize the name as Ephron with a long o.[4] Jerome's reading the second form

---

[2] See also *b. 'Erub.* 53a; Rahmer, *Die hebräischen Traditionen*, 36; and Ginzberg, 'Die Haggada' (*MGWJ* NS 7), 69–72.

[3] According to the Hebrew of the preceding verse, 'The sons of Heth answered Abraham, saying to him, *lō*'; LXX took that last word as *lō*, 'not', 'no'. The sense and order of words in Jerome's 'hear us, lord', is found also in Aquila's translation.

[4] Thus MT has long o written without *waw*; LXX use *omega*; and the Targums

of the name as Ephran may indicate how it was pronounced by Jews in his day; although it is equally likely that it is his own device, to indicate easily to his readers the difference between the two writings of the word. *Mekh. de R. Ishmael Amalek* 3: 49–53 explains that Ephron lost this letter after he had taken money from Abraham, contrasting this with persons who had letters added to their names, such as Abraham (see also above, on 17: 15 and 16). Rashi's commentary, following *b. BM* 87a, explains that Ephron promised much but actually did little; hence his name was deprived of the letter.[5] In *Gen. Rab.* 58: 7, R. Abba bar Judan in the name of R. Simon remarks that Ephron's shekels were in fact *centenaria*: he had charged Abraham overmuch, and to him is applied the verse in Prov. 28: 22 about the man of 'evil eye'. Jerome's use of this tradition to admonish those who sell burial grounds for money, even with the use of threats, owes much to these Jewish objections to Ephron's conduct.

CHAPTER 24

verse 9 PJ of this verse (cf. verse 2) says that the servant put his hand 'on the covenant (lit. cut) of the circumcision of Abraham'; TN refers to 'the covenant of Abraham', and the Ngl to 'the thigh of Abraham's covenant', the two latter being euphemistic expressions of the first interpretation. There is a reference to the same procedure in *Gen. Rab.* 59: 8 and *Sekhel Ṭov* on this verse.[1] But this interpretation was known quite widely among Christian exegetes, and is found in Ephraem's *Comm. in Gen.* 21. 2; Theodoret, *QG* 75; a Catena fragment in the name of Diodore quoting 'the Syrian and the Hebrew' (Petit, ii. 204); and in the fragments of Eusebius of Emesa (Devreesse, p. 74). This last states that it is a reading of 'the Hebrew', and Kamesar suggests that Jerome's comment in this

and the Syriac spell the second occurrence of the name with letter *waw* to indicate long o. The name is spelled with *waw* in MT once in this verse, twice in verse 10, and in verses 13 and 14. It is spelled without *waw* once in this verse, and at 25: 9; 49: 30; and 50: 13. Jerome gives as the meaning of Ephron 'dust of sorrow or unprofitable dust or their dust' in *Lib. Heb. Nom.* (p. 65).

[5] See also Rahmer, *Die hebräischen Traditionen*, 36–7, citing Naḥmanides on this verse.

[1] See Rahmer, *Die hebräischen Traditionen*, 37, and Albeck's explanation of *Gen. Rab.* 59: 8.

verse is to some degree directed against Eusebius, to make clear that the exegesis is not a reading of the Hebrew text of the Bible, but a Jewish tradition.[2] The Hebrew Bible says nothing about the mark of circumcision: therefore Jerome feels able to ground his Christian interpretation of the verse, at least by implication, in the words of the Hebrew Bible itself. See also *Adv. Jov.* 1. 10.

verse 22 LXX read: 'The man took golden earrings, each of a drachma weight', thus equating the Hebrew *beqaʿ* with the drachma; but Jerome may be following a MS of LXX of the type represented in Field, i. 39, and Wevers, p. 228, which read 'didrachma' instead of 'drachma'. The witnesses to VL reflect the same variants in reading. The Biblical *beqaʿ*, Jerome's *BACE*, was valued at half a shekel: Jerome understands this, and follows Josephus, *Ant.* 3. 195, in equating the shekel with four Attic drachmae. The half-shekel *beqaʿ* thus represents two drachmae, one didrachma.[3] There is a difficulty, however, with his conversion of the sums into Latin 'ounces'. Here he shows that one 'ounce', the whole shekel, will equal four drachmae; but in his commentary *In Hiez.* 1. 4: 9–12 he states that one 'ounce' equals eight drachmae. Either he has made a mistake in this latter equation, or he may unconsciously be converting the 'ounce' into the Rabbinic currency of his day, according to which one biblical shekel is the equivalent of two Rabbinic shekels.[4]

verse 43 Jerome's dispute with Jovinian (392) about the value of the monastic and ascetic life included further defence of the perpetual virginity of Christ's Mother which Jovinian, like Helvidius before him, had denied. Hence Jerome's interest in the precise meaning of *ʿalmāh* and his reference to the Immanuel prophecy of Isa. 7: 14 are directed not only against Jewish arguments about the meaning of the word: see *Adv. Jov.* 1. 32, where Rebecca as *ʿalmāh*, one who is truly chaste, is given as a type of the Church and brought as witness against Jovinian's position. There is in Hebrew a common root *ʿlm*, 'to conceal', which Jerome presses into service

---

[2] See Kamesar, *Jerome*, 153–5, who cites other Christian writers as knowing the tradition. The servant's action was understood by Christian exegetes as pointing forward to Baptism, or the union between Christ and the Church or the soul: see Harl, *Bible d'Alexandrie*, i. 199.

[3] See also his commentary *In Hiez.* on 4: 9–12, where he states unambiguously that a shekel equals four drachmae. He thus disagrees with Eusebius of Emesa, who valued the shekel at two drachmae: see Kamesar, 'Thesis', 135–6.

[4] See Aberbach and Grossfeld, *Targum Onkelos*, 141.

here and in *In Esa.* 3. 7: 14, to argue that the word *ʿalmāh* means
'hidden'.[5] Indeed, in his comment on Isa. 7: 14, he records Aquila's
translation of the word in this verse of Genesis as *apokruphos*,
'hidden'. His first proof text is Job 28: 20–1, where the *niphʿal* form
neʿelmāh, 'hidden', occurs: the verses are appropriate, given that the
Blessed Virgin was identified with Wisdom, the subject under discussion there.[6] Next he quotes 2 Kgs. (LXX, 4 Reigns) 4: 27, where
the form *heʿlīm* occurs in respect of the Lord's hiding information
from Elisha.

The idea that an *ʿalmāh* is a hidden girl leads Jerome to argue that
such a one possesses some extra quality in addition to mere physical
virginity: she is virgin in spirit as well as in body. (Philo, *QG* 4. 99
had already interpreted the fact that Gen. 24: 16 twice refers to
Rebecca as a virgin as meaning that she was a virgin both in body
and in respect of her incorruptible soul). His authority is 1 Cor. 7:
34, which says of the virgin that she is 'careful for the things of the
Lord, that she may be holy both in body and in spirit': see also *Ep.*
22. 38. He adds Exod. 2: 8 to show that *ʿalmāh* is used of Miriam,
sister of Moses, and ends with a call to Jews to challenge his
argument if they will.

He gives a much longer defence of his arguments in *In Esa.* 3. 7:
14, where he uses as proof texts Ps. 9: 1; Gen. 24: 16, 43; and the
passage from 2 Kings. He even resorts to comparative philology,
suggesting that Hebrew borrowed words from other languages, like
the word *ʾappiryōn* at Song 3: 9, which he explains as Greek
phoreion (sedan-chair). So he declares that *alma* in Punic means
'virgin' and in Latin 'holy', and that Hebrew may have borrowed
the word. In all this, his arguments are philological, and are based
on the Hebrew text of Scripture: Jerome does not resort to what
was perhaps the most famous Christian defence for understanding
'young woman' in Isa. 7: 14 as 'virgin', the claim of Fathers like
Irenaeus (*Adv. Haer.* 3. 21. 1, 5) that the Jews had falsified the text.

More widespread among Christians, however, was the view that
the Greek word *neanis*, 'young woman', could have the meaning
'virgin' in certain circumstances. The LXX of Deut. 22: 23–9,
which gives the law concerning a man who in good faith marries a

---

[5] In fact, *ʿalmāh* probably derives from an homonymous root *ʿlm*, 'to be mature'.
On Jerome's exposition of Isa. 7: 14, see Jay, *L'Exégèse de saint Jérôme*, 117.

[6] This is expressed clearly in the Old Roman rite, and may be traced back as far
as Ambrose, *De Spiritu Sancto* 2. 51 (PL 16: 753).

young woman whom he later suspects was not a virgin at the time
of marriage, is a case in point. In this Greek text 'young woman'
and 'virgin' seem to be used interchangeably, and as ancient a work
as the *Dialogue of Timothy and Aquila* (111) used these verses to
prove the point.[7] But Origen, in one of the best known of his
writings (*Contra Celsum* 1. 34 ff.), had gone further and had invoked the Hebrew of Deut. 22: 23–9 to support his contention that
ʿalmāh in Isa. 7: 14 means 'virgin'. Since, however, the word *ʿalmāh*
nowhere appears in Deut. 22: 23–9, but only the words *naʿărāh*,
'young woman' and *bĕtūlāh*, 'virgin', his argument could only fail.
Jerome himself (*Adv. Jov.* 1. 32) recognized the true meanings of
the Hebrew words in Deut. 22: 23–9, and that text plays no part in
his elucidation of the meaning of *ʿalmāh*.[8]

verse 59 Jerome's rendering of Hebrew *mēniqtāh* as 'nurse',
which he uses also in Vg, is shared with Aquila, Symmachus, TO,
and TN, deriving it from root *ynq*, 'to suckle'. LXX had taken it
from root *qnh*, 'to acquire, possess', and translated with *ta
huparchonta*. The latter encompasses as one of its possible meanings 'people', but that is not its necessary sense.[9]

verses 62–3 On Gerar and Isaac's place of residence, see above,
21: 30–1; 22: 3–4. The Hebrew *lāśūaḥ* occurs only here in Scripture, and its sense is uncertain even to modern scholars. Among the
ancients, it was rendered by LXX as 'to busy himself', *adoleschēsai*,
a word with negative overtones of idle prattling and vain reasoning.
It therefore posed much the same difficulty as LXX's use of 'wise'
to describe the serpent in the Garden of Eden, as noted above at 3:
1. Amongst the Jews, however, it was usual to relate the word to
root *śyḥ*, 'to muse', in the sense of commune with God: Philo had
already understood even the LXX to have this sense, *Leg. All.* 3. 43,
Quod Det. 29–31, *QG* 4. 140. Christian exegetes were troubled by
the pejorative sense of *adoleschēsai*, and sought to explain it as
meaning that Isaac prayed or meditated: see, for example, Origen,

[7] See de Lange, *Origen and the Jews*, 99, 191, n. 61, and Kamesar, 'Thesis', 197–
202, for references to Eusebius of Caesarea, John Chrysostom, Theodoret, Basil, and
John of Jerusalem. The latter notes (p. 202) that Basil even regarded *neanis* as
common language for 'virgin'.

[8] According to Kamesar, 'Thesis', 205–6, Origen failed to verify the Hebrew text
of Deut. 22, and depended simply on Greek texts which he then 'Hebraized',
assuming that *ʿalmāh* was the only Hebrew equivalent of Greek *neanis*.

[9] See Harl, *Bible d'Alexandrie*, i. 204. Indeed, Wevers, p. 237, notes that some
witnesses to Symmachus read not *trophon*, 'nurse', but *trophēn*, 'victuals'.

Sel. in Gen. 24: 62. Augustine, *QG* 69, clearly stated the problem, which was compounded by VL's translation of the Greek as *exerceri*, 'to exercise himself' physically, rather than spiritually or mentally.

Jerome invokes the Hebrew against LXX and translates it exactly as does Symmachus, whom he does not acknowledge: it is not clear that Symmachus' 'to speak' is meant to suggest prayer by Isaac.[10] But the Rabbinic interpretation of this verb is 'to pray': so, for example, TO, PJ, TN, and *Mekh. de R. Ishmael Beshallah* 3: 30–2. It is entirely probable, given his words here, that Jerome reflects this Rabbinic understanding: in Vg he translated as 'to meditate'. Significant is his note that Isaac went out at the ninth hour,[11] the regular time for the evening prayer which Isaac was said to have instituted: *b. Ber.* 26b; *jer. Ber.* 4: 1; *b. ʿAZ* 7b; *Gen. Rab.* 60: 14; *PRE* 16: 3; *Tanh. Beshallah* 9. Jerome's clarification of this word on the basis of the Hebrew text and Jewish tradition was possibly directed at Ambrose, who had anguished over *adoleschēsai*, and had understood it as *hallucinari*, 'to talk idly, dream'; *abalienari*, 'to be estranged', or even 'to be driven mad'; *exerceri*, 'to exercise oneself' (in line with VL); or *deambulare*, 'to walk about' (all listed by Fischer, p. 259). Throughout his investigation, Ambrose, like Augustine, had sought for a positive sense of *adoleschēsai*. For Christ's prayer alone on the mountain, see Matt. 14: 23; Luke 6: 12; Jerome's description of prayer as 'spiritual victims' recalls 1 Peter 2: 5.

verse 65 LXX, followed by VL, translated the Hebrew word *ṣāʿīp* as *theristron*, 'veil', which is the explanation given in TO, PJ, TN, FTP, and FTV. Jerome describes the garment more closely, from his own observation of Arab life: see *In Esa.* 2. 3: 22. He refers to it as *pallium*, 'mantle', both here and in Vg. It is of interest to him as symbolically representing virginal purity: see his comments on Song 1: 3; 8: 10 in *Ep.* 107. 7.

CHAPTER 25

verses 1–6 Jerome has followed the Hebrew, not LXX, for the names of these people: the latter add the names Thaima after Saba;

[10] See Salvesen, *Symmachus*, 46. For the original Hebrew and its LXX translation, see le Déaut, *Targum du Pentateuque*, i. 240 and the literature cited there.
[11] See Rahmer, *Die hebräischen Traditionen*, 38.

Ragouel and Nabdeēl after Dadan; and read Abira and Elraga for
Abida and Aledea respectively. LXX also describe Isaac as 'his son',
which Jerome, like the Hebrew, does not have. PJ, the second Ngl,
FTP, and FTV of 25: 1 identify Keturah with Hagar, the first two
named Targums specifying that she was bound *qtyrh* or *qtyr'* to him
formerly. The same identification is found in *PRE* 30: 4; *MHG* and
Yalquṭ Shim'oni on this verse. Jerome says not that the Hebrews
hand on a tradition (*tradunt*), only that they suppose (*suspicantur*)
that the women are one and the same. In fact, the matter was
disputed, as *Gen. Rab.* 61: 4 indicates: R. Jehudah accepted the
identification, whereas R. Nehemiah did not.[1] Further, the meaning
of her name as 'bound' was not espoused by all sources. *PRE*, for
example, related it also to *qtwrt*, the 'incense' offered in the Temple, as did Origen, *Hom. in Gen.* 11. 1; and in *Lib. Heb. Nom.* (p.
64) Jerome himself had interpreted it as 'one offering incense or
coupled or joined'. But the identification of Keturah and Hagar is
probably ancient, in that *Jub.* 20: 13 already speaks of the descendants of Keturah and of Ishmael (Hagar's son) as having mixed
together: they may, in time, have come to be regarded as identical.
For an attempt to defend Abraham from allegations of sexual
incontinence, see also Augustine, *QG* 70.

Jerome depends on Josephus, *Ant.* 1. 239–40, for his remarks
about the sons of Keturah 'according to the historians of the
Hebrews': it is only when he begins to speak of the sons of Dadan
that he leaves Josephus' record. Troglodytis was the shores of the
Red Sea, both on the African and Arabian sides; Arabia Eudaimon,
Latin Arabia Felix, was the Arabian peninsula itself. Origen, *Sel. in
Gen.* 25: 1, says that Keturah's descendants lived there, but adds a
reference to the Midianites, among whom was Jethro, the father-in-
law of Moses. The story of Afer seems to derive from Alexander
Polyhistor, who was born *c.* 105 BC. During the latter part of the
first century BC he wrote at great length about a number of nations,
including the Jews and Samaritans. His work sometimes quotes
Jewish and Samaritan sources.[2] Cleodemus Malchus, about whom
very little is known, is most probably the original source of the

---

[1] See further Rahmer, ibid. 38–9, citing *Yalquṭ Shim'oni* 2. 904 to the effect that
she was either a daughter or granddaughter of Japheth.

[2] Jerome used not only the writings of Josephus, but was also familiar with the
works of Herodotus, Xenophon, and Berossus: see Jay, *L'Exégèse de saint Jérôme*,
182–3. For Alexander's work, see J. Freudenthal, *Alexander Polyhistor und die von
ihm erhaltenen Reste jüdischer und samaritanischer Geschichtswerke* (Hellenistische
Studien, 1–2; Breslau, 1874–5); and discussion of his writings in Schürer, *History of*

story, however: if Alexander Polyhistor used his work, then clearly
he must have been writing some time before 50 BC. The material is
preserved also by Eusebius, *Praep. Evang.* 9. 20. 2–4. But much
obscurity surrounds Josephus' use of Alexander Polyhistor, and it is
not clear from where he derived the material he attributes to him
and Malchus.[3] Jerome seems content to follow Josephus without
question.

While LXX and Josephus took the sons of Dadan in 25: 3
(Asshurim, Letushim, and Leummim) as names of peoples, Jerome
quotes unnamed Jewish authorities that they refer to occupations.
See also his *Lib. Heb. Nom.* (p. 68) for the meaning of Laomim. In
fact, FTV interprets them as merchants, craftsmen (*'wmnyn*), and
heads of peoples, which almost exactly corresponds with Jerome's
information. PJ and TN are very similar, but both read *'mpwryn*, a
word whose meaning has been much debated, in the second place.
It may be a Greek loan-word *emporoi*, 'traders'; but in that case it
would repeat the sense of the first word, and consequently other
suggestions have included its identification with *empeiroi*, 'skilled
ones', or even *empuroi* in the sense of 'smiths'.[4] It may even be the
case that Jerome and FTV represent the original Palestinian
Targum which has been slightly garbled by PJ and TN, possibly
because they were using Greek loan-words which the compilers or
scribes of those Targums have not fully understood.

Be this as it may, Jerome's words coincide in some measure with
FTV; and his manner of introducing them is striking. He says that
'they think, they suppose', not defining who 'they' might be; but
'they' report something very close to information found in a known
text of Targum. And Jerome says that 'they' think that the Hebrew

the *Jewish People*, iii/1. 510–12. Whether Jerome knew his work or the work of
pagan historians directly may be doubted: see Courcelle, *Late Latin Writers*, 78–86.

[3] On Cleodemus Malchus, see R. Doran in J. H. Charlesworth (ed.), *The Old
Testament Pseudepigrapha*, ii (London, 1985), 883–6, esp. 883 for his comments
on Josephus' sources for this passage; Schürer, *History of the Jewish People*, iii/1.
526–8.

[4] On the Greek loan-words, see further Rahmer, *Die hebräischen Traditionen*,
39–41, and McNamara, *New Testament and Palestinian Targum*, 54–6, who also
discusses the relationships of the various Targums to one another, and St Jerome's
possible knowledge of Targums. Kamesar, 'Thesis', 93, notes that a fragment
attributed to Origen, but anonymous in the manuscripts, *Sel. in Gen.* (PG 12: 120C–
121B) interprets the name Letushim as *sphurokopoi*, 'beaters with the hammer', i.e.
'smiths'. Thus Jerome may have derived his interpretation of the names from a
Greek source; although Kamesar allows that the similarities between FTV and
Jerome suggest a link with Rabbinic tradition.

words should be 'translated' (*transferri*) in a particular sense. Remarkably, R. Samuel bar Nahman is recorded in *Gen. Rab.* 61: 5 as having attacked the Targum: 'R. Samuel bar Nahman said: Even though they translate (*mtrgmyn*) and say "traders and *'npryn* and heads of peoples", all of them are, in fact, heads of peoples.' That Jerome knows of an interpretation of this verse which is so very close to that found in an Aramaic Targum is important evidence in assessing his familiarity with Targumic tradition. The Targums seem to have understood Asurim on the basis of Prov. 9: 6, 'and walk (*'šrw*) on the road'; Latosim through Gen. 4: 22, 'he was the forger (*lōtēš*) of all bronze and iron cutting instruments'; and Laomim as *l'mym*, 'peoples'.[5]

For the view that the Syrians are named after Asurim, and that Keturah's sons went east, Jerome possibly had in mind Demetrius the Chronographer, fr. 3 in Eusebius, *Praep. Evang.* 9. 29. 1–3. It is otherwise not clear who may be meant.[6]

verse 8 The Hebrew reads: 'And Abraham expired (*wayyigwa'*) and died in a good old age, old and full; and he was gathered to his people'. LXX have not added 'grew weak', but with it have translated *wayyigwa'*. It may be an inappropriate rendering, although Jerome retains it in Vg. He took LXX's 'full of days' to refer to Abraham's good works: see also a similar addition in PJ, which has 'old and full of all that was good'. His comments on the apparent redundancy of the scriptural language are close to similar remarks of Philo, *QG* 4. 152, on the fully virtuous life of the righteous man.

The technical exegetical term *anagōgē*, whose Greek form Jerome almost always retains whenever he uses it, means literally 'elevated' or 'superior' and refers to the 'spiritual' sense of a word or passage of Scripture, most often as opposed to its literal sense. His understanding and use of the word may have developed over the years: in some of his writings it seems almost identical with *tropologia*, while in his latest work, the commentary *In Hieremiam*, it is applied to the moral and allegorical exegesis of Scripture almost exclusively.[7] Here, Jerome suggests that LXX have in reality limited the full range of possible meanings of the text with their addition 'of days':

---

[5] See Albeck's note to *Gen. Rab.* 61: 5 for these, and other possibilities.

[6] See J. Hanson, 'Demetrius the Chronographer', in J. H. Charlesworth (ed.), *The Old Testament Pseudepigrapha*, ii (London, 1985), 853 (fr. 3).

[7] See Jay, *L'Exégèse de saint Jérôme*, 226–32.

the Hebrew is thus superior in that it allows for a fuller and more 'spiritual' understanding.

verses 13–18   As Jerome explains later, he has not initially translated LXX, the majority of whose witnesses read: 'according to the name of his generations . . . and he dwelt from Evilat . . . until one comes to the Assyrians; over against the face of all his brothers he dwelt'. The note about the location of Ishmael's sons up to the words 'it is a region of Arabia' depends on Josephus, *Ant.* 1. 220–1. On the villages and 'little forts', see PJ and FTP of verse 16, which reflect closely Jerome's description of the Arab settlements.[8] On Duma, see *In Esa.* 5. 21: 11–12, where he identifies it as a region of Idumaea in the south, twenty miles from Eleutheropolis, near the mountains of Seir. The word for 'south' in Hebrew is *tēmān*, itself also a geographical location in Edom (Jer. 49: 7, 20); and 'east' is often expressed as *qedem*, hence the expression *bᵉnē qedem*, 'those who live in the East country'.

   The comment on verse 18 begins with a quotation of LXX, against which he sets the Hebrew that he dwelt 'in the presence of' (*coram*, rather than *in conspectu*, 'in the sight of', as he rendered Hebrew *ʿal pᵉnē* at the beginning of this section) his brothers. Thus he supports his contention that 'brethren' here means sons, using Gen. 31: 36–7 in accordance with the interpretation of those verses in *Gen. Rab.* 74: 13. Jacob had only one brother, Esau; yet Laban spoke of his brothers, and the only possible meaning of the word here is 'sons'. Eusebius of Emesa makes a similar point commenting on Gen. 27: 37 (Devreesse, p. 76). So Jerome transferred this to Ishmael, who had no brothers, but many sons.[9]

verses 21–2   The word used by LXX (*eskirtōn*) would be better rendered as 'leaped'. Aquila, according to Field, read *sunethlasthēsan*, which means 'struggled with one another', doubtless a reference to the future rivalry and hostility of the brothers. TO says that they 'were pushing about'; PJ and TN that they 'jostled one another'. The reading ascribed to Symmachus finds echoes in the *MHG*: 'they were going down and coming up in her womb like the waves of the sea'. But other witnesses to Symmachus

---

[8] See further Hayward, 'Targum Pseudo-Jonathan and Anti-Islamic Polemic', 84–5. Josephus seems to be the earliest of Jewish writers to equate the Ishmaelites with the Arabs: for the implications of this, see F. Millar, 'Hagar, Ishmael, Josephus and the Origins of Islam', *JJS* 44 (1993), 23–45.

[9] See also Rahmer, *Die hebräischen Traditionen*, 41.

read *diepalaion*, 'they wrestled'.[10] Vg has *collidebantur*, 'they were hostile, at variance with one another'; see also Jerome's *Ep.* 125. 15, where he says that they waged war with one another. *Sekhel Ṭov* of this verse says that they pushed one another like two mighty men.

verse 25 LXX describe Esau as 'first-born', *prōtotokos*; Jerome here and in Vg simply has 'first', following the Hebrew text (*hārī'šōn*). He restricts his comment to the meaning of Seir, which also comes to refer to Edom: see 36: 19. 'Hairy', *pilosus*, is one of the meanings he gives for the name in *Lib. Heb. Nom.* (p. 72), the other being *hispidus*, 'hairy, bristly', which he uses in Vg. He is silent about the ruddy (Hebrew *'admōnī*) appearance of Esau expressed in LXX by the rare word *purrhakēs*, which conveys a sense of savagery and bestial character noted by Philo, *QG* 4. 160. Is his treatment of Esau deliberately restrained?[11]

verse 30 In *Lib. Heb. Nom.* (p. 65), Edom is interpreted as 'red' or 'earthen'.

CHAPTER 26

verses 12–13 The consonantal text of the Hebrew may be vocalized as *šᵉ'ōrīm*, 'barley', as LXX and Pesh have understood the word; but MT reads *šᵉ'ārīm*, from root *š'r*, 'to reckon, value', hence 'valuations, reckonings'. Aquila indicates the antiquity of MT, Jerome essentially agreeing in Vg with 'one hundredfold'. TO and PJ have 'one hundred times what he had estimated'; see also *t. Ber.* 7(6): 8, *Gen. Rab.* 64: 6, *Sekhel Ṭov*, and Rashi's commentary on this verse.[1] Jerome takes the verse as referring to an increase in Isaac's virtues, using 26: 13 as further proof of this: he may have derived the idea from Philo, *De Mut. Nom.* 268–9, *QG* 4. 189–90. He may also be engaging with Origen, who had seen prefigured in

---

[10] See Salvesen, *Symmachus*, 207.

[11] See Feldman, 'Josephus' Portrait of Jacob', 123–4.

[1] See also *Pes. Rab.* 25; *PRK* 11; *Tanḥ. Rᵉeh* 12; *b. Ta'an.* 8; *Num. Rab.* 12: 11. Most of these Rabbinic sources indicate that Abraham's 'estimations' or 'valuations' were undertaken so that he might separate the correct amount of tithe or priestly offering. Jerome ignores this interpretation, even though it is strongly implied in Philo's exegesis of the number one hundred and this verse, *De Mut. Nom.* 189–92. He evidently approves of Aquila's version, which he cites some thirty-two times in *QHG*: see further Jay, *L'Exégèse de saint Jérôme*, 103–5.

Abraham's increasing barley stocks the miraculously multiplied barley loaves which Christ fed to the Five Thousand (*Hom. in Gen.* 12. 5; *Comm. in Joh.* 6. 9) and Christ's own growth in greatness (*Comm. in Matt.* 13. 15). Again, Jerome argues that it is the Hebrew itself which properly conveys these same truths about Christ; rather than LXX, which in this case offers the pedestrian and material business of barley stock as the proposed *locus* of a spiritual truth about Christ.

verses 17, 19 The Hebrew *nḥl* may mean both a 'torrent, seething stream' and 'wadi', the valley created by such a rushing torrent. The wadi may dry up and remain without water until a sudden violent storm of rain. Jerome thinks it fit that Isaac should live by the side of water, not in a parched land; accordingly, he quotes Ps. 110: 7 to show that *nḥl* refers to a torrent of water. In Vg he translated the word as 'torrent' in both these verses. 1 Kgs. 17: 6 also shows that Elijah drank from the *nḥl* Cedron during a famine. This became dry (1 Kgs. 17: 7); but Jerome recalls how, according to John 18: 1, Christ had crossed the Cedron on the night when he was handed over to his Passion. And it was during his Passion that Christ sanctified baptism, since water as well as blood flowed from his side, John 19: 34.

verse 21 LXX in most witnesses has 'and he dug another well'; Jerome here and in Vg follows the Hebrew. LXX translated Hebrew *śiṭnāh* as 'enmities', which Jerome retains in Vg: see also Philo, *De Somn.* 1. 40; Josephus, *Ant.* 1. 262; and *Jub.* 24: 20. His aim is to explain the meaning of the word Satan: thus he records the renderings of Aquila and Symmachus to show that Satan is properly the adversary.

verse 22 Both LXX and Hebrew have 'and he dug another well, and they did not contend about it'; whereas Jerome here and in Vg puts 'and they dug . . . they did not contend about them'. On the meaning of Hebrew *rᵉḥōbōt*, see above, comment on 10: 11.

verse 26 The Hebrew *ᵃḥuzzat mērēᵉḥū* could signify a name, 'Ahuzzath his companion': LXX, Vg, Pesh, and Symmachus have so understood it. R. Jehudah in *Gen. Rab.* 64: 9 is of the same opinion; and LXX chose to add this name to 21: 22. But both TO and TN explain the phrase as 'a company of his friends', and with them agrees R. Nehemiah in *Gen. Rab.* 64: 9. This is Rashi's preferred interpretation. PJ has: 'he laid hold of his friends to go with him'. All these explanations depend on the root Hebrew *'ḥz*, 'to grasp, seize', and the noun *'ḥzh* derived from it, 'what is possessed, held', i.e. 'company'.[2]

verses 32–3 LXX made a mistake, having read: 'and they said, We have not (*lō*) found water' rather than what is in the Hebrew: 'and they said to him (*lō*), We have found water'. Jerome rightly points out that their translation is devoid of sense for a literal or an allegorical interpretation of the verse.[3] Indeed, if the discovery of the wells refers spiritually to Abraham's increase in virtues, then LXX's statement that this well had no water is utterly incredible. By contrast with Jerome's simple and logical appeal to the Hebrew, Augustine's attempts to justify LXX lead him into all manner of mental contortions, *QG* 78.

'And he called its name Abundance' does not render the Hebrew, which Jerome otherwise follows here. MT has: 'And he called it *šibʿāh*'. This form of the word, spelled with *shin*, is unique in the Bible, occurring here as the proper name of the well; and it may mean 'oath', as LXX took it. On the meaning of Beer-Sheba, and the play on words involved, see above, comments on 21: 30–1. But to explain the Hebrew Jerome went to Aquila and Symmachus, both of whom seem to have taken the first root letter of *šibʿāh* not as *shin*, but as *sin* (which sounds almost exactly like *samech*), so that the word can be derived from root *śbʿ*, 'to be satisfied'. There are indeed nouns *śōbaʿ*, *śibʿāh*, 'abundance', *śobʿāh*, 'satiety', and *śābāʿ*, 'plenty'; and this last he put in Vg. Jerome comments again on this word at 41: 29; *In Esa.* 18. 65: 15–16; and *In Hier.* 3. 51. 1.

CHAPTER 27

verse 11 See Jerome's comment on 25: 25. 'Behold' is not found in LXX, but in the Hebrew.

verse 15 LXX have the singular 'robe'; Jerome has given the Hebrew with plural 'garments', in common with Aquila. For the first-born functioning as priests in pre-Aaronic times, see comments on 14: 18–19. That Esau's garments were the priestly robes is a tradition found (e.g.) in *jer. Meg.* 1: 11, *Tanḥ. Toledot* 12,

---

[2] See Rahmer, *Die hebräischen Traditionen*, 42. R. Nehemiah's words in *Gen. Rab.* 64: 9, *syʿh mn rḥmwy*, closely resemble TN, *syʿʿ mn rḥmwy*.

[3] For Jerome's use of the term 'allegory' and its meaning, see the discussion in Jay, *L'Exégèse de saint Jérôme*, 217–26.

Aggadath Bere'shith 42, although other sources such as *Num. Rab.*
4: 8 tell how Esau's vicious character debarred him from priestly
service. It was also believed that these garments had belonged to the
First Man: the tradition that they were priestly vestments stood
alongside another, that they were royal robes, and that Nimrod had
once possessed them. Jerome says nothing of this here, although his
account of the pre-Aaronic priesthood in *Ep.* 72 is more detailed.
Early Christian writers showed keen interest in the latter; and
Jerome is a key witness to the antiquity of the Haggadah found
attached to this verse of Scripture.[1] Esau's 'robe', as LXX have it,
was regarded as symbolic of the Old Testament, and a prefigure-
ment of the Church: see Ambrose, *De Jac.* 2. 9.

verse 36 Esau here comments on the name Jacob, Hebrew *ya⁽ᵃ⁾qōb*,
by referring to the verb *'qb*, 'to follow at the heel, to overreach' and
thus 'to supplant, trip up'; *Lib. Heb. Nom.* (pp. 67, 157) understands it as 'supplanter' and (p. 136) 'one who supplants'. The
Hebrew has a rhetorical question, 'is his name called Jacob . . .?',
which both LXX and TO make into a statement. This chapter has
told how Jacob, with his mother's help, had deceived Esau and
cheated him of Isaac's blessing (27: 5–29). Jerome here says that
Jacob deceived Esau by cunning ('arte deceperit'): TO of this verse,
along with *Gen. Rab.* 67: 4 and the vast majority of Rabbinic
commentators, go out of their way to avoid this, and speak instead
of Jacob having acted 'in wisdom', 'cleverly'.[2] But TN translated
literally, using root *'qb*; and PJ comes close to Jerome's interpretation with 'he has defrauded me'. But there is also the word *'āqēb*,
'heel', to be considered, for Gen. 25: 26 tells how Jacob was born
grasping hold of Esau's heel; not unnaturally, Jerome links the two
scriptural passages.

verse 40 Since Jewish exegesis of Jerome's day saw in Esau a code-
name for the Roman Empire, it is hardly surprising that this verse,
which prophesies Jacob's rule over Esau, presented problems and
opportunities for commentators both Jewish and Christian.[3] It is
therefore remarkable that Jerome is so brief in what he has to say.

---

[1] For analysis of this Haggadah in its various forms, see C. T. R. Hayward, 'The
Date of Targum Pseudo-Jonathan: Some Comments', *JJS* 40 (1989), 16–18.

[2] See Grossfeld, *Targum Onqelos to Genesis*, 101.

[3] See the literature cited at ch. 9 n. 4 above, and on this verse in particular, C. T.
R. Hayward, 'A Portrait of the Wicked Esau in the Targum of Codex Neofiti 1', in
The Aramaic Bible, ed. D.R.G. Beattie and M.J. McNamara (Sheffield, 1994), 300–
303.

He regards the sense of LXX as incomplete, and sets against it the
Hebrew, which reads: 'And you shall serve your brother; and it
shall come to pass that, when you wander (*tārīd*), you shall break
his yoke from upon your neck.' The opening translation is presumably meant to represent this Hebrew, and here he translates *tārīd* as
depones, literally 'you shall lay down'; and gives the second verb as
solves, 'you shall break'. In the light of what Jerome says, we
should probably best construe his translation as meaning: 'and it
shall happen, when you lay it down, then you shall break his yoke
from off your neck'.

His second rendering uses the future perfects *deposueris*, 'you
shall have laid down' and *solveris*, 'you shall have broken' to
translate LXX: this tense is used by Ambrose in his quotation of the
verse (*De Jac.* 2. 13; *Ep.* 77. 4), and his version is almost identical
with Jerome's second rendering. It most likely represents a form of
VL. A literal rendering of it illustrates Jerome's point about its
incompleteness: 'So when you shall have laid it down, and shall
have broken his yoke from your neck.' It is probable that Jerome
regarded VL as the real source of the problem.

He does not comment directly on the precise meaning of *tārīd*.[4]
Rather, he translates it 'lay down' as LXX had done, as if from root
yrd, 'go down': PJ and Aquila had invoked the same root in their
versions. In Vg, however, he translated it as 'shake off, discard'. But
his words, 'they shall cast off the yoke of servitude from their neck
and reject their dominion (*imperium*)', suggest that he may have
known more about Jewish understandings of this verse than is
apparent. Some exegetes took *tārīd* as if from root *rdh*, 'to rule', to
indicate the dominion and monarchical rule of one brother over
another: see TN, and R. Jose bar Halafta in *Gen. Rab.* 67: 7, and
what Jerome seems to have in mind here. Further, the expression
'yoke of servitude' is found exactly in TN and its gloss, FTP, and
FTV of this verse.[5] And FTP, like Jerome, refers specifically to the
Jews in this address to Esau: 'And by your weapons you shall live;

[4] See Salvesen, *Symmachus*, 47–8.
[5] Thus TN reads: 'And by your sword you shall live, and before your brother you
shall serve and *be in servitude* . . . but when the sons of Jacob forsake the
commandments . . . *you shall exercise dominion* (*tšlṭ*) over him and break off the
yoke of servitude from your neck.' The verb *šlṭ* may refer to the exercise of kingly
rule. For the meaning of *imperium* in Jerome's writings, see S. Fanning, 'Jerome's
Concepts of Empire', in L. Alexander (ed.), *Images of Empire* (Sheffield, 1991),
239–50.

and before your brothers the Jews you shall be serving ...', a
sentiment shared with the marginal gloss of TN. Although the
Targums and the Midrashim which expound Gen. 27: 40 do not
exactly coincide with Jerome's remarks, it is curious that both he
and they use similar vocabulary, which is not explicit in the Hebrew
Bible, to give the sense of the verse.

CHAPTER 28

verse 19 Quoting verse 17, Jerome explains that Bethel means
'house of God', and that Jacob called the place by that name. For
the meaning of the former name of the place, Luz, as 'nut' or
'almond', see also *Gen. Rab.* 69: 8. He is concerned to remove the
misconception that the place had three names, Luz, Ulammaus, and
Bethel, which LXX suggest: see Augustine, *QG* 85. The Hebrew
reads: 'And he called the name of that place Bethel; whereas
(*wᵉûlām*) Luz was the name of the city formerly (*lāri'šōnāh*).' LXX
had perpetrated what Jerome calls an absurdity, by stating that the
place was first called Ulammaus. In fact, they read Oulamlouz, and
translated Bethel literally as 'house of God': Oulamlouz is their
Graecized transliteration of Hebrew *'ûlām lûz*. VL has Ulamaus.[1]

While Jerome is right to point out that *'ûlām* means 'forecourt',
he here follows Aquila (Petit, ii. 223; cf. p. 224, the comment of an
unknown author) in thinking that it means 'formerly'. He says
nothing of a different Hebrew word with exactly the same form,
meaning 'however, but'. Jerome none the less knew this other sense
of *'ûlām* (see e.g. Vg of Exod. 9: 16), and he could have translated
the Hebrew as '*but* Luz was the name of the city formerly'. It may
be that, in his eagerness to point out the LXX's mistake, he has
adopted Aquila's reading, overlooking the fact that 'formerly' is
expressed by *lārî'šōnāh* standing at the end of the sentence.[2] On the
other hand, Jerome's words suggest another possible explanation of
what was in his mind: since there is a word *'ûlām* which means
'forecourt', he may have thought of that word as having a spread of
meanings deriving from its fundamental sense of 'what stands in
front', that is, what is before or prior to some other thing: hence,

---

[1] Wevers, pp. 273–4, enumerates a host of variant readings in witnesses to LXX.
They include *oulammaus*, *lammaous*, *oulmaous*, and *oulambanous*. The Greek
tradition clearly experienced difficulty with the word.

[2] See Burstein, 'La Compétence de Jérôme', 4–5.

'formerly'. Such a train of thought may have occurred to him as an explanation of Aquila's translation. He would then have omitted a translation of *lāri'šōnāh* as redundant. Indeed, Aquila seems also to have omitted the last word of the Hebrew.[3] LXX had made one composite word out of *'ūlām* and *lūz*, and Jerome seems to have been especially keen to distinguish these two words from one another.

CHAPTER 29

verse 27 Jerome's disagreement is with Josephus, *Ant.* 1. 302. He espouses common Jewish tradition that Jacob received Rachel as wife after seven days of marriage to Leah, the seven days being the period of the marriage feast.[1] Verse 30 is adduced to show that Jacob had, in fact, married Rachel. See also *Jub.* 28: 8; PJ, TN, FTV, and GM (Klein, p. 43) of this verse; Augustine, *QG* 89; *PRE* 16: 2; 36: 3; *jer. Ket.* 1: 1; *jer. MQ* 1. 80d; and *Midrash Pss.* 90.

verse 32 The Hebrew of this verse states that Reuben's mother Leah so called him because 'the Lord *rā'āh*, has seen my affliction'. Jerome here derives the word from *bēn*, 'son', and *rā'āh*, 'see', as does Philo in *Leg. All.* 1. 81 and *De Somn.* 2. 33. In *Lib. Heb. Nom.* (p. 71) he explains it as either 'a son who sees', or 'one who sees in the midst', this last derived from *rā'āh* and from *bēyn*, 'between'; the same work also has variant explanations of the name as an imperative, 'see the son!' (p. 77) and 'see in the midst!' (p. 160).

verse 33 Simeon is here derived from the root *šm'*, 'to hear', interpreted by Jerome as 'hearing': see also Philo, *De Ebr.* 94 and *De Somn.* 2. 34. *Lib. Heb. Nom.* (p. 72) has this sense, to which it adds 'name of the dwelling', from *šēm*, 'name' and *mā'ōn*, 'dwelling'. The second explanation reappears in the same work (p. 77) along with 'he heard sadness' (cf. p. 160), as also 'one who hears or he heard sadness' (p. 141). Jerome translates neither LXX nor Hebrew, and may be quoting from memory: his only concern is with the name Simeon.

verse 34 The Bible uses *yillāweh* to explain Levi's name. It means 'he shall become attached, joined', which Aquila attempted to

[3] See Field, i. 43.
[1] See also Pesh, and Geiger, *Urschrift*, 460.

translate exactly. Vg has *copulabitur*, 'will be joined'. The sense
'will accompany' is implied in this translation; but another rendering of Jerome's Latin version of what the 'instructors of the Hebrews' say, 'prosequetur me vir meus', would be 'my husband shall
honour me'. Such an understanding of the words may be implied in
b. Ber. 60a. In *Lib. Heb. Nom.* (p. 68), Levi is said to mean 'added'
(so also pp. 76, 157, 160) or 'taken up'; 'contiguous' is also given
(p. 140).

verse 35 As here, so in *Lib. Heb. Nom.* (p. 67) Judah is understood as 'acknowledgement' or 'praise'. The root *yādāh* in the
hiph'il means both 'praise' and 'confess', hence Jerome's comment
and illustration of the sense of the word by means of Matt. 11: 25.
See also the explanation of the name as 'one who acknowledges or
glorifies' and 'one who acknowledges or one who praises' in *Lib.
Heb. Nom.* (pp. 152, 157). His words are close to those of TN of
this verse: 'This time we shall praise and glorify before the Lord.
Therefore she called his name Judah.' GM has: 'This time I shall
give thanks and utter praise before the Lord'; and see Philo, *Leg.
All.* 1. 80, 2. 96; *De Plant.* 134; *De Somn.* 2. 34.

CHAPTER 30

verses 5–6 Probably following the Hebrew text of these verses,
Jerome omits the description of Bala as 'Rachel's handmaid'. The
root *dyn* means 'to judge', and in *Lib. Heb. Nom.* (pp. 64, 74) Dan
is explained as 'judgement' or 'one who judges'. See also Philo, *Leg.
All.* 2. 96, *De Somn.* 2. 35; Josephus, *Ant.* 1. 305.

verses 7–8 Jerome has not at first translated LXX, which have:
'and she bore a second son for Jacob. And Rachel said, God has
helped me, and I contended with my sister and prevailed . . .' In *Lib.
Heb. Nom.* (p. 70) we read: 'Neptalim—He has preserved me, or
He has expanded me [cf. Philo, *De Somn.* 2. 36], or He has surely
entwined me'; but elsewhere in that work the meaning is given as
'breadth' (p. 76) and 'kept apart or separated or he turned or he
intertwined me'. In Vg, Jerome renders as: 'God has put me together (*comparavit*) with my sister.' The Hebrew of verse 8 actually
reads: 'And Rachel said, I have wrestled wrestlings of God with my
sister, and I have prevailed, *naptūlē ᵉlōhīm niptaltī 'im ᵃhōtī gam
yākōltī*.' Aquila's translation of the first three words runs: 'God has

turned me around with a turning around', and Jerome notes how the Greek may also carry the significance of a 'bringing together'.

verses 10–11 The Hebrew text is written (*K'thib*) as *bgd*, vocalized as *beḡād*, meaning 'by chance, by fortune': LXX and Jerome in Vg so translate it. But what by tradition is actually read out (*Q're*) in public recitation of the Hebrew is *bāʾ gād*: this means 'luck has come', and is so rendered by TO. The other Targums, PJ, TN, FTV, FTP, and GM all understood *gd* in the sense of 'luck, fortune', which is one of the meanings given to Gad in *Lib. Heb. Nom.* (p. 67) along with 'temptation or brigand' (cf. pp. 75, 160). The *K'thib* and *Q're* sound very similar in actual pronunciation.[1] Aquila derives the meaning 'troop' (so also *Lib. Heb. Nom.*, p. 75, second translation) by interpreting Gad through the root *gdd*, 'to cut', and its derived noun *gedūd*, 'band, troop': he takes the first element of the expression in the sense of the *Q're*, *bāʾ*, 'has come, comes'. Similar is Symmachus: 'Gad, a band of pirates, has come'.[2] Thus another meaning of Gad in *Lib. Heb. Nom.* (p. 67) is 'brigand'; see also Philo, *De Somn.* 2. 35. Jerome, however, next reverts to the *K'thib*, and suggests the form *beḡād*, meaning 'in, under troop/ arms'. Throughout, Jerome seems to prefer the *K'thib*, and to recognize the ambiguity of the Hebrew. The third sense of Gad given in *Lib. Heb. Nom.* (p. 67) is 'trial'; but it does not feature here. LXX's rendering is problematic, in that it might seem to give authority to the notion that Fortune or Luck was a divine entity: for attempts to combat this, see Augustine, *QG* 91, who regards Leah's words in that version as merely a *façon de parler* which she innocently retained from her heathen past.

verses 12–13 The meaning of Asher, Hebrew *ʾāšēr*, as 'riches' arises from the similar-sounding Hebrew word *ʿōšer*, 'riches'. It is to this similarity in sound that Jerome refers at the end of his comment (see also *Ep.* 54. 16), when he speaks of the twofold meaning, literally 'ambiguity' of the word.[3] But the name Asher, whose meaning in *Lib. Heb. Nom.* (p. 61) is given as 'blessedness' (also pp. 130, 159) or 'blessed' (also pp. 73, 89, 139, 159), is of course from root *ʾšr*, meaning 'go straight', and the curious form *ʾašrē*, meaning literally 'the blessedness, happiness of . . .'. As Jerome says, verse 13 evidently expects us to understand the name as

---

[1] See further Rahmer, *Die hebräischen Traditionen*, 42.
[2] For discussion of Symmachus' reading, see Salvesen, *Symmachus*, 48.
[3] See Rahmer, *Die hebräischen Traditionen*, 42–3.

'blessed'. See also the comments of Philo, *De Somn.* 2. 35, *De Mig. Abr.* 95. We should note that many witnesses of LXX do not add 'riches' as an explanation of the name; but VL clearly favoured this interpretation, which is evident in the work of Ambrose and Cyril.[4]

verses 17–18 LXX and VL have: 'and she called his name Issachar, *which is a reward*.' The italicized words form no part of the Hebrew nor of Jerome's translation of the verse; and he will show that they are not only unnecessary, but misleading. The unvocalized Hebrew form of the name is *ysskr*. As in the case of Gad's name (above, verses 10–11), tradition presents us with a difference between *K'thib* and *Q're*. The former, what is written in the Hebrew text and its expected vocalization, is *yiśśākār*. It seems that Jerome has taken this as *yēš śākār*, 'there is a reward', following the *K'thib*; this he has done earlier in *Lib. Heb. Nom.* (pp. 67, 160). *Gen. Rab.* 72: 5 states that some Jews held this view. See further 49: 14–15, and the commentary on those verses.[5]

verses 19–20 'My husband shall love (or: choose) me' is read by some witnesses to VL as interpretation of LXX's 'shall choose me'. Jerome understands the word in a manner close to PJ: 'The Lord has presented (*zbd*) me with good gifts (*zbwdyn*) of children: this time my husband's dwelling shall be with me'; and Hebrew root *zbl* is understood by TO and Aquila also as 'dwell', probably in the light of 1 Kgs. 8: 13 and its association of *zbl* with 'house'.[6] Aquila also translates the verb as 'will dwell with me'. In *Lib. Heb. Nom.* (p. 73), Zabulon is explained as 'their dwelling', or 'his oath', or 'dwelling of beauty (v.l. of strength)', or 'night's flowing': this last, Jerome now states, is incorrect. It is Philo's explanation of the name (*De Somn.* 2. 34), and seems to be based on *zwb* 'to flow' and *lylh* 'night'. Jerome had adopted it, and it is found also in Ambrose, *Eps.* 12 (30). 10, 19 (71). 5. The phrase is unfortunate, and may mean 'nocturnal emission'.[7]

verse 21 Like Dan, Dinah derives from root *dyn*, 'to judge': see also *Lib. Heb. Nom.* (p. 64), 'this judgement'. Jerome relates the name to the incident described in Gen. 34, where the attempt of Shechem son of Hamor to marry her after he had raped her led to

---

[4] See Wevers, p. 285, first apparatus, and Kamesar, *Jerome*, 108–9.

[5] The readings of *K'thib* and *Q're* (which has *yiśśākār*) are discussed in full by Kasher, *Torah Shelemah*, 1197; see also Rahmer, *Die hebräischen Traditionen*, 43.

[6] On the Targumic renderings of *zbl*, see Grossfeld, *Targum Onqelos to Genesis*, 109.

[7] See Kamesar, *Jerome*, 109–10.

violent reprisals by Dinah's brothers Simeon and Levi. The Greek *dikē* includes the senses of lawsuit, trial, and the penalty exacted from the guilty party, and seems to Jerome to express more directly the full import of the name Dinah. Here, Leah is understood as 'working'; in *Lib. Heb. Nom.* (p. 68) she is called 'industrious', both words from Hebrew root *l'h*, 'to be weary'. Rachel is 'ewe' here and in *Lib. Heb. Nom.* (p. 70), where the word is also taken as: 'seeing the beginning' (roots *r'h*, 'to see', and *ḥll* in *hiph'il*, 'to begin'); 'vision of crime, wicked deed' (again *r'h*, and *r'*, 'evil'); or 'seeing God' (*r'h* and *'l*, 'God'). The meanings 'ewe' and 'seeing God' are adduced again in the same work (pp. 104, 138). Joseph is 'increase' (root *ysp*, 'to add') also in *Lib. Heb. Nom.* (p. 67).

verses 32–3 LXX have: 'Let your flocks pass by today, and separate from there every grey sheep among the rams, and every speckled and spotted among the goats: it shall be my wages. And my righteousness shall answer for me on the next day, because my wages are before you. All whatsoever is not spotted or speckled among the goats, and grey among the rams, shall be stolen with me.'[8] The lengthy exposition of these and the verses following arises, as Jerome says, because LXX is disordered, and clearly had difficulty in translating an awkward Hebrew text. For a valiant attempt to make sense of LXX, see Augustine, *QG* 93. The latter, given here in a very literal translation to reveal the difficulties, reads: 'I shall pass through all your flock today, removing from there each speckled and spotted animal, and every dark animal among the sheep, and the spotted and speckled among the goats: and it shall be my wage. And my righteousness shall answer for me on the following day, when you shall come over my hire before you. Every one that is not speckled and spotted among the goats, and dark among the sheep, it shall be stolen with me.'

Jerome gives a lengthy paraphrase of the Hebrew, attempting to make sense of things through a rational explanation of what happened, adducing as evidence Spanish equestrian lore: see Augustine, *QG* 93, and Oppian, *Cynegetica*.[9] The material from Quintilian is unidentified. It is, however, unlikely that Jerome derived his information directly from Oppian, Quintilian, or any other non-Christian source: much of what he knows about animals and their

[8] On LXX's translation, see further Harl, *Bible d'Alexandrie*, i. 232–3.

[9] See Vallarsi, PL 23 ad loc. for these references, and the mistaken addition of material from Hippocrates in Erasmus' edition of *QHG*.

behaviour seems to have come to him from these writers by way of other Church Fathers.[10] But the same kind of explanation is found also in Jewish sources: some MSS and editions of *Gen. Rab.* 73: 10 have a story of an Ethiopian man—the parallel in *Tanḥ. B. Naśo'* 13 refers to a king of the Arabs—whose wife bore a white son: R. Akiba proceeds to discover that the man had pictures of white men in his house, on which his wife had looked during sexual intercourse.[11] Naḥmanides has a similar explanation in his commentary on this verse. Eusebius of Emesa (Devreesse, p. 77) opposed this explanation of events on the grounds that Laban could have imitated them if natural forces alone were at work; rather, an angel showed Jacob what to do, and the result was God's activity.

verses 41–2 LXX have: 'And it happened at the time when the flocks became pregnant, conceiving in the belly, that Jacob placed the rods before the flocks in the drinking troughs, so that they should conceive by the rods. But whenever the flocks brought forth he did not put them in; but the unmarked ones were Laban's and the marked ones were Jacob's.'[12] This is very different from the Hebrew, of which a literal translation would be as follows: 'And it happened, when the stronger (*hmqšrwt*) sheep became heated, then Jacob would put the rods in front of the sheep in the drinking troughs, so that they should become heated by means of (or: among) the rods. But when the sheep were weak (*wbhʿṭyp*), he did not put them; and the weak ones (*hʿṭpym*) were for Laban, and the strong (*whqšrym*) were for Jacob.' LXX had difficulty with the two roots *ʿṭp* and *qšr*, which mean, respectively, 'to be weak' and 'to be vigorous'. On the assumption that first-born animals are the stronger, all the Targums of these verses, Pesh, and Symmachus render the root *qšr* as 'first-born', and refer *ʿṭp* to 'later born', i.e. weaker animals. Jerome here and in Vg agrees with this interpretation, which may also be found in *Gen. Rab.* 73: 10 (Resh Lakish); *PRK* 27: 3; and *Bereshith Zuṭṭa*.[13] It should be noted that Jerome is concerned to defend the superiority of the Hebrew and to explain

---

[10] See Courcelle, *Late Latin Writers*, 87–9; and further Jay, *L'Exégèse de saint Jérôme*, 190–4.

[11] See also the very similar Haggadah, with detailed description of the circumstances, in *Num. Rab.* 9: 34.

[12] See further Harl, *Bible d'Alexandrie*, i. 232–5.

[13] For the last reference, see the discussion in M. Goshen-Gottstein, *Fragments of Lost Targumim*, i (Ramat-Gan, 1983), 97–8 (in Hebrew). Note that in *Gen. Rab.* R. Johanan understands root *ʿṭp* to refer to 'first-born' animals.

what it means: quite different is Origen, *Sel. in Gen.* 30: 37, who ventures on a complex allegorical exposition of LXX.

The word which we have translated as 'that they should become heated', and which Jerome renders as 'that they might conceive', is *l^eyaḥmēnnāh*: Jerome's exegesis of the word is not known to me from any other source.

CHAPTER 31

verses 7–8 Both Hebrew and LXX have 'your father has deceived me', for which Jerome has put 'your father has lied to me'. LXX's translation of Hebrew *mnym* as 'lambs' may be the result of homoeophony: the Greek *amnos* sounds not unlike *mōnīm*.[1] But the word is *hapax legomenon*: hence the variety of meaning given to it by ancient commentators, including LXX. PJ translated it as 'parts', and Rashi, in tune with *Gen. Rab.* 73: 9, related it to the more common *minyan*, a 'sum' or 'quorum' of not fewer than ten: thus the wages were changed one hundred times. Otherwise, the meaning 'times, occasions', is favoured by TO, TN, Vg, and Pesh, and is given by Eusebius of Emesa (Devreesse, pp. 77–8) and Diodore (Petit, ii. 229) as the readings of 'the Syrian'. Origen, *Sel. in Gen.* 31: 7, notes the readings of Aquila, 'ten numbers', Symmachus, 'ten times in number', and the Hebrew, 'ten times', but persists in attempting to explain the LXX reading. See also Augustine, *QG* 95. Virgil, *Georgics* 2. 150, is adduced to prove that sheep may give birth twice in one year; and Jerome (cf. Augustine, *QG* 95) points out that the Bible is here relaying the same scientific information as the Roman poet.

verse 19 The *t^erāpīm* were sometimes regarded as figures or figurines, not least because of the incident described in 1 Sam. 19: 13–17, where David's wife Michal put *t^erāpīm* in the bed to deceive

---

[1] See further Harl, *Bible d'Alexandrie*, i. 235, and Salvesen, *Symmachus*, 241, who cites G. B. Caird, 'Homoeophony in the Septuagint', in W. D. Davies, R. G. Hammerton-Kelly, and R. Scroggs (eds.), *Jews, Greeks, and Christians—Religious Cultures in Late Antiquity: Essays in Honour of W. D. Davies* (Leiden, 1976), 74–88; E. Tov, 'Loanwords, Homophony, and Transliteration in the Septuagint', *Biblica*, 60 (1979), 216–36; J. de Waard, 'Homophony in the Septuagint', *Biblica*, 62 (1981), 551–61; and J. Barr, 'Doubts about Homoeophony in the Septuagint', *Textus*, 12 (1985), 1–77. For the possibility that Jerome's understanding of the problem here and in 31: 41 owes something to Eusebius of Emesa and Diodore of Tarsus, see Kamesar, *Jerome*, 128–9.

Saul's henchmen into believing that David was sick. Aquila's translation, which Jerome further discusses in *Ep.* 30. 6, may imply that
they were statues in human form: Vg has 'idols', and TO, TN, Ngl,
and PJ of this verse also regard them as images.[2] Origen, *Sel. in
Judg.* 17: 5, adopts the same interpretation. Jerome suggests that
this verse may help us to understand Judg. 17: 5; 18: 14, 17, 18, 20,
where the word refers to a cult object set up in the newly founded
sanctuary at Dan.

verse 21   For the principle of 'anticipation', see the commentary
on 14: 7. The mountain does not receive its name until later in this
chapter, at verse 47.

verse 41   With 'you have changed', Jerome here and in Vg follows
the Hebrew and Symmachus, while LXX have 'you have
misreckoned'. See above on verses 7–8. For Augustine's attempts to
expound LXX of this verse and verse 7, see *QG* 95.

verses 46–7   LXX translated: 'And Jacob said to his brothers:
Gather stones. So they gathered stones and made a mound; and
they ate and drank there upon the mound ... And Laban called it
Mound of Witness; but Jacob called it Mound is Witness.' The
Hebrew for witness is *ēd*, which Jerome has transcribed as *aad*.
Verse 47 contains the only portion of Aramaic in the Pentateuch,
which Jerome refers to here as 'Syrian'. It consists of two words,
vocalized in MT as *yᵉgar sāhᵃdūtā*. MT reads: 'And Laban called it
yᵉgar sāhᵃdūtā, but Jacob called it *galʿēd*.' Jerome notes that Laban
had adopted the Syrian language after the family's departure from
Mesopotamia, having referred already to the Aramaic language in
QHG 14: 2–3; 22: 20–2. His translation of the Hebrew closely
follows LXX, but in Vg he adds at the end of the verse a note, 'each
according to the characteristic idiom of his own language', which
effectively summarizes his comment here. The LXX have obliter-
ated the distinction between Laban's Aramaic and Jacob's Hebrew,
which Jerome strives to retain. Augustine, *QG* 97, gives exactly the
same translations of the Aramaic and Hebrew as Jerome, whose
interpretation he probably follows: he says that it has been handed
down 'by those who know the Syrian and Hebrew tongue'.

Jerome's remarks are entirely concerned with the languages used
and the meanings of words. By contrast Origen (*Sel. in Gen.* 31: 46)
offers no linguistic comment, but presents Jacob as a type of Christ

---

[2] For other interpretations of the word within the Targumic tradition, see
Grossfeld, *Targum Onqelos to Genesis*, 112.

who gathers stones to be built up on the foundation of the prophets
and Apostles with Christ as chief corner-stone: they are living
stones, a spiritual house and holy priesthood (cf. Eph. 2: 19–22; 1
Pet. 2: 4–5).

CHAPTER 32

verses 2–3 The Hebrew *maḥᵃnāyim* is a dual form meaning 'two
camps', and is found as a place-name elsewhere, e.g. Josh. 13: 26,
30; 2 Sam. 2: 8, 12; 1 Kgs. 2: 8. Jerome follows what seems to be
the plain meaning of the biblical text, that the camps consist of
angels: see also Augustine, *QG* 101. But the Targums PJ, TN, FTP,
FTV report that Jacob also considered the possibility that they
might be troops sent by Esau or Laban to oppose him. Jerome may
have been aware of this Targumic tradition, in that TN, FTP, and
FTV state that the angels have been sent to rescue Jacob from Esau
and Laban. But it should be noted that Eusebius of Emesa suggests
that the angels were a proof of God's help for him against Esau
(Devreesse, p. 78). Of particular interest is his description of the
angels as a *chorus*: the being who has dealings with Jacob later on
in this chapter is one of the angels who praise God in song,
according to TN, PJ, FTP, FTV, GM of verse 27. This tradition
originated in pre-Rabbinic times, as *LAB* 18: 6 makes clear. It is
found also in *b. Ḥullin* 91b; *Gen. Rab.* 78: 2; *PRE* 37: 2; and TN
actually names the angel as Sariel, 'Prince of God'.[1] On Jacob as
'prince', see further the comments on verses 28–9 below. Origen,
Sel. in Gen. 32: 2, speaks of Christ as the Way, and of the angels as
meeting such as follow that Way. His concerns are quite different
from Jerome's in these verses.

verses 10–11 The sense of the Hebrew, which Jerome tries to
capture here and in Vg, and which reads literally 'I am too little for
all the mercies . . .', is: 'I am unworthy of all the mercies . . .'. The
full translation of the Hebrew reads: 'And Jacob said, O God of my
father Abraham and God of my father Isaac, O Lord, who said to
me, Return to your land and to your birthplace, and I shall do good

[1] See G. Vermes, 'The Archangel Sariel: A Targumic Parallel to the Dead Sea
Scrolls', in J. Neusner (ed.), *Christianity, Judaism and Other Greco-Roman Cults*,
pt. iii: *Studies for Morton Smith at Sixty* (Leiden, 1975), 159–76; id. 'The Impact of
the Dead Sea Scrolls on Jewish Studies', *JJS* 26 (1975), 12–14.

for you: I am unworthy of all the mercies and of all the truth which you have done for your servant.'

But the various witnesses of LXX present a confused picture. Thus we read: 'let there be for me sufficiency of all the justice . . .'; 'I am satisfied with all the justice . . .'; or 'sufficient for me is all the justice . . .'; and VL, for the most part, opted for the last of these renderings.[2] These translations distort the Hebrew and yield no proper sense.

verses 28–9 Josephus, *Ant.* 1. 333, explained that God ordered Jacob to call himself Israel: 'this, according to the language of the Hebrews, signifies one who opposes an angel of God.' Jerome, however, goes straight to the Hebrew, which explains the name with the words: 'because *śārītā* with God'. But what might this untranslated verb signify? Ancient translators had different opinions, such that Jerome's researches would need to be wide-ranging. As first-fruits of these he quotes Aquila, who took the words to mean 'because you have ruled with God' on the basis of root *śrr*, 'to rule, to be a prince' and *'l*, 'God'. Jerome adopts this explanation here: it is the basis of all the Targumic translations of this verse (TO, PJ, TN, Ngl, GM), which speak of Jacob as prince (Hebrew *śar*) or great one with God or his angels. Likewise, *b. Ḥullin* 32a says that Jacob was made a prince (*śar*) over the angel. Jacob is therefore no longer 'the one who trips men up': see comments on 27: 36.

Symmachus translated *śārītā* as *ērxō*, the second person singular aorist middle of *archō*, which means 'you have begun': he seems to have derived the word from the Aramaic root *šry*, 'begin', to yield: 'because you have begun with God'. It is possible that Symmachus chose the verb *archō* with the notion of 'rule' in mind; or that Jerome understood his rendering as suggesting 'rule'; or the form in which his reading has come down to us is corrupt: if that is so, then we may yoke his translation with Aquila's.[3] But whatever Jerome's understanding of him in this verse, Symmachus may still have interpreted Hebrew *śārītā* as if it derived from Aramaic *šry*, 'to begin', choosing the aorist middle form deliberately to give the sense of 'to begin a religious act' and translating Hebrew *'im*, 'with', as *pros*, 'in relation to' God. If, as seems probable in the light of

---

[2] See Harl, *Bible d'Alexandrie*, i. 240–1, and Wevers, p. 310 for other variants and Aquila's version of the Hebrew, to which Jerome's is very similar.

[3] See Kamesar, *Jerome*, 121–2.

recent research, Symmachus was a Jew, then he probably knew traditions which related Jacob's change of name to divine promises about Israel's priesthood and sacral status encapsulated in this event.[4]

Theodotion's 'because you have striven (or: prevailed) with God' is close to LXX and Pesh, which understood the word through root *šrr*, 'to be hard, be firm'. This last Jerome also takes seriously, combining, it seems, the understanding of Israel as *prince* and as one who *strives* both with God and men. With this, we might compare *Gen. Rab.* 78: 3,

> You have wrestled with those above, and have prevailed over them; with those below, and you have prevailed over them. 'With those above'—this refers to the angel. R. Hama bar Hanina said: It was Esau's angel ... 'With those below and you have prevailed over them'—this refers to Esau and his troops. Another explanation of 'for you have ruled with God'—You are the one whose image is engraved above.

Theodoret, *QG* 93, also envisaged the events as encouragement for Jacob to confront Esau. In Vg, Jerome renders this verse as: 'For if against God you have been strong, how much the more shall you prevail against men!' He presents Jacob's partner here as God; but notes that there is disagreement among interpreters, and that an angel may be spoken of: such is the opinion of Eusebius of Emesa (Devreesse, p. 78). This difference of opinion is evident even in Jewish tradition: TO can say of Jacob 'you are a prince before the Lord', while TN (cf. Ngl, GM) goes further in toning down the anthropomorphism of the original Hebrew with 'you have been superior over angels from before the Lord'.

When Jerome says that *śarith* means 'prince', however, he interprets this verb as a noun, even though he has been quoting the Three who, without exception, translate the word as a verb. Given the use he has made of the Three and the comments which follow it seems highly unlikely that this note indicates a view of his own different from theirs, or even an attack on them.[5] Jerome is either

---

[4] For Symmachus as a Jew, see above, n. 31 to the Commentary on the preface. Jacob's change of name to Israel occurs at the same time and in the same place as Levi's appointment to the priesthood, while Jacob plans to build a temple, according to *Jub.* 32: 16–18. For the change of name associated with Israel's future priestly status, see also Philo, *De Abr.* 56; and PJ of Gen. 35: 11.

[5] See A. Butterweck, *Jakobs Ringkampf am Jabbok* (Judentum und Welt, 3; Frankfurt am Main, 1981), 185–6 (Jerome's comment owes nothing to the Three);

rather loosely giving the overall meaning of the word in a down-to-
earth fashion, or has been influenced by Rabbinic exegesis like *b.*
Ḥullin 92a cited above which interpreted the verb as 'he was made
a prince'.[6]

The meaning of Israel as 'a man, (or: mind) seeing God', noted in
Lib. Heb. Nom. (pp. 75, 139, 152, 155), can be traced back to
Philo: see, for example, *Leg. All.* 2. 34, 3. 15. Philo's influence was
very great,[7] and his explanation of the name was followed by most
Christian scholars, as Clement of Alexandria, *Stromateis* 2. 20. 2,
Paid. 1. 9. 57; Origen, *De Prin.* 4. 3, *Hom. in Num.* 11. 4. 7;
Eusebius, *Praep. Evang.* 11. 6. 31; Basil, *Comm. on Isaiah* 15;
Hilary, *De Trin.* 4. 31; and Eusebius of Emesa (Devreesse, p. 78)
can testify—to name but a few.[8] Jerome explains simply and clearly
why, in terms of the Hebrew language, this etymology is incorrect.
But he did not consign this sense of the name to oblivion; years later
he remarks that Israel might be understood as 'a man seeing God'
not in terms of the actual letters making up the name, but in the
way it sounds (*In Esa.* 12. 44: 1 ff.).

In passing, however, he refers to another possible meaning of the
name Israel as 'most honest one of God' (cf. *Lib. Heb. Nom.*, p.
139), thereby deriving it from root *yšr*, 'to be straight, to be right',
yielding the adjective *yāšār*, 'upright', and *'ēl*, 'God'. The clue to this
explanation is found in Hos. 12: 2–4, where the prophet gives his
own account of the naming of Israel. In 12: 3(4)–4(5) he para-
phrases the Genesis story with the words *śārāh 'et 'elōhīm: wayyāśar*
'el mal'āk ..., which RSV translates as 'he strove with God. He

and Miller, *Mysterious Encounters*, 215 n. 66 (Jerome criticizes the Three as well as
Josephus and LXX).

[6] For the latter explanation, see Kamesar, *Jerome*, 122, quoting *b. Ḥullin* 92a and
Gen. Rab. 78: 3; see also Butterweck, *Jakobs Ringkampf*, 29, 186, who cites TO's
rendering 'you are a prince before the Lord'.

[7] For a convenient summary of passages in Philo where he treats of the name
Israel, see the Loeb edition of his works, vol. x (Cambridge, Mass. and London,
1971), 334.

[8] See also *The Prayer of Joseph*, fr. A, translated by J. Z. Smith in J. H.
Charlesworth (ed.), *The Old Testament Pseudepigrapha*, ii (London, 1985), 713; for
Smith's discussion of 'a man seeing God' and Christian use of it, and the episode
recounted in Gen. 32, see ibid., pp. 703, 705–9. For a further list of authorities who
followed this explanation so that it became a cliché, see Kamesar, *Jerome*, 119–20.
Years after having written *QHG*, in his commentary *In Esa.* 12. 44: 1 ff., Jerome
remarks that the name Israel sounds in pronunciation as if it were 'a man who sees
God', even though its spelling does not warrant the interpretation: see discussion by
Jay, *L'Exégèse de saint Jérôme*, 295–6.

strove with the angel, and prevailed.' In Vg, however, Jerome took these words to mean, 'he was *upright* with the angel. And he prevailed over the angel . . .'. For the rendering of the first verb, there is little doubt that he followed Aquila (see Field, ii. 959–60), who translated both verbs as *katōrthōse*, which has a basic sense of 'he was upright'.

Jerome records this meaning of the name at *In Osee* 3. 12: 2–6, and *In Esa.* 12. 44: 1 ff. In the latter, the name Israel is qualified by a rare description of the Jews as Jeshurun, which LXX translated as 'beloved' but which 'the rest' took as '*euthutatos*, most upright' (Field, ii. 519, on Isa. 44: 2). Jeshurun occurs also in Deut. 33: 5 in the expression 'and He was king in Jeshurun': once more LXX translated as 'beloved', but Symmachus and Theodotion (Field, i. 324–5) have *en tōi euthei*. Jerome, in Vg, translated as 'in the presence of the most upright'. Given the definition of Israel as Jeshurun, which is a scriptural datum, Jerome no doubt felt justified in proposing a further derivation of the name from root *yšr*, a proposal which the translations of the Three clearly substantiated.[9]

verses 30–1   The Hebrew has *pᵉnîʾēl*, not *pᵉnûʾēl*, which is what Jerome seems to have read here and in Vg in common with the Samaritan Pentateuch, TO, Symmachus, Pesh, and Josephus, *Ant.* 1. 334. This latter form, as Jerome notes, is found elsewhere in Scripture: see Judg. 8: 8, 9, 17, and 1 Kgs. 12: 25. Scribal confusion of the vowel letters *yodh* and *waw*, representing long i and long u respectively, was fairly common; and it is also possible that the Hebrew text which Jerome knew had assimilated the reading of the word in this verse to the more common form Penuel found in the other biblical passages we have noted.

Jerome insists that Penuel is the name of a place, and in *Lib. Loc.* 914 he lists it under Fanuel as the place alongside the wadi Jabbok where Jacob wrestled and earned the name Israel: he says the word means 'the face of God' because it was there that Jacob saw God (see also his *Comm. in Esa.* 3. 6: 1). For the meaning 'face of God', see also *Lib. Heb. Nom.* (pp. 66, 100, 140). Neither LXX nor VL had transliterated Peniel as a proper name: the former has *eidos theou*, which might mean 'the form, appearance, look, shape, figure of God', and the latter tries to reproduce these nuances.[10] The way

---

[9] See also Jay, ibid.; Kamesar, *Jerome*, 123–5. For discussion of other passages in Jerome's works which refer to these verses, see Miller, *Mysterious Encounters*, 128–9.   [10] See Fischer, p. 353.

was open for Christian exegetes to refer this expression to Christ, who is the image of God: see Clement of Alexandria, *Paid*. 1. 57. 2; but Jerome appears to rule this out of order.

CHAPTER 33

verses 1–3 The Hebrew *wayyaḥaẓ* indeed means 'and he divided'; but the noun from this root, *ḥẓy*, means 'a half', and Aquila has translated the verb accordingly. Jerome follows this, to argue that Jacob's company was in two groups, not three. He directs his remarks against writers such as Josephus (*Ant.* 1. 328–30), who envisaged a threefold division, with the two groups of Jacob's family preceded by an advance party bearing gifts.

verse 17 The Hebrew reads: 'And Jacob journeyed to Sukkoth, and built a house for himself; and for his flocks he made booths (or: tents, Hebrew *sukkōt*). Therefore he called the name of the place Sukkoth.' LXX had reproduced this as: 'And Jacob departed to tents (*skēnai*), and made there houses for himself; and for his flocks he made tents. Therefore he called the name of that place Tents.' The name of the place is Sukkoth, which does indeed signify 'booths, tabernacles': see also *Lib. Heb. Nom.* (pp. 77, 85). *The Book of Places* has a reference to Sene, *Lib. Loc.* 967. This is presumably an error for Skenai, 'tents', which LXX read for Sukkoth in this verse. The entry is as follows: 'That is, tabernacles, the place where Jacob lived when he returned from Mesopotamia; which in the Hebrew language is called Soccoth.' In Vg at the end of this verse, Jerome puts the Hebrew name Soccoth, and adds 'that is, Tents'.

verse 18 The city of Melchizedech was called Salem, according to Gen. 14: 18; and in his comments above on that verse (q.v.), as well as here, Jerome appears to accept the traditional Jewish identification of that place with Jerusalem. By contrast, in *Ep.* 73. 7 he tells of 'a town opposite Scythopolis which is called Salem up to this day; and Melchizedech's palace is shown there: it consists of a vast set of ruins, displaying the grandeur of the ancient construction. Moreover, in the latter part of Genesis there is written concerning it: And Jacob crossed over into Salem.' The *Lib. Loc.* 966 is more complicated, and refers to one Salem as a city of the Shechemites, 'which is Shechem' (see also *Ep.* 73. 8); and to another Salem west of Aelia at the eighth milestone from Scythopolis: the latter is presumably the Salem spoken of in *Ep.* 73. 7. Finally, he refers to Josephus' identification of Salem, where Melchizedech was king, with Jerusalem.

Jerome here admits that there may be two or possibly more places called Shechem, and seems to stand aside from his earlier identification of this Salem with Jerusalem. But he notes that the word may be understood as a qualification of Shechem, since Hebrew root *šlm* has connotations of 'whole, perfect, complete' on the one hand, and of 'peace' on the other. For the interpretation of the name Jerusalem with reference to peace, he had before him Heb. 7: 2, which has influenced *Lib. Heb. Nom.* (pp. 72, 157). He explains that the meaning of the word depends on the vocalization of the root: thus *šālēm* is 'whole, complete', while *šālōm* is 'peace'.

The tradition that Jacob's thigh was healed here is found in *Gen. Rab.* 79: 5; *b. Shabb.* 33b; *Tanḥ. Wayyišlaḥ* 9. His thigh had been put out of joint after his encounter with the celestial being, a matter described earlier in Gen. 32: 32. The Targums give a general description of his 'perfection' without specifying that his thigh was healed. Thus for PJ he came 'complete in respect all that was his'; for TN 'perfect in good deed'; and for TO 'safely'. In the Vg, however, Jerome retains Salem as the name of the place, the city of the Sichimites.[1]

CHAPTER 34

verses 20–1 The Hebrew has: 'There men are *šlmym* with us', meaning, as Rashi points out, both 'peaceable' (so LXX, Vg) and 'whole-hearted'. Aquila may have tried to reproduce this in his translation. Jerome refers to 33: 18; so does TN, by describing the men as 'perfect in good deed with us' (cf. GM of this verse).

verse 25 The Hebrew word is *beṭaḥ*, which properly means 'in security', as LXX and Pesh have rendered it; so also TO, PJ, and TN, 'in safety'. Vg has 'confidently', here put last of all as a possible rendering: it is also the translation of Aquila, and Jerome derives it from the root *bṭḥ* in its sense of 'trust, be confident'.

---

[1] See also Rashi and *Leqaḥ Ṭov* on this verse: the name of the city is Shechem, and Salem refers to Jacob. The verse is discussed by Rahmer, *Die hebräischen Traditionen*, 43.

CHAPTER 35

verse 6   See above, comments on 28: 19.

verse 8   Jerome has translated the Hebrew, which has the words 'and was buried' not found in LXX. The Hebrew for 'nurse', *mēneqet*, occurs here and in 24: 59. In the latter verse, LXX translated it as 'property': see comments above.

verse 10   Jerome has not translated LXX, which does not include the final 'and He called his name Israel'. Nor does he fully translate the Hebrew, which has: 'And God said to him, Your name is Jacob. Your name shall no more be called Jacob, but Israel shall be your name. And He called his name Israel.' In Vg, Jerome omits 'and God said to him', replacing it with 'saying', and the following 'Your name is Jacob'. The events of Gen. 32: 24–32 are regarded as a renaming of Jacob 'by anticipation', a notion already discussed in 14: 7. Here, Jerome seems to agree with those who held that the being Jacob encountered was an angel, who merely tells in advance what is now realized by God Himself. This is the view also of *Leqah Tov* and *Sekhel Tov* on this verse; and *Gen. Rab.* 82: 3, R. Jose bar Haninah.

verse 16   Jerome has possibly reproduced VL, which specifies the land 'of Canaan' found neither in LXX nor in the Hebrew. It has probably been introduced into this verse under the influence of Gen. 48: 7. The Hebrew *kibrat hā'āreṣ*, a rare expression (only here; 48: 7; 2 Kgs. 5: 19) meaning, probably, 'a distance of land', puzzled LXX. As Jerome says, they rendered it here as the name of a place, Chabratha. In Gen. 48: 7, which says: 'Rachel died beside me in the land of Canaan on the road, while there was still *kibrat hā'āreṣ* to come to Ephratha', LXX have put 'in the land of Canaan, while I was approaching the hippodrome *chabratha* of the land to come to Ephratha'. It would seem that 'hippodrome' is an explanation of the transliterated Hebrew word. Even odder is their apparent use of 'hippodrome' as an explanation of the Hebrew place-name Ephratha in 35: 19, where they put 'the hippodrome of Ephratha'.[1]

---

[1] The similarity of the two words *kbrt* and *'prt* in Hebrew script may have encouraged LXX to interpret one in the light of the other: otherwise, LXX may have translated from Hebrew MSS with readings differing from our MT. In all cases, however, Chabratha and Ephratha are retained as place-names.

Aquila's translation seems to regard *kibrat* as a measure of distance, which is the view of Pesh and TO.[2] Jerome prefers an explanation which is paralleled in *Gen. Rab.* 82: 7, 'R. Eliezer ben Jacob said: When the land is hollow like a sieve (*kkbrh*) and the corn is found. The Rabbis said: When already the corn (*kbr hbr*) is found, and the rains are past, but summer heat has not yet come.'[3] PJ also interprets the phrase as a time of year, 'the full time of the harvest of the land', as does TN, 'the time of the harvest of the land'; but FTV combines the idea that *kibrat* is a measure of distance with a temporal sense, rendering 'the time of a measure of land'. Vg, like *QHG*, has 'springtime'. It seems probable that Jerome's exegesis owes something to Jewish understandings of the phrase still extant in Targum and Midrash; but his use of the words 'choice' and 'pick' may have come to him from other quarters. For he seems not entirely to abandon the LXX's notion that *kibrat* refers to a place, and considers the root *bḥr*, 'to choose', as its root: see *Lib. Heb. Nom.* (p. 64), where he gives the meaning of Chabratha as 'chosen' or 'heavy'. Jerome regards his overall understanding of the word as confirmed by the place-names Ephratha and Bethlehem. The first he derives from Hebrew root *prh*, 'be fruitful', as in *Ep.* 108. 10; and the second he translates literally as 'house of bread'. For the reference to Christ as the Bread from Heaven, see John 6: 32–58.

verse 18 Jerome describes the sounds of *ben 'ōnī* and *binyāmīn*, which are similar. He renders Benoni as 'son of my sorrow', and Benjamin as 'son of the right hand' also in *Lib. Heb. Nom.* (p. 62), *Ep.* 108. 10, and, for Benjamin, *Lib. Heb. Nom.* (pp. 79, 152, 155, 159). The right hand is, of course, a common symbol for strength, as in Exod. 15: 6. The final part of the comment disagrees with Philo, who regularly explained Benjamin as 'son of days': see *De Mut. Nom.* 92–6; *De Somn.* 2. 36; *De Mig. Abr.* 203. Since Gen. 44: 20 speaks of Benjamin as a son of Jacob's old age, such an interpretation of the name might seem reasonable, and is thus found in *Test. Ben.* 1: 5–6 and *Leqaḥ Ṭov* on this verse; but Jerome insists that the explanation is not consonant with what he knows of

---

[2] The sense of 'distance' may be original: see E. Vogt, 'Benjamin geboren "eine Meile" von Ephrata', *Biblica*, 56 (1975), 30–6.

[3] Quoted by Rahmer, *Die hebräischen Traditionen*, 44–5.

the Hebrew language.[4] Vg explains both names: 'Benoni, that is, Son of my sorrow'; and 'Beniamin, that is, Son of the right hand'. See also *Ep.* 140. 16.

verse 21 LXX have this verse as a preface to verse 16, and render: 'And Jacob set out from Bethel, and pitched his tent beyond the tower of Gader'. The Hebrew has: 'And Israel journeyed, and pitched his tent beyond Migdal Eder'. The place-name Migdal Eder is here understood as 'tower of the flock': see also *Lib. Heb. Nom.* (p. 61) for Ader as 'flock'. This may be yet another instance where Jerome relates a Jewish tradition unrecorded in early sources, since nothing earlier than the *MHG* on this verse identifies Migdal Eder with Jerusalem. None the less, the late collections *Leqaḥ Ṭov* and *Sekhel Ṭov* do connect this verse with Micah 4: 8, quoted here by Jerome, which speaks of 'the tower of the flock [Migdal Eder], the hill of the daughter of Zion'. This prophetic verse would have encouraged an early identification of Migdal Eder with Zion-Jerusalem. Jerome repeats LXX's translation of this verse, which took 'hill', Hebrew *ʿōpel* (which itself may be a proper name Ophel) as if it were *ʾōpel*, 'gloom' (cf. Aquila), or even, perhaps, *ᵃrāpel*, 'thick cloud'.

Against this, Jerome seems to set the geography of Jacob's journey: according to verse 19, he is located close to Bethlehem. Understanding Eder as 'flock', he could link Migdal Eder to Bethlehem, where the shepherds who heard of Christ's birth from the host of angels (Luke 2: 8–14) were tending flocks, and interpret the verse as a prophecy in a mystery (see above, 14: 18) of events in the Gospel: see also *Ep.* 108. 10. It is noteworthy that PJ of this verse describes Migdal Eder as 'the place from where the King Messiah is destined to be revealed at the end of days'.[5]

verse 27 LXX have: 'And Jacob came . . . to Mambre, to a city of the plain, this is Hebron in the land of Canaan' for the Hebrew 'And Jacob came . . . to Mamre, Kiriath Arba, which is Hebron'. Jerome had visited Hebron, and was able to speak of its position from his own experience. See also *Lib. Loc.* 934–5, where we are told that Hebron was once called Arbe, of which Arboc is a corrupt

---

[4] See further Kamesar, *Jerome*, 110–12, who contrasts Jerome's lucid correctness with the opaqueness of Greek sources dealing with this name.

[5] See P. Winter, 'The Cultural Background of the Narrative in Luke I and II', *JQR* 45 (1954), 238–40; le Déaut, *La Nuit pascale*, 277. On Jerome's use of *vaticinium* to designate the prophecy, see comments on 10: 24 and notes.

version (see above, 23: 2); and ibid. 955, where Mambre is both identified with Hebron and named as one of Abraham's friends.

CHAPTER 36

verse 4 Eliphaz is described in the Book of Job (2: 11) as a Temanite, here further identified as a descendant of Esau. *Sekhel Ṭov* on this verse says that he prophesied in the days of Job, but does not identify him as a son of Ada. See further below on verse 22.

verses 19–20 LXX of verse 19 differs from the Hebrew, which Jerome appears to have translated here. The former read: 'These are the sons of Esau, and these are their leaders. These are the sons of Edom', while the latter has 'These are the sons of Esau, who is Edom; and these are their chiefs'. See above on 25: 25, 30.

verse 20 Jerome begins his quotation of LXX in mid-sentence. That version reads: 'And these are the sons of Seir, of the Chorraean . . .'. Chorraean is an attempt to reproduce Hebrew *ḥōrī*, 'the Horites', which Jerome understands here and at *In Abdiam* 1 as 'free' in the light of the Mishnaic Hebrew root *ḥrr*, 'set free'. It is possible that he intends his explanation of the name to be understood as it is by R. Aha ben Jacob in *b. Shabb.* 85b, that they were 'set free from their property', since he tells how Esau dispossessed them according to Deut. 2: 21. He thus distances himself from his other attempts to explain the name in *Lib. Heb. Nom.* (pp. 64, 86) as 'irascible' (from root *ḥrh*, 'burn with anger'), or 'from the holes (i.e. of the rocks)', Troglodytes (from *ḥōr*, 'a hole'). In the same way he shows no knowledge of PJ's interpretation of the name as 'nobles'.

verse 22 Eliphaz the Temanite had a concubine named Thimna, according to Gen. 36: 12. Jerome may be quoting that verse from memory, since he has reproduced neither the Hebrew nor LXX, which read: 'And Thimna was concubine to Eliphaz, son of Esau, and she bore Amalek to Eliphaz.' The preceding verse also refers to Theman and Kenaz who, with Amalek, once gave their names to lands subsumed into Idumaean territory in Jerome's day.

verse 24 Jerome gives the names of the persons in this verse in forms closer to the Hebrew than LXX. The word which so puzzled him is vocalized in MT as *hayyēmim*; but the consonants may indeed be read as *hayyamīm*, 'seas', which he has already confirmed (see 1: 10) as Hebrew idiom for pools of water. Jerome is careful to note that the same consonants can be taken as 'seas', perhaps to distance himself from a garbled Christian etymology of the word based on Hebrew *hammayim*, 'the water', extant in the Catenae (Petit, ii. 239). That Iamin means water was the view of 'the Syrian' quoted by Theodoret, *QG* 94, and of 'the Syrian and the Hebrew' quoted by Diodore (Petit, ii. 241); indeed, it is the reading of Pesh and *Leqaḥ Ṭov* on this verse.[1] 'Hot waters' is the sense Jerome prefers in Vg: there is no known Jewish precedent for this, and his invocation of Punic in support of the opinion must remain doubtful.[2] Possibly the root *ḥmm*, 'be warm', has influenced his interpretation.

Two differing interpretations refer the word to animals. The first envisages the mating of male wild asses with female domesticated asses to produce swift-footed creatures: this partly corresponds with PJ of this verse, which says that Anah 'hybridized wild asses with she-asses'; but the Targum goes on to say that these produced mules. This cannot be the case, since mules are produced by crossing horses with asses. However, Jerome's final explanation of the word is that it means precisely 'mules', the offspring of female horses and male asses. This last compares with *jer. Ber.* 8: 5, although there we read of she-asses crossed with stallions; a little later, however, in *jer. Ber.* 8: 8, there is extended discussion on how to recognize a mule whose dam is a horse and sire an ass, and vice versa. PJ, incidentally, seems to have conflated the two interpretations which Jerome has carefully kept separate.[3] In fact, 'mules' is the most common Rabbinic understanding of the word: see also *Gen. Rab.* 82: 14; *b. Ḥullin* 7b, cited by Rashi on this verse. Aquila and Symmachus transliterated the word as a plural noun, LXX and Theodotion as a singular: these translators may not have known what the word meant or, being aware of different possible interpretations, opted to remain neutral.[4]

---

[1] 'Waters' is what the Syriac text actually reads. For discussion of conjectural emendations, see Rahmer, *Die hebräischen Traditionen*, 45–6; and Grossfeld, *Targum Onqelos to Genesis*, 125.

[2] See Rahmer, *Die hebräischen Traditionen*, 46–7.

[3] See also Rahmer, ibid. 47.

[4] The witnesses to Aquila, Symmachus, and Theodotion differ among themselves in the way the transliterated word is spelled; and a number ascribe a singular form of the word to Symmachus: see Wevers, pp. 345–6, second apparatus.

verse 33 See above on 22: 20–2. Some witnesses to VL add, after Jobab's name, the words 'who is the Patriarch Job':[5] see also Theodoret, *QG* 95, and Epiphanius, *Adv. Haer.* 1.

CHAPTER 37

verse 3 Joseph's 'coat of many colours' is Hebrew *keṭōnet passīm*. The first word of this pair means 'tunic', but the second is rare and occasioned discussion. Aquila's rendering is shared essentially with TO, TN, PJ, FTP, and FTV; Pesh; and *Leqaḥ Ṭov*: the tunic was richly decorated, and reached to the ankles. Symmachus regarded it as indicating long sleeves: so also *Gen. Rab.* 84: 8 and *Aggadath Bere'shith*. The word *passīm* occurs also in 2 Sam. 13: 18, and in his version of the narrative which includes that verse, Josephus (*Ant.* 7. 171) describes it as a sleeved tunic reaching to the ankles. Both ancient translators saw here the Hebrew word *pas*, 'sole' of the foot or, by extension, the 'palm' of the hand. Notwithstanding his remarks here, Jerome translated it in Vg as *polymitam*, 'brocaded, of many threads'; see also *Ep.* 130. 2. Jerome's technical and philological comments here owe nothing to, and differ entirely from, the allegorical and theological lessons perceived in this tunic by (e.g.) Clement of Alexandria, *Stromateis* 5. 53. 2–3; Origen, *Hom. in Ezech.* 6. 9.

verse 28 The Hebrew, Vg, and the Targums read 'silver' instead of LXX's 'gold'.[1] Jerome sees here an instance of the 'Hebrew truth', since it was unthinkable to him that Joseph could have been sold for more money than was Christ, whom Judas betrayed for thirty pieces of silver (Matt. 26: 15). See Jerome, *Comm. in Matt.* 4; *Comm. in Philemon* 613c.

verse 36 LXX have used *archimageiros* to translate Hebrew *sar haṭṭabbāḥīm* in this verse and at 40: 3 (Codex Alexandrinus); 41: 10, 12. The Greek verb *mageireuein* has a primary sense of 'to be a cook; to cook meat'; secondarily, it means 'to butcher'. Hebrew root *ṭbḥ* means primarily 'to slaughter', and the noun *ṭabbāḥ* from

---

[5] See Fischer, p. 380, citing an anonymous source and Gregory of Tours, *Hist.* 1. 8.

[1] LXX have probably altered the Hebrew in the light of the price of slaves at the time when the translators were working: see Harl, *Bible d'Alexandrie*, i. 262, and the literature there cited.

the root means 'cook' or 'guardsman'. LXX appear to have tried to find a translation which does justice to both senses of the Hebrew. Thus while *Jub.* 34: 11; 39: 2, VL of this verse and of 40: 3; 41: 10, 12, and *LAB* 8: 9 took the expression to mean 'chief of the cooks',[2] Philo and Josephus kept LXX's translation (e.g. Philo, *Leg. All.* 3. 236, *De Jos.* 23; Josephus, *Ant.* 2. 39) with its double meaning.

But we find elsewhere the phrase *rab ṭabbāḥīm* (e.g. 2 Kgs. 25: 8, 10; Jer. 39: 9), meaning a military commander, a chief guardsman who may also act as an executioner. It is probably with these passages in mind that TO of Gen. 37: 36 has 'chief of the killers, executioners', while TN and PJ read 'chief of the guardsmen'; and Jerome's Vg has 'chief of the army'.[3] See also his rendering of the phrase in Vg Gen. 40: 3; 41: 10 ('chief of the soldiers'); and 41: 12 ('leader of the soldiers'). Jerome's refusal to follow LXX and VL was apparently noted by Augustine, *QG* 127.

Potiphar is here called a eunuch; but later there are references to his notorious wife (e.g. 39: 7) and to his daughter (41: 45). The Jewish tradition which Jerome sets forth to explain Potiphar's situation is well represented in extant sources. Thus PJ of Gen. 39: 1 reads: 'And Potiphar bought him, because he saw that he was beautiful, with a view to committing sodomy with him; and immediately it was decreed [by God] against him that his testicles should shrivel up; and he became an eunuch.' The same account appears also in *Gen. Rab.* 86: 3; *b. Soṭ.* 13b; *Tanḥ. B.* ad loc. Jerome clearly prefers this Jewish resolution of the difficulty to the efforts of Diodore (Petit, ii. 256), who presents 'the Syrian' and 'the Hebrew' as making 'eunuch' do duty for 'faithful man', since the eunuch is most often in charge of royal possessions.[4]

---

[2] But see O. Wintermute, 'Jubilees', in J. H. Charlesworth (ed.), *The Old Testament Pseudepigrapha*, i (London, 1983), 121 note b. Further to the reading of LXX, Harl, *Bible d'Alexandrie*, i. 263, comments on the fact that in Gen. 40: 3 Codex Alexandrinus this same official's title is *archimageiros*, but Codex Vaticanus reads *desmophulax*, 'gaol-keeper'.

[3] TN and PJ use the Latin loan-word *spiculator*, here translated 'guardsman', in this verse and at 40: 3, 4; 41: 10, 12; see also GM of 41: 10, 12. The Latin is properly *speculator*, and in Rabbinic literature can have the sense of 'executioner'. See Schürer, *History of the Jewish People*, i. 371.

[4] Gennadius (Petit, ii. 255), explains the description of Potiphar as a eunuch as a *katachrēsis*, the 'abuse' of a term which might also include a quite radical adaptation of its meaning. One interpretation of the word 'eunuch' in this verse may be 'benevolent', *eunoun*, a sense which is clearly dependent on the Greek translation, not the Hebrew text of the Bible. For the understanding and use of *katachrēsis* among the Fathers, see Kamesar, *Jerome*, 164–7. Jerome's knowledge of the Hebrew

The position of Potiphar as high priest of Heliopolis receives further attention at 41: 45, where the Bible refers to him as priest of On; see also 41: 50; 46: 20. On is the native Egyptian name for Heliopolis, and is so understood by LXX; *Jub.* 34: 11; 40: 10; 44: 24; Artapanus, *ap.* Eusebius, *Praep. Evang.* 9. 23. 3; Demetrius *ap.* Eusebius, ibid. 9. 21. 12. It was the centre of worship of the gods Re-harakhty and Atum, with whom was associated the sacred bull Mnevis (Strabo, *Geography* 17. 1. 22, 27): for many years it was patronized by the Pharaohs, and offered sacral support and justification for their rule. But by classical times Heliopolis had become renowned as a centre of philosophical, scientific, and religious learning; thus Jerome is able to represent Potiphar as 'hierophant', that is, the revealer and teacher of religious mysteries, doctrines, and ceremonial actions.[5] Philo used this word to describe Moses (see especially *De Post.* 173) and his purity of body (*De Somn.* 2. 109). It should be noted that Jerome does not distinguish Potiphar the owner of Joseph from Potiphar the father-in-law of Joseph as two separate individuals: Origen, *Sel. in Gen.* 41: 45, records this distinction, but also refers to a Jewish apocryphal work asserting that they were identical.[6]

CHAPTER 38

verse 5 The Hebrew reads: 'and she called his name Selah; and he (not 'she', as LXX and VL read) was *bik^ezīb* when she bore him'. The root *kzb* means 'to lie' and, when applied to rivers or plants, 'to fail, give out': Jerome illustrates this latter sense at the end of his comment, by referring to Hab. 3: 17. Aquila takes the verse to mean that she failed to give birth to children after Selah, and Jerome follows his interpretation. But the Rabbinic tradition pointed to Chezib as the name of a place which signifies her failure to produce children thereafter. This interpretation is found in *Gen. Rab.* 85: 4, PJ, and FTP of this verse. TO reads simply

text of Scripture and the Jewish tradition meant that he did not have to resort to such devices.

[5] For the fame of the Heliopolitan priests and their learning, see Herodotus, *Hist.* 2. 3, and Strabo, *Geography* 17. 1. 29. The latter tells how philosophy and astronomy were taught there, and that Plato and Eudoxus were pupils of the priests.
[6] On this apocryphon, see further de Lange, *Origen and the Jews*, 129.

the name as if it were a place. Jerome, too, in *Lib. Loc.* 935 states that Chazbi is now 'a desert place near Adullam in the regions of Eleutheropolis', adding that the matter is debated more fully in *QHG*.

In *QHG*, however, he follows Aquila and interprets Chazbi in a manner very close to TN, which reads: 'and it was the case that she ceased (i.e. having children) after she bore him', words which are found almost exactly in Pesh, and recall the two words of FTV, 'and it came to pass that she ceased'. While the Jewish sources quoted above allow for Chazbi as the name of a place, these do not; and the likelihood of Jerome's indebtedness to Targumic tradition in this instance cannot be ruled out.[1] Jerome follows the general drift of *QHG* in the Vg, 'when he was born, she ceased from bearing children any more'.

verse 12 The Hebrew reads *rēʿēhū*, 'his friend', whereas LXX and VL vocalized the same consonants *rʿhw* as *rōʿēhū*, 'his shepherd'. Without the possessive suffixes, the words are *rēʿeh* and *rōʿeh* respectively; and an unvocalized consonantal Hebrew text could be interpreted with respect to either word. In Vg Jerome translated the word as *opilio*, 'shepherd'.

verse 14 The Hebrew *bᵉpetaḥ ʿēnayim*, literally 'at the gate of the two eyes', could be taken in different ways. Enayim might be the name of a place, as LXX 'at the gates (plural) of Ainan', VL (cf. Jerome's translation here) 'at the gate of Aenan', and *b. Soṭ.* 10a regard it. TO also thinks of Enayim as a place; but renders the preceding word 'gate' or 'entrance' as 'crossroads'. But PJ has: 'she sat at the crossroads, where all *eyes* are on the look-out . . .'; like Jerome in his comment here and in Vg, this Targum takes *ʿēnayim* as 'roads', as do TN and Pesh. Although Philo, *De Congr.* 124, has a similar understanding of the Hebrew, he differs from Jerome and the Targums in saying that Tamar sat at a place 'where three roads met'.[2]

verse 26 Judah had promised to give to Tamar his son Selah as husband (38: 11), but he had failed to do this. So Tamar assumed the guise of a prostitute, and seduced Judah himself. Her pregnancy

---

[1] On this verse, see further Geiger, *Urschrift*, 462; Rahmer, *Die hebräischen Traditionen*, 48–9; C. Peters, 'Peschitta und Targumim des Pentateuchs', *Le Muséon*, 48 (1935), 42; and Kamesar, *Jerome*, 186–7.

[2] Rahmer, *Die hebräischen Traditionen*, 49, notes that *Gen. Rab.* 85: 7 states that Enayim is not the name of a place. See also Ginzberg, 'Die Haggada' (*MGWJ* NS 7), 544.

caused scandal, but she was able to prove that Judah was the father of the child, he himself being compelled to recognize that his failure to give Selah to Tamar was the cause of her justifiable action. LXX stresses this, reading 'Tamar is justified rather than I . . .'. Jerome's point is that what Tamar had done was not right, but was justified only when set alongside the greater evil which Judah had done to her. He thus distances himself from the allegorizing of Philo, *De Mut. Nom.* 134–6.

verse 29 The Hebrew here reads, literally: 'And she said, How have you burst forth? A breach be upon you!' LXX rendered her words as 'Why has the wall been cut through because of you?', and VL attributed them to a midwife; cf. Jerome, *In Eph.* 1; *Eps.* 52. 3, 123. 12. The name *Pārez* is derived by Aquila and Symmachus from the root *prẓ*, 'to break through'. Quite what the child 'broke through' is not evident, so Jerome supplies the afterbirth as the object of the verb. However, Pharisee derives not from *prẓ*, but from root *prš*, 'to separate'; and the word is a transliteration not of a Hebrew, but of an Aramaic form *pᵉrišā'* meaning 'separated one'. Jerome's explanation of Pharez here and in *Dial. contra. Lucif.* 23 agrees on one level with that of Origen, who derives Pharisee from Pharez and explains it in the same way (*Comm. Series in Matt.* 9, 20, 27; *Comm. in Joh.* 1. 13). On another level, however, Origen's comments differ from Jerome's, in that they explore the nature of the Pharisees' division and segregation: they separate the spiritual meanings of the prophetic writings from the literal-historical sense, preferring the latter to the former. Jerome's exegesis is determined by the Christian use of Phares as a type of Christ, who had broken down the wall dividing Jew and Gentile (see Eph. 2: 14–16). This he also records in *Ep.* 52. 3.

verse 30 The name *Zāraḥ* Jerome derives from root *zrḥ*, 'to rise', from which comes the noun *mizrāḥ*, 'east'. Zerah's sons are listed in 1 Chr. 2: 6. They were renowned as men of great wisdom, and only Solomon seems to have been wiser than they, according to 1 Kgs. 4: 21. In *Ep.* 123. 12, however, Jerome also connects the name with Hebrew *zera'*, 'seed'. For Christian readers, both these explanations would have force: Christ is called *anatolē*, the eastern star, in Luke 1: 78 (cf. Matt. 2: 1); and is spoken of by Paul as the seed promised to Abraham, who is not Isaac, but Christ (Gal. 3: 16). Jerome is silent about the thread of scarlet tied to Zerah's hand, which, according to Origen (*Comm. Series in Matt.*

125) prefigured Christ's passion and the purple robe which he received.

CHAPTER 40

verse 1 The Hebrew word under consideration here is *mašqēh*, 'butler'. VL had 'he who was over the wine' or 'he who was over the wine-pourers'. See Jerome's comments above on 15: 2–3, where, however, the Hebrew word is *mešeq*, translated as 'steward' in Vg. The translation 'cupbearer' he uses in Vg of this verse. Where Jerome concentrates on the meaning of the word, Origen, *Sel. in Gen.* 40: 1 offers an understanding of the 'sin' of the butler and baker. Ganymede, son of Tros according to Homer, *Iliad* 5. 265, was famed for his outstanding beauty, and was said to have been carried off to Olympus to be the gods' cupbearer. Virgil (*Aeneid* 5. 255) says that he was borne aloft by an eagle; Ovid (*Met.* 10. 155–7) that Jupiter took him, having taken the form of an eagle. See also Horace, *Odes* 4. 4. 1–12.

verses 9–10 Hebrew *śārīg* is rare, found only here, in verse 12 of this same chapter, and in Joel 1: 7. In the two verses of Genesis, LXX translated it as *puthmenes*, 'stems': VL, which Jerome partly quotes for this verse, used *fundi*, 'vine-clusters'. The variety of meanings which he proposes for this word correspond largely to translations known from the different Targums. Thus TO has *šbšyn*, 'branches'; PJ *mzwgy*, 'vine-branches, tendrils'; and TN and GM *šrbyṯyn*, 'shoots, twigs, bunches'. Vg's *propagines*, which Jerome has used here also as his final rendering of the word, 'shoots', compares with TN and GM of this verse. Given the variety of meanings he proposes, it seems unlikely that he depended on Aquila and Symmachus, both of whom used *klēmatides*, a word commonly meaning 'brushwood', and only very rarely 'vine-branches'. Didymus the Blind, *De Trin.* 1. 18, referred these three shoots to the Trinity, which helps to account for Jerome's interest in the accurate translation of this particular verse.

verse 16 Hebrew has 'three baskets of *ḥōrī*, white bread', a word found only here in the whole Hebrew Bible. Jerome translated it as 'flour' in Vg: this corresponds neither with the Targums, all of which speak of bread, nor with Philo, *De Somn.* 2. 158, who speaks of 'purest loaves'; nor with Josephus, *Ant.* 2. 71, where the baskets contain loaves of bread and royal luxuries. Jerome's translation, in fact, coincides with Aquila's: he has 'fine meal' (*guris*). Note also the meaning given to the names Chorri and Chorraeus in *Lib. Heb. Nom.* (p. 64) as 'flour' or 'floured'.

Augustine, *QG* 131, shows the problem which LXX raise: they have rendered *ḥōrī* with *chondritos*, 'coarse bread', understood in Latin as the rations proper for a slave's food allowance. He rightly asks what need Pharaoh would have of such things, and therefore seeks to explain away the oddity of LXX. Jerome indicates that proper understanding of Hebrew *ḥōrī* eliminates any problem. Once more, Origen, *Sel. in Gen.* 40: 9, 16, has a different emphasis, discerning profound theological significance in the vine-shoots and the baskets, whereas Jerome strives to clarify the meaning of the actual word.

CHAPTER 41

verse 2 The Hebrew word is *'āḥū*, found here and at verse 18. LXX read it as *achei* on both occasions, and VL had translated it as 'river bank'. This is not a correct rendering, as Jerome shows. The word is possibly Egyptian, meaning 'Nile-grass', so Skinner, *Commentary on Genesis*, 465. TO's translation is 'reed-grass': TN has 'reeds', Ngl, PJ, and FTV 'papyrus'. Aquila and Symmachus, however, understood it as 'marsh', which is Jerome's preference in Vg of this verse ('marshy places') and at 41: 18 ('pasture of marsh'). Jerome explains how letter *waw* representing vowel u and letter *yodh* representing vowel i can easily be confused in Hebrew script, suggesting that LXX have misread the Hebrew which lay before them. He finally notes their use of Greek *chi* to represent the sound of the Hebrew letter *ḥeth*.

verse 16 Jerome's translation of the Hebrew is very literal, as in Vg; and the proper sense of it is given by Symmachus. TO is clearest of all as to the meaning of the phrase: 'Not through my wisdom, but from before the Lord shall the welfare of Pharaoh be restored.' PJ has Joseph say that it is not through him that the dream will be interpreted, but through God. LXX, like Pesh, seem to have read the Hebrew *bl'dy*, which means 'without me', simply as *bl'd*, and then to have translated the following word to produce 'without God . . .'. LXX also supply a negative later in the verse, to indicate that God is the interpreter of dreams.[1]

verse 29 For Jerome's discussion of the various ways of reading and understanding forms derived from the root *šbʿ*, see above, 21: 30–1 and 26: 32–3; and *In Esa*. 18. 65: 15–16.

verse 43 The Hebrew has: 'and they called out before him *ʾabrēk*'. The word is probably of Egyptian origin; but LXX and Jerome in Vg took it to mean 'herald', and placed it as subject of the sentence. TN and PJ may also have regarded it in this light, with their translations: 'and they proclaimed before him'; but see further below. Aquila, like Ibn Ezra centuries later, took the word as from root *brk*, 'kneel, bless', from which comes the noun *berek*, 'knee': this corresponds to R. Jose ben Durmaskit's interpretation in *Sifre Deut*. 1 that the word is equivalent to *birkayim*, 'knees', since at Joseph's authority everyone entered and went out. See also the second interpretation of the word offered by Origen, *Sel. in Gen*. 41: 43. Symmachus transliterated the word.

Jerome rejects all these translations in favour of the Jewish exegesis which sees in this one expression two separate words, *ʾāb*, 'father', and *rēk*, 'tender'. Thus in *Sifre Deut*. 1, R. Jehudah explains it as 'father in respect of wisdom, tender in respect of years'; see also *Gen. Rab*. 90: 3; and PJ, 'This is the father of the king, great in wisdom, but tender in years', which is almost identical with FTP, FTV, and GM. TO's translation, 'This is the father of the king' (cf. *b. BB* 4a), seems to be an abbreviation of the longer exegesis set out here, as is probably the reading of Pesh, 'father and ruler'.[2] It is probable that Jerome derived this knowledge directly from Jews;[3] for although Origen knew this tradition and recorded it along with Aquila's translation of *ʾabrēk* (*Sel. in Gen*. 41: 43), he does not state that it is Jewish.[4]

verse 45 LXX made an attempt to transliterate the name Zaphnath-paneah (*ṣpnt pʿnḥ*), as did Aquila and most witnesses to TO; Pesh reproduced the name, and added an explanation, 'the one

---

[1] See Salvesen, *Symmachus*, 52–3.

[2] See Vermes, 'Bible and Midrash', 203–4; id., 'Haggadah in the Onkelos Targum', *JSS* 8 (1963), 162; Geiger, *Urschrift*, 463–4.

[3] See Rahmer, *Die hebräischen Traditionen*, 50–1; Kamesar, *Jerome*, 101–3.

[4] For the claim that Origen was Jerome's source, see Ginzberg, 'Die Haggada' (*MGWJ* NS 7), 546; R. Bardy, 'Les Traditions juives dans l'œuvre d' Origène', *RB* 34 (1925), 230.

to whom hidden things are revealed'. Symmachus certainly reproduced the name, but may also have added an explanation, 'being
hidden, he revealed', or, possibly, 'he revealed hidden things'.[5] The
element *ṣpn* in his name could be taken as the Hebrew root 'to
hide', and the sense of 'revealer of hidden things' was widely
accepted. Jerome in *Lib. Heb. Nom.* (p. 72) gives it as the meaning
of the Hebrew form of the name. Thus TN (cf. GM) has 'the man
to whom hidden things are revealed';[6] PJ, 'the man who uncovers
hidden things'; and 'the Syrian', 'he who knows the hidden things'.
Gen. Rab. 90: 4 records the same meanings; and Josephus, *Ant.* 2.
91, took it to mean 'finder of hidden things'. Augustine, *QG* 135
(like Theodoret, *QG* 94), explained the name as 'he revealed hidden things' because he interpreted the king's dreams, something he
may have derived from Philo;[7] he adds that in Egyptian the name
means 'saviour of the world'.

The Egyptian sense of the name has been explored by modern
scholars: probably it means 'The god speaks and he lives'.[8] But
Jerome here and in Vg took it as 'saviour of the world', having
already expressly stated in *Lib. Heb. Nom.* (p. 72): 'But we have
learned from the Egyptians that in their language the word means
the saviour of the world.' This rendering is most likely influenced
by Christian thinking, which regarded Joseph as a type of Christ in
that he alone preserved alive the whole of Egypt and those who
visited it during the famine.[9]

verses 50–2 Jerome seems to translate the Hebrew here, since
LXX read: 'And two sons were born to Joseph before the seven
years of famine came, whom Aseneth the daughter of Petephres,
priest of Heliopolis bore for him . . .' He was much exercised about
the number of Israelites who went into Egypt, and discusses the
matter at length at 46: 26–7 and 48: 1. By contrast, Origen, *Sel. in
Gen.* 41: 52 says nothing of this problem. According to *b. Taʿan.*

---

[5] On the question of what Symmachus read, see Salvesen, *Symmachus*, 53–4.

[6] A few witnesses to TO also have this, as does Origen, *Sel. in Gen.* 41: 45. See
Grossfeld, *Targum Onqelos to Genesis*, 138–9; de Lange, *Origen and the Jews*, 129;
Bowker, *The Targums*, 254–5; Vermes, 'Bible and Midrash', 204; and L. Ginzberg,
The Legends of the Jews, 7 vols. (Philadelphia, 1909–38), v. 345.

[7] See de Lange, *Origen and the Jews*, 129, 206 n. 69; in *De Mut. Nom.* 91, Philo
explains the name as 'a mouth judging in answer'.

[8] See especially Skinner, *Commentary on Genesis*, 470–1; G. von Rad, *Genesis*
(London, 1963), 372–3; and cf. Rahmer, *Die hebräischen Traditionen*, 51.

[9] But see Salvesen, *Symmachus*, 54, for the suggestion that Jerome may have had
in mind the root *pdh*, 'deliver, redeem', in his explanation of Zaphnath-paneah.

11a, *Tanḥ. Noaḥ* 11, it is improper to engender children in a time of famine. The name Manasseh, *menaššeh*, he here derives from root *nšh*, 'to forget'; he gives essentially the same derivation in *Lib. Heb. Nom.* (p. 69), adding another interpretation, 'necessity'. Ephraim he takes from root *prh*, 'be fruitful', as in *Lib. Heb. Nom.* (p. 65), 'fruitful, or one who is growing'.

CHAPTER 43

verse 11 The last word in this verse is *šeqēdīm*, properly, as Aquila, Symmachus, and Vg took it, 'almonds'. Jerome quotes the verse to illustrate the meaning of the word *nekʼōt*, which LXX translated as 'incense', Aquila and Vg as 'storax'. It is not common, and means 'spices, aromatics'. It occurs in Gen. 37: 25, where Rashi understands it as 'spices', quoting 2 Kgs. 20: 13 as proof: this latter verse is an almost exact doublet of Isa. 39: 2, the passage to which Jerome alludes here. But the word presented difficulties to ancient commentators, since *Jub.* 42: 20 and Josephus, *Ant.* 2. 118, seem to have ignored it; and TO, PJ, and TN here and at 37: 25 translated it as 'wax, gum'. Likewise for this verse *Gen. Rab.* 91: 11 gives its meaning as 'wax'. Hence, perhaps, Jerome's concern to elucidate its sense.

verse 34 Kamesar notes that this comment is typical of the genre *Quaestiones*, seeking to solve the problem which would be created if it were said that the brothers became drunk and behaved in an unseemly manner.[1] Indeed Philo, *De Jos.* 205–6, so bowdlerized the episode as to make it entirely wholesome. The verb used here is *škr*, which means nothing other than 'become drunk, inebriated'; but Jerome interprets it in the light of Ps. 65: 11. At first sight, this presents a puzzle, because this verse does not contain the verb *škr*; furthermore, Jerome has probably quoted the verse from memory, since it occurs in this form in no known version. But the verse does contain the Hebrew verb *rwh*, as follows: 'Her furrows Thou dost saturate abundantly (*rawweh*), her ridges Thou dost lower; Thou dost make it soft with showers; Thou blessest its springing up.' The root *rwh* has the primary meaning 'be saturated', and a secondary

---

[1] See Kamesar, 'Thesis', 76, citing Augustine on the problem of unseemly conduct attributed to Joseph's brothers. For Origen, *Comm. in Joh.* 1. 206, the story refers to spiritual intoxication: see Harl, *Bible d'Alexandrie*, i. 286.

sense of 'be intoxicated', such that LXX in this verse rendered it as *methouson*, 'make drunk'. Why Jerome should invoke this verse here may be explained by the fact that Aramaic has a root *rwy* cognate with Hebrew *rwh*, which the Targums of this verse use to translate *škr*: thus TO, 'and they drank and had their fill (or: became drunk) with him'; see also TN and PJ. The Hebrew verb *škr*, 'become drunk', occurs only twice elsewhere in the Pentateuch, and *rwy* is the usual Aramaic translation of it: see TO and TN of Gen. 9: 21; and FTV, PJ, TO, TN, and GM of Deut. 32: 42; also Targum 2 Sam. 11: 13; Isa. 29: 9; Jer. 25: 27. One possible way of explaining Jerome's comment, then, would be to assume that he knew a traditional rendering of Hebrew *škr*, 'become drunk', by Aramaic *rwy*, 'be saturated', which he himself sought to justify on the basis of a Psalm verse in which the Hebrew cognate of the Aramaic verb occurred. But even the use of this slightly less explicit verb in the Targums did not seem to go far enough in exonerating Joseph's brothers, in the opinion of some authorities: thus *b. Shabb.* 139a and *Gen. Rab.* 92: 5 explain that the brothers had not drunk wine since the day that Joseph had been separated from them. Augustine, *QG* 144, seems to follow Jerome's explanation of the 'drunkenness'.

CHAPTER 44

verses 1–2 LXX, whom Jerome follows in Vg, have correctly understood the Hebrew as 'sack', but Jerome adduces two other meanings of the word: see also PJ, which reads 'his bag', *ṭwnyh*; TO (cf. TN) has 'his bag, burden, load', *ṭwʿnyh*.[1] The cup, Hebrew *gᵉbīaʿ*, was translated as *kondu* by the LXX:[2] Aquila preferred *scyphum*, 'goblet', which was taken up by Ambrose, *De Josh.* 61, and by Jerome in Vg. Symmachus rendered the word with *phialē*, a broad flat bowl used for drinking. The word *kondu* is found again in Isa. 51: 17, where LXX had used it to represent Hebrew *kōs*, a common word for 'cup'; Symmachus in that verse put *kratēr*, 'a mixing-bowl for wine'. Interestingly, the Targum of Isa. 51: 17 used the Greek loan-word *phialē* to render the expression

---

[1] Fischer, p. 453, notes a Hexaplaric marginal note which reads *thula<kia>*, 'little sacks', and compares this with Jerome's interpretation of the Hebrew.

[2] For LXX's translation, *kondu*, see Harl, *Bible d'Alexandrie*, i. 286.

qubbaʿat kōs, 'bowl of the cup', translating 'the broad bowl of the cup'.

CHAPTER 45

verses 9–10   The word in question is vocalized in the MT as Goshen. LXX read Gesem at this point, and 'of Arabia' was probably added, as it is again at 46: 34, under the influence of Neh. 2: 19, where we hear of Geshem the Arab. But Arabia was actually the name of one of the nomes of Graeco-Roman Egypt, according to Ptolemy and Strabo, and LXX may equally be attempting to offer a contemporary identification of the site.[1] Hebrew *gesem*, as Jerome records, means 'rain'.

verse 17   The Hebrew is *bᵉ ʿîrᵉkem*, which means 'beasts', and is so rendered by *Jub.* 43: 22, Vg, Pesh, Allos, TO, PJ, and TN. Aquila and Symmachus have *ktēnē*, which means 'property', but again also 'cattle, herds'; and some witnesses of LXX also read 'beasts of burden', *phoreia*.[2] Theodotion and most witnesses to LXX read 'wagons, carriages', which is also the understanding of Josephus, *Ant.* 2. 167.

verse 21   The Hebrew *ṣēdāh* means 'provision, food for a journey', and so it has rightly been understood here by all the Greek versions, as well as Vg, Pesh, and Targums. It also occurs in Ps. 132: 15, where Aquila and Symmachus treat it as 'food', but most witnesses to LXX have translated with *thēra*, which, as Jerome says, implies food taken in hunting, 'game'; they had in mind the root *ṣdh* which means 'to hunt'. Other MSS have 'widow', which some modern scholars suggest may represent the original text.[3] Jerome once more displays his ostensible knowledge of Egyptian and its contemporary pronunciation, as if to imply that the LXX translators may have been influenced to some degree by the local Egyptian language. But he almost certainly derived his information from Pliny, *Nat. Hist.* 22. 121, who speaks of a two-grained wheat called *olyra* or *arinca*:

---

[1] So Skinner, *Commentary on Genesis*, 488; however, see further Harl, *Bible d'Alexandrie*, i. 291.

[2] See Field, i. 64, who also notes that some witnesses to the text of *QHG* at this point also read *phoreia*.

[3] See A. A. Anderson, *Psalms*, New Century Bible, ii (London, 1972), 884. The word supplies a good parallel to 'poor' in the second half of the line.

he says that the Egyptians make out of this grain a medicine which they call *athera*.

CHAPTER 46

verses 26–7   LXX read: 'all the souls of the house of Jacob who went into Egypt were seventy-five.' Jerome tries to deal with two separate, related difficulties. First, LXX and the Hebrew disagree on the numbers who went into Egypt: LXX have seventy-five, while the Hebrew has seventy. Second, the Hebrew text has its own difficulty, since this verse says that sixty-six sons of Jacob went down; Joseph was already there, and had two sons (verse 27); thus the total was sixty-nine, although verse 27 lists seventy. Who was the missing person?

Jerome begins with the sixty-six who went down with Jacob, and notes that there is no disagreement about that number. It can be calculated by referring back to earlier information in Genesis. LXX, however, say that Joseph had nine sons in Egypt. About two of these, there can be no disagreement: the Hebrew of 41: 50–2 is plain, as Jerome has already noted on those verses. But LXX, in their rendering of 46: 20 which Jerome quotes here, have added to the list 'by anticipation' (see above, notes on 14: 7) Joseph's grandsons, the sons of Manasseh and Ephraim: see further 1 Chr. 7: 14. Five of these are listed here; with Ephraim and Manasseh the number increases to seven, and we have eight if we include Joseph himself. It is not clear how LXX account for the number nine.[1]

By contrast, the Hebrew is clear, apart from the question asked earlier: who is the seventieth person? Jerome names Jacob himself: this is the opinion of *Jub.* 44: 12–13; *Gen. Rab.* 94: 9 ('there are some who say . . .'); *Leqaḥ Ṭov*; *Sekhel Ṭov*; and *MHG* on this

---

[1] While the state of LXX's text is not our primary concern, on this numerical problem see the remarks of Marguerite Harl, *Bible d'Alexandrie*, i. 296. She records that at Exod. 1: 5, LXX, a Qumran Bible MS, and MT give the numbers as seventy, the figure found also at Deut. 10: 22 MT and LXX, apart from Codex Alexandrinus, which has seventy-five. She notes the possibility that the MT of Gen. 46: 26–7 may have been 'corrected' to agree with Deut. 10: 22, noting that the number seventy would correspond also to the number of the Gentile nations (Deut. 32: 8–9) divided according to the number of the 'sons of Israel'.

verse.[2] But there were other opinions: the seventieth person was thought to be Jochebed, the mother of Moses (to name but a few sources: *b. BB* 123; *Gen. Rab.* 94: 9; *Num. Rab.* 3: 8; 13: 20; *Tanḥ. Bᵉmidbar* 16, 19; *PRK* 2: 10; and PJ on this verse); or God Himself (*Gen. Rab.* 94: 9; *PRE* 39: 1); or Serah, daughter of Asher (*Gen. Rab.* 94: 9; *Midrash Sam.* 32; *Eccles. Rab.* 9: 18; *Tanḥ. Wayyera'* 12; *Aggadath Bere'shith* 22: 3); or a son of Dan (*Midrash Sam.* 32). Josephus, *Ant.* 2. 176–83, so calculated the numbers that there was no missing person.

Jerome reiterates the principle of anticipation which LXX have used. They witness to the number seventy as having gone into Egypt at Deut. 10: 22. They have added the five sons of Manasseh and Ephraim to the list in these verses of Genesis. But explaining LXX is one task: defending the New Testament another, since Stephen in his speech (Acts 7: 14) quotes the LXX numbers as stated in Genesis. Jerome makes the following points: first, that the Gentiles would have known the Greek Bible, and it would have been inopportune for Luke to differ from it; second, that Luke himself was then an unknown author, whereas LXX had the status of Holy Scripture. He seems to leave open here the question of whether Luke knew Hebrew, although Jerome himself may have believed that he did: see *De Scrip. Ecc.* 7. Jerome's solution of this problem, however, was disputed by Augustine, *QG* 152, who not only urged that LXX were correct and their numbers full of mystical significance, but also was frankly sceptical of 'Hebrew truth', which he regarded as offering no resolution of the problem and as raising its own particular difficulties.

verse 28 The Hebrew has: 'And he sent Judah before him to Joseph, to direct (*lᵉhōrōt*) him to Goshen; so they came to the land of Goshen.' LXX translated: 'to Joseph, to meet him at the city of Heroes, into the land of Ramesses'. Apparently they translated *lᵉhōrōt* first as 'to meet', and then the sound of the word may have suggested also Heroopolis.[3] Josephus, *Ant.* 2. 184, followed LXX in this reading. The land of Goshen is taken as the land of Ramesses, no doubt because Gen. 47: 11 (Hebrew and LXX) tells

---

[2] See also Rahmer, *Die hebräischen Traditionen*, 51–2.

[3] Jerome does not comment on the meaning of this word, which elicited many different interpretations: see Grossfeld, *Targum Onqelos to Genesis*, 151–3; Salvesen, *Symmachus*, 56–7. His Vg rendering interprets the word twice, 'to inform him and to meet him', reflecting ancient debates: Aquila rendered it as 'to show', Symmachus 'to enlighten'.

that Joseph settled his family there.[4] Jerome's quotation of 47: 11 corresponds neither with Hebrew nor LXX. The former reads: 'And he gave them a possession in the land of Egypt, in the best of the land, in the land of Ramesses', which LXX faithfully rendered into Greek.

For the identity of Goshen with the Thebaid, and Ramesses with Arsinoë, see especially PJ, Ngl, and FTV: they took the place to be Pelusium. Arsinoë was capital of the nome of Heroopolis, on the Pelusium side of the Nile.

CHAPTER 47

verse 31 The problem is caused by the Hebrew word *mṭh*: it may be vocalized as *maṭṭeh*, 'staff, rod', or as *miṭṭāh*, 'bed, couch'. The former was read by LXX and Pesh, and was copied by Heb. 11: 21. This in its turn caused a problem. Whose staff was meant: Israel's own, or Joseph's? Augustine posed the question in these terms (*QG* 162), and seems to have accepted Jerome's Hebrew solution. But he would not agree that the LXX version has little or no meaning, and accordingly echoes earlier commentators who argued that it was Joseph's staff to which Israel had bowed, and that he had thus worshipped Joseph, who was a type of Christ (see comments on 41: 45), through the latter's staff or sceptre. Such was Origen's interpretation (*Hom. in Gen.* 15. 4), and it found an echo in the work of Eusebius of Emesa (Devreesse, p. 79), who, however, declares that other exegetes regarded the staff as Jacob's own: when Joseph swore the oath, his father bowed his head over his staff, and worshipped Joseph through it. Jerome may be concerned to refute Eusebius here, and in any case cuts through all the confusion engendered by the Greek translations.[1] For 'bed' is the vocalization of MT, and is the reading of Aquila, Symmachus, and 'the Hebrew'. The Targums agree with this; both PJ and the Ngl (cf. *Sifre Deut.* 31) make the point that Jacob was worshipping. But his homage

---

[4] See also Harl, *Bible d'Alexandrie*, i. 297.

[1] See Kamesar, *Jerome*, 155–7; he notes that Jerome arrives at an interpretation similar to that of Gennadius and Diodore (Petit, ii. 262–5), but by a different route (p. 156). Theodoret, *QG* 109, had also regarded the staff as Joseph's and had seen Jacob's action as fulfilling the dream prophecy of Joseph recorded in Gen. 37: 5–10.

was directed towards the Shekhina, which was there revealed to him.

CHAPTER 48

verse 1   See above, comments on 41: 50–2 and 46: 26–7.

verse 2   LXX read: 'your father is troubled . . .'; Jerome follows the Hebrew, and the renderings of Aquila and Symmachus. See above, comments on 47: 31, for the different translations 'staff' and 'bed' of the one Hebrew word *mṭh*. Pesh here follows LXX, reading 'couch'.

verses 5–6   See above, comments on 41: 50–2; 46: 26–7; 48: 1, *Leqaḥ Ṭov*, and *Sekhel Ṭov* on these verses, for the number of Joseph's sons. Jacob's insistence that Joseph's sons Ephraim and Manasseh will be equal with Jacob's own sons as tribes of Israel is handled by Jerome in a manner very close to that of the Targums: thus, where the Hebrew has Jacob say of Ephraim and Manasseh 'they shall be mine', PJ states that 'they shall be reckoned like Reuben and Simeon', (cf. Vg: 'they shall be counted', *reputabuntur*); and in TN Jacob twice insists that they shall be 'for my name', that is, most certainly mine. Particularly important is the fragmentary text GM, which agrees with Jerome further in making any future children of Joseph members of the tribes of Ephraim and Manasseh. In Klein's translation, it reads: '[   ] shall be called by my name; Ephraim and Manasseh like Reuben [and Simeon shall receive] a portion and an inheritance with us, in the division of the land. *And [your] progeny*: And the seed of your progeny, which you begot after them, shall be [attributed] to you; they shall be named after their brothers, in their inheritance.' See also *PR* 3; Josephus, *Ant.* 2. 195; Augustine, *QG* 145.

verse 22   Hebrew Shechem (*šᵉkem*) became *Sikima* in this verse of LXX as if it were a noun in the accusative case; similarly, it is Sicimam in VL. The place features in John 4: 5 as Sychar, as he notes also in *In Osee* 2. 6: 8–9, *Ep.* 108. 13. It was the chief city of the Samaritans, whose temple had once stood on Mount Gerizim adjacent to the town. In Roman times it was called Neapolis (see also *Lib. Loc.* 965–6), and was the home of Justin Martyr.

Jerome notes *šᵉkem* as meaning 'shoulder', qualified by *'aḥad*, 'one': this is the literal sense of the Hebrew, as Aquila has it. He says nothing here of an exegetical tradition that these words mean 'one portion' in the sense, perhaps, of a special gift: such is the interpretation of TO, and it appears in Vg, 'I am giving to you one portion more than to your brothers'. TO does not identify this portion as Shechem, as do PJ and, eventually, TN; and its translation may be related to interpretations which regarded *šᵉkem* as a birthright, or the garment of the First Adam.[1]

Jerome may, however, know another Jewish tradition, that the 'bow and sword' are symbolic of righteousness: thus TN, Ngl, FTP, FTV, and GM interpret them variously as good deeds or virtuous conduct. *Mekh. de R. Ishmael Beshallah* 3: 40–4, and some witnesses of TO regard the sword as prayer, and the bow as supplication; see also *Tanh. Beshallah* 9; *Mekh. de R. Šimeᶜon bar Yoḥai*, p. 53, lines 4–6; and *b. BB* 123a for similar explanations.

Jacob explains his deliverance after the incident at Shechem (Gen. 34), where his sons Simeon and Levi had killed the inhabitants and he had consequently feared reprisals (Gen. 34: 30). Jerome's interpretation of the sword and bow as 'bravery', meaning money, is not attested in Jewish sources. He finally notes that Shechem was not given to the tribe of Joseph by lot, but as a personal grant by Jacob; and as proof he cites the existence of Joseph's tomb there: see also *Lib. Loc.* 965–6 as cited above.

CHAPTER 49

verses 3–4 The Hebrew contains a number of rare and difficult words which Jerome seems to have interpreted with the help of Jewish exegesis. First, he translates *wᵉrēʾšīt ʾōnī* as 'the head among my children', using the word *capitulum*, 'little head, chapter' as in his comments on *bᵉrēʾšīt* in Gen. 1: 1. At the root of his translation lies the perception that *ʾōnī* here means 'my strength, vigour', and the phrase 'the beginning of my vigour' is thus taken to mean 'the first of the children whom I fathered'. The same approach to the phrase is found in LXX, Theodotion, Pesh, TO, and PJ: in *Gen. Rab.* 98: 3 and *b. Yeb.* 76a we are told that Reuben was the product of Jacob's first act of sexual intercourse. In Vg, however, Jerome

---

[1] See TN and FTV of this verse.

translates as 'the beginning of my sorrow, my pain' in agreement
with Aquila, Symmachus, FTV, FTP, and GM.

The words 'the one greater to be borne and greater in strength'
represent Hebrew *yeter šᵉᵉēt wᵉyeter ʿāz*: the phrase probably means
'superiority, excellence of dignity, superiority of strength'. Jerome's
interpretation is very similar to that of the Targums PJ, FTP, FTV,
GM, and TN, which is given here as an example:

It was destined that you should take three portions more (*ytyr*) than your
brothers: the right of the first-born was yours, and the kingship and the
high priesthood were destined for you. Because you sinned, Reuben my
son, the right of first-born was given to my son Joseph, and the kingship to
Judah, and the high priesthood to the tribe of Levi.

The beginnings of this Haggadah may be traced in Scripture itself,
at 1 Chr. 5: 1–2; the developed version of the Palestinian Targums
is found in slightly different form in *Gen. Rab.* 98: 4, *b. BB* 123a,
and abridged in TO.[1] Jerome tries to capture the sense of this in his
Vg with 'first in gifts, greater in sovereignty (*in imperio*)'; possibly
he was influenced by Aquila's rendering, 'superior in bearing and
superior in power'.[2]

The Hebrew *paḥaz kammayim ʾal tōtar* proved problematic for
the ancient translators. It probably should be rendered: 'liable to
flood like water, you shall not excel'; here and in Vg Jerome renders
the first word as 'pour out' (LXX and Theodotion are similar), and
the last as 'increase, grow': see also TO, 'get benefit'; Aquila and
Symmachus, 'excel'. The Targums understood this imagery as
sexual in content, and consequently referred the verse to Reuben's
seduction of his father's concubine Bilhah (Gen. 35: 22). For this
Reuben was punished and ordered not to sin again: Jerome's interpretation is very close to that of PJ and TN, although the latter, in
failing to translate the words 'for you went up to your father's
couch . . .', reveals a tendency to exonerate Reuben found also in
TO and other sources.[3] Jerome's words are markedly different from

---

[1] See Rahmer, *Die hebräischen Traditionen*, 52; le Déaut, *Targum du
Pentateuque*, i. 435; and Grossfeld, *Targum Onqelos to Genesis*, 160, who also
notes *Tanḥ. B. Wayeḥi* 11.

[2] Symmachus had: 'excellent things to take and to hold abundantly'. See Salvesen,
Symmachus, 58–9, who notes that Symmachus' wording seems close to that of the
Targums. Perhaps something of the Jewish understanding of the verse was mediated
to Jerome through the Three.

[3] See especially Grossfeld, *Targum Onqelos to Genesis*, 160–1 on this whole
section. The attempts to minimize Reuben's error (*see Gen. Rab.* 98: 4; *b. Shabb.*

Origen, *Hom. in Gen.* 17. 2, who sees in Reuben a type of the Jews, who are hard of heart. The concubine he understands as Hagar, and Reuben's attempted ravishing of her as typifying his failure to obey the Old Testament Law.

verses 5–6 LXX, whom VL followed with greater and lesser degrees of success, seem to have read *kbry* 'my liver' for *kbdy*, 'my glory', either having a different *Vorlage* or having confused *daleth* with *resh* in the reading of the latter. Jerome's 'be laid waste', *desoletur*, is read as *dissolvatur* in some witnesses, to give 'lest my renown be broken'.[4] His translation of the Hebrew text, which he calls the 'Hebrew truth', here differs from his Vg in other details, but the overall thrust of the two renderings is the same. The verses were commonly explained as referring to the incident at Shechem (Gen. 34), and this in turn led to the reading of the Hebrew (*'iqq^{e}rū šōr*), correctly rendered by LXX's 'they hamstrung a bull,' as 'they overturned the wall'. That is to say, Jerome has vocalized *šwr* as *šūr*, 'wall', rather than *šōr*, 'bull, ox', in common with Aquila, Symmachus, PJ, TN, TO, and Pesh. The Shechem incident is to the fore in all the Targums of these verses. With his translation of these verses, Jerome removes any possibility of identifying the bull with Christ, who was crucified (hamstrung) by the Jewish priests (Levi) and people (Simeon), an exegetical ploy found in Hippolytus, *Frg. in Gen.* (PG 10: 588). But see further below, comments on verse 7.

This verse is another of those traditionally said to have been altered for King Ptolemy; it may be that Jerome knew of this and accordingly set out the full Hebrew text in translation. But he says nothing to suggest that he knew of the alleged alteration, and it is indeed questionable whether the LXX in truth altered the Hebrew text at all.[5]

verse 7 For 'tribes' Jerome has 'sceptres': see above on 47: 31; 48: 2. Simeon's dispersal among the tribe of Judah is recorded in Josh. 19: 1 and further elaborated in 1 Chr. 4: 42. For the last sentence of his comment Jerome returns to LXX of verse 6, according to which Simeon and Levi hamstrung a bull. For the interpretation of

55b), which are found also in PJ and TN, suggest that it was merely regarded as though he had defiled Bilhah: in actual fact, he had placed his father's bed in Leah's tent.

[4] Vg has: 'Let my soul not come into their plan, and let my renown not be in their assembly.'

[5] On this, see details in Tov, 'Rabbinic Tradition concerning the "Alterations" ', 79–80, 87–8.

these Patriarchs as Pharisees, and the bull as Christ done to death by them, see Tertullian, *Adv. Marc.* 3. 18, *Adv. Iud.* 10; Hippolytus, *Frg. in Gen.* (PG 10: 588); and Origen, *Hom. in Gen.* 17. 3. But within Jewish tradition we find the record that the descendants of Simeon and Levi were scribes and teachers of the Torah: thus FTP, FTV, and Ngl have the tribe of Simeon scattered as scribes and Torah-teachers among the assembly of Jacob, and the Levites among the Study Houses of Israel.

verses 8–9 On root *ydh* as meaning both 'acknowledge' and 'praise' see 29: 35. Jerome understood the verse in a Messianic sense in common with his predecessors. On 'mystery' see 14: 18. For the idea that all should pay homage to Judah, see also TO and TN. The word which LXX translated as 'tender shoot' is *ṭerep*, and has the sense of 'prey'. 'Captivity', which Jerome prefers, may echo *ṭerep* if it is understood in the sense of 'a taking', which is Aquila's rendering. With this word, Jerome is able to draw a connection with Ps. 68: 19, long understood by Christians as reference to Christ's Resurrection and Ascension. Indeed, his exegesis of this verse in one sense reflects that of Origen, *Hom. in Gen.* 17. 5, who takes the 'tender shoot' of LXX as a type of Christ, and the verse as a whole as prefiguring his Death and Resurrection. Jerome's attention to the Hebrew, however, enables him to make an association of the verse with the Resurrection and the Ascension, thus significantly expanding the use to which the text might be put.

verse 11 It is useful to compare Jewish exegesis of this verse with Jerome's remarks. Thus in *Tanḥ. Wayeḥi* 10, we read:

> The vine refers to Israel, as it is said: Thou didst bring a vine out of Egypt (Ps. 80: 9); the colt refers to the Holy City. And 'to the Soreqah' refers to Israel, as it is said: And I planted you as Soreq (Jer. 2: 21). 'The foal of his ass'—this means that they shall rebuild the ass-gate.

But much more so than in earlier comments, Jerome's Christian presuppositions are evident. The foal and the ass recall Christ's triumphal entry into Jerusalem (Matt. 21: 1–11; Mark 11: 1–10; Luke 19: 29–38; John 12: 12–18) as well as the patristic interpretations of the details of the narratives, e.g. Justin, *Apol.* 32. 5–6, *Dial.* 53. 1–2. He singles out the word *śōrēq* (choice vine), because of its use in prophetic literature as a symbol of Israel; see Isa. 5: 2; Jer. 2: 21, and Jerome, *In Esa.* 2. 5: 2, *In Hier.* 1. 2. 21. Israel he understands as the Church itself, following St Paul in Gal. 6: 16;

Rom. 9: 6–8. His eulogy of Judah assumes a Messianic interpret-ation of the verse: this is found in Jewish tradition (e.g. *Gen. Rab.* 56: 2; 98: 9; *b. Ber.* 56b), but the Targums TN and PJ speak of a warrior Messiah, victorious in battle, which does not enter Jerome's line of vision.[6]

The Hebrew which Jerome translated as 'and his ass, my son, to the choice vine' is written *wᵉlaśśōrēqāh bᵉnī ᵃtōnō*, and is commonly rendered as: 'and the colt of his ass to the choice vine'. In such a translation, which LXX and VL adopt, the word *bᵉnī* is regarded as an unusual, but not unprecedented form of the noun *bēn* in its singular construct state: the phrase *bᵉnī ᵃtōnō* then means, literally, 'the son of his she-ass'.[7] But *bᵉnī* may also represent a singular form of the same noun with a first person pronominal suffix, 'my son': such is Jerome's reading, and it allows him to imagine the Patriarch breaking off from his main speech and turning to deliver a direct address to his son Judah. The technical term for such a rhetorical device is the Greek *apostrophē*, which passed into Latin, was used by orators like Quintilian, and appears here in Jerome's comment. Two manuscripts of *QHG* put the word in Greek characters. By translating the Hebrew text in this way both here and in the Vg, Jerome is able to argue for a powerful Christological interpretation of a kind not possible given the renderings of LXX and VL.

The comment on *ʿīrōh*, which may, as Jerome notes, be translated as 'his colt' or 'his city', further illustrates his Christian exegesis: he thinks of the City of God 'set on a hill' (Matt. 5: 14) which is also Zion, so described in Ps. 46: 5, a figure of the Church. This last piece of exegesis is not found in Origen, *Hom. in Gen.* 17. 7, an intricate comment which Jerome seems at pains to correct in the light of the Hebrew. For Origen, the colt represents the Gentiles who did not possess the Law (since no man had sat on the colt); the foal refers to the Jews, carrying the burden of the Law but faith-lessly, such that they were replaced by the Gentiles. The vine is Christ's human nature, to which was bound the colt representing the Logos. Jerome no doubt sensed that his own exegesis based on the original Hebrew was much clearer, more consistent and in-

---

[6] On the Targums of this verse and their relationship to Isa. 63: 1–6 and Rev. 19: 13–15, see McNamara, *New Testament and Palestinian Targum*, 230–3. But Jerome says nothing of the Messianic possibilities of these verses, unlike Justin, *Apol.* 32. 7–11; *Dial.* 54. 1–2, 63. 2, 76. 2.

[7] See Gesenius, *Hebrew Grammar*, ed. E. Kautzsch, rev. A. E. Cowley (Oxford, 1910), 253 § 90 I, m.

herently more probable than Origen's; it is also more detailed, allowing him to make use of the full range of meaning of *'īrōh* as 'his colt' or 'his city'.

verses 14–15 Jerome's translation of LXX makes clear how that version presented Issachar as a typical Platonist, desiring 'the Good', an idea developed by *Test. Iss.* 4: 1–5: 2, and Philo, *De Ebr.* 94, *Leg. All.* 1. 78.[8] His rendering of the Hebrew owes something to Aquila: like the latter, he translates *gārem* as 'bony', and the final words *l^emas 'ōbēd* as 'serving for an allotted payment', suggesting the paying of tribute to kings. His interpretation of *lisbōl* as 'to carrying burdens', here and in Vg, differs from LXX, who had put 'to labour': the latter provide an excellent link with the Rabbinic interpretations of this verse which have Issachar *labouring* in the Torah, and the verb *laborare* and noun *labor* are, in any case, used by Jerome in this comment to describe Issachar's activities. This same word also features in Ambrose's comments on the verse, *De Abr.* 1. 5.

On the boundaries of Zebulon, see verse 13. For Issachar fed by Zebulon's trading, see *Yalquṭ Shim'oni* 161, and 1069 for the note that his brother brought gifts to him. Although preferring Hebrew to LXX, Jerome does not dismiss the latter's picture of Issachar as a farmer, found also in *Test. Iss.* 3: 1; 5: 3–7. Jerome is apparently aware of Jewish exegesis of this verse which makes of Issachar one who labours in the Torah: see *Gen. Rab.* 98: 12 ('as an ass bears a burden, so Issachar bore the Torah'), PJ, TN, FTP, FTV. Issachar was regarded as a Torah scholar, whose tribe sat in the Sanhedrin: see *Sekhel Ṭov* on Gen. 30: 17. Jerome notes that the Hebrews understand the text at this point 'metaphorically'; their exegesis does not result in a 'spiritual' interpretation, but one which is essentially historical, the words of the Hebrew original being understood figuratively. For another 'metaphorical' reading of the text, see the following comment.[9]

verses 16–18 Jerome first gives a translation of the Hebrew, but reading 'prince' for *šepīpōn*, 'viper' (he reverts to 'serpent' in Vg), and 'your saviour' at the end of the verse for Hebrew 'your sal-

---

[8] So Harl, *Bible d'Alexandrie*, i. 310.
[9] See Rahmer, *Die hebräischen Traditionen*, 52–4; M. Beer, 'Issachar and Zebulon', *Bar-Ilan*, 6 (1968), 168–70; and add *Sekhel Ṭov*; Rashi; *Leqaḥ Ṭov* (Sanhedrin); and *Sifre Deut.* 354. On Jerome's use of the terms 'metaphor' and 'metaphorically' and their significance, see Jay, *L'Exégèse de saint Jérôme*, 153–9.

vation'. LXX, followed by VL, give verse 16 as: 'Dan shall judge his people, as also one tribe in Israel'; Vg puts, for the latter half of this verse, 'as also another tribe in Israel'. It is important to compare Jerome's comment with PJ of these verses, which we quote in full:

There shall be a man who shall be chosen, and he shall arise from those of the house of Dan. He is like a serpent which lies by the crossroads, and at the head of the snakes which lie in wait by the path, which bites the horses on the heels, so that their rider falls from fear through falling over backwards. So shall Samson the son of Manoah kill all the mighty men of the Philistines, cavalry and foot-soldiers; and he shall hamstring their horses, and throw those who are on them backwards. (18) When he saw Gideon son of Joash and Samson son of Manoah who were to arise as redeemers, Jacob said: Not for Gideon's redemption do I wait, nor for Samson's redemption do I long, since their redemption is the redemption of an hour; but for Your redemption do I wait and long, O Lord, for Your redemption is an everlasting redemption.

Similar exegesis is found in TN, FTV, FTP, and Ngl.[10] A Tosefta Targum (Klein, p. 171) refers to Messiah, son of David, as Jacob's hope; note the Messianic reference in Jerome's comment, which quotes Gen. 49: 10 as in his Vg translation: Hebrew has 'and his shall be the obedience of the peoples'. The verses naturally suggested Samson the Danite, who was bound by a Nazirite vow not to cut his hair (Judg. 13: 5; Num. 6: 5); his exploits in saving Israel from the Philistines (Judg. 14–15); and his deception by Delilah (Judg. 16: 17): see also *Gen. Rab.* 98: 14. Jerome regards the verses as being 'in the form of a metaphor', on which see comments to verses 14–15 above.

verse 19 Jerome claims to have translated the Hebrew, which actually reads: 'Gad, a troop shall maraud him; but he shall maraud (at) the heel'. He interprets the verse with reference to events spoken of in 1 Chr. 5: 18–22, in similar fashion to *Gen. Rab.* 98: 15, which says:

When Israel were conquering and dividing the land, the tribes of Reuben and Gad were with them, and they left their little sons behind. He who left his son aged 10 found him aged 24; He who left his son aged 20 found him

---

[10] All this is quite different from Philo's interpretation of the verses in *De Agr.* 94–110 and *Leg. All.* 2. 97–101, reported by Harl, *Bible d'Alexandrie*, i. 311: she also notes Origen (*Hom. in Ezech.* 11. 3) and Rufinus (*Apologia* 2. 16), both of whom refer the verses to Christ, while Hippolytus (*Frg. in Gen.* (PG 10: 593)) refers them to Jewish opposition to Christ.

aged 34. Three wicked clans joined in battle against them, Jetur, Naphish, and Qedemah [there follows a reference to 1 Chr. 5: 10].[11]

The meaning of Gad as 'armed man, troop' (see above, comments on 30: 10–11 and Vg) is given here also by Aquila and is assumed in *Gen. Rab.* 98: 15, with its remark: 'troops ravage them, but they ravage the ravaging troops'.[12] Similar is *jer. Soṭ.* 8: 10, and the notes in PJ, TO, and TN that Gad's house would go forth equipped and armed. The record of their inheritance in the land is found in Josh. 13: 24–8.

Jerome refers finally to further *mysteries* (see above, 14: 18) in this chapter, having in mind Origen's extended comments on Reuben, Simeon, Levi, and Judah in *Hom. in Gen.* 17. The latter, however, does not discuss any other Patriarch in that homily.

verse 21 LXX describe Naphtali as 'a spreading stem', which Jerome has put as 'an unbound thicket'.[13] The Hebrew, *'ayyālāh šᵉluḥāh*, is best translated as Jerome has it later in this comment and in Vg, 'a hind let loose': this is also Aquila's translation. LXX may have read the first word as *'ēlāh*, 'terebinth'; this reading allowed Hippolytus, *Frg. in Gen.* (PG 10: 597), to view the stem as Christ, the tree as the Church of the Gentiles. The rendering 'watered field' may depend on exegesis of the sort Jerome sets out here and which derives ultimately from Rabbinic sources. Thus *Gen. Rab.* 98: 17 understands the 'hind let loose' as irrigated land, *byt hšlḥyn*; and at 99: 12 the same text locates it in the valley of Gennesaret (cf. also *Sifre Deut.* 355) where fruit ripens quickly, a point made also in *Tanḥ. Wayehi* 13 and *MHG* on this verse.

The second half of the statement in Hebrew reads 'yielding *'imrē šāper*, deer of pleasantness': Jerome's translation 'eloquence' takes the word as if from root *'mr*, 'to say', in the same way as *Gen. Rab.* 97: 21, PJ, TN, FTV, FTP, and Ngl.[14] Tiberias was the site of a major Rabbinic academy throughout the third and fourth centuries.[15] The eloquence, therefore, is that of the Rabbis in the Schools, whom Jerome mentions elsewhere in his work.

---

[11] See also Rahmer, *Die hebräischen Traditionen*, 54–5.

[12] See further Goshen-Gottstein, *Fragments*, ii. 15–16.

[13] For an explanation of the translation, see Grossfeld, *Targum Onqelos to Genesis*, 169 n. 52, who suggests a link with Isa. 17: 10–11.

[14] See also Rahmer, *Die hebräischen Traditionen*, 55–6.

[15] See s.v. 'Tiberias', in *Jewish Encyclopaedia*, ed. I. Singer (New York and London, 1901–6), xii. 142–3, and in *Encyclopaedia Judaica*, ed. C. Roth (Jerusalem, 1971–2), xv. 1130–3; Neubauer, *Géographie du Talmud*, 208–14; Schürer, *History of the Jewish People*, ii. 181.

verses 22–6 The Hebrew reads:

A son of fruitfulness is Joseph, even a son of fruitfulness by a well: daughters tread on the wall. And they embittered him and were numerous; and the archers were hostile to him. But his bow abides in strength, and the arms of his hands remain supple and vigorous by the hands of the mighty God of Jacob; from thence he became the feeder, the stone of Israel: From the God of thy father . . .[16]

LXX read:

Joseph is a son increased; my beloved son is increased; my youngest son, turn to me. They took evil counsel against him and reviled him, and the archers pressed upon him. And their bows were consumed in strength, and the sinews of their arms were made slack by the hand of the mighty one of Jacob, from where is the one who strengthened Israel by the God of your father; and my God helped you . . .

On the meaning of the name Joseph as 'increase', see comments above on 30: 21; and on Ephraim, see 48: 5–6. The great fruitfulness of Joseph is heavily emphasized by TO, who uses the verb *śgy*, 'increase, become many' to translate the description of Joseph as a 'son of fruitfulness', Hebrew *ben pōrāt*; this Targum, like TN and PJ, took *pōrāt* from Hebrew root *prh*, 'be fruitful', and only here translates that root with Aramaic *śgy*.[17]

Unlike PJ and TN, who interpreted the 'archers' as the Egyptian magicians who opposed Joseph, TO suggests that they were his brothers: so also *Leqaḥ Ṭov* on this verse.[18]

verse 27 Jerome approves application of this verse to the Apostle Paul, using it again at *In Esa.* 2. 5: 2; *In Osee* 2. 5: 8–9; *Eps.* 38. 1, 70. 8. See also Hippolytus, *Frg. in Gen.* (PG 10: 604); Origen, *Sel. in Gen.* 43: 34; and Hilary, *Tractatus in Ps.* 67: 28. Diodore (Petit, ii. 288) summarizes the exegesis while questioning its propriety: he notes that those who accepted it applied LXX's 'in the morning he shall still eat' either to Paul's persecuting the Church, or to his tuition in the Law by Gamaliel; they then referred 'and in the evening he shall give food' either to his being persecuted after his conversion, or to his nourishing of those to whom he preached, or to his office as teacher of many nations after his tuition by Gamaliel.

---

[16] See further, Grossfeld, *Targum Onqelos to Genesis*, 169–70.
[17] See ibid. 170 n. 56.
[18] See also *Gen. Rab.* 98: 12; 99: 1; and Grossfeld, *Targum Onqelos to Genesis*, 173–4.

Paul's persecution of the Church is recorded in Acts 9: 1–3 and in his own writings at (e.g.) 1 Cor. 15: 9–10. The Hebrew of this verse speaks of eating and dividing, which suggested to ancient commentators the consumption and apportioning of sacrificial food, the more so since, by tradition, the Temple was located in the tribal territory of Benjamin. The first part of Jerome's comment is strikingly similar to TO of this verse, which runs:

Benjamin: in his land the Shekhina shall dwell, and the Sanctuary shall be built in his inheritance. In the morning and at evening the priests shall be offering the sacrifice; and at the time of the evening they shall be dividing the rest of their allotted portion from the remainder of the holy things (i.e. the sacrifices).

In his comment, however, Jerome does not explain why the Jews of his day interpreted the verse in this way; and he also compresses a good deal of exegetical material into a short compass. Two items are particularly worthy of note. First, Benjamin was credited with being the tribe on whose land the Temple was built because Deut. 33: 12 speaks of this tribe as the beloved of the Lord, who 'makes His dwelling between his (Benjamin's) shoulders'. Given this scriptural warrant, the idea that the Temple was built on Benjaminite territory is both widespread (see e.g. *Mekh. de R. Ishmael Beshallah* 6: 16–19; *Sifre Deut.* 352; *Sifre Num.* 78, 81; *b. Yoma* 12a; *b. Zeb.* 118b) and probably pre-Christian in origin, since it appears in *Test. Ben.* 9: 2. The Targums TN, FTP, FTV, and PJ all display knowledge of it.[19] For Origen's knowledge of this tradition, see *In Hier. Homilia* 18. 13 on Jer. 20: 2.

Second, the image of the wolf, a savage and ruthless beast, was distasteful and required interpretation such that it reflected well on Benjamin. The rapacious character of the animal readily suggested the altar, on which thousands of offerings were presented (*Lev. Rab.* 3: 5). Thus the references in the Hebrew to 'eating' and 'dividing' (Vg has 'divide' here instead of 'give', Jerome's rendering in *QHG*) were referred to the sacrifices: see *Gen. Rab.* 99: 3 (R. Pinhas); *Tanḥ. B. Wayehi* 14; *Tanḥ. Wayehi* 14; *Midrash Aggadah* and *Leqaḥ Ṭov* on this verse.

---

[19] See Rahmer, *Die hebräischen Traditionen*, 57–8, who also quotes the famous story of Miriam, the apostate daughter of the priestly course of Bilga: in the persecution of Antiochus Epiphanes, she reviled the altar, shouting at it 'Lukos! Lukos! How long will you devour the possessions of Israel, and not stand up for them in the time of persecution?' (*b. Sukk.* 56b; cf. *jer. Sukk.* 5: 8; *t. Sukk.* 4: 28).

Finally, it is possible that Jerome's comment reflects a point of law addressed particularly by TO, PJ, TN, and the other Targums. The Hebrew speaks of the wolf's activity at morning and evening: this suggested an interpretation referring to the daily morning and evening sacrifice of a lamb (Exod. 29: 38–42; Num. 28: 1–8) directly spoken of by the Targums and at least implied by Jerome. But this sacrifice was not divided between the altar and the priests: it was offered whole on the altar. Hence the dividing of the sacrifices could not refer to the daily burnt offering, and must refer to something else. The Targums say what this was: the remains of such other sacrifices offered during the day by the people to which the priests had a legitimate claim. Jerome may allude to this by saying that, in the evening, the priests ate 'those things which are by the law ascribed to themselves from the people'.[20] He ends by remarking that the ministers of the altar derived their livelihood from the altar, a point made by the Apostle Paul (1 Cor. 9: 13), to whom, as he has already said, the Christians apply this scriptural verse.[21]

'Lukos' is Greek for wolf: according to the story, Miriam had married a pagan. See also H. Grätz, 'Haggadische Elemente bei den Kirchenvätern', *MGWJ* 3 (1854), 430.

[20] See the detailed discussion of this in Grossfeld, *Targum Onqelos to Genesis*, 175.

[21] The language of 1 Cor. 9: 13 naturally suggests an allusion to Gen. 49: 27. It reads: 'Do you not know that those who minister the sacred things eat the things of the temple; that those who wait on the altar have their portion (*summerizontai*) from the altar?' The one occurrence of the verb *summerizesthai* in LXX (Prov. 29: 24) translates Hebrew *ḥlq*, the verb 'divide' used in Gen. 49: 27.

BIBLIOGRAPHY

ABERBACH, M., and GROSSFELD, B., *Targum Onkelos to Genesis: A Critical Analysis together with an English Translation of the Text* (New York, 1982).

ALEXANDER, P. S., 'The Targumim and Early Exegesis of "Sons of God" in Genesis', *JJS* 23 (1972), 60–71.

—— 'The Toponymy of the Targumim, with Special Reference to the Table of Nations and the Boundaries of the Land of Israel', D.Phil. thesis (Oxford, 1974).

—— 'Targum, Targumim', in *The Anchor Bible Dictionary*, vi (New York, 1992), 320–31.

BEN-AMI SARFATI, G., 'The Tent = The House of Study', *Tarbiz* 38 (1968), 87–9.

ANDERSON, A. A., *Psalms*, New Century Bible, ii (London, 1972).

AVI-YONAH, M., *The Jews of Palestine* (Oxford, 1976).

BARDY, R., 'Les Traditions juives dans l'œuvre d'Origène', *RB* 34 (1925), 217–52.

—— 'La Littérature patristique des "Quaestiones et Responsiones" sur l'Écriture Sainte', *RB* 41 (1932), 210–36; 341–69; 515–37; *RB* 42 (1933), 14–30; 211–29; 328–52.

—— 'Saint Jérôme et ses maîtres hébreux', *RB* 46 (1934), 145–64.

BARR, J., 'Doubts about Homoeophony in the Septuagint', *Textus*, 12 (1985), 1–77.

BARTHÉLEMY, D., *Les Devanciers d'Aquila* (SVT 10; Leiden, 1963).

—— 'La Place de la Septante dans l'Église', in *Aux grands carrefours de la révélation et de l'exégèse de l'Ancien Testament: Journées du Colloque Biblique de Louvain* (Recherches Bibliques, 8; Louvain, 1967), 13–28.

—— 'Origène et le texte de l'Ancien Testament', in J. Fontaine and C. Kannengiesser (eds.), *Epektasis: Mélanges patristiques offerts au Cardinal Jean Daniélou* (Paris, 1972), 247–61.

BASKIN, J. R., *Pharaoh's Counsellors: Job, Jethro and Balaam in Rabbinic and Patristic Tradition* (Chico, Calif., 1983).

BEER, M., 'Issachar and Zebulon', *Bar-Ilan*, 6 (1968), 168–70.

BORNECQUE, H., *Les Déclamations et les déclamateurs d'après Sénèque le Père* (Hildesheim, 1967).

BOTTERWECK, G. J., and RINGGREN, H. (eds.), *Theological Dictionary of the Old Testament*, 6 vols. (Grand Rapids, 1974–90).

BOWKER, J., 'Haggadah in the Targum Onkelos', *JSS* 12 (1967), 51–65.

BOWKER, J., *The Targums and Rabbinic Literature* (Cambridge, 1969).

BROWN, D., *Vir Trilinguis: A Study in the Biblical Exegesis of Saint Jerome* (Kampen, 1992).

BURNEY, C. F., 'Christ as the APXH of the Creation', *JTS* 27 (1926), 160–77.

BURSTEIN, E., 'La Compétence de Jérôme en hébreu: Explication de certaines erreurs', *REA* 21 (1975), 3–12.

BUTTERWECK, A., *Jakobs Ringkampf am Jabbok* (Judentum und Welt, 3; Frankfurt am Main, 1981).

CAIRD, J. B., 'Homoeophony in the Septuagint', in W. D. Davies, R. G. Hammerton-Kelly, and R. Scroggs (eds.), *Jews, Greeks, and Christians—Religious Cultures in Late Antiquity: Essays in Honour of W. D. Davies* (Leiden, 1976), 74–88.

CAVALLERA, F., *Saint Jérôme: Sa vie et son œuvre*, 2 vols. (Paris, 1922).

—— 'Les "Quaestiones Hebraicae in Genesim" de saint Jérôme et les "Quaestiones in Genesim" de saint Augustin', *Miscellanea Augustiniana*, pt. 2 (Rome, 1931), 359–72.

CLAUS, F., 'La Datation de l'Apologia Prophetae David et l'Apologia David Altera: Deux œuvres authentiques de saint Ambroise', *Studia Patristica Mediolanensia*, 7 (Milan, 1976), 168–93.

COHEN, G. D., 'Esau as Symbol in Early Medieval Thought', in A. Altman (ed.), *Jewish Medieval and Renaissance Studies* (Cambridge, Mass., 1967), 19–48.

COLLINS, J. J., 'Artapanus', in J. H. Charlesworth (ed.), *The Old Testament Pseudepigrapha*, ii (London, 1985), 889–903.

COURCELLE, P., *Late Latin Writers and their Greek Sources*, trans. H. E. Wedeck (Cambridge, Mass., 1969).

DANIÉLOU, J., *The Bible and the Liturgy* (Notre Dame, Ind., 1956).

—— *Théologie du Judéo-Christianisme*, i (Tournai, 1958).

DAVIES, W. D., *Paul and Rabbinic Judaism* (London, 1965).

LE DÉAUT, R., 'Traditions targumiques dans le Corpus paulinien? (Hebr 11, 4 et 12, 24; Gal 4, 29–30; II Cor 3, 16' *Biblica*, 42 (1961), 28–48.

—— 'Le Titre de Summus Sacerdos donné à Melchisédech est-il d'origine juive?', *RSR* 50 (1962), 222–9.

—— *La Nuit pascale* (Rome, 1963).

—— *Targum du Pentateuque*, 5 vols. (Paris, 1978–81).

DÍEZ MACHO, A., 'Targum y Nuevo Testament, in *Mélanges Eugène Tisserant* (Studi e Testi, 231. i; Rome, 1964), 153–85.

DIVJAK, J., *Sancti Aureli Augustini Opera*, sect. 2, pt. 6 (CSEL 88; Vienna, 1981).

DORAN, R., 'Aristeas the Exegete', in J. H. Charlesworth (ed.), *The Old Testament Pseudepigrapha*, ii (London, 1985), 855–9.

—— 'Cleodemus Malchus', ibid. 883–7.

DUCKWORTH, G. E., *The Nature of Roman Comedy* (Princeton, NJ, 1952).

Encyclopaedia Judaica, ed. C. Roth, 16 vols. (Jerusalem, 1971–2).

FANNING, S., 'Jerome's Concepts of Empire', in L. Alexander (ed.), *Images of Empire* (Sheffield, 1991), 239–50.

FELDMAN, L. H., 'Josephus' Portrait of Jacob', *JQR* 79 (1988–9), 101–51.

FRAADE, S. D., *Enosh and his Generation: Pre-Israelite Hero and History in Postbiblical Interpretation* (Chico, Calif., 1984).

FREUDENTHAL, J., *Alexander Polyhistor und die von ihm erhaltenen Reste jüdischer und samaritanischer Geschichtswerke* (Hellenistische Studien, 1–2; Breslau, 1874–5).

GEIGER, A., *Urschrift und Uebersetzung der Bibel* (Breslau, 1857).

GESENIUS, *Hebrew Grammar*, ed. E. Kautzsch, rev. A. E. Cowley (Oxford, 1910).

GINZBERG, L., *The Legends of the Jews*, 7 vols. (Philadelphia, 1909–38).

GINZBERG, R., 'Die Haggada bei den Kirchenvätern und in der apokryphischen Literatur', *MGWJ* NS 6 (1898), 537–50; *MGWJ* NS 7 (1899), 17–22, 61–75, 117–25, 149–59, 217–31, 292–303, 409–16, 461–70, 485–504, 529–47.

GOSHEN-GOTTSTEIN, M., *Fragments of Lost Targumim*, 2 vols. (Ramat-Gan, 1983–9 (in Hebrew)).

GRÄTZ, H., 'Haggadische Elemente bei den Kirchenvätern', *MGWJ* 3 (1854), 311–19, 352–5, 381–7, 428–31; *MGWJ* 4 (1855), 186–92.

GREENSPOON, L. J., 'Symmachus', in *The Anchor Bible Dictionary*, vi (New York, 1992), 251.

GRIBOMONT, J., 'Jerome', in A. di Bernardino (ed.), *Patrology*, iv, trans. P. Solari (Westminster, Md., 1991), 195–245.

GROSSFELD, B., 'Targum Onkelos and Rabbinic Interpretation to Genesis 2:1, 2', *JJS* 24 (1973), 176–8.

—— *The Targum Onqelos to Genesis*, The Aramaic Bible, vi (Edinburgh, 1988).

—— *The Targum Onqelos to Leviticus and the Targum Onqelos to Numbers*, The Aramaic Bible, viii (Edinburgh, 1988).

GRUENWALD, I., *Apocalyptic and Merkavah Mysticism* (Leiden, 1980).

GRÜTZMACHER, G., *Hieronymus: Eine biographische Studie zur alten Kirchengeschichte*, 3 vols. (Studien zur Geschichte der Theologie und der Kirche; i, Leipzig, 1901; ii–iii, Berlin, 1906–8).

HANSON, J., 'Demetrius the Chronographer', in J. H. Charlesworth (ed.), *The Old Testament Pseudepigrapha*, ii (London, 1985), 843–54.

HARL, M., *La Bible d'Alexandrie*, i: *La Genèse* (Paris, 1986).

VON HARNACK, A., *Porphyrius, 'Gegen die Christen' 15 Bücher: Zeugnisse, Fragmente, und Referate* (Abhandlungen der königlich preussischen Akademie der Wissenschaften, 1; Berlin, 1916).

HAYWARD, C. T. R., *The Targum of Jeremiah*, The Aramaic Bible, xii (Wilmington, Del. 1987).

HAYWARD, C. T. R., 'The Date of Targum Pseudo-Jonathan: Some Comments', *JJS* 40 (1989), 7–30.

—— 'Targum Pseudo-Jonathan and Anti-Islamic Polemic', *JSS* 34 (1989), 77–93.

—— 'Some Observations on Saint Jerome's "Hebrew Questions on Genesis" and the Rabbinic Tradition', *PIBA* 13 (1990), 58–76.

—— 'Pirqe de Rabbi Eliezer and Targum Pseudo-Jonathan', *JJS* 42 (1991), 215–46.

—— 'Inconsistencies and Contradictions in Targum Pseudo-Jonathan: The Case of Eliezer and Nimrod', *JSS* 37 (1992), 31–55.

—— 'A Portrait of the Wicked Esau in the Targum of Codex Neofiti I', in D.R.G. Beattie and M.J. McNamara (Ed.), *The Aramaic Bible. Targums in their Historical Context* (Sheffield, 1994), 291–309.

HUNZINGER, H., 'Babylon als Deckname für Rom und die Datierung des I. Petrusbriefes', in H. Reventlow (ed.), *Gottes Wort und Gottes Land: Festschrift für H.-W. Hertzberg* (Göttingen, 1965), 67–77.

JACKSON, H., '4Q252: Addenda', *JJS* 44 (1993), 118–20.

JAY, P., 'La Datation des premières traductions de l'Ancien Testament sur l'hébreu par saint Jérôme', *REA* 28 (1982), 208–12.

—— *L'Exégèse de saint Jérôme d'après son 'Commentaire sur Isaïe'* (Paris, 1985).

JELLICOE, S., *The Septuagint and Modern Study* (Oxford, 1968).

Jewish Encyclopaedia, ed. I. Singer, 12 vols. (New York and London, 1901–6).

KAMESAR, A., 'Studies in Jerome's *Quaestiones Hebraicae in Genesim*: The Work as seen in the context of Greek Scholarship', D.Phil. thesis (Oxford, 1987).

—— *Jerome, Greek Scholarship, and the Hebrew Bible* (Oxford, 1993).

KAMIN, S., 'The Theological Significance of the *Hebraica Veritas* in Jerome's Thought', in M. Fishbane and E. Tov (eds.), *'Sha'arei Talmon': Studies in the Bible, Qumran, and the Ancient Near East presented to Shemaryahu Talmon* (Winona Lake, Ind., 1992), 243–53.

KASHER, M., *Torah Shelemah* (Jerusalem, 1936–   (in Hebrew)).

KELLY, J. N. D., *Jerome: His Life, Writings, and Controversies* (London, 1975).

KRAUSS, S., 'The Jews in the Works of the Church Fathers', *JQR* 6 (1894), 225–61.

DE LANGE, N. R. M., *Origen and the Jews: Studies in Jewish–Christian Relations in third-century Palestine* (Cambridge, 1976).

LARSSON, G., 'The Chronology of the Pentateuch: A Comparison of the MT and LXX', *JBL* 102 (1983), 401–9.

LEWIS, J. P., *A Study of the Interpretation of Noah and the Flood in Jewish and Christian Literature* (Leiden, 1968).

LIEBERMAN, S., 'How Much Greek in Jewish Palestine?' in *Biblical and*

Other Studies (P. W. Lown Institute of Advanced Judaic Studies; Cambridge, Mass., 1963), 135–9.

LIM, T. H., 'The Chronology of the Flood Story in a Qumran Text (4Q252)', *JJS* 43 (1992), 288–98.

McNAMARA, M., *The New Testament and the Palestinian Targum to the Pentateuch* (Rome, 1966).

—— *Targum and Testament* (Shannon, 1972).

MARA, G. M., 'Ambrose of Milan, Ambrosiaster, and Nicetas', in A. di Bernardino (ed.), *Patrology*, iv, trans. P. Solari (Westminster, Md., 1991), 144–94.

MARTIN, M. F., 'The Palaeographical Character of Codex Neofiti I', *Textus*, 3 (1963), 1–35.

MILLAR, F., 'Hagar, Ishmael, Josephus and the Origins of Islam', *JJS* 44 (1993), 23–45.

MILLER, W. T., *Mysterious Encounters at Mamre and Jabbok* (Brown Judaic Studies, 50; Chico, Calif., 1984).

NAUROY, G., 'Jérôme, lecteur et censeur de l'exégèse d'Ambroise', in Y.-M. Duval (ed.), *Jérôme entre l'Occident et l'Orient* (Paris, 1988), 173–203.

NAUTIN, P., 'La Date du "De Viris Inlustribus" de Jérôme, de la mort de Cyrille de Jérusalem et de celle de Grégoire de Nazianze', *RHE* 56 (1961), 33–5.

—— 'Études de chronologie hiéronymienne', *REA* 20 (1974), 251–84.

—— *Origène*, i: *Sa vie et son œuvre* (Paris, 1977).

—— 'L'Activité littéraire de Jérôme de 387 à 392', *RTP* 115 (1983), 247–59.

—— 'Hieronymus', in *Theologische Realenzyklopädie*, xv/1–2 (Berlin, 1986), 304–15.

NEUBAUER, A., *La Géographie du Talmud* (Paris, 1868).

NIKOLASCH, F., 'Zur Ikonographie des Widders von Gen 22', *Vigiliae Christianae*, 23 (1969), 197–223.

O'LOUGHLIN, T., 'Adam's Burial at Hebron: Some Aspects of its Significance in the Latin Tradition', *PIBA* (forthcoming).

PETERS, C., 'Peschitta und Targumim des Pentateuchs', *Le Muséon*, 48 (1935), 1–54.

VON RAD, G., *Genesis* (London, 1963).

RAHLFS, A., 'Quis Sit Ho Suros?', *Kleine Mitteilungen: Mitteilungen des Septuaginta-Unternehmens der Akademie der Wissenschaft in Göttingen*, i/7 (Berlin, 1915).

RAHMER, M., *Die hebräischen Traditionen in den Werken des Hieronymus durch einen Vergleichung mit den jüdischen Quellen*, i: *Die 'Quaestiones in Genesin'*, (Breslau, 1861).

ROSENBAUM, M., and SILBERMANN, A. M., *Pentateuch with Targum Onkelos, Haphtaroth and Rashi's Commentary* (New York, n.d.).

ROUTH, M. J., *Reliquiae Sacrae*, i (Oxford, 1846).

SALVESEN, A., *Symmachus in the Pentateuch* (Manchester, 1992).

SCHADE, L., *Die Inspirationslehre des heiligen Hieronymus* (Freiburg i.B., 1910).

SCHÄFER, P., 'Die Termini "Heiliger Geist" und "Geist der Prophetie" in den Targumim und das Verhältnis der Targumim zu einander', *VT* 20 (1970), 304–14.

—— *Die Vorstellung vom Heiligen Geist in der Rabbinischen Literatur* (Munich, 1972).

SCHÜRER, E., *The History of the Jewish People in the Age of Jesus Christ*, rev. and ed. G. Vermes, F. Millar, *et al.*, 3 vols. (Edinburgh 1973–87).

SCHWARZ, W., *Principles and Problems of Biblical Translation* (Cambridge, 1955).

SILVERSTONE, A. E., *Aquila and Onkelos* (Manchester, 1931).

SKINNER, J., *A Critical and Exegetical Commentary on Genesis* (Edinburgh, 1912).

SMITH, J. Z., 'The Prayer of Joseph', in J. H. Charlesworth (ed.), *The Old Testament Pseudepigrapha*, ii (London, 1985), 699–714.

SPARKS, H. F. D., 'Jerome as a Bible Translator', in P. R. Ackroyd and C. F. Evans (eds.), *The Cambridge History of the Bible*, i (Cambridge, 1970), 517–26.

SPIEGEL, S., *The Last Trial* (New York, 1967).

SWETE, H. B., *Introduction to the Old Testament in Greek* (Cambridge, 1902).

TOV, E., 'Loanwords, Homophony, and Transliteration in the Septuagint', *Biblica*, 60 (1979), 216–36.

—— 'The Rabbinic Tradition concerning the "Alterations" inserted into the Greek Pentateuch and their Relation to the Original Text of the LXX', *JSJ* 15 (1984), 65–89.

—— *Textual Criticism of the Hebrew Bible* (Assen, 1992).

URBACH, E. E., *The Sages: Their Concepts and Beliefs*, 2 vols. (Jerusalem, 1979).

VERMES, G., 'Haggadah in the Onkelos Targum', *JSS* 8 (1963), 159–69.

—— 'The Targumic Versions of Genesis 4: 3–16', *Annual of the Leeds University Oriental Society*, 3 (1961–2) (Leiden, 1963), 81–114.

—— 'Bible and Midrash', in P. R. Ackroyd and C. F. Evans (eds.), *The Cambridge History of the Bible*, i (Cambridge, 1970), 199–231.

[NB: The above three articles are reprinted in *Post-Biblical Jewish Studies* (Leiden, 1975), 127–38; 92–126; 59–91 respectively.]

—— 'The Life of Abraham', in *Scripture and Tradition in Judaism*² (Leiden, 1973), 67–126.

—— 'The Story of Balaam: The Scriptural Origin of Haggadah', in *Scripture and Tradition in Judaism*² (Leiden, 1973), 127–77.

—— 'Redemption and Genesis xxii', in *Scripture and Tradition in Judaism*² (Leiden, 1973), 193–229.

—— 'The Archangel Sariel: A Targumic Parallel to the Dead Sea Scrolls', in J. Neusner (ed.), *Christianity, Judaism and Other Greco-Roman Cults*, pt. iii: *Studies for Morton Smith at Sixty* (Leiden, 1975), 159–76.

—— 'The Impact of the Dead Sea Scrolls on Jewish Studies', *JJS* 26 (1975), 12–14.

VOGT, E., 'Benjamin geboren "eine Meile" von Ephrata', *Biblica*, 56 (1975), 30–6.

DE WAARD, J., 'Homophony in the Septuagint', *Biblica*, 62 (1981), 551–61.

WACHOLDER, B. Z., *Essays on Jewish Chronology and Chronography* (New York, 1976).

WINTER, P., 'The Cultural Background of the Narrative in Luke I and II', *JQR* 45 (1954), 230–42.

WINTERMUTE, O., 'Jubilees', in J. H. Charlesworth (ed.), *The Old Testament Pseudepigrapha*, ii (London, 1983), 33–142.

WUTZ, F. X., *Onomastica Sacra: Untersuchungen zum Liber Interpretationis Nominum Hebraicorum des heiligen Hieronymus* (TU 41; Leipzig, 1914–15).

ZEITLIN, S., 'The Origin of the Term Edom for Rome and the Christian Church', *JQR* 60 (1969), 262–3.

OLD TESTAMENT

NEW TESTAMENT

RABBINIC LITERATURE

Index of Passages Cited

CHURCH FATHERS

JEWISH WRITERS IN GREEK

MEDIAEVAL JEWISH COMMENTATORS

CLASSICAL WRITERS

INDEX OF AUTHORS

GENERAL INDEX